# Exam Ref 70-533
# Implementing Microsoft Azure
# Infrastructure Solutions
## 2nd Edition

Rick Rainey
Michael Washam
Dan Patrick
Steve Ross

**Exam Ref 70-533 Implementing Microsoft Azure Infrastructure Solutions, 2nd Edition**

**Published with the authorization of Microsoft Corporation by:**
**Pearson Education, Inc.**

ISBN-13: 978-1-5093-0648-0
ISBN-10: 1-5093-0648-X

Library of Congress Control Number: 2017963305
1 18

**Trademarks**

Microsoft and the trademarks listed at *https://www.microsoft.com* on the "Trademarks" webpage are trademarks of the Microsoft group of companies. All other marks are property of their respective owners.

**Warning and Disclaimer**

**Special Sales**

For information about buying this title in bulk quantities, or for special sales opportunities (which may include electronic versions; custom cover designs; and content particular to your business, training goals, marketing focus, or branding interests), please contact our corporate sales department at corpsales@pearsoned.com or (800) 382-3419.

For government sales inquiries, please contact governmentsales@pearsoned.com.

For questions about sales outside the U.S., please contact intlcs@pearson.com.

| | |
|---|---|
| **Editor-in-Chief** | Greg Wiegand |
| **Senior Acquisitions Editor** | Laura Norman |
| **Development Editor** | Troy Mott |
| **Managing Editor** | Sandra Schroeder |
| **Senior Project Editor** | Tracey Croom |
| **Editorial Production** | Backstop Media |
| **Copy Editor** | Christina Rudloff |
| **Indexer** | Julie Grady |
| **Proofreader** | Christina Rudloff |
| **Technical Editor** | Tim Warner |
| **Cover Designer** | Twist Creative, Seattle |

# Contents at a glance

# Contents

---

**What do you think of this book? We want to hear from you!**

Microsoft is interested in hearing your feedback so we can continually improve our
books and learning resources for you. To participate in a brief online survey, please visit:

**https://aka.ms/tellpress**

## Chapter 3    Design and implement a storage strategy    155

**What do you think of this book? We want to hear from you!**

Microsoft is interested in hearing your feedback so we can continually improve our
books and learning resources for you. To participate in a brief online survey, please visit:

https://aka.ms/tellpress

# Introduction

The 70-533 exam focuses on Infrastructure as a Service (IaaS) features available in Microsoft Azure (storage, networking, and compute). The exam also covers some of the more common Platform as a Service (PaaS) services that an IT professional will experience in an Azure environment. It covers deploying and configuring virtual machines, virtual machine scale sets, containers, and web apps, with Azure App Services including integration with services like the Content Deployment Network (CDN). This exam also covers the intricacies of networking, including hybrid connectivity with technologies like ExpressRoute, site-to-site VPN, and point-to-site, as well as a broad range of storage related topics, such as choosing the right storage solution, and understanding how to scale and diagnose performance.

Other key capabilities measured by the exam include your ability to author and deploy ARM templates, and automate workloads using a wide variety of services and tools, such as the Azure command line tools, Azure Automation, and implementing monitoring solutions for infrastructure and services deployed in Azure. Security is a key topic that is interwoven throughout the subjects, including topics such as encryption at rest and in transit, as well as identity management with Azure AD and monitoring for security threats with Azure Security Center.

This book is written specifically for IT professionals who want to demonstrate their skills to implement and configure these services in Microsoft Azure.

This book covers every major topic area found on the exam, but it does not cover every exam question. Only the Microsoft exam team has access to the exam questions, and Microsoft regularly adds new questions to the exam, making it impossible to cover specific questions. You should consider this book a supplement to your relevant real-world experience and other study materials. If you encounter a topic in this book that you do not feel completely comfortable with, use the "Need more review?" links you'll find in the text to find more information and take the time to research and study the topic. Great information is available on MSDN, TechNet, and in blogs and forums.

# Organization of this book

This book is organized by the "Skills measured" list published for the exam. The "Skills measured" list is available for each exam on the Microsoft Learning website: *https://aka.ms/examlist*. Each chapter in this book corresponds to a major topic area in the list, and the technical tasks in each topic area determine a chapter's organization. If an exam covers six major topic areas, for example, the book will contain six chapters.

# Microsoft certifications

Microsoft certifications distinguish you by proving your command of a broad set of skills and experience with current Microsoft products and technologies. The exams and corresponding certifications are developed to validate your mastery of critical competencies as you design and develop, or implement and support, solutions with Microsoft products and technologies both on-premises and in the cloud. Certification brings a variety of benefits to the individual and to employers and organizations.

> **MORE INFO** **ALL MICROSOFT CERTIFICATIONS**
>
> For information about Microsoft certifications, including a full list of available certifications, go to *https://www.microsoft.com/learning*.

# Acknowledgments

**Rick Rainey**. It is a privilege to be a contributing author to such a valuable resource for the IT professional working in Azure. To the reader, it is my hope that the information in this text provides a rich learning experience. Thank you to everyone who has contributed to this second edition. To my family and dearest friends, thank you for your patience and support during this journey.

**Michael Washam**. Helping others learn about the cloud is always a great experience, and I hope this second edition helps readers learn more about Azure, and of course ultimately help them prepare for passing the exam! I would like to thank my wife Becky for being very patient with me when I take on projects like this, and my co-authors for making this book excellent by passing on their immense technical expertise. In addition to the tech gurus, I would like to thank James Burleson at Opsgility for editing assistance and the rest of the folks at the Opsgility team for being patient during the authoring and editing process. Finally, the editors and reviewers from Pearson provided fantastic support and feedback throughout the process.

**Dan Patrick**. Writing this book has taught me much more than probably anyone who reads it will ever learn. To Michael Washam, thank you for taking a chance on me. Finally, I want to thank my two girls Stella and Elizabeth, and the love of my life Michelle for being the reason why I continue to learn.

**Steve Ross**. This was my first foray into authoring a book, and it was quite a learning experience. Many thanks to Michael Washam and Dan Patrick for patiently answering a lot of questions during the process. I'm also thankful for the folks who accomplished the editing and technical reviews, as the work is much improved due to their diligence. Endeavors like this, done "off the side of the desk" require a lot of afterhours work, so thanks to my beautiful wife and kids for putting up with my late nights in the office. Finally, I'm thankful to God for a wonderful career in IT, and for many other kindnesses too numerous to mention. May He be honored in all I do.

## Microsoft Virtual Academy

Build your knowledge of Microsoft technologies with free expert-led online training from Microsoft Virtual Academy (MVA). MVA offers a comprehensive library of videos, live events, and more to help you learn the latest technologies and prepare for certification exams. You'll find what you need here:

*https://www.microsoftvirtualacademy.com*

## Quick access to online references

Throughout this book are addresses to webpages that the author has recommended you visit for more information. Some of these addresses (also known as URLs) can be painstaking to type into a web browser, so we've compiled all of them into a single list that readers of the print edition can refer to while they read.

Download the list at *https://aka.ms/examref5332E/downloads*.

The URLs are organized by chapter and heading. Every time you come across a URL in the book, find the hyperlink in the list to go directly to the webpage.

## Errata, updates, & book support

We've made every effort to ensure the accuracy of this book and its companion content. You can access updates to this book—in the form of a list of submitted errata and their related corrections—at:

> *https://aka.ms/examref5322E/errata*

> If you discover an error that is not already listed, please submit it to us at the same page.

> If you need additional support, email Microsoft Press Book Support at *mspinput@microsoft.com*.

Please note that product support for Microsoft software and hardware is not offered through the previous addresses. For help with Microsoft software or hardware, go to *https://support.microsoft.com*.

## We want to hear from you

At Microsoft Press, your satisfaction is our top priority, and your feedback our most valuable asset. Please tell us what you think of this book at:

> *https://aka.ms/tellpress*

> We know you're busy, so we've kept it short with just a few questions. Your answers go directly to the editors at Microsoft Press. (No personal information will be requested.) Thanks in advance for your input!

## Stay in touch

Let's keep the conversation going! We're on Twitter: *http://twitter.com/MicrosoftPress*.

# Preparing for the exam

Microsoft certification exams are a great way to build your resume and let the world know about your level of expertise. Certification exams validate your on-the-job experience and product knowledge. Although there is no substitute for on-the-job experience, preparation through study and hands-on practice can help you prepare for the exam. We recommend that you augment your exam preparation plan by using a combination of available study materials and courses. For example, you might use the Exam ref and another study guide for your "at home" preparation, and take a Microsoft Official Curriculum course for the classroom experience. Choose the combination that you think works best for you.

Note that this Exam Ref is based on publicly available information about the exam and the author's experience. To safeguard the integrity of the exam, authors do not have access to the live exam.

# CHAPTER 1

# Design and implement Azure App Service Web Apps

Microsoft Azure Web Apps is a fully managed Platform as a Service (PaaS) that enables you to build, deploy, and scale enterprise-grade web applications in seconds. Whether your organization requires a global web presence for the organization's .com site, a solution to a line-of-business intranet application that is secure and highly available, or a site for a digital marketing campaign, Web Apps is the fastest way to create these web applications in Azure. Of all the Azure compute options, Web Apps is among the simplest to implement for scalability and manageability, and for capitalizing on the elasticity of cloud computing.

> **IMPORTANT**
>
> **Have you read page xvii?**
>
> It contains valuable information regarding the skills you need to pass the exam.

> **MORE INFO   COMPARING AZURE COMPUTE CHOICES**
>
> A feature comparison between the different Azure compute choices is available at *https://docs.microsoft.com/en-us/azure/app-service-web/choose-web-site-cloud-service-vm*.

This chapter covers Azure Web Apps through the lens of an IT professional responsible for deploying, configuring, monitoring, and managing Web Apps. As such, the tools that will be used to demonstrate these functions will be as follows:

- Azure Portal
- Azure PowerShell Cmdlets, v4.2.1
- Azure CLI 2.0, v2.0.12

> **MORE INFO   AZURE POWERSHELL CMDLETS AND CLI TOOLS**
>
> The Azure PowerShell Cmdlets and CLI tools can be downloaded and installed at: *https://azure.microsoft.com/en-us/downloads/*. Scroll down to the command-line tools section for installation links and documentation.

## Skills covered in this chapter:

- Skill 1.1: Deploy web apps
- Skill 1.2: Configure web apps
- Skill 1.3: Configure diagnostics, monitoring, and analytics
- Skill 1.4: Configure scale and resilience

# Skill 1.1: Deploy web apps

As an IT professional, you need to understand how to create the *infrastructure* to host a web application. At a minimum, this means creating two resources: a web app and an App Service plan. The web app is the resource for which an application runs in. The App Service plan is the resource that defines the location, size, capacity, and features for which the web app will run on.

You will often need to create additional resources the application requires. For example, the application may require a SQL Database for storing data, a Redis cache for caching, a storage account for storing metadata, and perhaps a Contend Delivery Network (CDN) for serving static data to end users. Understanding the resource requirements for the application will help you determine the infrastructure you need to deploy to support it.

> **This skill covers how to:**
>
> - Create an App Service Plan
> - Create a web app
> - Create deployment slots
> - Swap deployment slots
> - Deploy an application
> - Migrate a web app to a different App Service Plan

## Create an App Service Plan

Azure Web Apps use App Service plans to group features and capacity settings that can be shared across one or more web apps. This enables you to more easily manage costs and resources for your web apps. App service plans are available in the following pricing tiers:

- Free
- Shared

- Basic
- Standard
- Premium
- Isolated

**EXAM TIP**

The Basic, Standard, Premium, and Isolated tiers offer you dedicated compute resources. The Free and Shared tiers use shared compute resources with other Azure tenants. Furthermore, with Free and Shared, you are throttled to not exceed certain limits, such as CPU time, RAM consumption, and network bandwidth. More information on limits, quotas and constraints is available at *https://docs.microsoft.com/en-us/azure/azure-subscription-service-limits*.

Within the Basic, Standard, Premium, and Isolated tiers, you have three types of plans to choose from that vary only in their capacity, such as the number of cores and amount of RAM. As an example, the three types of plans in the Premium tier are shown in Figure 1-1.

| P1 Premium | | P2 Premium | | P3 Premium | |
|---|---|---|---|---|---|
| 1 | Core | 2 | Core | 4 | Core |
| 1.75 | GB RAM | 3.5 | GB RAM | 7 | GB RAM |
| | 250 GB Storage | | 250 GB Storage | | 250 GB Storage |
| | Custom domains / SSL SNI Incl & IP SSL Support | | Custom domains / SSL SNI Incl & IP SSL Support | | Custom domains / SSL SNI Incl & IP SSL Support |
| | Up to 20 instance(s) * Subject to availability | | Up to 20 instance(s) * Subject to availability | | Up to 20 instance(s) * Subject to availability |
| | 20 slots Web app staging | | 20 slots Web app staging | | 20 slots Web app staging |
| | 50 times daily Backup | | 50 times daily Backup | | 50 times daily Backup |
| | Traffic Manager Geo availability | | Traffic Manager Geo availability | | Traffic Manager Geo availability |

**FIGURE 1-1** Premium tier options for web apps as shown in the Azure portal

You can create a new app service plan when you create a new web app using the Azure portal. Or, you can create an app service plan first and then use it later when creating one or more web apps.

## Create an app service plan (Azure portal)

In the Azure portal, search the Marketplace for App Service Plan and open the New App Service Plan blade. Specify a name, location, operating system type (Windows or Linux), and the pricing tier as shown in Figure 1-2.

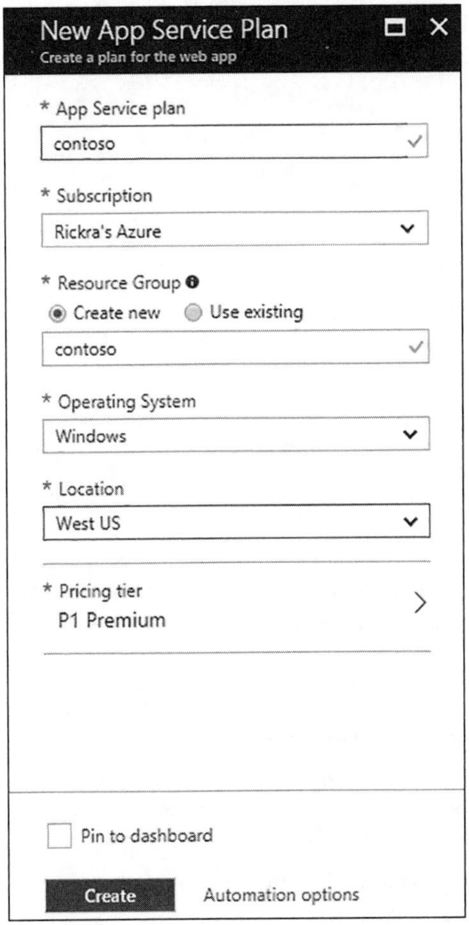

**FIGURE 1-2** New App Service Plan blade in the Azure portal

## Create an app service plan (PowerShell)

Use the New-AzureRmAppServicePlan cmdlet to create a new app service plan.

```
# Define properties for the app service plan
$resourceGroupName = "contoso"
$appServicePlanName = "contoso"
$location = "West US"
$tier = "Premium"
$workerSize = "small"

# Create a new resource group
New-AzureRmResourceGroup -Name $resourceGroupName -Location $location

# Create a new app service plan
New-AzureRmAppServicePlan -ResourceGroupName $resourceGroupName `
    -Name $appServicePlanName -Location $location -Tier $tier -WorkerSize $workerSize
```

### Create an app service plan (CLI)

Use the App Service plan create command to create a new app service plan.

```bash
#!/bin/bash

# Define properties for the app service plan
resourceGroupName="contoso"
appServicePlanName="contoso"
location="westus"
sku="P1"

# Create a new resource group.
az group create --location $location --name $resourceGroupName

# Create a new app service plan
az appservice plan create --resource-group $resourceGroupName \
    --name $appServicePlanName --location $location --sku $sku
```

# Create a web app

When you create an Azure Web App, you create a unique DNS name, select an app service plan (or create a new one), and select an operating system type (Windows or Linux).

> **EXAM TIP**
>
> Docker containers are used to support Linux on web apps. There are built-in Docker images to support various versions of Node.js, PHP, .Net Core, and Ruby runtime stacks. You can also choose to use runtime stacks from Docker Hub or a private registry of images, if your organization has one.
>
> If you select Linux for your operating system type, you must select an app service plan that was configured for Linux, or create a new app service plan with Linux support.

It is common when creating a web app environment to create additional resources to support things like caching, storage, monitoring, and diagnostics. When you create a web app environment, you are essentially defining the *infrastructure* for the web application to run in. In an on-premises environment, a similar analogy creates a website on Windows Server using IIS Manager. When you do this, you simply create the site without any code. Later, application code is published to the site that users can reach through their browser. That is the same for web apps. Creating a web app doesn't mean you have a working web application. It means you have the infrastructure in place to host a web application.

### Create a web app (Azure portal)

In the Azure portal, search the Marketplace for web app and open the New Web App blade. Specify a name, operating system type (Windows or Linux), select an app service plan (or create a new one), and optionally choose to add Application Insights as shown in Figure 1-3. Application Insights is a resource that collects telemetry data about your application running in the web app, which can be useful for troubleshooting performance issues, application errors, and even insights into how end users are using the application.

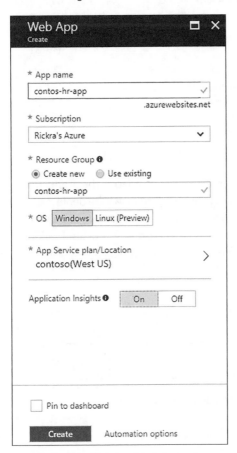

**FIGURE 1-3** New Web App blade in the Azure portal

## Create a web app (PowerShell)

Use the New-AzureRmWebApp cmdlet to create a new web app.

```
# Define properties for the web app
$resourceGroupName = "contoso"
$appServicePlanName = "contoso"
$location = "West US"
$webAppName = "contoso-hr-app"

# Create a new web app using an existing app service plan
New-AzureRmWebApp -ResourceGroupName $resourceGroupName -Location $location `
    -AppServicePlan $appServicePlanName -Name $webAppName
```

## Create a web app (CLI)

Use the webapp create command to create a new web app.

```
# Define properties for the web app
resourceGroupName="contoso"
appServicePlanName="contoso"
webAppName="contoso-hr-app"

# Create a new web app using an existing app service plan
az webapp create --resource-group $resourceGroupName \
    --name $webAppName --plan $appServicePlanName
```

# Define deployment slots

Every Azure web app, by default, includes one deployment slot, referred to as the production deployment slot, and is where the production version of your application will be deployed. You can add additional deployment slots as needed. When you have two or more deployment slots, you can swap the contents of the deployment slots as new versions of your application are being developed. An example of how the deployment slots for a web app might be configured is shown in Figure 1-4.

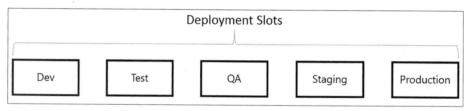

**FIGURE 1-4** Example of how deployment slots can be used for different environments

**EXAM TIP**

Adding additional deployment slots to an Azure Web App requires that the App Service Plan it is running on be configured for Standard or Premium pricing tier. You can add up to 10 deployment slots in Standard. You can add up to 20 deployment slots in Premium.

## Create a deployment slot (Azure portal)

In the Azure portal, click on Deployment Slots in the web app blade. This will open the deployment slots blade showing all your deployment slots. Click the +Add Slot button at the top of the blade. In the add a slot blade, provide a Name for the deployment slot and select Configuration Source as shown in Figure 1-5.

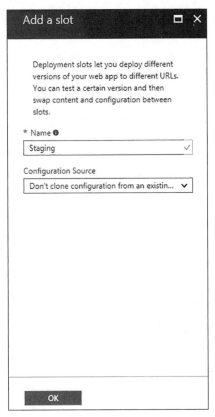

**FIGURE 1-5** Adding a deployment slot named Staging using the Azure portal

> **NOTE**  **CLONING AN EXISTING DEPLOYMENT SLOT**
>
> When you create a deployment slot, you can choose to clone an existing deployment slot's configuration settings. For example, if you have a database connection string setting in a 'Dev' deployment slot and you want to use the same setting in new deployment slot called 'Test', you can choose to clone the 'Dev' deployment slot settings.

## Create a deployment slot (PowerShell)

Use the New-AzureRmWebAppSlot cmdlet to create a new deployment slot. The code below creates a deployment slot with default configuration settings.

```
$resourceGroupName = "contoso"
$webAppName = "contoso-hr-app"
$stagingSlotName = "Staging"

# Create a new web app deployment slot
New-AzureRmWebAppSlot -ResourceGroupName $resourceGroupName `
    -Name $webAppName -Slot $stagingSlotName
```

To create new deployment slot that clones an existing deployment slot, use the
Get-AzureRmWebAppSlot cmdlet to get a reference to the slot you want to clone. Then,
pass it in using the SourceWebApp parameter of the New-AzureRmWebAppSlot cmdlet.
The code below creates a new deployment slot that clones the production deployment slot.

```
$resourceGroupName = "contoso"
$appServicePlanName = "contoso"
$webAppName = "contoso-hr-app"
$stagingSlotName = "Staging"
$productionSlotName = "Production"

# Get a reference to the production deployment slot
$productionSite = Get-AzureRmWebAppSlot -ResourceGroupName $resourceGroupName `
    -Name $webAppName -Slot $productionSlotName

# Create a deployment slot that clones the production deployment slot settings
New-AzureRmWebAppSlot -ResourceGroupName $resourceGroupName `
    -Name $webAppName -Slot $stagingSlotName `
    -AppServicePlan $appServicePlanName -SourceWebApp $productionSite
```

## Create a deployment slot (CLI)

Use the webapp deployment slot create command to create a new deployment slot with
default settings.

```
#!/bin/bash

resourceGroupName="contoso"
webAppName="contoso-hr-app"
stagingSlotName="Staging"

az webapp deployment slot create --resource-group $resourceGroupName \
    --name $webAppName --slot $stagingSlotName
```

### EXAM TIP

A deployment slot is actually a completely separate Azure web app linked to your production slot website. For example, if you create your web app using the name contoso-web and
then later add a deployment slot named staging, then the web app name for the staging
slot would be called contoso-web-staging. Each website would be reachable from its unique
URL. For example: *http://contoso-web.azurewebsites.net/* and *http://contoso-web-staging.
azurewebsites.net/.*

# Swap deployment slots

When swapping deployment slots, you are swapping the contents of one slot with another. For example, you may have version 2.0 of an application in your staging slot and version 1.0 of the application in the production slot. Using deployment slots gives you the flexibility to test your version 2.0 application before pushing it to production. It also gives you a way to roll back (swap back) to the version 1.0 application if necessary. Figure 1-6 illustrates swapping between a staging and production environment.

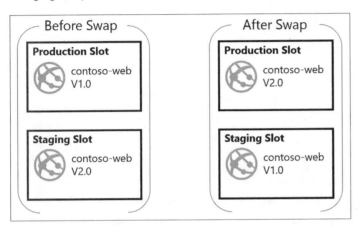

**FIGURE 1-6** Swapping between production and staging deployment slots

Deployment slot swaps can be executed as an immediate swap as explained above. Or, you can perform a multi-phase swap, also known as Swap with preview. In the latter case, your destination slot (for example, production) settings are first applied to your source slot (for example, staging) without making any changes to your destination slot. This gives you the opportunity to test the source slot using the settings from the destination slot. After verifying the application is working as expected in the source slot, you can perform the second phase by completing the swap. If the application is not working as expected, you can cancel the swap in the second phase.

**EXAM TIP**

**Multi-phase deployment swaps are recommended for mission critical workloads. To learn more see:** *https://docs.microsoft.com/en-us/azure/app-service-web/web-sites-staged-publishing#swap-with-preview-multi-phase-swap.*

## Swap deployment slots (Azure Portal)

In the Azure portal, click on Deployment Slots in the web app blade for your source web app (for example, the Staging web app). Click the Swap button at the top of the Deployment Slots blade.

In the Swap blade, choose a Swap type, which can be either Swap or Swap With Preview. Set the Destination to the deployment slot you want to swap into. If there are configuration setting differences between the two slots, you can review those by clicking on Preview Changes as shown in Figure 1-7.

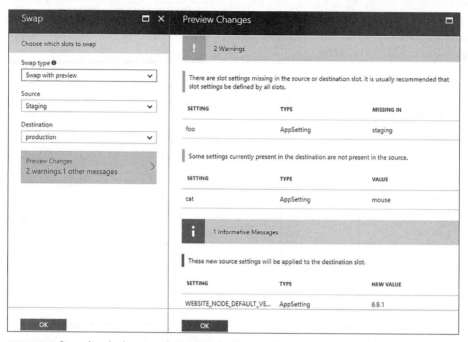

**FIGURE 1-7** Swapping deployment slots and reviewing warnings in the Azure portal

When you are ready to proceed with the swap, click the Ok button at the bottom of the Swap blade. Since this is a multi-phase swap, the configuration settings have been updated in the source (Staging) slot. Now, you should do some final testing and validation of the application before proceeding to the second phase.

After validating the application, you need to complete the swap. To do so, open the Deployment slots blade and click the Complete swap button at the top of the blade. In the Swap blade, set the Swap action to Complete swap if you want to proceed with the swap. Or, set it to Cancel Swap if you want to cancel. Finally, click OK to complete the second phase, as shown in Figure 1-8.

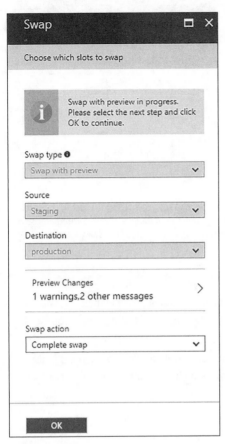

**FIGURE 1-8** Completing a multi-phase deployment swap in the Azure portal

## Swap deployment slots (PowerShell)

Use the Swap-AzureRmWebAppSlot cmdlet to swap deployment slots. If you want to initiate a multi-phase swap, include the `SwapWithPreviewAction` parameter with a value of ApplySlot-Config. The following code shows a simple single-phase swap.

```
$resourceGroupName = "contoso"
$webAppName = "contoso-hr-app"
$stagingSlotName = "Staging"
$productionSlotName = "Production"

# Swap staging and production deployment slots (single phase)
Swap-AzureRmWebAppSlot -ResourceGroupName $resourceGroupName -Name $webAppName `
    -SourceSlotName $stagingSlotName -DestinationSlotName $productionSlotName
```

## Swap deployment slots (CLI)

Use the `webapp deployment slot swap` command to swap deployment lots. If you want to initiate multi-phase swap, set the action parameter to preview. The following code shows a simple single-phase swap.

```bash
#!/bin/bash

resourceGroupName="contoso"
webAppName="contoso-hr-app"
stagingSlotName="Staging"
productionSlotName="Production"
swapAction="swap"

# Swap staging and production deployment slots (single phase)
az webapp deployment slot swap --resource-group $resourceGroupName --name $webAppName \
    --slot $stagingSlotName --target-slot $productionSlotName --action $swapAction
```

# Deploy an application

Deploying an application to an Azure web app is the process by which the web application (or code) is copied to one of the deployment slots, usually a test or staging slot. A web app can be published using a variety of tools, such as the following:

- Source control systems are often used in a continuous delivery (or deployment) model where the applicate is deployed as code changes are checked into the source control system
- FTP clients, such as FileZilla
- Azure PowerShell
- Web Deploy
- Visual Studio
- Local Git
- GitHub
- Visual Studio Team Services
- Azure Resource Manager Template (using the MSDeploy web app extension)
- More...

# Migrate a web app to separate App Service Plan

A web app may be moved to a different App Service Plan. This may be necessary if you need to isolate resources for a single web app or set of web apps. For example, you may have internal applications that consume high amounts of memory and external customer facing applications that need to be able to scale out at time to meet demand spikes. In situations like this, it is recommended to create separate app service plans that are configured appropriately for each workload. Also, by having separate app service plans, the web apps in each App Service Plan are isolated from web apps in other App Service Plans.

> **MORE INFO**  **APP SERVICE PLANS IN DEPTH**
>
> An in-depth overview of App Service Plans is available at: *https://docs.microsoft.com/en-us/azure/app-service/azure-web-sites-web-hosting-plans-in-depth-overview*.

## Migrate a web app to a separate App Service Plan (Azure portal)

In the Azure portal, click on Change App Service Plan under the App Service Plan section of the web app blade. In the App Service Plan blade, click on the App Service Plan you want to move the web app to. Figure 1-9 shows a choice of two App Service Plans available to migrate the web app to. The web app will be moved when you click on an available App Service Plan.

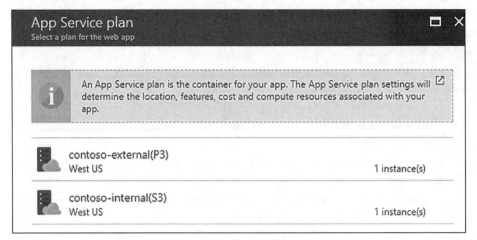

**FIGURE 1-9** Migrating a web app to a separate App Service Plan in the Azure portal

**EXAM TIP**

If you have multiple deployment slots defined for your web app, then you must migrate each slot separately to a different App Service Plan. Migrating one deployment slot to a separate App Service Plan does not automatically migrate all of the deployment slots.

**EXAM TIP**

A web app can be migrated to an App Service Plan in the same resource group and region as the existing App Service Plan it is linked to. If you need to move a web app to an App Service Plan in a different region and/or resource group, then you can choose the Clone App option under the Development tools section. The Clone App feature is only available on the Premium pricing tier.

## Skill 1.2: Configure web apps

Every web app has unique characteristics that need to be taken into consideration when configuring the infrastructure that the application will run in. With Azure web apps, you have many choices when it comes to configuration settings and the tools you use to configure the web app.

# Configuring application settings

An application targeting a web app in Azure will usually have some configuration settings it depends on to run properly. For example, you may need to configure the infrastructure for a specific version of the .NET Framework, PHP, or Java. Or, you may need to define a connection string to a database. The application settings section of Azure Web Apps is where these, and many more, configuration settings will be made. Table 1-1 shows some common settings and their possible values.

**EXAM TIP**

Configuring application settings for a web app differs depending on your OS type (Windows or Linux). For this section of the text, the only application settings applicable to web apps running on Linux are Always On, ARR Affinity, app settings, and connection strings.

**TABLE 1-1** Application settings for Azure Web Apps

| SETTING | VALUES |
| --- | --- |
| .NET Framework Version | V3.5, V4.7 (default) |
| PHP Version | OFF, 5.5 (default), 5.6, 7.0, 7.1 |
| Java Version | OFF (default), Java 7, Java 8 |
| Python Version | OFF (default), 2.7, 3.4 |
| Platform | 32-bit (default), 64-bit |
| Web Sockets | OFF (default), ON |
| Always On | OFF (default), ON |
| ARR Affinity | OFF, ON (default) |

**MORE INFO** **APPLICATION SETTINGS FOR AZURE WEB APPS**

For a complete overview of application settings and configuration options is available at: *https://docs.microsoft.com/en-us/azure/app-service-web/web-sites-configure.*

## Connection strings and application settings

Just about any web application will have a database for storing data. Azure Web Apps has a unique way of configuring *connection strings* to databases by enabling you to provide a connection string setting as part of the web app environment. By storing a connection string as a site setting, the application can retrieve the connection string at runtime as an environment variable rather than storing it in a configuration file, such as a web.config or php.ini file. This approach is more secure because it avoids storing sensitive information, such as user id and password, in the configuration files for the application. Azure Web Apps support the following types of database connection strings:

- SQL Database
- SQL Server
- MySQL
- PostgreSQL
- Notification Hub
- Service Bus
- Event Hub
- API Hub
- Document DB
- Redis Cache
- Custom

Azure Web Apps use this same technique for *application settings* that a web application may depend on. Application settings can be anything, such as a URL to a third party web service or a custom runtime setting that the application code understands.

Application settings for *connection strings* and application settings are defined as key/value pairs. The key can be any name you want. The name you choose for a setting is how you and your developers will reference the setting in code. For example, the following is a sample of how a key/value pair could be defined for a connection string to a SQL database.

```
Key = "ContosoDBConnStr"
Value = "Server=tcp:contosodbsrv01.database.windows.net,1433;Database=contoso-database;
User ID=AdminUser@contosodbsrv01;Password={your_password_here};Trusted_Connection=False;
Encrypt=True;Connection Timeout=30;"
```

The value for a connection string defined as a site setting can be retrieved at runtime by referencing the name of the environment variable for the setting. The name of the environment variable is a combination of a constant string based on the type of database connection string plus the name of the key. The constant strings are as follows:

- SQLAZURECONNSTR_
- SQLCONNSTR_
- MYSQLCONNSTR_
- CUSTOMCONNSTR_

Using the example from earlier, the environment variable name for the ContosoDBConnStr connection string is SQLAZURECONNSTR_ContosoDBConnStr.

Similarly, the value for an application setting defined as a site setting can also be retrieved at runtime by referencing the name of the environment variable for the setting. The constant string for application settings is APPSETTING_. As an example, if an application setting key is defined as ContosoHRWebServiceURL, then the environment variable name for the setting is APPSETTING_ ContosoHRWebServiceURL.

> **MORE INFO  CONNECTION STRINGS AND APPLICATION SETTINGS**
>
> Although it's not a requirement to store connection strings and application settings as site settings for an Azure web app, it's generally recommended to do so. Application developers still have the option of storing these settings in application configuration files such as Web. config or php.ini files.
>
> When it comes to storing secrets, an even better option would be to store the secret in Azure Key Vault and store the secret URI to the setting in Key Vault as an app setting.  For an example on this scenario see: *https://docs.microsoft.com/en-us/azure/key-vault/key-vault-use-from-web-application*.

**EXAM TIP**

If an app setting or connection string is defined in both an application configuration file and as a site setting in the Azure website, the site setting value takes precedence over the setting in the application configuration file.

By default, app settings and connection strings are swapped when performing a deployment swap. However, there may be cases where you want a setting to stick to the deployment slot it is defined in and not be swapped. This is achieved by marking an app setting or connection string as a slot setting, as shown in Figure 1-10. In this example, SettingX will not be swapped to another deployment slot during a swap operation because it has been marked as a slot setting.

| App settings | | |
| --- | --- | --- |
| WEBSITE_NODE_DEFAULT_VERSI... | 6.9.1 | ☐ Slot setting |
| settingX | value-x | ☑ Slot setting |
| settingY | value-y | ☐ Slot setting |

**FIGURE 1-10**  Slot settings for a web app in the Azure portal

## Configure application settings (PowerShell)

Use the Set-AzureRmWebApp cmdlet to set application settings such as Always On, ARR Affinity, app settings, connection strings and more. When setting app settings and connection strings, use Get-AzureRmWebApp first to get the current settings, append/modify the settings, and then apply the settings. The following code demonstrates adding new settings to existing app settings for a web app.

```
$resourceGroupName = "contoso"
$webAppName = "contoso-hr-app"

# Get current app settings
$webApp = Get-AzureRmWebApp -ResourceGroupName $resourceGroupName -Name $webAppName
$settings = $webApp.SiteConfig.AppSettings

# Add new settings to the current set of settings
$newSettings = New-Object Hashtable
$newSettings["setting1"] = "value-1"
$newSettings["setting2"] = "value-2"
foreach ($setting in $settings) {
    $newSettings.Add($setting.Name, $setting.Value)
}

# Apply the new app settings to the web app
Set-AzureRmWebApp -ResourceGroupName $resourceGroupName -Name $webAppName -AppSettings
$newSettings
```

## Configure application settings (CLI)

Use the webapp config appsettings set command to set application settings.

```
#!/bin/bash

resourceGroupName="contoso"
webAppName="contoso-hr-app"

# Add a new app setting to a web app
az webapp config appsettings set -resource-group $resourceGroupName --name $webAppName \
    --settings setting3=value-3
```

# Configure a custom domain for a web app

Azure Web Apps are assigned to the *azurewebsites.net* domain. So, if your site name is contoso-web, then it is reachable at the URL *contoso-web.azurewebsites.net*. During development and testing this may be acceptable. However, as you approach the release of your web app, you will generally want to configure a custom domain for the site, such as contoso.com.

Configuring a custom domain name requires the following steps:

1.  Obtain a custom domain from a domain registrar of your choice.

2.  Add DNS records for your domain using your domain registrar.

3.  Associate the custom domain with your Azure web app.

## Adding DNS records

The DNS records you add with your domain registrar can be either an A record or CNAME record. An A record resolves a domain to a specific IP address. For Azure Web Apps, that IP address is the IP address of the cluster of servers your website is running in. It is not the IP address of a specific virtual machine. You can obtain the IP address you should use for your A record from the Azure portal by clicking on Custom domains in the web app blade, as shown in Figure 1-11.

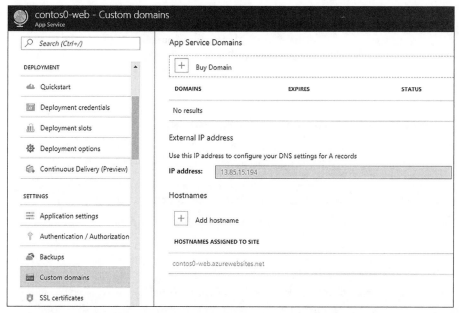

**FIGURE 1-11** Locating the IP address to use for A records in the Azure portal

If you use an A record, then Azure requires that you first add a TXT record mapped to the web app's hostname to verify that you own the domain. Table 1-2 illustrates how the A record and TXT record are defined for the custom domain contoso.com.

**TABLE 1-2** Example DNS records when using A records to configure a custom domain

| RECORD TYPE | NAME | VALUE |
|---|---|---|
| A | @ | 13.85.15.194 |
| TXT | @ | Contos0-web.azurewebsites.net |

If you use CNAME records, then your DNS records only indicate the custom domain and the Azure Web App URL (or hostname) it maps to. It is also possible to map subdomains. Table 1-3 shows an example of how a CNAME record is defined for a custom domain contoso.com.

**TABLE 1-3** Example DNS record when using CNAME records to configure a custom domain

| RECORD TYPE | NAME | VALUE |
|---|---|---|
| CNAME | contoso.com | Contos0-web.azurewebsites.net |

## Associating the custom domain with the web app

After the CNAME records have been verified, the last step is to associate your custom domain with your Azure Web App. This can be done using the Azure portal as shown previously.

> **NOTE  MODE SETTING REQUIREMENTS FOR CUSTOM DOMAINS**
>
> Custom domains are not supported in the free tier for an app service plan.

> **MORE INFO  CUSTOM DOMAINS AND AZURE WEB APPS**
>
> More information and detailed steps on how to configure custom domains is available at *https://docs.microsoft.com/en-us/azure/app-service-web/app-service-web-tutorial-custom-domain#map-a-cname-record*.

# Configure SSL certificates

Azure Web Apps provide SSL support for every site by default. If your website is named contoso-web, you can open a browser and access it using http or https. However, the azurewebsites.net domain is a shared domain and therefore the wildcard certificate providing SSL is also shared, making it less secure than if you had a custom domain and your own SSL certificate for the custom domain.

Most sites will have a custom domain and therefore will need to configure SSL with this in mind. The site must also be in Standard mode to support this configuration. Configuring SSL for an Azure Web App with a custom domain requires the following steps:

1. Obtain an SSL certificate.
2. Upload the SSL certificate to Azure.
3. Configure the SSL bindings.

**EXAM TIP**

**SSL support for an Azure Web App with a custom domain is not provided in the Free and Shared pricing tiers of App Service Plans.**

A certificate authority must sign your SSL certificate, and the certificate must adhere to the following requirements:

- The certificate contains a private key.
- The certificate must be created for key exchange that can be exported to a Personal Information Exchange (.pfx) file.
- The certificate's subject name must match the custom domain. If you have multiple custom domains for your website, the certificate will need to be either a wildcard certificate or have a subject alternative name (SAN).
- The certificate should use 2048-bit (or higher) encryption.

There are two methods for configuring an SSL certificate. One option is to create an App Service Certificate. Another is to obtain an SSL certificate from a third party.

**EXAM TIP**

**Regardless of which method you choose to configure an SSL certificate, be advised that neither forces HTTPS only traffic to the application running in the web app. This means users can still access the application using HTTP. To enforce HTTPS, a rewrite rule must be defined in the application configuration files to redirect HTTP requests to HTTPS. More information is available at: *https://docs.microsoft.com/en-us/azure/app-service-web/app-service-web-tutorial-custom-ssl#enforce-https*.**

## Configure an SSL certificate using an App Service Certificate

In the Azure portal, search for App Service Certificate in the marketplace. Provide a resource name, host name, and select a certificate SKU. The certificate SKU can be a *standard* certificate or a *wildcard* certificate. Figure 1-12 illustrates creating a new App Service Certificate in the Azure portal.

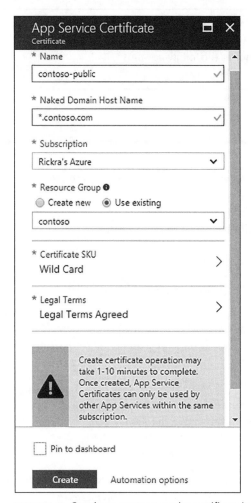

**FIGURE 1-12** Creating a new app service certificate in the Azure portal

After creating the app service certificate, you must perform the following three steps:

1. Store the certificate in Azure Key Vault.

2. Verify domain ownership. This refers to ownership of the host name you specified when creating the app service certificate.

3. Import the certificate into your web app and add SSL bindings, which can be SNI SSL or IP-based SSL.

> **MORE INFO**   **CONFIGURE SSL USING AN APP SERVICE CERTIFICATE**
>
> For additional information and detailed steps on how to configure an SSL certificate using an App Service Certificate, see *https://docs.microsoft.com/en-us/azure/app-service-web/web-sites-purchase-ssl-web-site*.

**EXAM TIP**

An app service certificate can only be used with other app services (web apps, API apps, mobile apps) in the same subscription. It also must be stored in an Azure Key Vault instance.

## Configure a third party SSL certificate

After obtaining an SSL certificate from a third party, you must perform the following two steps:

1. Upload the SSL certificate to Azure.
2. Configure the SSL bindings in your web app.

You can upload your SSL certificate to Azure using the Azure portal. Open the web app blade and click on SSL certificates under the Settings section. This will open a blade where you can upload the certificate and configure SSL bindings as shown in Figure 1-13.

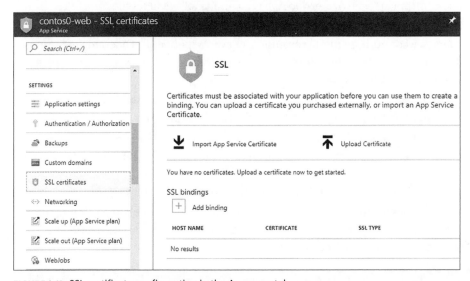

**FIGURE 1-13** SSL certificate configuration in the Azure portal

After the SSL certificate has been uploaded, the last step in the process is to configure the SSL bindings. Azure Web Apps support *Server Name Indication* (SNI) SSL and the traditional *IP-based SSL*. You can configure the SSL bindings in the Azure portal in the SSL Certificates blade referenced earlier in Figure 1-13. For each binding you must specify the following:

- The custom domain name
- The SSL certificate to use for the custom domain
- Select either SNI SSL or IP-based SSL

If you choose IP-based SSL for your SSL binding and your custom domain is configured using an A record, Azure will assign a new dedicated IP address to your website. This is a different IP address than what you previously used to configure the A record. Therefore, you must update the A record with your DNS registrar using the new virtual IP address. The virtual IP address can be found in the management portal by clicking the Properties part of the Website blade.

## Configuring handler mappings

Depending on the tools and language used to build a web application, it may be necessary for you to configure additional handlers (or interpreters) to support the web app's code. To configure a handler mapping for an Azure Web App requires the following settings:

- **Extension**   The file extension that you want to be handled by the script processor. This can be a wildcard, a specific file extension, or even a specific file. For example, *, *.php, and Handler.fcgi. The script processor defined in the script processor path will process requests that match this pattern.

- **Script Processor Path**   The absolute path to the script processor that will process requests for files matching the pattern in the extension property.

- **Optional Arguments**   This can be a path to a script for the script processor to process or any other argument that you may need to define when invoking the script processor.

### Configuring handler mappings using the management portal

In the Azure portal, you can add handler mappings by opening the Application Settings blade for your web app. Scroll down towards the bottom of the blade until you find the Handler Mappings section, as shown in Figure 1-14.

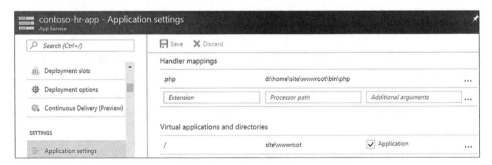

**FIGURE 1-14** Handler mappings in Azure portal

# Configuring virtual applications and directories

Some web applications require virtual applications or directories be added as part of the web app configuration. Azure Web Apps supports these configuration requirements. Configuring a virtual application or directory for an Azure Web App requires the following settings:

- **Virtual Directory**   The path that users will use to access the directory or application.
- **Physical Path**   The path to the physical directory or application.
- **Application**   If selected, the virtual directory is configured as a web application. If the checkbox is clear, it will be a virtual directory.

In the Azure portal, you can add virtual applications and directories by opening the Configuration Settings blade for your web app. Scroll down towards the bottom of the blade until you find the Virtual Applications And Directories section, as shown previously in Figure 1-14.

# Skill 1.3: Configure diagnostics, monitoring, and analytics

Monitoring web apps to identify failures, potential performance issues, or metrics used to determine application health is a necessary function for IT. Azure Web Apps provides a rich set of monitoring and diagnostic features that you can use to easily monitor the application and quickly retrieve diagnostic data when you need to probe deeper into how the site is performing.

---

**This skill covers how to:**

- Enable application and site diagnostics
- Retrieve diagnostic logs
- View streaming logs
- Monitor web app resources
- Monitor App Service Plan resources
- Monitor availability, performance, and usage
- Monitor Azure services
- Configure backup

---

## Enabling application and web server diagnostics

Diagnostic logging is not enabled by default. It is up to you to enable and configure logging in a way that provides the information you need to troubleshoot issues. There are two categories of Azure Web App Diagnostic logs:

- Application diagnostic logs
- Web server diagnostic logs

*Application diagnostic logs* contain information produced by the application code. This can be tracing that the developers instrumented when writing the code, or exceptions that were raised by the application. When you enable application logs, you must specify the logging level, which can be one of the following:

- Error
- Warning
- Information
- Verbose

*Web server diagnostic logs* contain information produced by the web server that the web application is running on. Three types of web server diagnostic logs can be enabled:

- **Web Server Logging**  Contains all HTTP events on a website and is formatted using the W3C extended log file format.
- **Detailed Error Messages**  Contains information on requests that resulted in a HTTP status code of 400 or higher.
- **Failed Request Tracing**  Contains detailed traces for any failed requests. This log also contains traces for all the IIS components that were involved in processing the request. This can be useful when trying to isolate where in the system a failure is occurring.

## Enabling diagnostics logs (Azure portal)

In the Azure portal, enable application and web server diagnostic logs by opening the web app blade and clicking Diagnostics Logs under the Monitoring section. This will open the Diagnostic Logs blade, where you can enable the logs and configure the logging level, as shown in Figure 1-15.

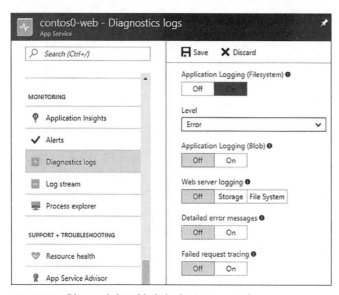

**FIGURE 1-15** Diagnostic logs blade in the Azure portal

## Enabling diagnostics logs (PowerShell)

Use the Set-AzureRmWebApp cmdlet to configure diagnostic logs. For example, the code shown here enables the *web server logging* and the *failed request tracing*.

```
$resourceGroupName = "contoso"
$webAppName = "contos0-web"

# Get a reference to an existing web app
$webApp = Get-AzureRmWebApp -ResourceGroupName $resourceGroupName -Name $webAppName

# Configure diagnostic logging
Set-AzureRmWebApp -ResourceGroupName $resourceGroupName -Name $webAppName `
    -RequestTracingEnabled $true -HttpLoggingEnabled $true
```

## Enabling diagnostic logs (CLI)

Use the webapp log config command to configure diagnostic logs. For example, the code shown here enables application logging and disables failed request tracing.

```
#!/bin/bash

resourceGroupName="contoso"
webAppName="contos0-web"

# Configure diagnostic logging
az webapp log config --resource-group $resourceGroupName --name $webAppName \
    --application-logging true --failed-request-tracing false
```

> **MORE INFO** **DIAGNOSTIC LOGGING FOR AZURE WEB APPS**
>
> Additional information about the diagnostic logging options, what is logged, and how to configure the logs is available at: *https://docs.microsoft.com/en-us/azure/app-service-web/web-sites-enable-diagnostic-log*.

# Retrieving diagnostic logs

You have many choices when it comes to retrieving diagnostic logs or just viewing the contents of the logs. Regardless of how you choose to retrieve diagnostic logs, it's helpful to understand where the logs are stored on the web app's file system. Table 1-4 lists the different logs and their location in the file system.

**TABLE 1-4** Diagnostic log file locations on the file system for an Azure website

| LOG FILE TYPE | LOCATION |
| --- | --- |
| Application Diagnostics | D:\Home\LogFiles\Application\ |
| SITE DIAGNOSTICS (WEB SERVER) | D:\HOME\LOGFILES\HTTP\RAWLOGS\ |
| Site Diagnostics (Detailed Errors) | D:\Home\LogFiles\DetailedErrors\ |
| SITE DIAGNOSTICS (FAILED REQUEST TRACES) | D:\HOME\LOGFILES\W3SVC<RANDOM#>\ |

> **NOTE  FAILED REQUEST LOGS STYLE SHEET FILE**
>
> When failed request logging is enabled, the folder where the logs are stored contains an .xml file and a file named Freb.xsl file. The .xml file contains the log data generated by the server. The Freb.xsl file is a style sheet document that enhances viewing the .xml file in your browser. When downloading failed request logs to your local computer, save the Freb.xsl in the same folder with a .xml file. Then, open the .xml file using your browser for an enhanced viewing experience. This makes identifying errors and warnings in the log much easier.

## Using FTP to retrieve log files

In the Diagnostic logs blade of the Azure portal are settings identifying the FTP user and a URL that you can use to access the web app's file system. Using this information, you can connect using any FTP client you choose, navigate the file system, and download diagnostic logs.

## Using Site Control Manager (Kudu) to retrieve log files

Site Control Manager, often referred to as "Kudu", is a web app extension that you can use to retrieve log files, browse the file system, edit files, delete files, view environment variables, and even capture process dump files.

To access the Site Control Manager, open your browser and navigate to: *https://<your site name>.scm.azurewebsites.net*.

**EXAM TIP**

Every Azure web app gets the Site Control Manager site extension installed by default. There is nothing you have to do to enable it.

The URL is the same as the URL for your web app, with the added scm immediately after the website name. Figure 1-16 is an example of what the Site Control Manager (SCM) home page looks like for a web app running on a Windows App Service Plan. For a web app running on a Linux app service plan, the SCM features are not as rich.

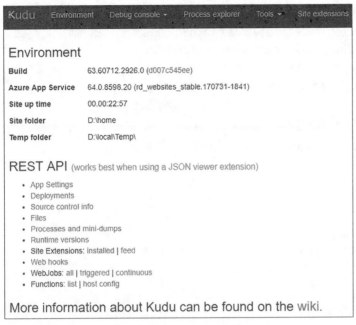

**FIGURE 1-16** The home page of the site control manager "Kudu" extension

Using Site Control Manager, select the Debug Console and then select the CMD option. This opens a debug console (Bash or SSH for Linux App Service Plans) that you can type directly into or use the navigation above. As you click the navigation links, the console will update to your current directory. Figure 1-17 shows the contents of the LogFiles folder.

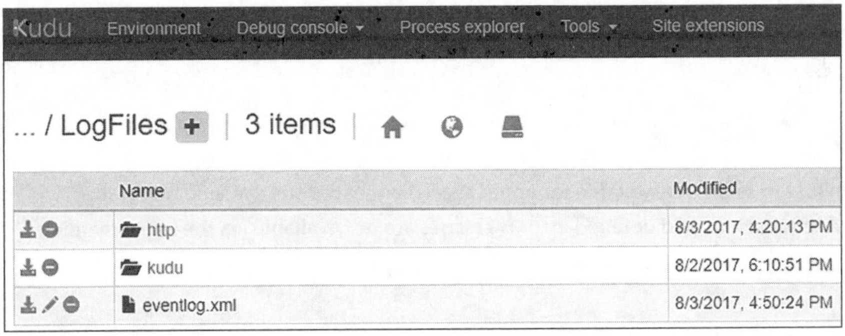

| ... / LogFiles + \| 3 items | | | | | | |
| --- | --- | --- | --- |

| | Name | | Modified |
| --- | --- | --- | --- |
| 📥 ⊖ | 📁 http | | 8/3/2017, 4:20:13 PM |
| 📥 ⊖ | 📁 kudu | | 8/2/2017, 6:10:51 PM |
| 📥 ✎ ⊖ | 📄 eventlog.xml | | 8/3/2017, 4:50:24 PM |

**FIGURE 1-17** The debug console in Site Control Manager and viewing the LogFiles folder

Using Site Control Manager, you can download an entire folder or individual files by clicking the download link to the left of the directory or file name.

### Retrieve diagnostic logs (PowerShell)

Use the Save-AzureWebsiteLog cmdlet to download diagnostic logs. This code will download the log files and store them in E:\Weblogs.zip on the client computer.

```
$wsName = "contoso-web"
Save-AzureWebsiteLog -Name $wsName -Output e:\weblogs.zip
```

### Retrieve diagnostic logs (CLI)

Use the webapp log download command to download diagnostic logs.

```
#!/bin/bash

resourceGroupName="contoso"
webAppName="contos0-web"

# Configure diagnostic logging
az webapp log download --resource-group $resourceGroupName --name $webAppName \
    --log-file ./webapplogs.zip
```

## Viewing streaming logs

Sometimes it is preferable to view log data as it is being collected (almost real-time). Azure Websites provides a feature to enable streaming of log data via the log-streaming service. You can connect to the log-streaming service using the following methods:

- Management portal
- Azure PowerShell Cmdlets
- Command-Line Tools
- Site Control Manager (Kudu)
- Visual Studio

**EXAM TIP**

The streaming log service is available for application diagnostic logs and web server logs only. Failed request logs and detailed error messages are not available via the log-streaming service.

### Viewing streaming logs (Azure portal)

The streaming log service is accessible from the web app blade. Scroll down to the Monitoring section and click on Log stream. In the Log stream blade, you can toggle between application and web server logs, pause and start the log-streaming service, and clear the logs in the console. Figure 1-18 shows example output for the web server logs in the Log stream blade.

**FIGURE 1-18** The Logs stream blade in the Azure portal showing web server logs

### Viewing streaming logs (PowerShell)

Use the Get-AzureWebsiteLog cmdlet to stream logs directly in the Azure PowerShell console window. The code shown here connects to the log-streaming service to start streaming the web server logs.

```
Get-AzureWebsiteLog -Name "contoso-web-west" -Tail -Path http
```

The Get-AzureWebsiteLog also supports a Message parameter that you can use to filter the output when streaming application logs. For example, the code shown here filters the log-streaming output to just application logs that are categorized as errors.

```
Get-AzureWebsiteLog -Name "contoso-web-west" -Tail -Message Error
```

### Viewing streaming logs (CLI)

Use the web app log tail command to view logs directly in a bash shell.

```
az webapp log tail -resource-group "contoso" -name "contos0-web"
```

## Monitor web app resources

The Azure portal provides rich and visually appealing screens to monitor your web app. The web app blade is where you can quickly and easily get access to information, click through metrics, parts and graphs, and in some cases just hover over part items to drill deeper into the data.

The web app blade displays web parts for five categories of metrics as follows:

- Number of requests
- HTTP server errors
- Data in
- Data out
- Average response time

The graphs in these web parts are useful to get a quick all up view of how things are performing. However, you can also click into these web parts to get a deeper look into the data, change the chart type, go back further in history, and view any alerts you may have for a particular metric. Figure 1-19 shows the Average Response Time metric (after clicking on the web part in the web app blade) with the CPU Time metric added to the graph.

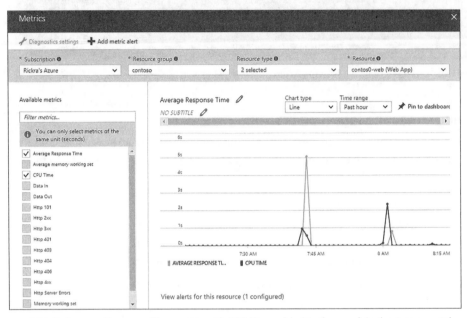

**FIGURE 1-19** Average Response Time metric with CPU Time added to the graph in the Azure portal

## Monitor App Service Plan resources

The App Service Plan your web app is running on should also be monitored to insure you are properly sized to support the app services (web apps, API apps, mobile apps) running on the App Service Plan. The App Service Plan metrics provide insight on how resources such as CPU, memory, HTTP queue length, and others are consumed across all instances. For example, if memory is sustaining a value of 85% or more, then you may want to consider scaling up the plan to the next pricing tier or increasing the number of instances.

The app service plan blade displays a monitoring web part showing CPU Percentage and Memory Percentage. You can click into the web part and explore the data further as shown in Figure 1-20.

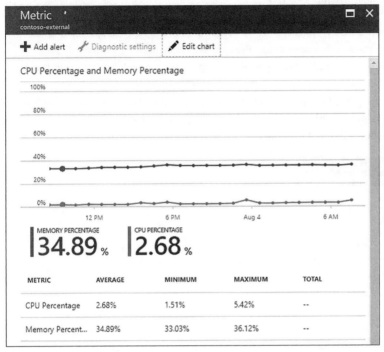

**FIGURE 1-20** App Service Plan CPU and memory percentage metrics in the Azure portal

---

**MORE INFO**  **AZURE WEB APP AND APP SERVICE PLAN METRICS**

For a complete list of metrics available for web apps and app service plans see: *https://docs.microsoft.com/en-us/azure/app-service-web/web-sites-monitor/*.

## Monitor availability, performance, and usage

Application Insights provides deeper monitoring of your web app, enabling you to monitor application performance, availability for end users, and even provide insight into how your users are using the application.

To get started, create a new Application Insights resource in the Azure portal. Search for Application Insights in the Azure Marketplace. Provide a friendly name for the application Insight resource and select an application type. If your application developer included the Application Insights SDK in the application code, then you can get deeper insights by selecting an application type matching the framework/code that the developer used. If you don't have this information, you can select a General application type. Figure 1-21 illustrates creating a new application insight resource in the Azure portal.

**FIGURE 1-21**  Creating a new Application Insights resource in the Azure portal

A common monitoring task is to setup availability tests to monitor your web application from several locations around the world. This gives you data on the availability and responsiveness of your application from the perspective of users in different regions of the world.

There are two types of availability tests you can configure. The simplest is the URL Ping test whereby Azure will simply ping your web app URL using an HTTP GET request. To create an availability test, scroll down on the Application Insights blade and click on Availability Tests. In the Availability Tests blade, click Add Test at the top. Even a simple URL Ping test has many properties to configure, such as parsing dependent links, retries, test locations, HTTP success criteria, setup alerts, and more as shown in Figure 1-22.

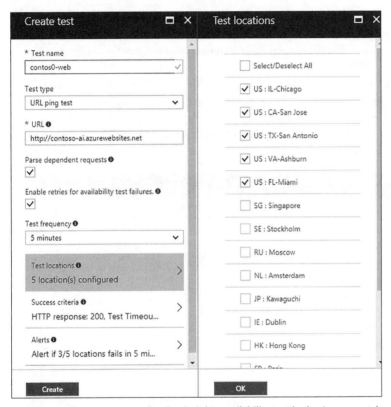

FIGURE 1-22 Create a new application insights availability test in the Azure portal

The other type of availability test is a Multi-step web test. This type of test requires that you create a Web Performance and Load Test Project in Visual Studio, configure the tests, and then upload the test file to Azure.

Availability tests run at configured intervals (default is five mins) across all of the test locations you configured. As a result, it will take several minutes before you start to see data from your availability test. Figure 1-23 shows the availability blade for a simple URL Ping Test. Each green dot represents a successful test from a test location. You can also click on the green dots to see details about that specific test.

**FIGURE 1-23**  Availability test summary for a web app configured with a URL Ping Test

When you create an availability test you can also create an alert. The default alert for the URL Ping Test triggers an alert if three of the test locations fail within a five minute window. If this happens, then subscription administrators get an automated email about the alert.

Three types of alerts are available as follows:

- **Metric Alert**   Triggered when some metric crosses a threshold value for a sustained period of time.
- **Web Tests Alert**   Triggered when a site becomes unavailable or has response times exceeding a threshold value.
- **Proactive Diagnostic Alert**   Warns you of potential application failure, application performance, and app service issues.

You can add new alerts from the Application Insights blade. Scroll down to the Configure section and click Alerts to open the Alerts blade.

> *MORE INFO*   **CONFIGURING ALERTS IN APPLICATION INSIGHTS**
>
> Further guidance on the types of alerts, how to configure them, and when to use them is available at: *https://docs.microsoft.com/en-us/azure/application-insights/app-insights-alerts*.

Application Insights can also be used to capture client-side telemetry data. This enables you to get metrics such as page load time, out-bound AJAX call durations, browser errors, and more. To enable this, you (or your developer) will need to add a small amount of JavaScript to the pages you want to capture client-side telemetry data on. Application Insights provides the JavaScript for you with full integration with your storage account where the telemetry data is stored. All you have to do is cut/paste it into your code.

> *MORE INFO*   **APPLICATION INSIGHTS FOR CLIENT-SIDE TELEMETRY DATA**
>
> Information and guidance on how to capture and analyze client-side telemetry data is available at: *https://docs.microsoft.com/en-us/azure/application-insights/app-insights-javascript*.

## Monitor Azure services

To effectively monitor web apps that you are responsible for means you also need monitor the Azure services your web app depends on. The Microsoft Azure platform is very transparent when it comes to service availability and places a Service Health (in preview at the time of this writing) web part on dashboard of the Azure portal. In the Service Health blade, you can get a global map view of regions with service issues, review planned maintenance, be informed of health advisories, and see health history. Figure 1-24 shows a heal history report where you can review the issue, download an issue summary and learn if there are mitigation steps you need to take.

**FIGURE 1-24** Service health blade in the Azure portal

---

> **MORE INFO   AZURE SERVICES STATUS**
>
> You can view Azure service status information on the Azure website without signing into your Azure subscription. The public Azure service status page is available at: *https://azure.microsoft.com/en-us/status/*.

## Configure backup

Having a solid backup plan is a best practice for any application running on-premises or in the cloud. Azure Web Apps offer an easy and effective backup service that can be used to back up your web app configuration, file content, and even databases that your application has a dependency on.

To configure backup for a web app, you must have an Azure Storage account and a container where you want the backups stored. Open the web app blade and click on Backups under the Settings section.

Backups can be invoked on-demand or based on a schedule that you define when configuring the backup. When configuring a backup schedule you can also specify retention period for the backup.

## Restore an Azure web app backup

At some point, it may be necessary to restore a web app from a backup. The Azure portal pro-vides an intuitive interface to guide you through the process. As you start the restore process, you can select which backup to restore from and where to restore to, such as overwriting the existing web app or to a new web app environment as shown in Figure 1-25.

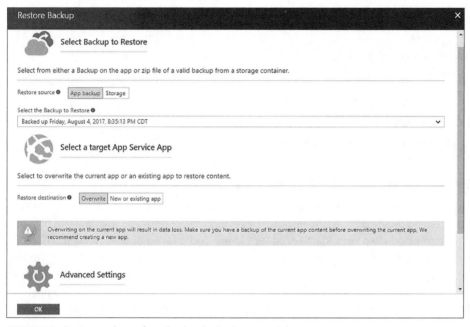

**FIGURE 1-25** Restore web app from backup in the Azure portal

# Skill 1.4: Configure web apps for scale and resilience

The Microsoft Azure platform is an extremely resilient platform. By leveraging the services and features available, you can implement highly available solutions to meet demand from users in a way that is cost effective for the business. The notion of elastic scale is a key driver for moving to the cloud, and Azure App Service Plans deliver this through a rich set of scalability features in the platform.

Using the Autoscale feature, you can scale out and in the number of instances of your app service plan based on schedules you set or metrics you define. You can also manually scale the number of instances in situations where you want a constant number of instances to host your app services.

> **This skill covers how to:**
> - Scale up or down an app service plan
> - Scale app service instances manually
> - Scale app service instances using Autoscale
> - Configure Azure Traffic Manager

## Scale up or down an app service plan

The decision to scale up or down an app service plan is driven by the resource needs of the app services running on the plan. As the resource needs increase or decrease you may find that you need to scale up or down your App Service Plan. When you scale up or down an app service plan, the only properties that change are the number of cores and the amount of RAM. For example, if you have an S1 App Service Plan, scaling it up to an S3 simply increases the number of cores from 1 to 4 and the amount of RAM from 1.75 GB to 7 GB. The features, such as amount of storage, maximum number of instances, maximum number of slots, custom domain support, and more remain the same.

To scale up or down an App Service Plan, open the app service plan blade and click on Scale up (App Service Plan) as shown in Figure 1-26.

**FIGURE 1-26** Scale up option under Settings in the App service plan blade

Selecting this option opens up the pricing tier blade, where you can scale up or down your App Service Plan. It is also possible to choose an entirely different pricing tier, such as changing from a Standard tier to a Premium tier.

## Scale app service instances manually

The maximum number of instances you can scale out an App Service Plan to is defined by the pricing tier of the app service plan as follows:

- 3 instances in Basic
- 10 instances in Standard
- 20 instances in Premium (subject to availability)
- 100 instances in Isolated (used with App Service Environment)

These limits apply whether you scale out manually or using Autoscale, which will be discussed in the next section.

To scale in or out the number of instances in an app service plan, open the App Service Plan blade and click on Scale out (App service plan) as shown above in Figure 1-26. In the Scale out blade, adjust the Instance count slider to the desired number of instances as shown in Figure 1-27.

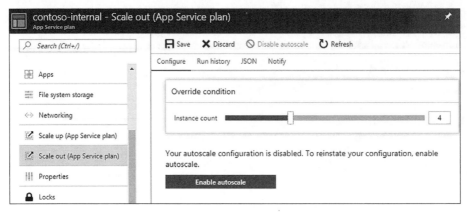

**FIGURE 1-27** Manually scaling out app service plan instances

## Scale app service instances using Autoscale

Azure's Autoscale feature enables you to define scale conditions that contain rules and configuration settings that are used to rigger scale out actions. Autoscale conditions can be based on a metric, such as CPU, or based on a schedule. An App Service Plan can have multiple scale conditions defined, meaning you can combine different metric conditions and schedule conditions simultaneously.

To get started, you first have to enable Autoscale for an app service plan. To enable this, click the Enable Autoscale button in the Scale out blade as shown above in Figure 1-27.

### Create a metric-based scale condition

Open the Scale Out Blade for the App Service Plan. In the scale condition web part, set the Scale mode to Scale based on a metric. Define the Minimum, Maximum and Default Instance limits for the scale condition. Figure 1-28 illustrates a scale condition that will scale in and out instances within a range of 1 to 5.

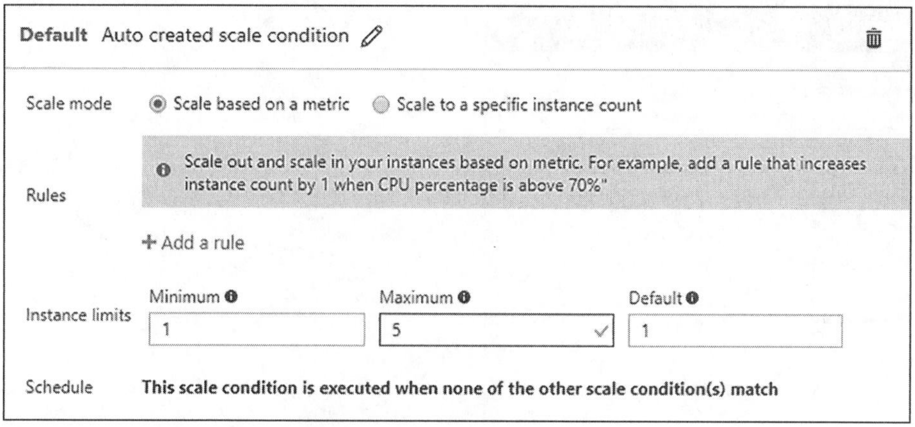

**FIGURE 1-28** Scale by metric condition in the Azure portal

Next, click the +Add a rule link to define a new scale rule. The first property in a scale rule you need to set is the Metric Source, which defaults to the App Service Plan resource. This means the metrics you can base your scale rule on are those provided by the App Service Plan, such as CPU Percentage.  However, you can choose a different metric source that will provide different metrics to base your rule on. For example, you may want to define a rule based on a metric in an Application Insights resource, such as Server response time.

Next, choose the metric to base your rule on, configure the criteria for the metric, and the scale action to execute when the criteria is met. Figure 1-29 shows a scale rule based on CPU Percentage, whereby the instance count will increase by one when the CPU percentage across all instances exceeds 70% for a period of 10 minutes or more.

**FIGURE 1-29**  Scale rule based on CPU Percentage

## Create a schedule-based scale condition

Sometimes you may want to scale out your app service plan instances when you can predict increased demand. For example, an organization needs additional resources during the day to support business demand but in the evening hours can get by with a minimum set of resources when there are significantly fewer users of the system. This situation is easily addressed by creating a schedule-based scale condition that increases app service plan instances early in the morning and then decreases them in the evening.

To create a schedule-based scale condition using the example above, open the Scale out blade for the app service plan. In the scale condition web part, set the Scale mode to Scale to a specific instance count. Set the instance count to the number of instances needed during working hours. Figure 1-30 shows a scale condition that sets the instance count to 3 between the hours of 6AM and 6PM for working for workdays.

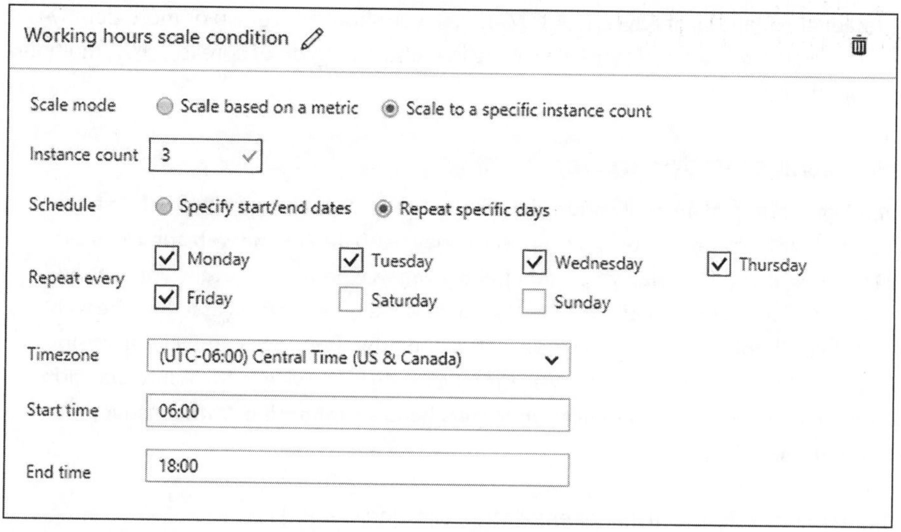

**FIGURE 1-30** Scale by schedule condition in the Azure portal

When the schedule criteria is not met, such as in the evenings and on weekends, the default scale condition created in the previous section is applied. This would have the effect of scaling back down to one instance if the CPU percentage stays below 70%.

> **MORE INFO   AUTOSCALE BEST PRACTICES**
>
> Additional information on Autoscale concept and guidance on best practices is available at: *https://docs.microsoft.com/en-us/azure/monitoring-and-diagnostics/insights-autoscale-best-practices*.

## Configure Azure Traffic Manager

Azure Traffic Manager is a network service that you can use to route users to web app endpoints (deployments) in potentially different datacenters around the world. It provides services and settings that you can use to improve availability, performance for users, or load-balance traffic. It works by applying a policy engine to DNS queries for the domain names of your web app.

> **MORE INFO  AZURE TRAFFIC MANAGER OVERVIEW**
>
> For more information on when Traffic Manager is, how it works, and scenarios it is intended for, see: *https://docs.microsoft.com/en-us/azure/traffic-manager/traffic-manager-overview*.

To leverage the features of Azure Traffic Manager, you should have two or more deployments of your web app. The deployments can be in the same region or spread across multiple regions around the world.

> **NOTE  MULTIPLE DEPLOYMENTS FOR THE SAME WEB APP**
>
> The implementation of an application will greatly influence how Azure Traffic Manager can be used for that application. As simple as it may be to deploy the web app to multiple locations, careful consideration should be given to whether or not the application was designed for multiple deployments. How data is managed and accessed by the web app, whether or not application state is a factor, and other important application design aspects need to be reviewed. Traffic Manager is a powerful service in the Azure platform that should be reviewed with application owners before configuring Traffic Manager for the application.

Configuring Azure Traffic Manager entails the following steps:

- Create an Azure Traffic Manager profile
- Add endpoints to the profile
- Update DNS records for your custom domain

## Create an Azure Traffic Manager profile

To create an Azure Traffic Manager profile, you must select a unique DNS name for your profile. All Azure Traffic Manager profiles use the shared domain *.trafficmanager.net. Therefore, your DNS name must be unique because it will form the Azure Traffic Manager domain name that you will use when updating your DNS records. As an example, a DNS name for Contoso might be *contoso-web-tm.trafficmanager.net*.

Related to the DNS name setting is the *DNS Time-To-Live (TTL)*, which tells DNS clients and resolvers on DNS servers how long to cache the name resolved by Azure Traffic Manager. The default value for this setting is five minutes.

You must select a routing method. The routing method options are as follows:

- **Performance**   Choose this option when your web app is deployed in different regions and you want users to be routed to the deployment closest to them.
- **Weighted**   Choose this option when you want to distribute the load across multiple deployments.  If you set the weights of each endpoint to the same value, then this would achieve round-robin routing.  Increasing the weight of one endpoint increases the frequency users are routed to it over lower weighted endpoints.
- **Priority**   Choose this option when you want one deployment to be the primary for all traffic and the others to be available as backup if the primary becomes unavailable. If you have more than two deployments, then you can prioritize the order of the endpoints that you want Traffic Manager to failover to.

**MORE INFO**   **TRAFFIC MANAGER ROUTING METHODS**

For further information on each of the routing methods and detailed walkthroughs of how DNS queries are resolved, see: *https://docs.microsoft.com/en-us/azure/traffic-manager/traffic-manager-routing-methods*.

For Azure Traffic Manager to determine the health of your web app endpoints (deployments) you need to provide configuration settings so Azure Traffic Manager can query your endpoints to determine if an endpoint should be taken out of the rotation. The configuration settings consist of the following:

- **Protocol**   This can be HTTP, HTTPS, or TCP.
- **Port**   Defaults to standard HTTP and HTTPS ports, such as 80 or 443.  You may choose to use a different port to separate normal web traffic from endpoint monitoring traffic.
- **Path**   This is the path in the application that the monitoring service will perform an HTTP GET request against (if using HTTP/S). This can be the root of the application, such as "/". Or, it could be a specific health check page the application may make available, such as /Healthcheck.aspx.
- **Probing interval**   Determines how frequent Azure probes your endpoint.
- **Tolerated number of failures**   Nmber of times a health probe can fail before the endpoint is considered to be down/unavailable.
- **Probe timeout**   Timeout period for a probe request.  Must be smaller than the probing interval setting.

**NOTE**   **USING HEALTH CHECK PAGES TO DETERMINE ENDPOINT HEALTH**

Some web applications provide a health check page as part of the application and may name the page Healthcheck.aspx. The advantage of having a health check page is that the page can check the health of other services the application depends on, such as SQL Database connections, web service availability, or internal metrics the application developers have added as part of the health monitoring of the application. Just because a request for a page such as the root at "/" may return an HTTP 200 (OK), doesn't necessarily mean the application is healthy. By using a custom health check page, applications can more accurately determine the health of the application instance and return an error code, such as HTTP 503 (Service Unavailable). As a result, Azure Traffic Manager will remove the endpoint from the rotation until the application instance returns HTTP 200 (OK).

To create an Azure Traffic Manager profile using the management portal, specify the unique DNS name and the load balancing method. Next, configure the settings for the profile. Figure 1-31 shows the Configure page for an Azure Traffic Manager profile.

**FIGURE 1-31** Configuring a traffic manager profile in the Azure portal

To create a Traffic Manager profile using Azure PowerShell, use the New-AzureRmTraffic-ManagerProfile cmdlet. For example, the code below creates a profile named contoso-public with a domain name of *contoso-public-tm.trafficmanager.net*, Performance routing method, and TCP monitoring on port 8082.

```
# Properties for the traffic manager profile
$tmName = "contoso-public"
$tmDnsName = "contoso-public-tm"
$ttl = 300
$monitorProtocol = "TCP"
$monitorPort = 8082

# Create the traffic manager profile
New-AzureRmTrafficManagerProfile -ResourceGroupName $resourceGroupName -Name $tmName `
    -RelativeDnsName $tmDnsName -Ttl $ttl -TrafficRoutingMethod Performance `
    -MonitorProtocol $monitorProtocol -MonitorPort $monitorPort
```

# Add endpoints to an Azure Traffic Manager profile

The endpoints are where Azure Traffic Manager will resolve DNS queries to for your domain. After creating the Azure Traffic Manager profile, you must add the endpoints to the profile that you want Azure Traffic Manager to resolve DNS queries to. In the Azure portal, you can add, delete, and disable endpoints on the Endpoints page of the Azure Traffic Manager profile, as shown in Figure 1-32.

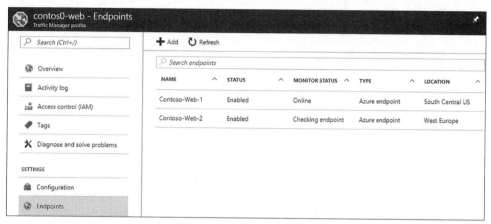

**FIGURE 1-32** Traffic manager endpoints in the Azure portal

You can use PowerShell to add an endpoint by using the Get-AzureRmTrafficManagerProfile and New-AzureRmTrafficManagerEndpoint. The code below demonstrates adding an existing web app as an endpoint to a traffic manager profile.

```
$resourceGroupName = "contoso"
$webAppName = "contos0-web"
$newTmEndpointName = "Contoso-Web-1"
$newTmEndpointTarget = "contos0-web.azurewebsites.net"

# Get the current traffic manager profile
$tmProfile = Get-AzureRmTrafficManagerProfile -ResourceGroupName $resourceGroupName
-Name $tmName

# Get a reference to an existing web app
$webApp = Get-AzureRmWebApp -ResourceGroupName $resourceGroupName -Name $webAppName

# Add the web app endpoint to the traffic manager profile
New-AzureRmTrafficManagerEndpoint -ResourceGroupName $resourceGroupName -ProfileName
$tmProfile.Name `
    -Name $newTmEndpointName -Type AzureEndpoints -EndpointStatus Enabled `
    -TargetResourceId $webApp.Id
```

To remove an endpoint, use the Remove-AzureRmTrafficManagerEndpoint cmdlet as shown here.

```
# Get the current traffic manager profile
$tmProfile = Get-AzureRmTrafficManagerProfile -ResourceGroupName $resourceGroupName
 -Name $tmName

Remove-AzureRmTrafficManagerEndpoint -ResourceGroupName $resourceGroupName
-ProfileName $tmProfile.Name `
    -Name $newTmEndpointName -Type AzureEndpoints -Force
```

To disable an endpoint, use the Disable-AzureRmTrafficManagerEndpoint cmdlet as shown here.

```
# Get the current traffic manager profile
$tmProfile = Get-AzureRmTrafficManagerProfile -ResourceGroupName $resourceGroupName
 -Name $tmName

Disable-AzureRmTrafficManagerEndpoint -ResourceGroupName $resourceGroupName -ProfileName
 $tmProfile.Name `
    -Name $newTmEndpointName -Type AzureEndpoints -Force
Update DNS records for your custom domain
```

The last step to configuring Azure Traffic Manager is to update your custom domain to point to the Azure Traffic Manager DNS name using a CNAME record. As an example, assume your custom domain is contoso.com and your Azure Traffic Manager DNS name is *contoso-web-tm.trafficmanager.net*. Table 1-5 shows how the CNAME record should be configured in this scenario.

**TABLE 1-5** Example DNS record for a custom domain and an Azure Traffic Manager DNS name

| RECORD TYPE | NAME | VALUE |
| --- | --- | --- |
| CNAME | www.contoso.com | contoso-web-tm.trafficmanager.net |

**EXAM TIP**

As users navigate to an application configured with Azure Traffic Manager, there is not any actual traffic routed through Traffic Manager. When a user browses to a website configured with Azure Traffic Manager, such as www.contoso.com, the user's DNS server will send a new DNS query to the DNS name for the Traffic Manager profile, such as contoso-web-tm. trafficmanager.net. The Traffic Manager DNS name servers receive this query. Based on the load balancing method in the Azure Traffic Manager profile, Traffic Manager will select an endpoint from the profile, and return a CNAME record mapping contoso-web-tm.traf-ficmanager.net to the DNS name for the selected endpoint, such as contoso-web-east. azurewebsites.net. The user's DNS server will then resolve the endpoint DNS name to an IP address and return it to the user. The user's browser then calls the selected website using the IP address. The domain and IP address are cached on the client machine, so subsequent requests to the website are sent directly to the website until the local DNS cache expires.

# Thought experiment

In this thought experiment, apply what you have learned about this chapter. You can find answers to these questions in the next section.

You are the IT Administrator for Contoso and responsible for managing the Contoso website. The public-facing website today is running in a Shared mode hosting plan. The development team is about to release a new version of the web app that will require 3.5 GB of memory to perform as designed.

As part of this new release, the marketing team is planning to run some television commercials and radio ads to notify new and existing customers of the new features and services offered by Contoso. The expectation is that these ads will generate large demand spikes as they are run during the campaign.

Due to the frequency of changes, the business has indicated that the web application should be backed up 3 times per day (once every 8 hours).

You need to provide a solution to meet the resource requirements for the new website version and to support the traffic spikes expected during the marketing campaign.

1. How will you scale the app service plan to meet the new resource requirements?
2. How will you configure the web app to support the traffic spikes during the marketing campaign?

# Thought experiment answers

This section contains the solution to the thought experiment.

1. The best pricing tier SKU for the app service plan to meet these requirements would be the Premium (P2) SKU. It meets the memory requirement of 3.5 GB. It also supports Autoscale which will be needed to support demand spikes. Finally, the requirement to backup multiple times per day is also met in the Premium tier. If the business only required daily backups, then the Standard (S2) SKU would be more cost effective. However, supporting multiple backups per day pushes this into the Premium tier.

2. You should use Azure Autoscale to sale out and in the number of instances to support the marketing campaign. You can create a metric-based autoscale condition and scale based on the number of requests, CPU, http queue length, or another metric that is useful for measuring load on the app service plan. Another option is to use a schedule-based autoscale condition, whereby you scale out the number of instances during the campaign and scale in the number of instances afterwards. Without additional information, it's not possible to determine what the right number of instances should be before, during, and after the campaign. So, a combination of metric-based and scheduled-based autoscale conditions would be best.

# Chapter summary

- Azure web apps are created under the *.azurewebsites.net shared domain.

- Adding deployment slots to a web app requires that the app service plan it runs on be in the Standard, Premium, or Isolated pricing tier.

- App Service Environment is a feature of App Service that provides a virtual network for your app service application (web app for example) to run in. This allows you to use virtual network security controls such as network security groups, virtual appliances, user defined routes, etc. to protect the web app.

- A web app has an implied production deployment slot by default. You can add additional deployment slots if your app service plan is standard, premium, or isolated.

- When creating new deployment slots, you can clone the configuration settings from another deployment slot or create a new deployment slot with empty settings.

- When swapping deployment slots, you can perform a single-phase swap or a multi-phase swap. The latter is recommended for mission critical workloads.

- An app service plan defines the capacity (cores, memory, or storage) and features available to the web apps running on it.

- Migrating web apps to a different app service plan requires that the target app service plan be in the same region and resource group as the source app service plan.

- Web App Application Settings is where you can configure language versions for .NET Framework, PHP, Java, and Python. This is also where you can set the site to run in 32-bit or 64-bit mode, enable web sockets and the Always-On feature, and configure handler mappings.

- Application settings and connection strings can be defined in the web app infrastructure and retrieved at application runtime using environment variables.

- To configure a custom domain, you must first add an A record and/or CNAME record using your DNS registrar. For A records, you must also add a TXT record to verify domain ownership.

- Azure Web Apps support Server Name Indication (SNI) SSL and IP-based SSL for web apps with a custom domain.

- App Service Certificate SKU can be either Standard or Wild Card.

- You can obtain an SSL certificate using App Service Certificate or separately through a 3rd party.

- An App Service Certificate can only be used by other app services in the same subscription.

- When you configure a SSL certificate for a web app, users can still access the web app using HTTP. To force HTTPS only traffic, a rewrite rule must be defined in the applications configuration file (or code).

- Azure Web Apps provides two categories of diagnostic logs: application diagnostics and web server diagnostics. There are three web server diagnostic log files available: Web Server, Detailed Errors, and Failed Request.

- When enabling application diagnostic logging, you must specify the logging level, which can be Error, Warning, Information, or Verbose.

- Monitor web app resources when you need to monitor just the web app.

- Monitor app service plan resources when you need to monitor metrics such as compute and memory that your web apps are running on.

- Site Control Manager (Kudu) is a web app extension and is installed by default for every web app. It is accessible at https://<your site name>.scm.azurewebsites.net. To authenticate, sign-in using the same credentials you use to sign-in to the Azure portal.

- Use Application Insights to monitor performance metrics, availability, and how users are using the application.

- Use Application Insights and client-side JavaScript to capture client-side telemetry data such as page load times, outbound AJAX call duration, and browser exceptions.

- Availability tests enable you to test the availability of your web app from multiple regions and monitor the duration of the tests.

- Use alerts to notify subscription administrators or others of potential performance, availability, or Azure service issues.

- Azure Web App backups can be used to back up web app configuration, file content, and databases.

- Azure Web App backups can be performed on-demand or on a schedule.

- Azure Web App backups can be restored over the existing web app or to a different web app environment.

- Scaling up an app service plan within a pricing tier increases the number of cores and RAM.

- Scaling out an app service plan increases the number in instances.

- Autoscale can be configured to scale on a schedule or based on a metric.

- The metric source of a metric-based scale rule determines the metrics available.

- Traffic Manager provides support for the following routing methods: Performance, Weighted, Priority, and Geographic.

- Traffic Manager is not a load balancer. It is an advanced DNS query resolver that resolves DNS queries based on the traffic manager profile settings.

# CHAPTER 2

# Create and manage Compute Resources

Microsoft Azure offers many features and services that can be used to create inventive solutions for almost any IT problem. Two of the most common services for designing these solutions are Microsoft Azure Virtual Machines (VM) and VM Scale Sets. Virtual machines are one of the key compute options for deploying workloads in Microsoft Azure. Virtual machines can provide the on-ramp for migrating workloads from on-premises (or other cloud providers) to Azure, because they are usually the most compatible with existing solutions. The flexibility of virtual machines makes them a key scenario for many workloads. For example, you have a choice of server operating systems, with various supported versions of Windows and Linux distributions. Azure virtual machines also provide you full control over the operating system, along with advanced configuration options for networking and storage. VM Scale Sets provide similar capabilities to VMs, and provide the ability to scale out certain types of workloads to handle large processing problems, or to just optimize cost by only running instances when needed. The third option covered in this module is Azure Container Service (ACS). Azure Container Service optimizes the configuration of popular open source tools and technologies, specifically for Azure. ACS provides a solution that offers portability for both container-based workloads and application configuration. You select the size, number of hosts, and choice of orchestrator tools and ACS handles everything else.

## Skills covered in this chapter:

- Skill 2.1: Deploy workloads on Azure Resource Manager (ARM) virtual machines (VMs)
- Skill 2.2: Perform configuration management
- Skill 2.3: Design and implement VM Storage
- Skill 2.4: Monitor ARM VMs
- Skill 2.5: Manage ARM VM Availability
- Skill 2.6: Scale ARM VMs
- Skill 2.7: Manage containers with Azure Container Service (ACS)

# Skill 2.1: Deploy workloads on Azure Resource Manager (ARM) virtual machines (VMs)

Microsoft Azure Virtual Machines is a flexible and powerful option for deploying workloads into the cloud. The support of both Windows and Linux-based operating systems allows for the deployment of a wide variety of workloads that traditionally run in an on-premises environment.

> **This skill covers how to:**
> - Identify and run workloads in VMs
> - Create virtual machines
> - Connect to virtual machines

## Identify and run workloads in VMs

Due to the flexible nature of virtual machines, they are the most common deployment target for workloads that are not explicitly designed with the cloud in mind. Azure virtual machines are based on Windows Server Hyper-V. However, not all features within Hyper-V are directly supported because much of the underlying networking and storage infrastructure is much different than a traditional Hyper-V deployment.

With that in mind, it should not come as a total surprise that all workloads from Microsoft (including roles and features of Windows Server itself) are not supported when running within Azure Virtual Machines. Microsoft Azure supports running all 64-bit versions of Windows Server starting with Windows Server 2003 and on. In the event the operating system itself is not supported like Windows Server 2003, this support is limited to issues that don't require operating system-level troubleshooting or patches). Beyond Windows Server, much of the Microsoft server software portfolio is directly supported on Azure VMs, such as Exchange, CRM, System Center, and so on.

The best way to keep track of what is, and is not supported, is through the Microsoft support article at *http://support.microsoft.com/kb/2721672*. This article details which Microsoft workloads are supported within Azure. Also, the article is kept up-to-date as new workloads are brought online, or the support policy changes when new capabilities within Azure enhance what is supported.

There are several distributions of Linux that are endorsed and officially supported to run in Microsoft Azure Virtual Machines. At the time of this writing, the following distributions have been tested with the Microsoft Azure Linux Agent and have pre-defined images in the Azure Marketplace with the agent pre-configured. Table 2-1 shows the current endorsed Linux distributions.

**TABLE 2-1** Endorsed Linux distributions for Azure VMs

| Distribution | Version |
|---|---|
| CentOS | CentOS 6.3+, 7.0+ |
| CoreOS | 494.4.0+ |
| Debian | Debian 7.9+, 8.2+ |
| Oracle Linux | 6.4+, 7.0+ |
| Red Hat Enterprise Linux | RHEL 6.7+, 7.1+ |
| SUSE Linux Enterprise | SLES/SLES for SAP<br>11 SP4<br>12 SP1+ |
| openSUSE | openSUSE Leap 42.1+ |
| Ubuntu | Ubuntu 12.04, 14.04, 16.04, 16.10 |

This list is updated as new versions and distributions are on-boarded and can be accessed online at *https://docs.microsoft.com/en-us/azure/virtual-machines/linux/endorsed-distros*.

You can also bring your own custom version of Linux if you deploy the Microsoft Azure Linux agent to it. You should be aware that the Microsoft Azure support team offers various levels of support for open source technologies including custom distributions of Linux. For more details see *https://support.microsoft.com/en-us/help/2941892/support-for-linux-and-open-source-technology-in-azure*.

Running Linux on Microsoft Azure Virtual Machines requires an additional piece of software known as the Microsoft Azure Linux Agent (waagent). This software agent provides much of the base functionality for provisioning and communicating with the Azure Fabric Controller including the following:

- Image provisioning
- Creation of a user account
- Configuring SSH authentication types
- Deployment of SSH public keys and key pairs
- Setting the host name
- Publishing the host name to the platform DNS
- Reporting SSH host key fingerprint to the platform
- Resource disk management
- Formatting and mounting the resource disk
- Configuring swap space
- Networking
- Manages routes to improve compatibility with platform DHCP servers
- Ensures the stability of the network interface name
- Kernel

- Configures virtual NUMA (disable for kernel <2.6.37)
- Consumes Hyper-V entropy for /dev/random
- Configures SCSI timeouts for the root device (which could be remote)
- Diagnostics
- Console redirection to the serial port
- SCVMM deployments
- Detects and bootstraps the VMM agent for Linux when running in a System Center Virtual Machine Manager 2012 R2 environment
- Manages virtual machine extensions to inject component authored by Microsoft and Partners into Linux VM (IaaS) to enable software and configuration automation
- VM Extension reference implementation at *https://github.com/Azure/azure-linux-extensions*

The Azure Fabric Controller communicates to this agent in two ways:

- A boot-time attached DVD for IaaS deployments. This DVD includes an OVF-compliant configuration file that includes all provisioning information other than the actual SSH keypairs.
- A TCP endpoint exposing a REST API used to obtain deployment and topology configuration.

> **MORE INFO**   **MICROSOFT LINUX AGENT**
>
> For more information on how the Microsoft Azure Linux agent works and how to enable it on a Linux distribution see *https://docs.microsoft.com/en-us/azure/virtual-machines/linux/agent-user-guide.*

## Create virtual machines

There are multiple ways to create virtual machines depending on your intended use. The easiest way to create an individual virtual machine is to use the Azure portal. If you have a need for automated provisioning (or you just enjoy the command line) the Azure PowerShell cmdlets and the Azure cross-platform command-line tools (CLI) are a good fit. For more advanced automation that could even include orchestration of multiple virtual machines Azure Resource Manager templates could also be used. Each method brings with its own capabilities and trade-offs, and it is important to understand which tool should be used in the right scenario.

To create a virtual machine using the Azure portal, you first click the new button and you can then either search for an image or solution or you can browse by clicking Compute, as shown in Figure 2-1. Within the Compute category you will see the featured images, and if one of those images is not appropriate you can click the See all option to view a larger selection.

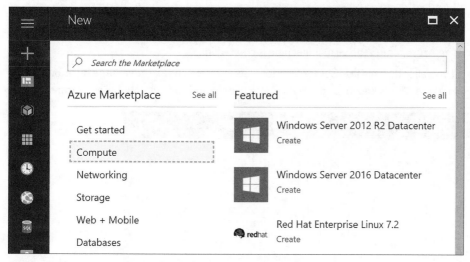

**FIGURE 2-1** The Azure Marketplace view for virtual machines

## Create an Azure VM (Azure portal)

The Azure portal allows you to provision virtual machines from a wide variety of virtual machine images, and pre-defined templates for entire solutions such as SQL Server Always On, or even a complete SharePoint farm using just your web browser. For individual virtual machines you can specify some, but not all, configuration options at creation time. Some options, such as configuring the load balancer, and specifying additional storage configuration such as adding data disks, are not available at creation time but can be set after the virtual machine is created. Using the Azure portal, you can create virtual machines individually or you can deploy an ARM template that can deploy many virtual machines (including other Azure resources as well). You can even use the Azure portal to export an ARM template from an existing deployed resource. Through the integrated Azure Cloud Shell, you can also execute commands from the command line that can also be used to provision virtual machines. After an image is selected, you navigate through several screens to configure the virtual machine.

The first blade to complete is the Basics blade, as shown in Figure 2-2. The basics blade allows you to set the following configuration options:

- The name of the virtual machine.
- Standard hard disk drive storage (HDD) or Premium solid-state disk (SSD) based storage.
- The administrator credentials.
- User name and password for Windows and Linux.
- Optionally an SSH key for Linux VMs.
- The Azure subscription to create the VM in (if you have more than one).

- The resource group name to deploy the virtual machine and its related resources in, such as network interface, public IP, etc.
- The Azure region the virtual machine is created in.
- If you already have licenses for Windows Server you can take advantage by using them in Azure. This is known as the Hybrid Use Benefit and can cut your bill significantly.

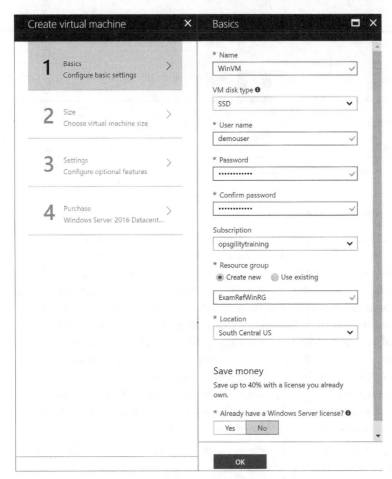

**FIGURE 2-2** The Basics blade of the portal creation process for a Windows-based virtual machine

You can specify an existing SSH public key or a password when creating a Linux VM. If the SSH public key option is selected you must paste in the public key for your SSH certificate. You can create the SSH certificate using the following command:

```
ssh-keygen -t rsa -b 2048
```

To retrieve the public key for your new certificate, run the following command:

```
cat ~/.ssh/id_rsa.pub
```

From there, copy all the data starting with ssh-rsa and ending with the last character on the screen and paste it into the SSH public key box, as shown in Figure 2-3. Ensure you don't include any extra spaces.

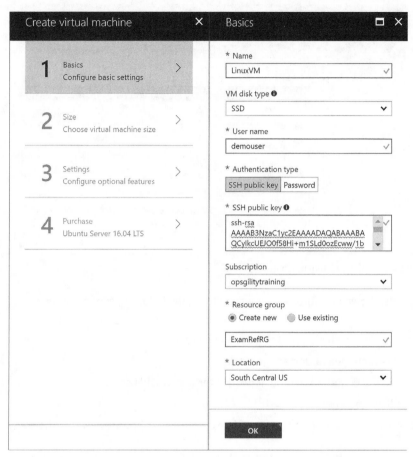

**FIGURE 2-3** The Basics blade of the portal creation process for a Linux-based virtual machine

After setting the basic configuration for a virtual machine you then specify the virtual machine size, as show in Figure 2-4. The portal gives you the option of filtering the available instance sizes by specifying the minimum number of virtual CPUs (vCPUs) and the minimum amount of memory, as well as whether the instance size supports solid state disks (SSD) or only traditional hard disk drives (HDD).

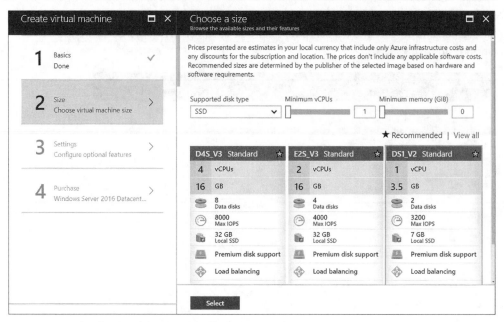

**FIGURE 2-4** Setting the size of the virtual machine

The Settings blade, shown in Figure 2-5, allows you to set the following configuration options:

- Whether the virtual machine is part of an availability set
- Whether to use managed or unmanaged disks
- What virtual network and subnet the network interface should use
- What public IP (if any) should be used
- What network security group (if any) should be used (you can specify new rules here as well)

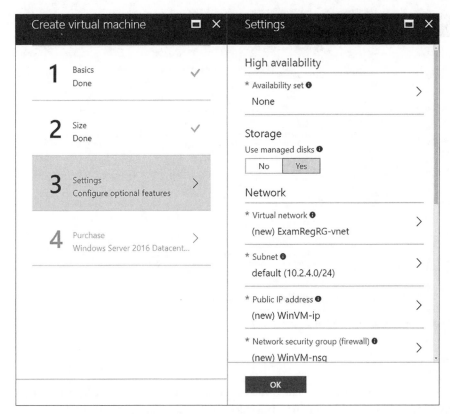

**FIGURE 2-5** Specifying virtual machine configuration settings

The last step to create a virtual machine using the Azure portal is to read through and agree to the terms of use and click the purchase button, as shown in Figure 2-6. From there, the portal performs some initial validation of your template, as well as checks many of the resources against policies in place on the subscription and resource group you are targeting. If there are no validation errors the template is deployed.

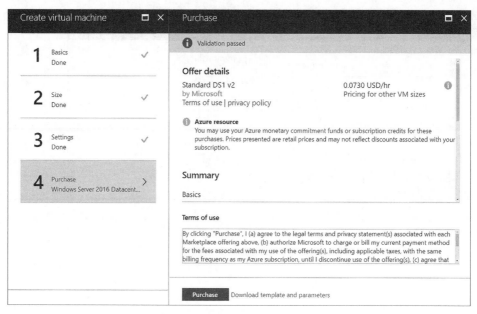

**FIGURE 2-6** Accepting the terms of use and purchasing

**EXAM TIP**

The link next to the purchase button allows you to download an Azure Resource Manager template and parameters file for the virtual machine you just configured in the portal. You can customize this template and use it for future automated deployments.

## Create an Azure VM (PowerShell)

The PowerShell cmdlets are commonly used for automating common tasks such as stopping and starting virtual machines, deploying ARM templates, or for making configuration settings on a vast number of resources at the same time. Using the Azure PowerShell cmdlets, you can also create virtual machines programmatically. Let's walk through creating a similar virtual machine to what was shown in the previous section using PowerShell.

The approach we'll use is to programmatically create the resources needed for the virtual machine such as storage, networking, availability sets and so on, and then associate them with the virtual machine at creation time.

Before you can create or manage any resources in your Azure subscription using the Azure PowerShell cmdlets you must login by executing the Login-AzureRmAccount cmdlet (which is an alias to the Add-AzureRmAccount cmdlet).

```
Login-AzureRmAccount
```

A virtual machine and all its related resources such as network interfaces, disks, and so on must be created inside of an Azure Resource Group. Using PowerShell, you can create a new resource group with the New-AzureRmResourceGroup cmdlet.

```
$rgName      = "Contoso"
$location    = "West US"
New-AzureRmResourceGroup -Name $rgName -Location $location
```

This cmdlet requires you to specify the resource group name, and the name of the Azure region. These values are defined in the variables $rgName, and $location. You can use the Get-AzureRmResourceGroup cmdlet to see if the resource group already exists or not, and you can use the Get-AzureRmLocation cmdlet to view the list of available regions.

Azure virtual machines must be created inside of a virtual network. Like the portal, using PowerShell, you can specify an existing virtual network or you can create a new one. In the code example below, the New-AzureRmVirtualNetworkSubnetConfig cmdlet is used to create two local objects that represent two subnets in the virtual network. The virtual network is actually created within the call to New-AzureRmVirtualNetwork. It is passed in the address space of 10.0.0.0/16, and you could also pass in multiple address spaces similar to how the subnets were passed in using an array.

```
$subnets = @()
$subnet1Name = "Subnet-1"
$subnet2Name = "Subnet-2"
$subnet1AddressPrefix = "10.0.0.0/24"
$subnet2AddressPrefix = "10.0.1.0/24"
$vnetAddresssSpace = "10.0.0.0/16"
$VNETName = "ExamRefVNET-PS"
$subnets += New-AzureRmVirtualNetworkSubnetConfig -Name $subnet1Name `
                                    -AddressPrefix $subnet1AddressPrefix
$subnets += New-AzureRmVirtualNetworkSubnetConfig -Name $subnet2Name `
                                    -AddressPrefix $subnet2AddressPrefix
$vnet = New-AzureRmVirtualNetwork -Name $VNETName `
                        -ResourceGroupName $rgName `
                        -Location $location `
                        -AddressPrefix $vnetAddresssSpace `
                        -Subnet $subnets
```

Virtual Machines store their virtual hard disk (VHD) files in an Azure storage account. If you are using managed disks (see more in Skill 2.3) Azure manages the storage account for you. This example uses unmanaged disks so the code creates a new storage account to contain the VHD files. You can use an existing storage account for storage or create a new storage account. The PowerShell cmdlet Get-AzureRmStorageAccount returns an existing storage account. To create a new one, use the New-AzureRmStorageAccount cmdlet, as the following example shows.

```
$saName     = "examrefstoragew123123"
$storageAcc = New-AzureRmStorageAccount -ResourceGroupName $rgName `
                                -Name $saName `
                                -Location $location `
                                -SkuName Standard_LRS
$blobEndpoint = $storageAcc.PrimaryEndpoints.Blob.ToString()
```

The $blobEndpoint variable is used in a later code snippet to specify the location of where the VMs disks are created.

Use the New-AzureRmAvailabilitySet cmdlet to create a new availability set, or to retrieve an existing one use Get-AzureRmAvailabilitySet.

```
$avSet = New-AzureRmAvailabilitySet -ResourceGroupName $rgName `
                                -Name $avSet `
                                -Location $location
```

To connect to the virtual machine remotely create a public IP address resource.

```
$pip = New-AzureRmPublicIpAddress -Name $ipName `
                                -ResourceGroupName $rgName `
                                -Location $location `
                                -AllocationMethod Dynamic `
                                -DomainNameLabel $dnsName
```

By default, adding a public IP to a VM's network interface will allow in all traffic regardless of the destination port. To control this, create a network security group and only open the ports you will use. The example below creates an array that will be used for the rules and populates the array with the New-AzureRmNetworkSecurityRuleConfig cmdlet.

```
# Add a rule to the network security group to allow RDP in
$nsgRules = @()
$nsgRules += New-AzureRmNetworkSecurityRuleConfig -Name "RDP" `
                                -Description "RemoteDesktop" `
                                -Protocol Tcp `
                                -SourcePortRange "*" `
                                -DestinationPortRange "3389" `
                                -SourceAddressPrefix "*" `
                                -DestinationAddressPrefix "*" `
                                -Access Allow `
                                -Priority 110 `
                                -Direction Inbound
```

The New-AzureRmNetworkSecurityGroup cmdlet creates the network security group. The rules are passed in using the SecurityRules parameter.

```
$nsgName    = "ExamRefNSG"
$nsg = New-AzureRmNetworkSecurityGroup -ResourceGroupName $rgName `
                                -Name $nsgName `
                                -SecurityRules $nsgRules `
                                -Location $location
```

Now that the public IP and the network security group are created, use the *New*-AzureRm-NetworkInterface cmdlet to create the network interface for the VM. This cmdlet accepts the unique ID for the subnet, public IP, and the network security group for configuration.

```
$nicName    = "ExamRefVM-NIC"
$nic = New-AzureRmNetworkInterface -Name $nicName `
                            -ResourceGroupName $rgName `
                            -Location $location `
                            -SubnetId $vnet.Subnets[0].Id `
                            -PublicIpAddressId $pip.Id `
                            -NetworkSecurityGroupId $nsg.ID
```

Now that all the resources are created that the virtual machine requires, use the New-AzureRmVMConfig cmdlet to instantiate a local configuration object that represents a virtual machine to associate them together. The virtual machine's size and the availability set are specified during this call.

```
$vmSize     = "Standard_DS1_V2"
$vm = New-AzureRmVMConfig -VMName $vmName -VMSize $vmSize `
                        -AvailabilitySetId $avSet.Id
```

After the virtual machine configuration object is created there are several configuration options that must be set. This example shows how to set the operating system and the credentials using the Set-AzureRmVMOperatingSystem cmdlet. The operating system is specified by using either the Windows or the Linux parameter. The ProvisionVMAgent parameter tells Azure to automatically install the VM agent on the virtual machine when it is provisioned. The Credential parameter specifies the local administrator username and password with the values passed to the $cred object.

```
$cred = Get-Credential
Set-AzureRmVMOperatingSystem -Windows `
                            -ComputerName $vmName `
                            -Credential $cred `
                            -ProvisionVMAgent `
                            -VM $vm
```

The operating system image (or existing VHD) must be specified for the VM to boot. Setting the image is accomplished by calling the Set-AzureRmVMSourceImage cmdlet and specifying the Image publisher, offer, and SKU. These values can be retrieved by calling the cmdlets Get-AzureRmVMImagePublisher, Get-AzureRmVMImageOffer, and Get-AzureRmVMImageSku.

```
$pubName    = "MicrosoftWindowsServer"
$offerName  = "WindowsServer"
$skuName    = "2016-Datacenter"
Set-AzureRmVMSourceImage -PublisherName $pubName `
                            -Offer $offerName `
                            -Skus $skuName `
                            -Version "latest" `
                            -VM $vm
```

```
$osDiskName = "ExamRefVM-osdisk"
$osDiskUri    = $blobEndpoint + "vhds/" + $osDiskName  + ".vhd"
Set-AzureRmVMOSDisk -Name $osDiskName `
                    -VhdUri $osDiskUri `
                    -CreateOption fromImage `
                    -VM $vm
```

The final step is to provision the virtual machine by calling the New-AzureRmVMConfig cmdlet. This cmdlet requires you to specify the resource group name to create the virtual machine in and the virtual machine configuration, which is in the $vm variable.

```
New-AzureRmVM -ResourceGroupName $rgName -Location $location -VM $vm
```

**EXAM TIP**

In addition to knowing how to provision a virtual machine from an image, it is good to understand how to create from an existing disk using the Set-AzureRmVMOSDisk -CreateOption attach parameter (for more information see *https://docs.microsoft.com/en-us/ powershell/module/azurerm.compute/set-azurermvmosdisk*) or using an existing managed operating system disk (for more information see *https://docs.microsoft.com/en-us/azure/ virtual-machines/windows/create-vm-specialized*).

## Create an Azure VM (CLI)

The Azure CLI tools are used in a similar fashion to the PowerShell cmdlets. They are built to run cross platform on Windows, Mac, or Linux. The syntax of the CLI tools is designed to be familiar to users of a Bash scripting environment. Let's walk through an example that creates the same resources as the previous PowerShell example, except creating a Linux-based virtual machine instead.

Like the PowerShell cmdlets, you first must login to access Azure using the CLI tools. The approach is slightly different, after executing the command az login, the tools provide you with a link to navigate to in the browser, and a code to enter. After entering the code and your credentials you are logged in to the command line.

```
az login
```

Create a new resource group by executing the az group create command and specifying a unique name and the region.

```
#!/bin/bash
rgName="Contoso"
location="WestUS"
az group create --name $rgName --location $location
```

The following command can be used to identify available regions that you can create resources and resource groups in.

```
az account list-locations
```

From here you have two options. You can create a virtual machine with a very simple syntax that generates much of the underlying configuration for you such as a virtual network, public IP address, storage account, and so on, or you can create and configure each resource and link to the virtual machine at creation time. Here is an example of the syntax to create a simple stand-alone virtual machine:

```
# Creating a simple virtual machine

vmName="myUbuntuVM"
imageName="UbuntuLTS"
az vm create --resource-group $rgName --name $vmName --image $imageName
 --generate-ssh-keys
```

**EXAM TIP**

The generate-ssh-keys **parameter dynamically generates keys to connect to the Linux virtual machine for you if they are missing. The new keys are stored in ~/.ssh. You can also specify a user name and password using the admin-username and admin-password parameters if you set the** authentication-type **parameter to password (default is ssh).**

To create all the resources from scratch, as shown in the section on creating a virtual machine using the PowerShell cmdlets, you can start with the virtual network. Use the az network vnet create command to create the virtual network. This command requires the name of the virtual network, a list of address prefixes, and the location to create the virtual network in.

```
vnetName="ExamRefVNET-CLI"
vnetAddressPrefix="10.0.0.0/16"
az network vnet create --resource-group $rgName -n ExamRefVNET-CLI
--address-prefixes $vnetAddressPrefix -l $location
```

The az network vnet subnet create command is used to add additional subnets to the virtual network. This command requires the resource group name, the name of the virtual network, the subnet name, and the address prefix for the subnet to create.

```
Subnet1Name="Subnet-1"
Subnet2Name="Subnet-2"
Subnet1Prefix="10.0.1.0/24"
Subnet2Prefix="10.0.2.0/24"
az network vnet subnet create --resource-group $rgName --vnet-name $vnetName -n
 $Subnet1Name --address-prefix $Subnet1Prefix
az network vnet subnet create --resource-group $rgName --vnet-name $vnetName -n
 $Subnet2Name --address-prefix $Subnet2Prefix
```

The az storage account create command is used to create a new storage account. In this example, the code uses the new storage account to store the VHD files for the Linux VM created later.

```
storageAccountName="examrefstoragew124124"
az storage account create -n $storageAccountName --sku Standard_LRS -l $location
--kind Storage --resource-group $rgName
```

The az vm availability-set create command is used to create a new availability set.

```
avSetName="WebAVSET"
az vm availability-set create -n $avSetName -g $rgName --platform-fault-domain-count
3 --platform-update-domain-count 5 --unmanaged -l $location
```

The az network public-ip create command is used to create a public IP resource. The allocation-method parameter can be set to dynamic or static.

```
dnsRecord="examrefdns123123"
ipName="ExamRefCLI-IP"
az network public-ip create -n $ipName -g $rgName --allocation-method Dynamic
--dns-name $dnsRecord -l $location
```

The az network nsg create command is used to create a network security group.

```
nsgName="webnsg"
az network nsg create -n $nsgName -g $rgName -l $location
```

After the network security group is created, use the az network rule create command to add rules. In this example, the rule allows inbound connections on port 22 for SSH and another rule is created to allow in HTTP port 80.

```
# Create a rule to allow in SSH
az network nsg rule create -n SSH --nsg-name $nsgName --priority 100 -g $rgName --access
Allow --description "SSH Access" --direction Inbound --protocol Tcp --destination-
address-prefix "*" --destination-port-range 22 --source-address-prefix "*" --source-
port-range "*"

# Create a rule to allow in HTTP
az network nsg rule create -n HTTP --nsg-name webnsg --priority 101 -g $rgName --access
Allow --description "Web Access" --direction Inbound --protocol Tcp --destination-
address-prefix "*" --destination-port-range 80 --source-address-prefix "*" --source-
port-range "*"
```

The network interface for the virtual machine is created using the az network nic create command.

```
nicname="WebVMNic1"
az network nic create -n $nicname -g $rgName --subnet $Subnet1Name --network-security-
group $nsgName --vnet-name $vnetName --public-ip-address $ipName -l $location
```

To create a virtual machine, you must specify whether it will boot from a custom image, a marketplace image, or an existing VHD. You can retrieve a list of marketplace images by executing the following command:

```
az vm image list
```

The command az image list is used to retrieve any of your own custom images you have captured.

Another important piece of metadata needed to create a virtual machine is the VM size. You can retrieve the available form factors that can be created in each region by executing the following command:

```
az vm list-sizes --location $location
```

The last step is to use the `az vm create` command to create the virtual machine. This command allows you to pass the name of the availability set, the virtual machine size, the image the virtual machine should boot from, and other configuration data such as the username and password, and the storage configuration.

```
imageName="Canonical:UbuntuServer:17.04:latest"
vmSize="Standard_DS1_V2"
containerName=vhds
user=demouser
vmName="WebVM"
osDiskName="WEBVM1-OSDISK.vhd"
az vm create -n $vmName -g $rgName -l $location --size $vmSize --availability-set
 $avSetName --nics $nicname --image $imageName --use-unmanaged-disk --os-disk-name
 $osDiskName --storage-account $storageAccountName --storage-container-name
 $containerName --generate-ssh-keys
```

> **MORE INFO**   **AZURE POWERSHELL CMDLETS AND CLI TOOL**
>
> The Azure PowerShell cmdlets and CLI tools can be downloaded and installed at *https://azure.microsoft.com/en-us/downloads/*. Scroll down to the Command-Line Tools section for installation links and documentation.

The Azure Cloud Shell, shown in Figure 2-7, is a feature of the Azure portal that provides access to an Azure command line (CLI or PowerShell) using the user credentials you are already logged into without the need to install additional tools on your computer.

**FIGURE 2-7** Starting the Cloud Shell

*EXAM TIP*

Stopping a virtual machine from the Azure portal, Windows PowerShell with the Stop-AzureRmVM cmdlet, or the `az vm deallocate` command puts the virtual machine in the Stopped (deallocated) state (az vm stop puts the VM in the Stopped state). It is important to understand the difference between Stopped (deallocated) and just Stopped. In the Stopped state a virtual machine is still allocated in Azure, and the operating system is simply shut down. You will still be billed for the compute time for a virtual machine in this state. A virtual machine in the Stopped (deallocated) state is no longer occupying physical hardware in the Azure region, and you will not be billed for the compute time (you are still billed for the underlying storage).

## Creating an Azure VM from an ARM template

Azure Resource Manager (ARM) templates provide the ability to define the configuration of resources like virtual machines, storage accounts, and so on in a declarative manner. ARM templates go beyond just providing the ability to create the resources; some resources such as virtual machines also allow you to customize them and create dependencies between them. This allows you to create templates that have capabilities for orchestrated deployments of completely functional solutions. Chapter 5, "Design and deploy ARM templates" goes in-depth on authoring templates. Let's start with learning how to deploy them.

The Azure team maintains a list of ARM templates with examples for most resources. This list is located at *https://azure.microsoft.com/en-us/resources/templates/,* and is backed by a source code repository in GitHub. If you want to go directly to the source to file a bug or any other reason you can access it at *https://github.com/Azure/azure-quickstart-templates.*

You can deploy ARM templates using the portal, the command line tools, or directly using the REST API. Let's start with deploying a template that creates virtual machines using the portal. To deploy a template from the portal, click the NEW button and search for Template Deployment, as shown in Figure 2-8, and select the Template Deployment name from the search results, and then click Create.

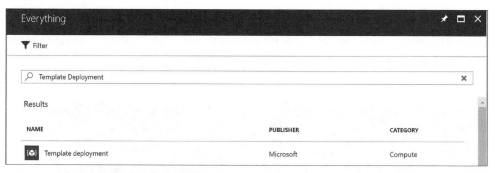

**FIGURE 2-8** The Template Deployment option

From there, you have the option to build your own template using the portal's editor (you can paste your own template in or upload from a file using this option too), or choose from one of the most common templates. Last of all, you can search the existing samples in the quickstart samples repository and choose one of them as a starting point. Figure 2-9 shows the various options after clicking the template deployment search result.

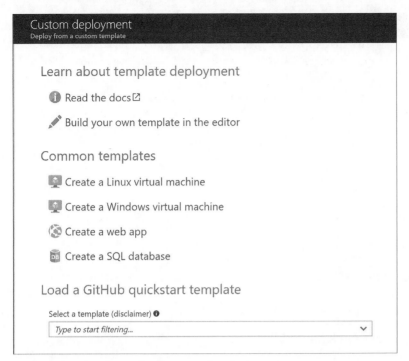

**FIGURE 2-9** Options for configuring a template deployment

Choosing one of the common templates links opens the next screen, which gives you the options for deploying the template. A template deployment requires you to specify a subscription and resource group, along with any parameters that the template requires. In figure 2-10 the Admin Username, Admin Password, DNS Label Prefix, and Windows operating system version values are all parameters defined in the template.

**FIGURE 2-10** Deploying a template

Clicking the Edit Template button opens the editor shown in Figure 2-11, where you can continue modifying the template. On the left navigation, you can see the parameters section that defines the four parameters shown in the previous screen, as well as the resource list, which defines the resources that the template will create. In this example, the template defines a storage account, public IP address, virtual network, network interface, and the virtual machine.

**FIGURE 2-11** The template editor view

The editor also allows you to download the template as a JavaScript Object Notation (.json) file for further modification or for deployment using an alternative method.

The Edit Parameters button allows you to edit a JSON view of the parameters for the template, as shown in Figure 2-12. This file can also be downloaded and is used to provide different behaviors for the template at deployment time without modifying the entire template.

Common examples of using a parameters file:

- Defining different instance sizes or SKUs for resources based on the intended usage (small instances for test environments for example)
- Defining different number of instances
- Different regions
- Different credentials

**FIGURE 2-12** Editing template parameters using the Azure portal

The last step to creating an ARM template using the portal is to click the Purchase button after reviewing and agreeing to the terms and conditions on the screen.

The Azure command line tools can also deploy ARM templates. The template files can be located locally on your file system or accessed via HTTP/HTTPs. Common deployment models have the templates deployed into a source code repository or an Azure storage account to make it easy for others to deploy the template.

This example uses the Azure PowerShell cmdlets to create a new resource group, specify the location and then deploy a template by specifying the URL from the Azure QuickStart GitHub repository.

```
# Create a Resource Group
$rgName   = "Contoso"
$location = "WestUs"
New-AzureRmResourceGroup -Name $rgName -Location $location

# Deploy a Template from GitHub
$deploymentName = "simpleVMDeployment"

$templateUri = "https://raw.githubusercontent.com/Azure/azure-quickstart-templates/
master/101-vm-simple-windows/azuredeploy.json"
New-AzureRmResourceGroupDeployment -Name $deploymentName `
                                   -ResourceGroupName $rgName `
                                   -TemplateUri $templateUri
```

If the template requires parameters without default values, the cmdlet will prompt you to input their values.

**EXAM TIP**

The parameters to a template can be passed to the New-AzureRmResourceGroupDeploy-ment cmdlet using the `TemplateParameterObject` parameter for values that are defined directly in the script as .json. The `TemplateParameterFile` parameter can be used for values stored in a local .json file. The `TemplateParameterUri` parameter for values that are stored in a .json file at an HTTP endpoint.

The following example uses the Azure CLI tools to accomplish the same task.

```bash
#!/bin/bash
# Create the resource group
rgName="Contoso"
location="WestUS"
az group create --name $rgName --location $location
# Deploy the specified template to the resource group
deploymentName="simpleVMDeployment"
templateUri="https://raw.githubusercontent.com/Azure/azure-quickstart-templates/
master/101-vm-simple-linux/azuredeploy.json"
az group deployment create --name $deploymentName  --resource-group $rgName --template-
uri $templateUri
```

**EXAM TIP**

The parameters to a template can be passed to the az group deployment create com-mand using the `parameters` parameter for values that are defined directly in the script as .json. The `template-file` parameter can be used for values stored in a local .json file. The `template-uri` parameter for values that are stored in a .json file at an HTTP endpoint.

# Connecting to virtual machines

There are many ways to connect to virtual machines. You should consider options such as connecting to VMs using their public IP addresses and protecting them with network security groups, and allowing only the port for the service you are connecting to. You should also un-derstand how to connect to a VM on its private IP address. This introduces additional connec-tivity requirements such as ExpressRoute, Site-to-Site, or Point-to-Site to put your client on the same network as your VMs. These technologies are discussed in Chapter 4, "Implement Virtual Networks." In this section we'll review the most common tools to connect and manage your VMs.

## Connecting to a Windows VM with remote desktop

The default connectivity option for a Windows-based virtual machine is to use the remote desktop protocol (RDP) and a client such as mstsc.exe. This service listens on TCP port 3389 and provides full access to the Windows desktop. This service is enabled by default on all Windows-based VMs. The Azure portal provides a connect button that will appear enabled for virtual machines that have a public IP address associated with them, as shown in Figure 2-13.

**FIGURE 2-13** The Connect button for an Azure VM

You can launch a remote desktop session from Windows PowerShell by using the Get-Azur-eRmRemoteDesktopFile cmdlet. The Get-AzureRmRemoteDesktopFile cmdlet performs the same validation as the Azure portal. The API it calls validates that a public IP address is associated with the virtual machine's network interface. If a public IP exists, it generates an .rdp file consumable with a Remote Desktop client. The .rdp file will have the IP address of the VIP and public port (3389) of the virtual machine specified embedded. There are two parameters that alter the behavior of what happens with the generated file.

Use the Launch parameter to retrieve the .rdp file and immediately open it with a Remote Desktop client. The following example launches the Mstsc.exe (Remote Desktop client), and the client prompts you to initiate the connection.

```
Get-AzureRmRemoteDesktopFile -ResourceGroupName $rgName -Name $vmName -Launch
```

The second behavior is specifying the LocalPath parameter, as the following example shows. Use this parameter to save the .rdp file locally for later use.

```
Get-AzureRmRemoteDesktopFile -ResourceGroupName $serviceName -Name $vmName -LocalPath
$path
```

## Connecting to a Windows VM with PowerShell remoting

It is also possible to connect to a Windows-based virtual machine using Windows Remote Management (WinRM), or more commonly known as Windows PowerShell remoting. The Set-AzureRmVMOperatingSystem supports two parameters that define the behavior of WinRM on a virtual machine at provision time.

- **WinRMHttps**   Enables connectivity over SSL using port 5986. If you connect to your virtual machine over the public internet, ensure this option is used to avoid man-in-the-middle attacks.

- **WinRMHttp**   Enables connectivity using 5985 (no SSL required). Enable this option if you want to connect to your virtual machines using PowerShell remoting from other virtual machines on the same private network.

To ensure your virtual machine is secure from man-in-the-middle attacks you must deploy a self-signed SSL certificate that your local computer trusts and that the virtual machine trusts. This is accomplished by creating the certificate using the New-SelfSignedCertificate cmdlet, or makecert.exe. After the certificate is created, it must be added to an Azure Key Vault to secure it as a secret.

During provisioning you reference the secret using the `WinRMCertificateUrl` parameter of the Set-AzureRmVMOperatingSystem cmdlet if you are creating the virtual machine Power-Shell, or if you are using a template you can specify the sourceVault and certificate information directly as part of the secrets configuration stored in the osProfile section.

```
"secrets": [
  {
    "sourceVault": {
      "id": "<resource id of the Key Vault containing the secret>"
    },
    "vaultCertificates": [
      {
        "certificateUrl": "<URL for the certificate>",
        "certificateStore": "<Name of the certificate store on the VM>"
      }
    ]
  }
],
```

> **MORE INFO** **CONFIGURING WINRM ON WINDOWS-BASED VIRTUAL MACHINES**
>
> For more information on enabling WinRM on your Windows-based virtual machines a complete walk through is available at: *https://docs.microsoft.com/en-us/azure/virtual-machines/windows/winrm.*

## Connecting to a Linux virtual machine using SSH

The default connectivity option for a Linux-based virtual machine is to use the secure shell (SSH) protocol. This service listens on TCP port 22 and provides full access to a command line shell. This service is enabled by default on all Linux-based VMs. When you click the Connect button on a Linux-based virtual machine with a public IP associated with it you see a dialog, like the one shown in Figure 2-14, advising you to use SSH to connect.

**FIGURE 2-14** The connect dialog advising how to connect to a Linux VM using SSH

Use the following command to connect to a Linux VM using the SSH bash client.

```
ssh username@ipaddress
```

If the virtual machine is configured for password access, SSH then prompts you for the password for the user you specified. If you specified the public key for an SSH certificate during the creation of the virtual machine it attempts to use the certificate from the ~/.ssh folder.

There are many options for SSH users from a Windows machine. For example, if you install the Linux subsystem for Windows 10, you will also install an SSH client that can be accessed from the bash command line. You can also install one of many GUI-based SSH clients like PuTTy. The Azure Cloud Shell shown in Figure 2-15 also provides an SSH client. So regardless of which operating system you are on, if you have a modern browser and can access the Azure portal you can connect to your Linux VMs.

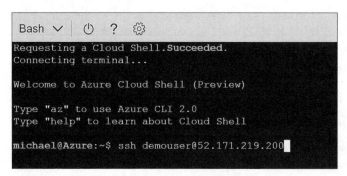

**FIGURE 2-15** Connecting to a Linux VM using SSH from within the Azure Cloud Shell

> **MORE INFO** **OPTIONS FOR USING SSH FROM WINDOWS**
>
> There are plenty of options to connect to your Linux-based virtual machines from Windows. The following link has more detail on SSH certificate management and some available clients at *https://docs.microsoft.com/en-us/azure/virtual-machines/linux/ssh-from-windows*.

## Skill 2.2: Perform configuration management

Azure virtual machines have a variety of built-in extensions that can enable configuration management as well as a variety of other operations such as installing software agents and even enabling remote debugging for live troubleshooting purposes. The two most common extensions for configuration management are the Windows PowerShell Desired State Configuration (DSC) extension and the more generic Custom Script Extension. Both extensions can be executed at provisioning time or after the virtual machine has already been started. The Windows PowerShell DSC Extension allows you to define the state of a virtual machine using the PowerShell Desired State Configuration language and apply it as well as perform continuous updates when integrated with the Azure Automation DSC service. The custom script extension can be used to execute an arbitrary command such as a batch file, regular PowerShell script, or a bash script. In addition to these extensions there are also more specific extensions that allow you to configure your virtual machines to use open source configuration management utilities such as Chef or Puppet and many others.

> **This skill covers how to:**
>
> - Automate configuration management by using PowerShell Desired State Configuration (DSC) and VM Agent (custom script extensions)
> - Enable remote debugging

***EXAM TIP***

To use virtual machine extensions like Windows PowerShell DSC, Custom Script Extension, Puppet, and Chef on Windows, the Azure virtual machine agent must be installed on the virtual machine. By default, the agent is installed on virtual machines created after February 2014 (when the feature was added). But, it's also possible to not install the agent on Windows-based virtual machines by not passing the `ProvisionVMAgent` parameter of the Set-AzureRmVMOperatingSystem cmdlet in PowerShell. If the agent is not installed at provisioning time, or if you have migrated a virtual hard disk from on-premises, you can manually install the agent on these virtual machines by downloading and installing the agent from Microsoft at *http://go.microsoft.com/fwlink/?LinkID=394789&clcid=0x409*.

## PowerShell Desired State Configuration

PowerShell Desired State Configuration (DSC) allows you to declaratively configure the state of the virtual machine. Using built-in resource providers or custom providers with a DSC script enables you to declaratively configure settings such as roles and features, registry settings, files and directories, firewall rules, and most settings available to Windows. One of the compelling features of DSC is that, instead of writing logic to detect and correct the state of the machine, the providers do that work for you and make the system state as defined in the script.

For example, the following DSC script declares that the Web-Server role should be installed, along with the Web-Asp-Net45 feature. The WindowsFeature code block represents a DSC resource. The resource has a property named Ensure that can be set to Present or Absent. In this example, the WindowsFeature resource verifies whether the Web-Server role is present on the target machine and if it is not, the resource installs it. It repeats the process for the Web-Asp-Net45 feature.

```
Configuration ContosoSimple
{
    Node "localhost"
    {
        #Install the IIS Role
        WindowsFeature IIS
        {
            Ensure = "Present"
```

```
          Name = "Web-Server"
        }
        #Install ASP.NET 4.5
        WindowsFeature AspNet45
        {
          Ensure = "Present"
          Name = "Web-Asp-Net45"
        }
    }
}
```

In addition to the default DSC resources included by default with PowerShell DSC, there is an open source DSC resource kit hosted in GitHub that has many more resources that are maintained and updated by the Windows PowerShell engineering, and of course you can write your own. To install a custom resource, download it and unzip it into the C:\Program Files\ WindowsPowerShell\Modules folder. To learn about and download the latest DSC resource kit from Microsoft see the following GitHub repo at: *https://github.com/PowerShell/DscResources*.

The example uses the xPSDesiredStateConfiguration module from the DSC resource kit to download a .zip file that contains the website content. This module can be installed using PowerShellGet by executing the following commands from an elevated command prompt:

```
Install-Module -Name xPSDesiredStateConfiguration
# ContosoWeb.ps1
configuration Main
{
    # Import the module that defines custom resources
    Import-DscResource -Module xPSDesiredStateConfiguration
    Node "localhost"
    {
        # Install the IIS role
        WindowsFeature IIS
          {
            Ensure        = "Present"
            Name          = "Web-Server"
          }
         # Install the ASP .NET 4.5 role
        WindowsFeature AspNet45
        {
            Ensure        = "Present"
            Name          = "Web-Asp-Net45"
        }
        # Download the website content
        xRemoteFile WebContent
        {
            Uri           = "https://cs7993fe12db3abx4d25xab6.blob.core.windows.net/
public/website.zip"
            DestinationPath = "C:\inetpub\wwwroot"
            DependsOn       = "[WindowsFeature]IIS"
```

```
    }
    Archive ArchiveExample
    {
        Ensure        = "Present"
        Path          = "C:\inetpub\wwwroot\website.zip"
        Destination   = "C:\inetpub\wwwroot"
        DependsOn     = "[xRemoteFile]WebContent"
    }
  }
}
```

Before the DSC script can be applied to a virtual machine, you must use the Publish-Azur-eRmVMDscConfiguration cmdlet to package the script into a .zip file. This cmdlet also import any dependent DSC modules such as xPSDesiredStateConfiguration into the .zip.

```
Publish-AzureRmVMDscConfiguration -ConfigurationPath .\ContosoWeb.ps1 -OutputArchivePath
  .\ContosoWeb.zip
```

The DSC configuration can then be applied to a virtual machine in several ways such as using the Azure portal, as shown in Figure 2-16.

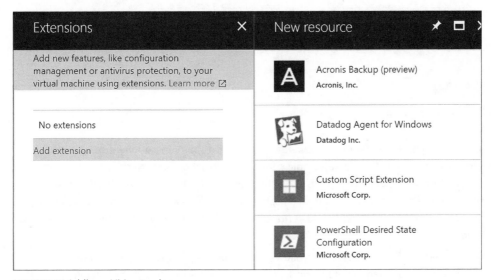

**FIGURE 2-16** Adding a VM extension

The Configuration Modules Or Script field expects the .zip file created by the call to the Publish-AzureRmVMDscConfiguration. The Module-Qualified Name Of Configuration field expects the name of the script file (with the .ps1 extension) concatenated with the name of the configuration in the script, which in the example shown in Figure 2-17 is ContosoWeb.ps1\Main.

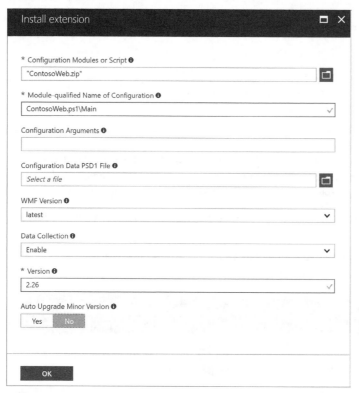

**FIGURE 2-17** Configuring a VM extension

One of the powerful features of PowerShell DSC is the ability to parameterize the configuration. This means you can create a single configuration that can exhibit different behaviors based on the parameters passed. The Configuration Data PSD1 file field is where you can specify these parameters in the form of a hashtable. You can learn more about how to separate configuration from environment data at *https://docs.microsoft.com/en-us/powershell/dsc/separatingenvdata*.

The PowerShell DSC extension also allows you to specify whether to use the latest version of the Windows Management Framework (WMF) and to specify the specific version of the DSC extension to use, and whether to automatically upgrade the minor version or not.

> **MORE INFO** **AZURE POWERSHELL DSC EXTENSION VERSIONS**
>
> You can find more about the DSC extension versions at *https://blogs.msdn.microsoft.com/powershell/2014/11/20/release-history-for-the-azure-dsc-extension/*. This blog post is actively maintained with new versions. PowerShell DSC configurations can also be applied programmatically during a PowerShell deployment by using the Set-AzureRmVmDscExtension cmdlet. In the example below, the Publish-AzureRmVMDscConfiguration cmdlet is used to publish the packaged script to an existing Azure storage account before applying the configuration using the Set-AzureRmVMDscExtension cmdlet on an existing virtual machine.

```
$rgName = "Contoso"
$location = "westus"
$vmName = "DSCVM"
$storageName = "erstorage"
$configurationName = "ContosoWeb"
$archiveBlob = "ContosoWeb.ps1.zip"
$configurationPath = ".\ContosoWeb.ps1"
#Publish the configuration script into Azure storage
Publish-AzureRmVMDscConfiguration -ConfigurationPath $configurationPath `
                              -ResourceGroupName $rgName `
                              -StorageAccountName $storageName
#Set the VM to run the DSC configuration
Set-AzureRmVmDscExtension -Version 2.26 `
                          -ResourceGroupName $resourceGroup `
                -VMName $vmName `
                 -ArchiveStorageAccountName $storageName `
                 -ArchiveBlobName $archiveBlob `
                 -AutoUpdate:$false `
                       -ConfigurationName $configurationName
```

The PowerShell DSC extension can also be applied to a virtual machine created through an ARM template by extending and adding the resource configuration in the virtual machine's resource section of the template. You learn more about authoring ARM templates in Chapter 5.

```
{
    "name": "Microsoft.Powershell.DSC",
    "type": "extensions",
    "location": "[resourceGroup().location]",
    "apiVersion": "2016-03-30",
    "dependsOn": [
      "[resourceId('Microsoft.Compute/virtualMachines', parameters('WebVMName'))]"
    ],
    "tags": {
      "displayName": "WebDSC"
    },
    "properties": {
      "publisher": "Microsoft.Powershell",
      "type": "DSC",
      "typeHandlerVersion": "2.26",
      "autoUpgradeMinorVersion": false,
      "settings": {
        "configuration": {
          "url": "[parameters('DSCUri')]",
          "script": "ContosoWeb.ps1",
          "function": "Main"
        },
        "configurationArguments": {
          "nodeName": "[parameters('WebVMName')]"
        }
      },
      "protectedSettings": {
        "configurationUrlSasToken": "[parameters('SasToken')]"
      }
    }
  }
```

The previous examples apply the PowerShell DSC configuration only when the extension is executed. If the configuration of the virtual machine changes after the extension is applied, the configuration can drift from the state defined in the DSC configuration. The Azure Automation DSC service allows you to manage all your DSC configurations, resources, and target nodes from the Azure portal or from PowerShell. It also provides a built-in pull server so your virtual machines will automatically check on a scheduled basis for new configuration changes, or to compare the current configuration against the desired state and update accordingly.

> **MORE INFO   AZURE AUTOMATION DSC**
>
> For more information on how to automatically apply PowerShell DSC configurations to your virtual machines see *https://docs.microsoft.com/en-us/azure/automation/automation-dsc-overview.*

## Using the custom script extension

The Azure custom script extension is supported on Windows and Linux-based virtual machines, and is ideal for bootstrapping a virtual machine to an initial configuration. To use the Azure custom script extension your script must be accessible via a URI such as an Azure storage account, and either accessed anonymously or passed with a shared access signature (SAS URL). The custom script extension takes as parameters the URI and the command to execute including any parameters to pass to the script. You can execute the script at any time the virtual machine is running.

### Using the custom script extension (Azure portal)

To add the custom script extension to an existing virtual machine, open the virtual machine in the portal, click the Extensions link on the left, and choose the Custom Script Extension option. The script file is specified as well as any arguments passed to the script. Figure 2-18 shows how to enable this extension using the Azure portal.

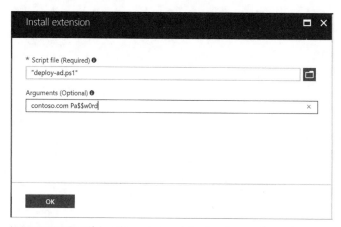

**FIGURE 2-18**  Specifying the custom script extension configuration

## Using the custom script extension (PowerShell)

Both the Azure PowerShell cmdlets and the Azure CLI tools can be used to execute scripts using the custom script extension. Starting with PowerShell, the following script deploys the Active Directory Domain Services role. It accepts two parameters: one is for the domain name and the other is for the administrator password.

```
#deployad.ps1
param(
  $domain,
  $password
)
$smPassword = (ConvertTo-SecureString $password -AsPlainText -Force)
Install-WindowsFeature -Name "AD-Domain-Services" `
                       -IncludeManagementTools `
                       -IncludeAllSubFeature
Install-ADDSForest -DomainName $domain `
                   -DomainMode Win2012 `
                   -ForestMode Win2012 `
                   -Force `
                   -SafeModeAdministratorPassword $smPassword
```

You can use the Set-AzureRmVMCustomScriptExtension cmdlet to run this script on an Azure virtual machine. This scenario can be used for installing roles or any other type of iterative script you want to run on the virtual machine.

```
$rgName      = "Contoso"
$scriptName = "deploy-ad.ps1"
$scriptUri = http://$storageAccount.blob.core.windows.net/scripts/$scriptName
$scriptArgument = "contoso.com $password"
Set-AzureRmVMCustomScriptExtension -ResourceGroupName $rgName `
                      -VMName $vmName `
                      -FileUri $scriptUri `
                      -Argument "$domain $password" `
                      -Run $scriptName
```

The FileUri parameter of the Set-AzureRmVMCustomScriptExtension cmdlet, accepts the URI to the script, and the Run parameter tells the cmdlet the name of the script to run on the virtual machine. The script can also be specified using the StorageAccountName, StorageAcountKey, ContainerName, and FileName parameters that qualify its location in an Azure storage account.

## Using the custom script extension (CLI)

You can also use the custom script extension for Linux-based virtual machines. The following example demonstrates a simple bash script that installs Apache and PHP. The script would need to be uploaded to an accessible HTTP location such as an Azure storage account or a GitHub repository for the custom script extension to access it and apply it to the virtual machine.

```
#!/bin/bash
#install-apache.sh
apt-get update
apt-get -y install apache2 php7.0 libapache2-mod-php7.0
apt-get -y install php-mysql
sudo a2enmod php7.0
apachectl restart
```

The following code example shows how this script can be applied to an Azure Virtual Machine named LinuxWebServer in the ExamRefRG-CLI resource group.

```
rgName="Contoso"
vmName="LinuxWebServer"
az vm extension set --resource-group $rgName --vm-name $vmName --name
$scriptName --publisher Microsoft.Azure.Extensions --settings ./cseconfig.json
```

The `az vm extension set` command can take the script to execute as a .json based configuration file as the previous example demonstrates. The contents of this .json file are shown for reference:

```
{
  "fileUris": [ "https://examplestorageaccount.blob.core.windows.net/scripts/apache.sh"
],
  "commandToExecute": "./apache.sh"
}
```

**EXAM TIP**

**There are many other ways of configuring and executing the custom script extension using the Azure CLI tools. The following article has several relevant examples that might be used in an exam, which you can find at** *https://docs.microsoft.com/en-us/azure/virtual-machines/linux/extensions-customscript.*

Like the PowerShell DSC extension, the custom script extension can be added to the resources section of an Azure Resource Manager template. The following example shows how to execute the same script using an ARM template instead of the CLI tools.

```
{
    "name": "apache",
    "type": "extensions",
    "location": "[resourceGroup().location]",
    "apiVersion": "2015-06-15",
    "dependsOn": [
        "[concat('Microsoft.Compute/virtualMachines/', parameters('scriptextensionNa
me'))]"
    ],
    "tags": {
        "displayName": "installApache"
    },
    "properties": {
        "publisher": "Microsoft.Azure.Extensions",
        "type": "CustomScript",
```

```
        "typeHandlerVersion": "2.0",
        "autoUpgradeMinorVersion": true,
      "settings": {
        "fileUris": [
          " https://examplestorageaccount.blob.core.windows.net/scripts/apache.sh "
        ],
        "commandToExecute": "sh apache.sh"
      }
    }
  }
}
```

> **MORE INFO**  **TROUBLESHOOTING USING VIRTUAL MACHINE EXTENSION LOGS**
>
> In the event your custom script extension fails to execute it's a good idea to review the log files. On Windows the logs are located at: C:\WindowsAzure\Logs\Plugins\Microsoft. Compute.CustomScriptExtension. On Linux at /var/log/azure/Microsoft.Azure.Extensions. CustomScript.

# Enable remote debugging

Sometimes a problem with an application cannot be reproduced on a developer's computer and only happens in a deployed environment. Azure Virtual Machines provides the ability to enable a developer using Visual Studio 2015 or above to attach a debugger directly to the offending process on the virtual machine and debug the problem as it happens.

To enable debugging, you should deploy a debug version of your application to the virtual machine, and then you can use the Visual Studio Cloud Explorer to find the virtual machine, right-click its name, and select the Enable Debugging option, as shown in Figure 2-19.

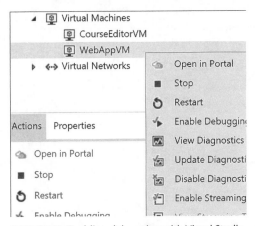

**FIGURE 2-19** Enabling debugging with Visual Studio

This step opens the necessary port on the network security group for your virtual machine, and then enables the virtual machine extension for remote debugging. After both tasks have completed, right-click the virtual machine once more and click the attach debugger option, as shown in Figure 2-20.

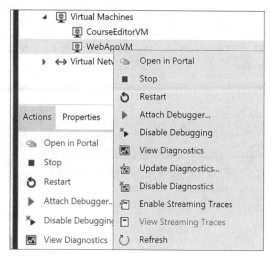

**FIGURE 2-20** Attaching the debugger

Visual Studio will prompt you to attach the process on the virtual machine to debug, as shown in figure 2-21. Select the process and click the Attach button. You are then able to set one or more breakpoints in the application and debug the problem directly on the offending virtual machine.

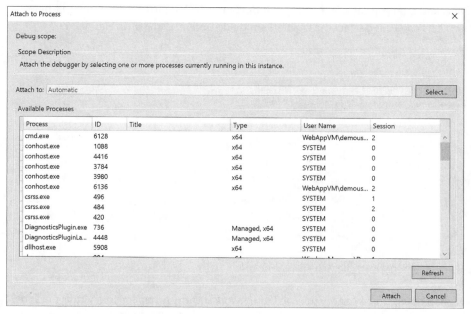

**FIGURE 2-21** Selecting the process to debug

# Skill 2.3: Design and implement VM Storage

There are many options to consider when designing a storage subsystem for your virtual machine infrastructure. Core requirements such as performance, durability, availability, security, and capacity must be considered, as well as what the requirements are for accessing the data from applications. Microsoft Azure offers a broad set of features and capabilities that solve each of these problems in their own way.

> **This skill covers how to:**
> - Configure disk caching
> - Plan storage capacity
> - Configure operating system disk redundancy
> - Configure shared storage using Azure File service
> - Configure geo-replication
> - Encrypt disks
> - Implement ARM VMs with Standard and Premium storage

## Virtual machine storage overview

It's important to understand that there are many features and capabilities to plan and design for when implementing virtual machines in Microsoft Azure. In this section we summarize some of these features and terms before we go deeper with how to put the pieces together to create a storage solution for your virtual machine infrastructure.

### Storage accounts and blob types

All persistent disks for an Azure Virtual Machine are stored in blob storage of an Azure Storage account. There are three types of blob files:

- Block blobs are used to hold ordinary files up to about 4.7 TB.
- Page blobs are used to hold random access files up to 8 TB in size. These are used for the VHD files that back VMs.
- Append blobs are made up of blocks like the block blobs, but are optimized for append operations. These are used for things like logging information to the same blob from multiple VMs.

An Azure Storage account can be one of three types:

- **Standard**   The most widely used storage accounts are Standard storage accounts, which can be used for all types of data. Standard storage accounts use magnetic media to store data.

- **Premium**   Premium storage provides high-performance storage for page blobs, which are primarily used for VHD files. Premium storage accounts use SSD to store data. Microsoft recommends using Premium Storage for all your VMs.

- **Blob**   The Blob Storage account is a specialized storage account used to store block blobs and append blobs. You can't store page blobs in these accounts; therefore you can't store VHD files. These accounts allow you to set an access tier to Hot or Cool; the tier can be changed at any time. The hot access tier is used for files that are accessed frequently—you pay a higher cost for storage, but the cost of accessing the blobs is much lower. For blobs stored in the cool access tier, you pay a higher cost for accessing the blobs, but the cost of storage is much lower.

Table 2-2 provides a mapping of what services are available and which blobs are supported by the storage account type.

**TABLE 2-2**  Services by Azure storage account type

| Account Type | General-purpose Standard | General-purpose Premium | Blob storage, hot and cool access tiers |
|---|---|---|---|
| Services | Blob, File, Queue Services | Blob Service | Blob Service |
| Types of blobs supported | Block blobs, page blobs, and append blobs | Page blobs | Block blobs and append blobs |

## Storage account replication

Each Azure storage account has built in replication to ensure the durability of its data. Depending on the storage account type these replication options can be changed for different types of behaviors.

- **Locally redundant storage (LRS)**   Each blob has three copies in the data center

- **Geo-redundant storage (GRS)**   Each blob has three copies in the data center, and is asynchronously replicated to a second region for a total of six copies. In the event of a failure at the primary region, Azure Storage fails over to the secondary region.

- **Read-access geo-redundant storage (RA-GRS)**   The same as (GRS), except you can access the replicated data (read only) regardless of whether a failover has occurred.

- **Zone redundant storage (ZRS)**   Each blob has three copies in the data center, and is asynchronously replicated to a second data center in the same region for a total of six copies. Note that ZRS is only available for block blobs (no VM disks) in general-purpose storage accounts. Also, once you have created your storage account and selected ZRS, you cannot convert it to use to any other type of replication, or vice versa.

## Azure disks

Azure VMs use three types of disks:

- **Operating System Disk (OS Disk)**  The C drive in Windows or /dev/sda on Linux. This disk is registered as an SATA drive and has a maximum capacity of 2048 gigabytes (GB). This disk is persistent and is stored in Azure storage.

- **Temporary Disk**  The D drive in Windows or /dev/sdb on Linux. This disk is used for short term storage for applications or the system. Data on this drive can be lost in during a maintenance event, or if the VM is moved to a different host because the data is stored on the local disk.

- **Data Disk**  Registered as a SCSI drive. These disks can be attached to a virtual machine, the number of which depends on the VM instance size. Data disks have a maximum capacity of 4095 gigabytes (GB). These disks are persistent and stored in Azure Storage.

There are two types of disks in Azure: Managed or Unmanaged.

- **Unmanaged disks**  With unmanaged disks you are responsible for ensuring for the correct distribution of your VM disks in storage accounts for capacity planning as well as availability. An unmanaged disk is also not a separate manageable entity. This means that you cannot take advantage of features like role based access control (RBAC) or resource locks at the disk level.

- **Managed disks**  Managed disks handle storage for you by automatically distributing your disks in storage accounts for capacity and by integrating with Azure Availability Sets to provide isolation for your storage just like availability sets do for virtual machines. Managed disks also makes it easy to change between Standard and Premium storage (HDD to SSD) without the need to write conversion scripts.

> *MORE INFO*  **DISKS AND VHDS**
>
> See the following for more information on Disks and VHDs *https://docs.microsoft.com/en-us/azure/virtual-machines/windows/about-disks-and-vhds*.

## Operating system images

In addition to using the VM images from the Azure marketplace, Azure also provides the ability to upload your own image or create a custom image directly in the cloud.

VM images are captured from an existing VM that has been prepared using the Windows program sysprep.exe or the Microsoft Azure Linux Agent (waagent) to make the operating system generalized. Generalized means that VM specific settings such as hostname, user accounts, domain join information, and so on are removed from the operating system so it is in a state to be provisioned on a new VM. Generalization does not remove customizations such as installation of software, patches, additional files, and folders. This capability is what makes VM images a great solution for providing pre-configured and tested solutions for VMs or VM Scale Sets.

Like Azure disks, there are managed and unmanaged images. Prior to the launch of Azure Managed Disks, unmanaged images were your only option. The primary problem that managed images solves over unmanaged images is storage account management. With unmanaged images, you can only create a new VM in the same storage account that the image resides in. This means if you wanted to use the image in another storage account you would have to use one of the storage tools to copy it to the new storage account first and then create the VM from it. Managed images solve this problem for the most part. Once a managed image exists you can create a VM from it using managed disks without worrying about the storage account configuration. This applies only to VMs created in the same region. If you want to create the VM in a remote region you must still copy the managed image to the remote region first.

To create a VM image you first generalize the operating system. In Windows this is using the sysprep.exe tool as shown in Figure 2-22. After this tool has completed execution the VM is in a generalized state and shut down.

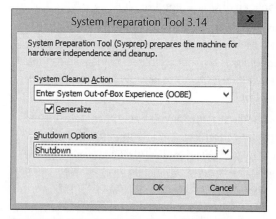

**FIGURE 2-22** Using the System Preparation tool to generalize a Windows VM

The command to generalize a Linux VM using the waagent program is shown here:

```
sudo waagent -deprovision+user
```

After the VM is generalized, you then deallocate the VM, set its status to generalized, and then use the Save-AzureRmVMImage cmdlet to capture the VM (including operating system disks) into a container in the same storage account. This cmdlet saves the disk configuration (including URIs to the VHDs) in a .json file on your local file system.

## Creating an unmanaged VM image (PowerShell)

The following example shows how to use the Azure PowerShell cmdlets to save an umanaged image using the Save-AzureRmVMImage cmdlet.

```
# Deallocate the VM
$rgName = "Contoso"
$vmName = "ImageVM"
```

```
Stop-AzureRmVM -ResourceGroupName $rgName -Name $vmName
# Set the status of the virtual machine to Generalized
Set-AzureRmVm -ResourceGroupName $rgName -Name $vmName -Generalized

$containerName = "vmimage"
$vhdPrefix     = "img"
$localPath     = "C:\Local\ImageConfig"
Save-AzureRmVMImage -ResourceGroupName $rgName -Name $vmName `
    -DestinationContainerName $containerName -VHDNamePrefix $vhdPrefix `
    -Path $localPath
```

## Creating a managed VM image (PowerShell)

This example shows how to create a managed VM image using PowerShell. This snippet uses the New-AzureRmImageConfig and New-AzureRmImage cmdlets.

```
# Deallocate the VM
# Deallocate the VM
$rgName = "Contoso"
$vmName = "ImageVM"
Stop-AzureRmVM -ResourceGroupName $rgName -Name $vmName
# Set the status of the virtual machine to Generalized
Set-AzureRmVm -ResourceGroupName $rgName -Name $vmName -Generalized
# Create a managed VM from a VM
$imageName = "WinVMImage"
$vm = Get-AzureRmVM -ResourceGroupName $rgName -Name $vmName
$image = New-AzureRmImageConfig -Location $location -SourceVirtualMachineId $vm.ID
New-AzureRmImage -Image $image -ImageName $imageName -ResourceGroupName $rgName
```

## Creating an managed VM image (CLI)

This example uses the `az vm generalize` and `az image` commands from the CLI tools to create a managed VM image.

```
# Create a Managed Image
rgName="Contoso"
vmName="ImageVM"
imageName="LinuxImage"
# Deallocate the VM
az vm deallocate --resource-group $rgName --name $vmName
# Set the status of the virtual machine to Generalized
az vm generalize --resource-group $rgName --name $vmName
az image create --resource-group $rgName --name $imageName --source $vmName
```

## Creating a VM from an image

Creating a VM from an image is very similar to creating an image using an Azure Marketplace image. There are differences depending on if you start with an unmanaged image or a managed image. For example, using an unmanaged image you must ensure that the destination operating system and data disk URIs for your VM references the same storage account that your image resides in and then you reference the operating system image by its URI in the storage account.

To specify an image using PowerShell, set the -SourceImageUri parameter of the Set-AzureRmOsDisk cmdlet.

```
$vm = Set-AzureRmVMOSDisk -VM $vm -Name $osDiskName -VhdUri $osDiskUri `
        -CreateOption fromImage -SourceImageUri $imageURI -Windows
```

Using the CLI tools, specify the URI using the image parameter of the `az vm create` command.

```
az vm create --resource-group $rgName --name $vmName --image $osDiskUri
--generate-ssh-keys
```

To create using a manage image with PowerShell, you first retrieve the image ID and pass it to Set-AzureRmVMOSDisk instead.

```
$image = Get-AzureRmImage -ImageName $imageName -ResourceGroupName $rgName
$vmConfig = Set-AzureRmVMSourceImage -VM $vmConfig -Id $image.Id
```

Using the CLI tools saves a step because it retrieves the image ID for you, you just need to specify the name of your managed image.

```
az vm create -g $rgName -n $vmName --image $imageName
```

### EXAM TIP

Image management is an incredibly important topic and having a solid understanding of the various options and techniques is undoubtedly valuable for passing the exam. Understanding how to create VMs from images, URIs, attach data disks, and copying disks from storage account to storage account will certainly not hurt your chances. You can learn more about managing images using the CLI tools at *https://docs.microsoft.com/en-us/azure/virtual-machines/linux/capture-image* and using PowerShell at *https://docs.microsoft.com/en-us/azure/virtual-machines/windows/capture-image-resource*.

## Virtual machine disk caching

Azure disks (operating system and data) have configurable cache settings that you should be aware of when designing systems for durability and performance. The caching behavior differs whether you are using Standard storage or Premium storage.

Caching works on Standard storage by buffering the reads and write on the local physical disk on the host server the virtual machine is running on. Virtual machines that use Azure Premium Storage have a multi-tier caching technology called BlobCache. BlobCache uses a combination of the Virtual Machine RAM and local SSD for caching. This cache is available for the Premium Storage persistent disks and the VM local disks. By default, this cache setting is set to Read/Write for operating system disks and Read Only for data disks hosted on Premium storage. With disk caching enabled on the Premium storage disks, virtual machines can achieve extremely high levels of performance that exceed the underlying disk performance.

There are three settings that can be applied to your disks (Standard and Premium):

- **None**   Configure host-cache as None for write-only and write-heavy disks.
- **Read Only**   Configure host-cache as ReadOnly for read-only and read-write disks.
- **Read Write**   Configure host-cache as ReadWrite only if your application properly handles writing cached data to persistent disks when needed.

You can set the host caching setting at any time, but understand that when the cache setting is changed that the disk will be unattached and then reattached to the virtual machine. For best practice, you should ensure that none of your applications are actively using the disk when you change the cache setting. Changing the operating system disk's host cache setting results in the virtual machine being rebooted.

The host cache setting can be modified for a disk by using the Azure portal as shown in Figure 2-23, the command line tools, an ARM template, or via a call to the REST API.

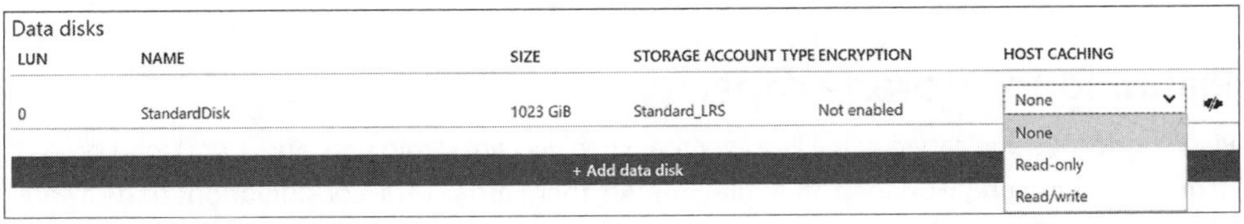

| Data disks | | | | | |
|------------|------|------|-----------------------|------------|--------------|
| LUN | NAME | SIZE | STORAGE ACCOUNT TYPE | ENCRYPTION | HOST CACHING |
| 0 | StandardDisk | 1023 GiB | Standard_LRS | Not enabled | None ∨ |
| | | | | | None |
| + Add data disk | | | | | Read-only |
| | | | | | Read/write |

**FIGURE 2-23** Setting the Host Caching options

With PowerShell, use the Set-AzureRmVMDataDisk cmdlet to modify the cache setting of a disk. In the following example, an existing virtual machine configuration is returned using the Get-AzureRmVM cmdlet, the disk configuration is modified using Set-AzureRmVMDataDisk, and then the virtual machine is updated using the Update-AzureRmVM cmdlet. You would use the Set-AzureRmVMOSDisk cmdlet instead to update the operating system disk. The Set-AzureRmVMDataDisk cmdlet also supports a `Name` parameter if you would rather update the disk by name instead of using the LUN.

```
$rgName = "StorageRG"
$vmName = "StandardVM"
$vm = Get-AzureRmVM -ResourceGroupName $rgName -Name $vmName
Set-AzureRmVMDataDisk -VM $vm -Lun 0 -Caching ReadOnly
Update-AzureRmVM -ResourceGroupName $rgName -VM $vm
```

Using the Azure CLI, there are two commands to use depending on whether the virtual machine is an unmanaged or a managed disk. Also, the host cache setting can only be specified when attaching a disk using the `az vm unmanaged-disk` for unmanaged disks, or `az vm disk attach` for managed and specifying the caching parameter. This means you would need to detach and then attach an existing VHD to modify the cache setting or you can specify during the creation of a new disk as the following example demonstrates.

```
rgName="StorageRG"
vmName="StandardVM"
diskName="ManagedDisk"
az vm disk attach --vm-name $vmName --resource-group $rgName --size-gb 128 --disk
 $diskName --caching ReadWrite –new
```

To configure the disk cache setting using an ARM template specify the caching property of the OSDisk, or each disk in the dataDisks collection of the virtual machine's OSProfile configuration. The following example shows how to set the cache setting on a data disk.

```
"dataDisks": [
  {
    "name": "datadisk1",
    "diskSizeGB": "1023",
    "lun": 0,
    "caching": "ReadOnly",
    "vhd": { "uri": "[variables('DISKURI')]" },
    "createOption": "Empty"
  }
]
```

# Planning for storage capacity

Planning for storage capacity is a key exercise when you are deploying a new workload or migrating an existing workload. In Azure Storage, there are several considerations to be aware of. The first is the size of the disks themselves. For an Azure virtual machine, the maximum capacity of a disk is 4095 GB (4 TB). Currently, the maximum number of data disks you can attach to a single virtual machine are 64 with the G5/GS5 instance size for a total storage capacity of 64 TB.

In addition to the size limitations, it is important to understand that capacity planning differs if you are using Standard or Premium storage, or if you are using Managed or Unmanaged disks. From a capacity planning perspective, the primary difference between Managed and Unmanaged disks is that Unmanaged disks must include the capacity of the storage accounts you are creating in with your planning, and with Managed disks you do not.

## Capacity planning with Standard storage

A Standard Azure Storage account supports a maximum of 20,000 IOPS. A Standard Tier Azure Virtual Machine using Standard storage supports 500 IOPS per disk and basic tier supports 300 IOPS per disk. If the disks are used at maximum capacity, a single Azure Storage account could handle 40 disks hosted on standard virtual machines, or 66 disks on basic virtual machines. Storage accounts also have a maximum storage capacity of 500 TB per Azure Storage account. When performing capacity planning, the number of Azure Storage accounts per the number of virtual machines can be derived from these numbers.

**TABLE 2-3** Standard unmanaged virtual machine disks

| VM Tier | Basic Tier VM | Standard Tier VM |
|---|---|---|
| Disk size | 4095 GB | 4095 GB |
| Max 8 KB IOPS per persistent disk | 300 | 500 |
| Max number of disks performing max IOPS (per storage account) | 66 | 40 |

Table 2-4 shows the disk sizes, IOPS, and throughput per disk for standard managed disks.

**TABLE 2-4** Standard managed virtual machine disks

| Standard Disk Type | S4 | S6 | S10 | S20 |
|---|---|---|---|---|
| Disk size | 32 GB | 64 GB | 128 GB | 512 GB |
| IOPS per disk | 500 | 500 | 500 | 500 |
| Throughput per disk | 60 MB/sec | 60 MB/sec | 60 MB/sec | 60 MB/sec |
| **Standard Disk Type** | **S30** | **S40** | **S50** | |
| Disk size | 1024 GB (1 TB) | 2048 GB (2TB) | 4095 GB (4 TB) | |
| IOPS per disk | 500 | 500 | 500 | |
| Throughput per disk | 60 MB/sec | 60 MB/sec | 60 MB/sec | |

## Capacity planning with Premium storage

For workloads that require a high number of IOPs or low latency I/O Premium storage is an ideal solution. For capacity planning purposes, know that Premium storage supports DS-series, DSv2-series, GS-series, Ls-series, and Fs-series VMs. You can use Standard and Premium storage disks with these virtual machine types. A Premium Azure Storage account supports a maximum of 35 TB of total disk capacity, with up to 10 TB of capacity for snapshots. The maximum bandwidth per account (ingress + egress) is <= 50 Gbps.

**TABLE 2-5** Premium unmanaged virtual machine disks: per account limits

| Resource | Default Limit |
|---|---|
| Total disk capacity per account | 35 TB |
| Total snapshot capacity per account | 10 TB |
| Max bandwidth per account (ingress + egress1) | <=50 Gbps |

This means that just like when using Standard storage, you must carefully plan how many disks you create in each storage account as well as consider the maximum throughput per Premium disk type because each type has a different max throughput, which affects the overall max throughput for the storage account (see Table 2-6).

**TABLE 2-6** Premium unmanaged virtual machine disks: per disk limits

| Premium Storage Disk Type | P10 | P20 | P30 | P40 | P50 |
|---|---|---|---|---|---|
| Disk size | 128 GiB | 512 GiB | 1024 GiB (1 TB) | 2048 GiB (2 TB) | 4095 GiB (4 TB) |
| Max IOPS per disk | 500 | 2300 | 5000 | 7500 | 7500 |
| Max throughput per disk | 100 MB/s | 150 MB/s | 200 MB/s | 250 MB/s | 250 MB/s |
| Max number of disks per storage account | 280 | 70 | 35 | 17 | 8 |

Table 2-7 shows the disk sizes, IOPS, and throughput per disk for premium managed disks.

**TABLE 2-7** Premium managed virtual machine disks: per disk limits

| Premium Disks Type | P4 | P6 | P10 | P20 |
|---|---|---|---|---|
| Disk size | 32 GB | 64 GB | 128 GB | 512 GB |
| IOPS per disk | 120 | 240 | 500 | 2300 |
| Throughput per disk | 25 MB/sec | 50 MB/sec | 100 MB/sec | 150 MB/sec |
| Premium Disks Type | P30 | P40 | P50 | |
| Disk size | 1024 GB (1 TB) | 2048 GB (2 TB) | 4095 GB (4 TB) | |
| IOPS per disk | 5000 | 7500 | 7500 | |
| Throughput per disk | 200 MB/sec | 250 MB/sec | 250 MB/sec | |

Each Premium storage-supported virtual machine size has scale limits and performance specifications for IOPS, bandwidth, and the number of disks that can be attached per VM. When you use Premium storage disks with VMs, make sure that there is sufficient IOPS and bandwidth on your VM to drive disk traffic.

**MORE INFO**   **VIRTUAL MACHINE SCALE LIMITS FOR STORAGE**

For the most up-to-date information about maximum IOPS and throughput (bandwidth) for Premium storage-supported VMs, see Windows VM sizes at: *https://docs.microsoft.com/ en-us/azure/virtual-machines/windows/sizes* or Linux VM sizes: *https://docs.microsoft.com/ en-us/azure/virtual-machines/linux/sizes.*

## Implementing disk redundancy for performance

If your workload throughput requirements exceed the maximum IOPS capabilities of a single standard disk (500 IOPS on Standard or 500 IOPS (P10) to 7500 IOPS (P30 and P50) for Premium), or your storage requirements are greater than 4 TB per disk, you do have options. The first option is to add multiple data disks (depending on the virtual machine size) and implement RAID 0 disk striping, and create one or more volumes with multiple data disks. This provides increased capacity (up to 4 TB times the maximum number of disks for the virtual machine size) and increased throughput.

If your virtual machine is hosted on Server 2012 or above, you can use storage pools. You can use storage pools to virtualize storage by grouping industry-standard disks into pools, and then create virtual disks called Storage Spaces from the available capacity in the storage pools. You can then configure these virtual disks to provide striping capabilities across all disks in the pool, combining good performance characteristics. Storage pools make it easy to grow or shrink volumes depending on your needs (and the capacity of the Azure data disks you have attached).

This example creates a new storage pool named VMStoragePool with all the available data disks configured as part of the pool. The code identifies the available data disks using the Get-PhysicalDisk cmdlet and creates the virtual disk using the New-VirtualDisk cmdlet.

```
# Create a new storage pool using all available disks
New-StoragePool -FriendlyName "VMStoragePool" `
        -StorageSubsystemFriendlyName "Windows Storage*" `
        -PhysicalDisks (Get-PhysicalDisk -CanPool $True)
# Return all disks in the new pool
$disks = Get-StoragePool -FriendlyName "VMStoragePool" `
            -IsPrimordial $false |
            Get-PhysicalDisk
# Create a new virtual disk
New-VirtualDisk -FriendlyName "DataDisk" `
        -ResiliencySettingName Simple `
        -NumberOfColumns $disks.Count `
        -UseMaximumSize -Interleave 256KB `
        -StoragePoolFriendlyName "VMStoragePool"
```

The NumberOfColumns parameter of New-VirtualDisk should be set to the number of data disks utilized to create the underlying storage pool. This allows IO requests to be evenly distributed against all data disks in the pool. The Interleave parameter enables you to specify the number of bytes written in each underlying data disk in a virtual disk. Microsoft recommends that you use 256 KB for all workloads. After the virtual disk is created, the disk must be initialized, formatted, and mounted to a drive letter or mount point just like any other disk.

> **MORE INFO   STRIPING DISKS FOR PERFORMANCE ON LINUX**
>
> The previous example shows how to combine disks on Windows for increased throughput and capacity. You can do the same thing on Linux as well. See the following to learn more at *https://docs.microsoft.com/en-us/azure/virtual-machines/linux/configure-raid.*

**EXAM TIP**

Mounting data disks may come up on the exam. It is important to remember that on Windows, the drive D is mapped to the local resource disk, which is only for temporary data because it is backed by the local physical disk on the host server. The resource disk will be mounted on the /Dev/sdb1 device on Linux with the actual mount point varying by Linux distribution.

# Disk encryption

Protecting data is critical whether your workloads are deployed on-premises or in the cloud. Microsoft Azure provides several options for encrypting your Azure Virtual Machine disks to ensure that they cannot be read by unauthorized users.

## Azure Storage Service Encryption for files and disks

Azure Storage Service Encryption offers the ability to automatically encrypt blobs and files within an Azure storage account. This capability can be enabled on ARM based Standard or Premium storage accounts and automatically encrypts all new files and disks created within the storage account. This is important because if you enable encryption after you have placed files or disks in the storage account, that data will not be encrypted. All Managed disks and snapshots are automatically encrypted. Because they are managed you do not see the underlying storage account. Note that the keys for Azure Storage Service Encryption are managed by Microsoft and are not directly accessible to you. Figure 2-24 shows how to enable Azure Storage Service Encryption on an Azure storage account.

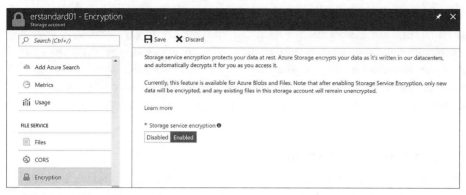

**FIGURE 2-24** Enabling Azure Storage Service Encryption on a storage account

> **MORE INFO** **AZURE STORAGE SERVICE ENCRYPTION**
>
> For more information on how the Microsoft Azure Storage Service Encryption feature works visit *https://docs.microsoft.com/en-us/azure/storage/common/storage-service-encryption.*

## Azure Disk Encryption

You can also take direct control of key management by enabling disk-level encryption directly on your Windows and Linux VMs. Azure Disk Encryption leverages the industry standard BitLocker feature of Windows, and the DM-Crypt feature of Linux to provide volume encryption for the operating system and the data disks. The solution is integrated with Azure Key Vault and Azure Active Directory to help you control and manage the disk-encryption keys and secrets in your key vault subscription.

Encryption can be enabled using PowerShell or the Azure CLI tools:

- See the following walkthrough to enable disk encryption on a Windows VM with PowerShell at *https://docs.microsoft.com/en-us/azure/virtual-machines/windows/encrypt-disks.*

- See the following walkthrough to enable disk encryption on a Linux VM with CLI at *https://docs.microsoft.com/en-us/azure/virtual-machines/linux/encrypt-disks.*

*EXAM TIP*

One of the key differences between Azure Disk Encryption and Storage Service Encryption is with Storage Service Encryption Microsoft owns and manages the keys, and with Azure Disk Encryption you do. Understanding this difference could come up on an exam.

## Using the Azure File Service

Azure File Service is a fully managed file share service that offers endpoints for the Server Messaging Block (SMB) protocol, also known as Common internet File System or CIFS 2.1 and 3.0.
This allows you to create one or more file shares in the cloud (up to 5 TB per share) and use the
share for similar uses as a regular Windows File Server, such as shared storage or for new uses
such as part of a lift and shift migration strategy.

Common use cases for using Azure Files are:

- **Replace or supplement on-premises file servers**   In some cases Azure files can be
  used to completely replace an existing file server. Azure File shares can also be replicated with Azure File Sync to Windows Servers, either on-premises or in the cloud, for
  performant and distributed caching of the data where it's being used.

- **"Lift and shift" migrations**   In many cases migrating all workloads that use data on
  an existing on-premises file share to Azure File Service at the same time is not a viable
  option. Azure File Service with File Sync makes it easy to replicate the data on-premises
  and in the Azure File Service so it is easily accessible to both on-premises and cloud
  workloads without the need to reconfigure the on-premises systems until they are
  migrated.

- **Simplify cloud development and management**   Storing common configuration
  files, installation media and tools, as well as a central repository for application logging
  are all great use cases for Azure File Service.

### Creating an Azure File Share (Azure portal)

To create a new Azure File using the Azure portal, open a Standard Azure storage account (Premium is not supported), click the Files link, and then click the + File Share Button. On the dialog
shown in Figure 2-25, you must provide the file share name and the quota size. The quota size
can be up to 5120 GB.

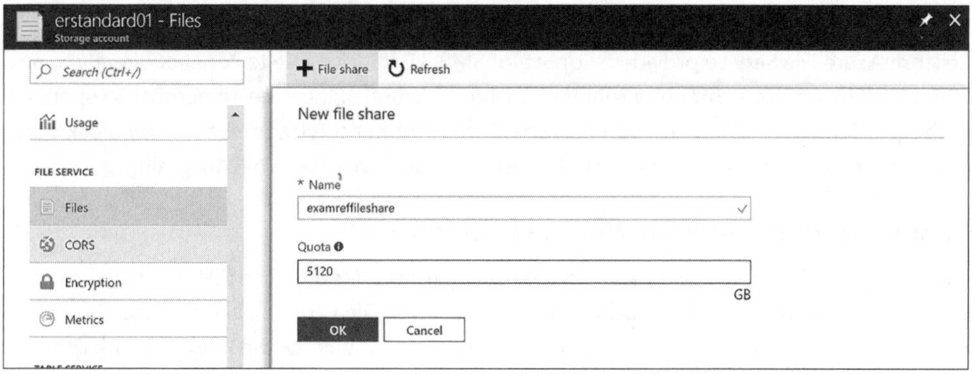

**FIGURE 2-25** Creating a new Azure File Share

## Creating an Azure File Share (PowerShell)

To create a share, first create an Azure Storage context object using the New-AzureStorage-Context cmdlet. This cmdlet requires the name of the storage key, and the access key for the storage account which is retrieved by calling the Get-AzureRmStoragerAccountKey cmdlet or copying it from the Azure portal. Pass the context object to the New-AzureStorageShare cmdlet along with the name of the share to create, as the next example shows.

```
# Create a storage context to authenticate
$rgName = "StorageRG"
$storageName = "erstandard01"
$storageKey = (Get-AzureRmStorageAccountKey -ResourceGroupName $rgName -Name
$storageName).Value[0]
$storageContext = New-AzureStorageContext $storageAccountName $storageKey
# Create a new storage share
$shareName = "logs"
$share = New-AzureStorageShare $shareName -Context $storageContext
```

## Creating an Azure File Share (CLI)

To create an Azure File Share using the CLI first retrieve the connection string using the az show connection string command, and pass that value to the az storage share create command as the following example demonstrates.

```
# Retrieve the connection string for the storage account
rgName="StorageRG"
storageName="erstandard01"
current_env_conn_string=$(az storage account show-connection-string -n $storageName
-g $rgName --query 'connectionString' -o tsv)

# Create the share
shareName="logscli"
az storage share create --name files --quota 2048 --connection-string
 $current_env_conn_string
```

## Connecting to Azure File Service outside of Azure

Because Azure File Service provides support for SMB 3.0 it is possible to connect directly to an Azure File Share from a computer running outside of Azure. In this case, remember to open outbound TCP port 445 in your local network. Some internet service providers may block port 445 so check with your service provider for details if you have problems connecting.

## Connect and mount with Windows Explorer

There are several ways to mount an Azure File Share from Windows. The first is to use the Map network drive feature within Windows File Explorer. Open File Explorer, and find the This PC node in the explorer view. Right-click This PC, and you can then click the Map Network Drive option, as shown in Figure 2-26.

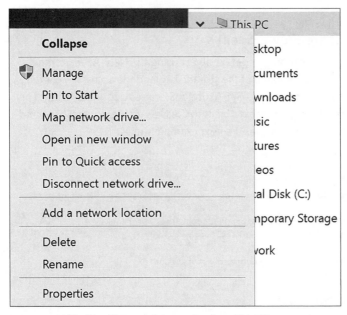

**FIGURE 2-26**  The Map Network Drive option from This PC

When the dialog opens, specify the following configuration options, as shown in Figure 2-27:

```
Folder: \\[name of storage account].files.core.windows.net\[name of share]
```

- Connect using different credentials: Checked

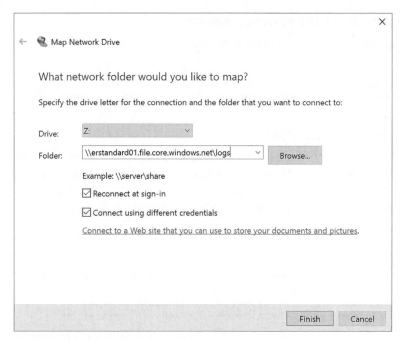

**FIGURE 2-27** Mapping a Network Drive to an Azure File Share

When you click finish, you see another dialog like the one shown in Figure 2-28 requesting the user name and password to access the file share. The user name should be in the following format: Azure\[name of storage account], and the password should be the access key for the Azure storage account.

**FIGURE 2-28** Specifying credentials to the Azure File Share

### Connect and mount with the net use command

You can also mount the Azure File Share using the Windows net use command as the following example demonstrates.

```
net use x \\erstandard01.file.core.windows.net\logs  /u:AZURE\erstandard01
r21Dk4qgY1HpcbriySWrBxnXnbedZLmnRK3N49PfaiL1t3ragpQaIB7FqK5zbez/sMnDEzEu/dgA9Nq/W7IF4A==
```

### Connect and mount with PowerShell

You can connect and mount an Azure File using the Azure PowerShell cmdlets. In this example, the storage account key is retrieved using the Get-AzureRmStorageAccountKey cmdlet. The account key is the password to the ConvertTo-SecureString cmdlet to create a secure string, which is required for the PSCredential object. From there, the credentials are passed to the New-PSDrive cmdlet, which maps the drive.

```
$rgName = "StorageRG"
$storageName = "erstandard01"
$storageKey = (Get-AzureRmStorageAccountKey -ResourceGroupName $rgName -Name
$storageName).Value[0]
$acctKey = ConvertTo-SecureString -String "$storageKey" -AsPlainText -Force
$credential = New-Object System.Management.Automation.PSCredential -ArgumentList
"Azure\$storageName", $acctKey
New-PSDrive -Name "Z" -PSProvider FileSystem -Root "\\$storageName.file.core.windows.
net\$shareName" -Credential $credential
```

### Automatically reconnect after reboot in Windows

To make the file share automatically reconnect and map to the drive after Windows is rebooted using the following command (ensuring you replace the place holder values):

```
cmdkey /add:<storage-account-name>.file.core.windows.net /user:AZURE\<storage-account-
name> /pass:<storage-account-key>
```

### Connect and mount from Linux

Use the mount command (elevated with sudo) to mount an Azure File Share on a Linux virtual machine. In this example, the logs file share would be mapped to the /logs mount point.

```
sudo mount -t cifs //<storage-account-name>.file.core.windows.net/logs /logs -o
vers=3.0,username=<storage-account-name>.,password=<storage-account-
key>,dir_mode=0777,file_mode=0777,sec=ntlmssp
```

# Skill 2.4: Monitor ARM VMs

Azure offers several configuration options to monitor the health of your virtual machines. In this skill, we'll review how to configure monitoring and alerts as well as how to setup storage for diagnostics information.

# Monitoring options in Azure

There are several tools and services in Azure designed to help you monitor different aspects of an application or deployed infrastructure. In addition to the built-in tools, you also can monitor your virtual machines using existing monitoring solutions such as Systems Center Operations Manager, or many other third-party solutions. Let's review at a high level some of the options that are available before going deeper into virtual machine specific monitoring.

## Azure Monitor

This tool allows you to get base-level infrastructure metrics and logs across your Azure subscription including alerts, metrics, subscription activity, and Service Health information. The Azure Monitor landing page provides a jumping off point to configure other more specific monitoring services such as Application Insights, Network Watcher, Log Analytics, Management Solutions, and so on. You can learn more about Azure Monitor at *https://docs.microsoft.com/en-us/azure/monitoring-and-diagnostics/monitoring-overview-azure-monitor*.

## Application Insights

Application Insights is used for development and as a production monitoring solution. It works by installing a package into your app, which can provide a more internal view of what's going on with your code. Its data includes response times of dependencies, exception traces, debugging snapshots, and execution profiles. It provides powerful smart tools for analyzing all this telemetry both to help you debug an app and to help you understand what users are doing with it. You can tell whether a spike in response times is due to something in an app, or some external resourcing issue. If you use Visual Studio and the app is at fault, you can be taken right to the problem line(s) of code so you can fix it. Application Insights provides significantly more value when your application is instrumented to emit custom events and exception information. You can learn more about Application Insights including samples for emitting custom telemetry at *https://docs.microsoft.com/en-us/azure/application-insights/*.

## Network Watcher

The Network Watcher service provides the ability to monitor and diagnose networking issues without logging in to your virtual machines (VMs). You can trigger packet capture by setting alerts, and gain access to real-time performance information at the packet level. When you see an issue, you can investigate in detail for better diagnoses. This service is ideal for troubleshooting network connectivity or performance issues.

## Azure Log Analytics

Log Analytics is a service in that monitors your cloud and on-premises environments to maintain their availability and performance. It collects data generated by resources in your cloud and on-premises environments and from other monitoring tools to provide analysis across multiple sources. Log Analytics provides rich tools to analyze data across multiple sources, allows complex queries across all logs, and can proactively alert you on specified conditions. You can even collect custom data into its central repository so you can query and visualize it. You can learn more about Log Analytics at *https://docs.microsoft.com/en-us/azure/log-analytics/log-analytics-overview*, as well as in Chapter 7.

## Azure Diagnostics Extension

The Azure Diagnostics Extension is responsible for installing and configuring the Azure Diagnostics agent on both Windows and Linux VMs to provide a richer set of diagnostics data. On Windows, this agent can collect a comprehensive set of performance counter data, event and IIS log files, and even crash dumps. It also provides the ability to automatically transfer this data to Azure Storage as well as surfacing telemetry to the Azure portal for visualization and alerts. The capabilities on Linux are more limited, but they still expose a broad range of performance telemetry to act on for reporting and alerts.

# Configuring Azure diagnostics

There are two levels of VM diagnostics: host and guest. With host diagnostics you can view and act on the data surfaced from the hypervisor hosting your virtual machine. This data is limited to high-level metrics involving the CPU, Disk, and Network. Enabling guest-level diagnostics involves having an agent running on the virtual machine that can collect a richer subset of data.

## Enabling and configuring diagnostics (Windows)

During the creation of a VM, you can enable both guest operating system diagnostics and boot diagnostics. During this time, you need to select a Standard storage account that the diagnostics agent will use to store the diagnostics data like shown in Figure 2-29.

**FIGURE 2-29** Enabling boot and guest operating system diagnostics during VM creation

You can also enable diagnostics on a VM after it is created. Figure 2-30 shows what it looks like to enable the diagnostic extension on a Windows VM.

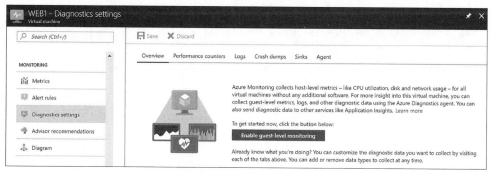

**FIGURE 2-30** Enabling diagnostics on a Windows VM

After the diagnostics extension is enabled, you can then capture performance counter data. Using the portal, you can select basic sets of counters by category, as Figure 2-31 shows.

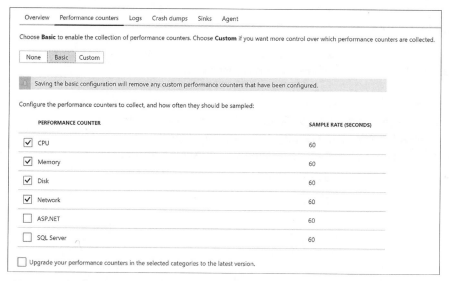

**FIGURE 2-31** Configuring the capture of performance counters

You can also configure diagnostics at a granular level by specifying exactly which counters to sample and capture including custom counters, as Figure 2-32 shows.

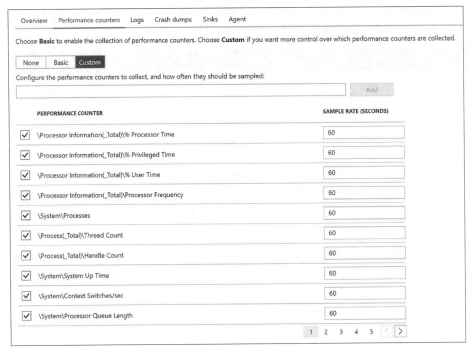

**FIGURE 2-32** Specifying a custom performance counter configuration

The Azure portal allows you to configure the agent to transfer IIS logs and failed request logs to Azure storage automatically, as Figure 2-33 demonstrates. The agent can also be configured to transfer files from any directory on the VM. However, the portal does not surface this functionality, and it must be configured through a diagnostics configuration file.

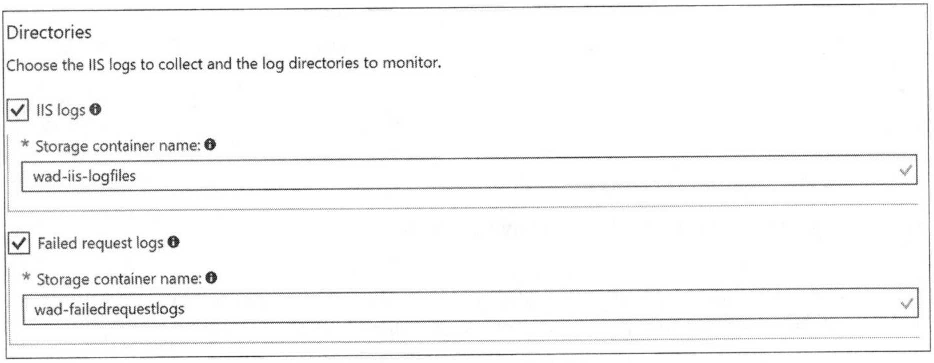

Directories

Choose the IIS logs to collect and the log directories to monitor.

☑ IIS logs ❶

  * Storage container name: ❶

    wad-iis-logfiles   ✓

☑ Failed request logs ❶

  * Storage container name: ❶

    wad-failedrequestlogs   ✓

**FIGURE 2-33** Configuring the storage container location for IIS and failed request logs

Like capturing performance counters, the diagnostics extension provides the option of collecting basic event log data, as Figure 2-34 shows. The custom view for capturing event logs supports a custom syntax to filter on certain events by their event source or the value.

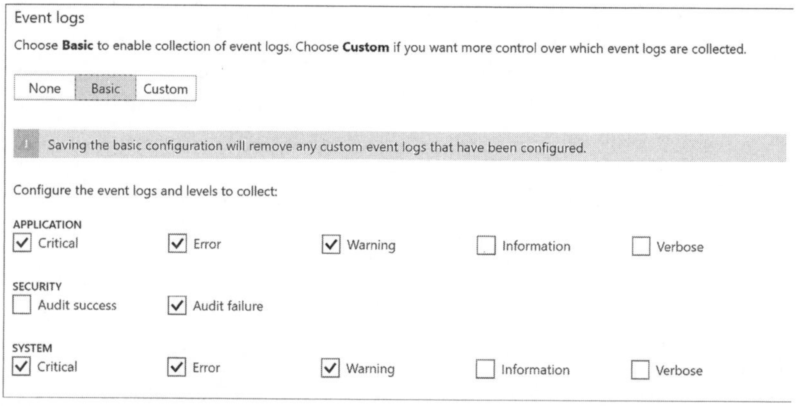

**FIGURE 2-34** Capturing event logs and levels to capture

For .NET applications that emit trace data, the extension can also capture this data and filter by the following log levels: All, Critical, Error, Warning, Information, and Verbose, as Figure 2-35 shows.

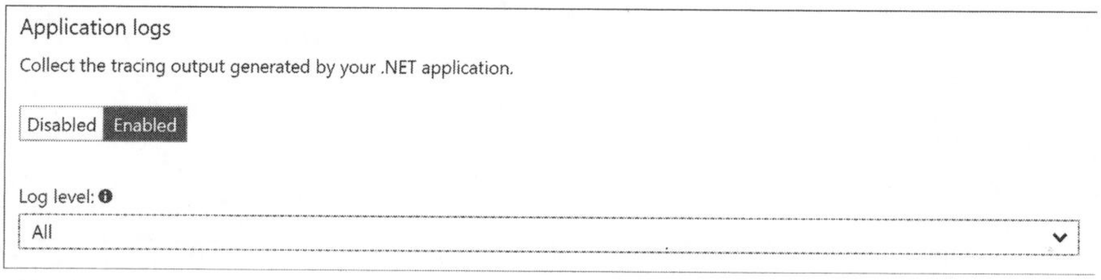

**FIGURE 2-35** Specifying the log level for application logs

Event Tracing for Windows (ETW) provides a mechanism to trace and log events that are raised by user-mode applications and kernel-mode drivers. ETW is implemented in the Windows operating system and provides developers a fast, reliable, and versatile set of event tracing features. Figure 2-36 demonstrates how to configure the diagnostics extension to capture ETW data from specific sources.

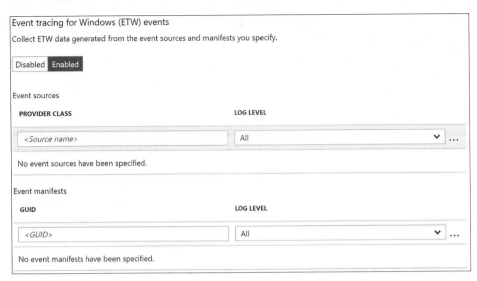

**FIGURE 2-36** Collecting Event Tracing for Windows (ETW)

Figure 2-37 demonstrates the portal UI that allows you to specify which processes to monitor for unhandled exceptions, and the container in Azure storage to move the crash dump (mini or full) to after it is captured.

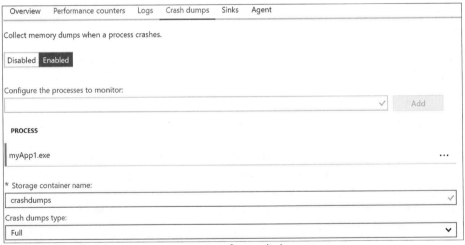

**FIGURE 2-37** Configuring processes to capture for crash dump

The agent optionally allows you to send diagnostic data to Application Insights, as Figure 2-38 shows. This is especially helpful if you have other parts of an application that use Application Insights natively so you have a single location to view diagnostics data for your application.

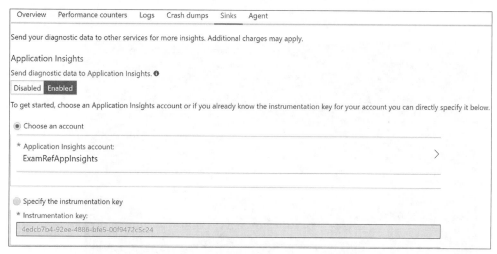

**FIGURE 2-38** Sending diagnostics data to Application Insights

The final diagnostics data to mention is boot diagnostics. If enabled, the Azure Diagnostics Agent captures a screenshot to a specific storage account of what the console looks like on the last boot. This helps you understand the problem if your VM does not start. Figure 2-39 shows a VM with boot diagnostics enabled.

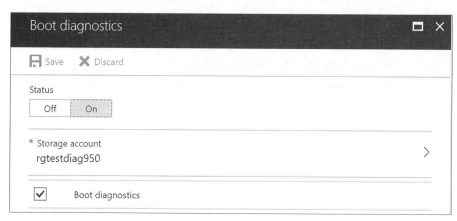

**FIGURE 2-39** Configuring boot diagnostics

Clicking the Boot Diagnostics link in the portal shows you the last captured screen shot of your VM, as Figure 2-40 shows.

Updated: Tuesday, October 3, 2017, 11:05:51 AM UTC

**FIGURE 2-40** The screen shot from the last boot for a Windows VM with boot diagnostics configured

## Enabling and configuring diagnostics (Linux)

The diagnostics agent on Linux does not support the same rich functionality that the Azure Diagnostics Agent for Windows does, so the blade for enabling and configuring the diagnostics extension for Linux is much simpler, as Figure 2-41 shows.

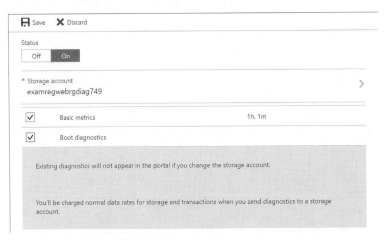

**FIGURE 2-41** Enabling diagnostics on a Linux VM

The output for boot diagnostics on Linux is different than the Windows output. In this case you get the log data in text form, as Figure 2-42 demonstrates. This is useful for downloading and searching output.

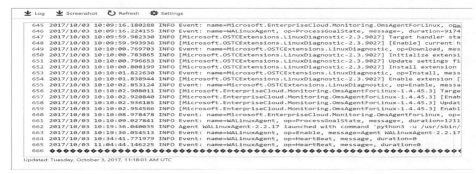

FIGURE 2-42  Boot diagnostics logs for a Linux VM

*EXAM TIP*

The Azure Diagnostics agent can also be configured through ARM templates and the command line tools by specifying a configuration file. For the exam you should be aware of the schema of this configuration and how to apply it using automated tools. You can learn more about the diagnostics schema at *https://docs.microsoft.com/en-us/azure/monitoring-and-diagnostics/azure-diagnostics-schema.*

## Configuring alerts

You can configure and receive two types of alerts.

- **Metric alerts**   This type of alert triggers when the value of a specified metric crosses a threshold you assign in either direction. That is, it triggers both when the condition is first met and then afterwards when that condition is no longer being met.

- **Activity log alerts**   This type of event occurs when a new activity log event occurs that matches the conditions specified in the alert. These alerts are Azure resources, so they can be created by using an Azure Resource Manager template. They also can be created, updated, or deleted in the Azure portal.

### Creating a metric alert

You create a metric alert by clicking Alert Rules, and then Add metric alert on a VM in the Azure Portal, as shown in Figure 2-43.

**FIGURE 2-43** Adding a metric alert to a VM

On the new dialog, you specify the name, description, and the criteria for the alert. Figure 2-44 shows the name and description for a new rule.

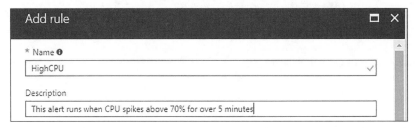

**FIGURE 2-44** Configuring the criteria for an alert

The next step is to configure the alert criteria. This is the metric to use, the condition, threshold, and the period. The alert shown in Figure 2-45 will trigger an alert when the Percentage CPU metric exceeds 70 percent over a five-minute period.

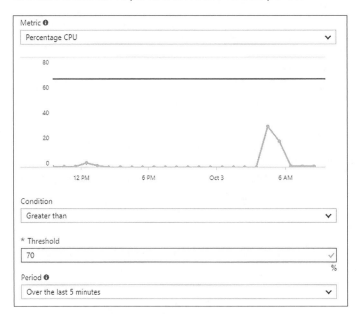

**FIGURE 2-45** The configuration of the alert

When an alert is triggered there are several actions that can be taken to either trigger further notifications, or to remediate the alert. These range from simply emailing users in the owners, contributors, and reader roles, or sending emails to designated administrator email addresses. Alerts can also call a webhook, run an Azure Automation runbook, or even execute a logic app for more advanced actions.

Webhooks allow you to route an Azure alert notification to other systems for post-processing or custom actions. For example, you can use a webhook on an alert to route it to services that send text messages, log bugs, notify a team via chat/messaging services, or do any number of other actions. You can learn more about sending alert information to webhooks at *https://docs.microsoft.com/en-us/azure/monitoring-and-diagnostics/insights-webhooks-alerts*.

A runbook is a set of PowerShell code that runs in the Azure Automation Service. See the following to learn more about using Runbooks to remediate alerts at *https://azure.microsoft.com/en-us/blog/automatically-remediate-azure-vm-alerts-with-automation-runbooks/*.

Logic Apps provides a visual designer to model and automate your process as a series of steps known as a workflow. There are many connectors across the cloud and on-premises to quickly integrate across services and protocols. When an alert is triggered the logic app can take the notification data and use it with any of the connectors to remediate the alert or start other services. To learn more about Azure Logic Apps visit *https://docs.microsoft.com/en-us/azure/logic-apps/logic-apps-what-are-logic-apps*. Figure 2-46 shows the various actions that can take place when an alert is triggered.

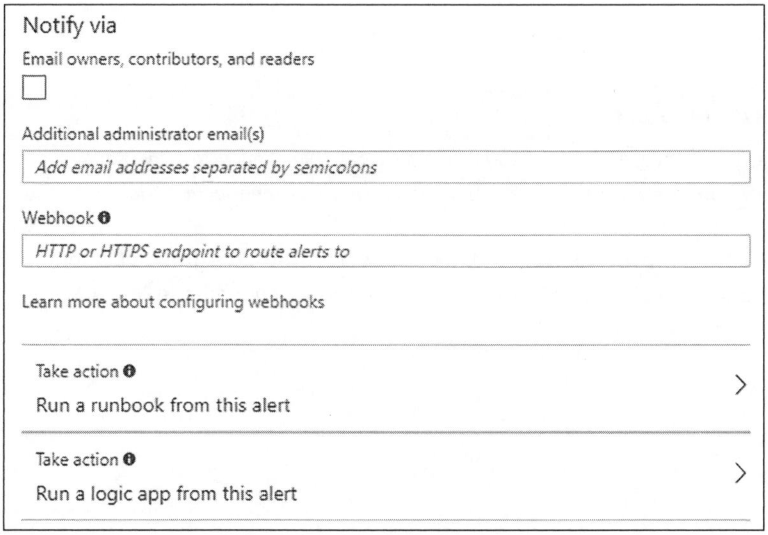

**FIGURE 2-46** Configuring notifications for an alert

## Creating an activity log alert

You create an activity alert by clicking Alert Rules, and then Add Activity Log Alert on a VM in the Azure portal, as shown in Figure 2-47.

**FIGURE 2-47** Creating an activity log alert

On the creation dialog, you must specify the resource group to create the new alert in, and then configure the criteria starting with the event category. The event category contains the following categories that expose different types of event sources.

- Administrative
- Security
- Security Health
- Recommendation
- Policy
- Autoscale

> **MORE INFO** **EVENT CATEGORIES**
>
> For a detailed review of what events are contained in each category see: *https://docs.micro-soft.com/en-us/azure/monitoring-and-diagnostics/monitoring-overview-activity-logs.*

After the event category is specified, you can filter to a specific resource group or resource as well as the specific operation. In Figure 2-48, the alert will trigger anytime the LinuxVM virtual machine is updated.

**FIGURE 2-48** Configuring an activity log alert

After the criteria is established, you define the actions that take place. Like the alerts, these are actual resources created in the resource group. You can add one or more actions from the following available options: Email, SMS, Webhook, or ITSM. Figure 2-49 demonstrates how to configure an Email action type.

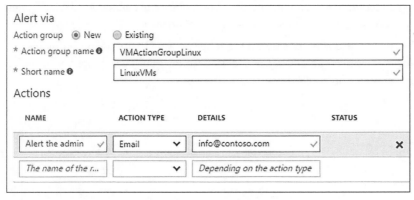

**FIGURE 2-49** Specifying the actions for an activity log alert

# Skill 2.5: Manage ARM VM availability

Resiliency is a critical part of any application architecture, whether the servers are physical or virtual Azure provides several features and capabilities to make virtual machine deployments resilient. The platform helps you to avoid single point of failure at the physical hardware level, and provides techniques to avoid downtime during host updates. Using features like availability zones, availability sets, and load balancers provides you the capabilities to build highly resilient and available systems.

> **This skill covers how to:**
> - Configure availability zones
> - Configure availability sets
> - Configure each application tier into separate availability sets
> - Combine the load balancer with availability sets

## Configure availability zones

Availability zones is a feature that at the time of this writing is in preview and is only available in a limited number of regions. Over time this feature will become more prevalent and will likely be integrated into the exam. At a high level, availability zones help to protect you from datacenter-level failures. They are located inside an Azure region, and each one has its own independent power source, network, and cooling. To ensure resiliency, there's a minimum of three separate zones in all enabled regions. The physical and logical separation of availability zones within a region protects applications and data from zone-level failures. Availability zones are expected to provide a 99.99 percent SLA once it is out of preview.

To deploy a VM to an availability zone, select the zone you want to use on the Settings blade of the virtual machine creation dialog, as shown in Figure 2-50. If you choose an availability zone, you cannot join an availability set.

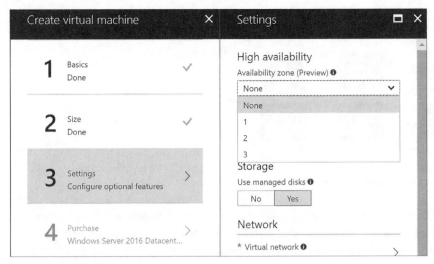

**FIGURE 2-50** Specifying the availability zone for a VM

At the time of this writing the following services are supported with availability zones:

- Linux virtual machines
- Windows virtual machines
- Zonal virtual machine scale sets
- Managed disks
- Load balancer

Supported virtual machine size families:

- Av2
- Dv2
- DSv2

## Configure availability sets

Availability sets are used to control availability for multiple virtual machines in the same application tier. To provide redundancy for your virtual machines, it is recommended to have at least two virtual machines in an availability set. This configuration ensures that at least one virtual machine is available in the event of a host update, or a problem with the physical hardware the virtual machines are hosted on. Having at least two virtual machines in an availability set is a requirement for the service level agreement (SLA) for virtual machines of 99.95 percent.

Virtual machines should be deployed into availability sets according to their workload or application tier. For instance, if you are deploying a three-tier solution that consists of web servers, a middle tier, and a database tier, each tier would have its own availability set, as Figure 2-51 demonstrates.

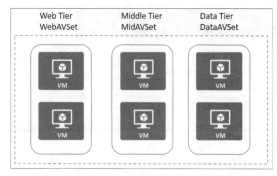

**FIGURE 2-51** Availability set configurations for a multi-tier solution

Each virtual machine in your availability set is assigned a fault domain and an update domain. Each availability set has up to 20 update domains available, which indicates the groups of virtual machines and the underlying physical hardware that can be rebooted at the same time for host updates. Each availability set is also comprised of up to three fault domains. Fault domains represent which virtual machines will be on separate physical racks in the datacenter for redundancy. This limits the impact of physical hardware failures such as server, network, or power interruptions. It is important to understand that the availability set must be set at creation time of the virtual machine.

## Alignment with Managed disks

For VMs that use Azure Managed Disks, VMs are aligned with managed disk fault domains when using an aligned availability set, as shown in Figure 2-52. This alignment ensures that all the managed disks attached to a VM are within the same managed disk fault domain. Only VMs with managed disks can be created in a managed availability set. The number of managed disk fault domains varies by region, either two or three managed disk fault domains per region.

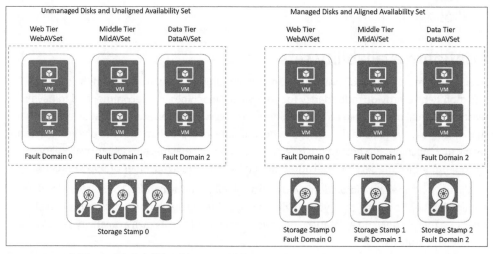

**FIGURE 2-52** Aligning managed disks with an availability set

## Create an availability set (Azure portal)

To create an availability set, specify a name for the availability set that is not in use by any other availability sets within the resource group, the number of fault and updates domains, as well as whether you will use managed disks with the availability set or not. Figure 2-53 demonstrates the Create Availability Set blade in the portal.

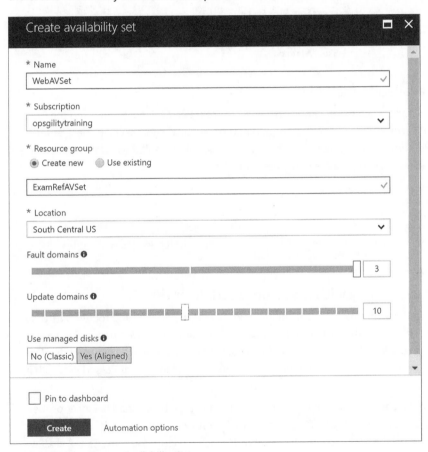

**FIGURE 2-53**  Creating an Availability Set

## Create an availability set (PowerShell)

The New-AzureRmAvailabilitySet cmdlet is used to create an availability set in PowerShell. The `PlatformUpdateDomainCount` and `PlatformFaultDomainCount` parameters control the number of fault domains and upgrade domains. The `Sku` parameter should be set to Aligned if you intend to deploy VMs that use managed disks.

```
# Create an availability set

$rgName     = "ExamRefRG"
$avSetName  = "WebAVSet"
$location   = "West US"
New-AzureRmAvailabilitySet  -ResourceGroupName $rgName `
                            -Name $avSetName `
                            -Location $location `
                            -PlatformUpdateDomainCount 10 `
                            -PlatformFaultDomainCount 3 `
                            -Sku "Aligned"
```

## Create an availability set (CLI)

The az vm availability-set create command is used to create an availability set using the CLI tools. The `platform-update-domain-count` and `platform-fault-domain-count` parameters are used to control the number of fault and upgrade domains. By default an availability set is created as aligned unless you pass the parameter unmanaged.

```
# Create an availability set
rgName="ExamRefRGCLI"
avSetName="WebAVSet"
location="WestUS"
az vm availability-set create --name $avSetName --resource-group $rgName --platform-
fault-domain-count 3 --platform-update-domain-count 10
```

## Managing availability with the Azure Load Balancer

The Azure Load Balancer provides availability for workloads by distributing requests across multiple virtual machines that perform the same task such as serving web pages. The Azure Load Balancer provides a feature called health probes that can automatically detect if a VM is problematic and removes it from the pool if it is. The load balancer is discussed in-depth in Chapter 4.

Each load balancer can be configured to have a TCP or HTTP based load balancer probe. The default probe behavior is for a TCP probe to make a socket connect on the port specified as the probe port. If the socket connect receives a TCP acknowledgement (ACK), the virtual machine continues receiving traffic in the load balancer rotation. If the probe does not receive a response (two failures, 15 seconds each by default), the load balancer takes the virtual machine in question out of the load balancer rotation. The load balancer does continue to probe, and if the service starts to respond, the virtual machine will be put back into rotation.

An HTTP probe works in a similar manner, except instead of looking for a TCP ACK, the HTTP probe is looking for a successful response from HTTP (HTTP 200 OK). This option allows you to specify the probe path, which is a relative path to an HTTP endpoint that responds with the code. For example, you could write custom code that responds on the relative path of /Health-check.aspx that checks whether the application on the virtual machine is functional (database connectivity and queue access). This allows a much deeper inspection of your application, and programmatic control over whether the virtual machine should be in rotation or not.

When you configure the backend pool of a load balancer you can associate it with the network interfaces of the virtual machines in your availability set, as shown in Figure 2-54.

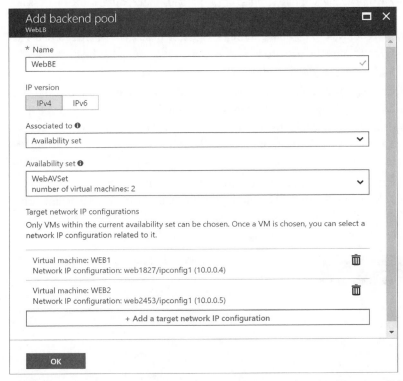

**FIGURE 2-54** Creating the backend pool of the load balancer using VMs from an availability set

# Skill 2.6 Scale ARM VMs

One of the more compelling benefits of Azure VMs is the ability to apply elasticity to any workload by providing the capability to flexibly scale up or out quickly. With Azure VMs there are two key ways to take advantage of this elasticity. The first is to change the size of your VMs as needed (up or down), and the second option is to use the virtual machine scale set (VMSS) feature to allow Azure to automatically add and remove instances as needed by your workload. In this skill we'll review these two techniques.

# Change VM sizes

There are many situations where the amount of compute processing a workload needs varies dramatically from day to day or even hour to hour. For example, in many organizations line of business (LOB) applications are heavily utilized during the workweek, but on the weekends, they see little to any actual usage. Other examples are workloads that require more processing time due to scheduled events such as backups or maintenance windows where having more compute time may make it faster to complete these tasks. Azure Resource Manager based VMs make it relatively easy to change the size of a virtual machine even after it has been deployed. There are a few things to consider with this approach.

The first consideration is to ensure that the region your VM is deployed to supports the instance size that you want to change the VM to. In most cases this is not an issue, but if you have a use case where the desired size isn't in the region the existing VM is deployed to, your only options are to either wait for the size to be supported in the region, or to move the existing VM to a region that already supports it.

The second consideration is if the new size is supported in the current hardware cluster your VM is deployed to. This can be determined by clicking the Size link in the virtual machine configuration blade in the Azure portal of a running virtual machine, as Figure 2-55 demonstrates. If the size is available you can select it. Changing the size reboots the virtual machine.

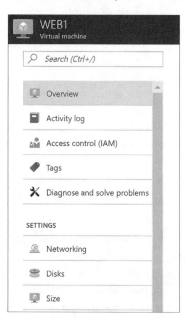

FIGURE 2-55 Creating the backend pool of the load balancer using VMs from an availability set

If the size is not available, it means either the size is not available in the region or the current hardware cluster. You can view the available sizes by region at *https://azure.microsoft.com/en-us/regions/services/*. In the event you need to change to a different hardware cluster you must first stop the virtual machine, and if it is part of an availability set you must stop all instances of the availability set at the same time. After all, when the VMs are stopped you can change the size, which moves all of the VMs to the new hardware cluster where they are resized and started. The reason all VMs in the availability set must be stopped before performing the resize operation to a size that requires different hardware. is that all running VMs in the availability set must use the same physical hardware cluster. Therefore, if a change of physical hardware cluster is required to change the VM size, all VMs must be first stopped and then restarted one-by-one to a different physical hardware cluster.

A third consideration is the form factor of the new size compared to the old size. Consider scaling from a DS3_V2 to a DS2_V2. A DS3_V2 supports up to eight data disks and up to four network interfaces. A DS2_V2 supports up to four data disks and up to two network interfaces. If the VM you are sizing from (DS3_V2) is using more disks or network interfaces then the target size, the resize operation will fail.

## Resizing a VM (PowerShell)

Use the Get-AzureRmVMSize cmdlet and pass the name of the region to the location parameter to view all the available sizes in your region to ensure the new size is available. If you specify the resource group and the VM name, it returns the available sizes in the current hardware cluster.

```
# View available sizes
$location = "WestUS"
Get-AzureRmVMSize -Location $location
```

After you have identified the available size, use the following code to change the VM to the new size.

```
$rgName = "EXAMREGWEBRG"
$vmName = "Web1"
$size = "Standard_DS2_V2"
$vm = Get-AzureRmVM -ResourceGroupName $rgName -VMName $vmName
$vm.HardwareProfile.VmSize = $size
Update-AzureRmVM -VM $vm -ResourceGroupName $rgName
```

If the virtual machine(s) are part of an availability set, the following code can be used to shut them all down at the same time and restart them using the new size.

```
$rgName = "ExamRefRG"
$vmName = "Web1"
$size = "Standard_DS2_V2"
$avSet = "WebAVSet"
```

### Resizing a VM (CLI)

The `az vm list-vm-resize-options` command can be used to see which VM sizes are available in the current hardware cluster.

```
rgName="ExamRefRG"
vmName="Web1"
az vm list-vm-resize-options --resource-group $rgName --name $vmName --output table
```

The `az vm list-sizes` command is used to view all sizes in the region.

```
az vm list-sizes --location westus
```

The `az vm resize` command is used to change the size of an individual VM.

```
az vm resize --resource-group $rgName --name $vmName --size Standard_DS3_v2
```

# Deploy and configure VM scale sets (VMSS)

For workloads that support the ability to dynamically add and remove instances to handle increased or decreased demand VM scale sets (VMSS) should be considered. A VMSS is a compute resource that you can use to deploy and manage a set of identical virtual machines.

By default, a VMSS supports up to 100 instances. However, it is possible to create a scale set up to 1000 instances if they are deployed with the property singlePlacementGroup set to false. A placement group is a construct like an Azure availability set, with its own fault domains and upgrade domains. By default, a scale set consists of a single placement group with a maximum size of 100 VMs. If the scale set property called singlePlacementGroup is set to false, the scale set can be composed of multiple placement groups and has a range of 0-1,000 VMs. When set to the default value of true, a scale set is composed of a single placement group, and has a range of 0-100 VMs.

Using multiple placement groups is commonly referred to as a large scale set. The single-PlacementGroup property can be set using ARM templates, the command line tools, or during portal creation.) Working with large scale sets does have a few conditions to be aware of. If you are using a custom image instead of a gallery image, your scale set supports up to 300 instances instead of 1000. Another scalability factor for consideration is the Azure Load Balancer. The basic SKU of the Azure Load Balancer can scale up to 100 instances. For a large scale set (> 100 instances) you should use the Standard SKU or the Azure Application Gateway.

### Creating a virtual machine scale set (Azure portal)

Figure 2-56 shows a portion of the creation dialog for creating a new VM scale set using the Azure portal. Like other Azure resources, you must specify a name and the resource group to deploy to. All instances of the VMSS will use the same operating system disk image specified here.

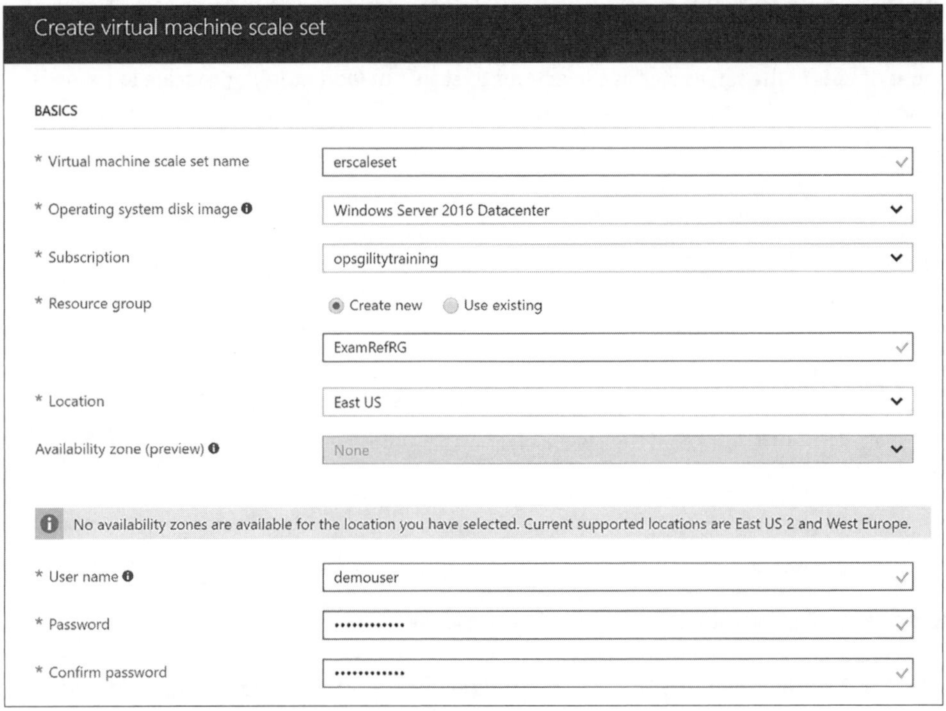

## Create virtual machine scale set

**BASICS**

| | |
|---|---|
| * Virtual machine scale set name | erscaleset ✓ |
| * Operating system disk image ❶ | Windows Server 2016 Datacenter ⌄ |
| * Subscription | opsgilitytraining ⌄ |
| * Resource group | ● Create new  ○ Use existing |
| | ExamRefRG ✓ |
| * Location | East US ⌄ |
| Availability zone (preview) ❶ | None ⌄ |

> ❶ No availability zones are available for the location you have selected. Current supported locations are East US 2 and West Europe.

| | |
|---|---|
| * User name ❶ | demouser ✓ |
| * Password | •••••••••••• ✓ |
| * Confirm password | •••••••••••• ✓ |

**FIGURE 2-56** Creating a VM scale set

Further down the page is where you specify the initial instance count, and instance size, as shown in figure 2-57. You can also choose to use managed or unmanaged disks, assign a public IP, and a DNS label. Creating a VMSS using the Azure portal also creates an instance of the Azure Load Balancer. Choosing Enable scaling beyond 100 instances creates the VMSS using the singlePlacementGroup property set to false. This change will also not create and associate the Azure Load Balancer with the scale set.

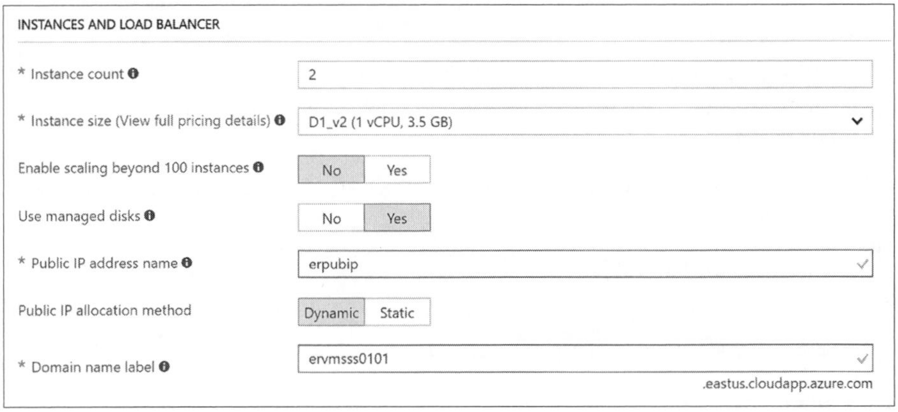

**INSTANCES AND LOAD BALANCER**

| | |
|---|---|
| * Instance count ❶ | 2 |
| * Instance size (View full pricing details) ❶ | D1_v2 (1 vCPU, 3.5 GB) ⌄ |
| Enable scaling beyond 100 instances ❶ | No \| Yes |
| Use managed disks ❶ | No \| **Yes** |
| * Public IP address name ❶ | erpubip ✓ |
| Public IP allocation method | **Dynamic** \| Static |
| * Domain name label ❶ | ervmsss0101 ✓ |
| | .eastus.cloudapp.azure.com |

**FIGURE 2-57** Configuring the instances and the load balancer for a VM scale set

When Autoscale is enabled you are presented with a set of configuration options for setting the default rules, as shown in figure 2-58. Here you can specify the minimum and maximum number of VMs in the set, as well as the actions to scale out (add more) or to scale in (remove instances).

AUTOSCALE

| | |
|---|---|
| Autoscale ❶ | Disabled  Enabled |
| * Minimum number of VMs ❶ | 1 |
| * Maximum number of VMs ❶ | 10 |
| **Scale out** | |
| * CPU threshold (%) ❶ | 75 |
| * Number of VMs to increase by ❶ | 1 |
| **Scale in** | |
| * CPU threshold (%) ❶ | 25 |
| * Number of VMs to decrease by ❶ | 1 |

**FIGURE 2-58** Configuring auto scale rules for a virtual machine scale set

The Azure portal creation process does not directly support applying configuration management options like VM extensions. However, they can be applied to a VMSS later using the command line tools or an ARM template.

## Creating a virtual machine scale set (PowerShell)

Creating a VM scale set using PowerShell is very similar to creating a regular virtual machine. You create a VMSS configuration object using the New-AzureRmVmssConfig cmdlet. From there, you either create or retrieve existing dependent resources and set them on the returned configuration object. Typically, virtual machine scale sets use a VM extension to self-configure themselves during the instance startup. The Add-AzureRmVmssExtension cmdlet is used to specify the extension configuration.

The following example is detailed, and creates all of the resources such as virtual network, load balancer, public IP address, as well as demonstrates how to apply a custom script extension to configure the VM instances on boot.

```
# Create a virtual machine scale set with IIS installed from a custom script extension
$rgName      = "ExamRefRGPS"
$location    = "WestUS"
$vmSize      = "Standard_DS2_V2"
$capacity    = 2

New-AzureRmResourceGroup -Name $rgName -Location $location

# Create a config object
$vmssConfig = New-AzureRmVmssConfig `
```

```
    -Location $location `
    -SkuCapacity $capacity `
    -SkuName $vmSize `
    -UpgradePolicyMode Automatic

# Define the script for your Custom Script Extension to run
$publicSettings = @{
    "fileUris" = (,"https://raw.githubusercontent.com/opsgility/lab-support-public/
master/script-extensions/install-iis.ps1");
    "commandToExecute" = "powershell -ExecutionPolicy Unrestricted -File install-iis.
ps1"
}

# Use Custom Script Extension to install IIS and configure basic website
Add-AzureRmVmssExtension -VirtualMachineScaleSet $vmssConfig `
    -Name "customScript" `
    -Publisher "Microsoft.Compute" `
    -Type "CustomScriptExtension" `
    -TypeHandlerVersion 1.8 `
    -Setting $publicSettings
$publicIPName = "vmssIP"

# Create a public IP address
$publicIP = New-AzureRmPublicIpAddress `
  -ResourceGroupName $rgName `
  -Location $location `
  -AllocationMethod Static `
  -Name $publicIPName

# Create a frontend and backend IP pool
$frontEndPoolName = "lbFrontEndPool"
$backendPoolName = "lbBackEndPool"
$frontendIP = New-AzureRmLoadBalancerFrontendIpConfig `
  -Name $frontEndPoolName `
  -PublicIpAddress $publicIP
$backendPool = New-AzureRmLoadBalancerBackendAddressPoolConfig -Name $backendPoolName

# Create the load balancer
$lbName = "vmsslb"
$lb = New-AzureRmLoadBalancer `
  -ResourceGroupName $rgName `
  -Name $lbName `
  -Location $location `
  -FrontendIpConfiguration $frontendIP `
  -BackendAddressPool $backendPool

# Create a load balancer health probe on port 80
$probeName = "lbprobe"
Add-AzureRmLoadBalancerProbeConfig -Name $probeName `
  -LoadBalancer $lb `
  -Protocol tcp `
  -Port 80 `
  -IntervalInSeconds 15 `
  -ProbeCount 2 `
  -RequestPath "/"
```

```
# Create a load balancer rule to distribute traffic on port 80
Add-AzureRmLoadBalancerRuleConfig `
  -Name "lbrule" `
  -LoadBalancer $lb `
  -FrontendIpConfiguration $lb.FrontendIpConfigurations[0] `
  -BackendAddressPool $lb.BackendAddressPools[0] `
  -Protocol Tcp `
  -FrontendPort 80 `
  -BackendPort 80

# Update the load balancer configuration
Set-AzureRmLoadBalancer -LoadBalancer $lb

# Reference a virtual machine image from the gallery
Set-AzureRmVmssStorageProfile $vmssConfig `
  -ImageReferencePublisher MicrosoftWindowsServer `
  -ImageReferenceOffer WindowsServer `
  -ImageReferenceSku 2016-Datacenter `
  -ImageReferenceVersion latest

# Set up information for authenticating with the virtual machine
$userName = "azureuser"
$password = "P@ssword!"
$vmPrefix = "ssVM"
Set-AzureRmVmssOsProfile $vmssConfig `
  -AdminUsername $userName `
  -AdminPassword $password `
  -ComputerNamePrefix $vmPrefix

# Create the virtual network resources
$subnetName = "web"
$subnet = New-AzureRmVirtualNetworkSubnetConfig `
  -Name $subnetName `
  -AddressPrefix 10.0.0.0/24
$ssName = "vmssVNET"
$subnetPrefix = "10.0.0.0/16"
$vnet = New-AzureRmVirtualNetwork `
  -ResourceGroupName $rgName `
  -Name $ssName `
  -Location $location `
  -AddressPrefix $subnetPrefix `
  -Subnet $subnet
$ipConfig = New-AzureRmVmssIpConfig `
  -Name "vmssIPConfig" `
  -LoadBalancerBackendAddressPoolsId $lb.BackendAddressPools[0].Id `
  -SubnetId $vnet.Subnets[0].Id

# Attach the virtual network to the config object
$netConfigName = "network-config"
Add-AzureRmVmssNetworkInterfaceConfiguration `
  -VirtualMachineScaleSet $vmssConfig `
  -Name $netConfigName `
  -Primary $true `
  -IPConfiguration $ipConfig
$scaleSetName = "erscaleset"
```

```
# Create the scale set with the config object (this step might take a few minutes)
New-AzureRmVmss `
    -ResourceGroupName $rgName `
    -Name $scaleSetName `
    -VirtualMachineScaleSet $vmssConfig
```

## Creating a virtual machine scale set (CLI)

The Azure CLI tools takes a different approach than PowerShell by creating resources like load balancers and virtual networks for you as part of the scale set creation.

```
# Create a VM Scale Set with load balancer, virtual network, and a public IP address
rgName="Contoso"
ssName="erscaleset"
userName="azureuser"
password="P@ssword!"
vmPrefix="ssVM"
az vmss create --resource-group $rgName --name $ssName --image UbuntuLTS
--authentication-type password --admin-username $userName --admin-password $password
```

The az vmss create command allows you to reference existing resources instead of creating them automatically by specifying the resources as parameters if you want to differ from the default behavior. Applying a vm extension is like what was seen in Skill 2.2. For a VMSS use the az vmss extension set command as shown in the following example.

```
#settings.json
{
  "fileUris": [
    "https://raw.githubusercontent.com/Azure/azure-quickstart-templates/master/
201-vmss-bottle-autoscale/installserver.sh"
  ],
  "commandToExecute": "bash installserver.sh"
}
az vmss extension set --publisher Microsoft.Compute --version 1.8 --name
CustomScriptExtension --resource-group $rgName --vmss-name $ssName --settings
@settings.json
```

## Upgrading a virtual machine scale set

During the lifecycle of running a virtual machine scale set you undoubtedly need to deploy an update to the operating system. The VMSS resource property upgradePolicy can be set to either the value manual or automatic. If automatic, when an operating system update is available all instances are updated at the same time, which causes downtime. If the property is set to manual, it is up to you to programmatically step through and update each instance using PowerShell with the Update-AzureRmVmssInstance cmdlet or the Azure CLI tools az vmss update-instances command.

> **MORE INFO  UPGRADING A VIRTUAL MACHINE SCALE SET**
>
> You can learn more about upgrading virtual machine scale sets at *https://docs.microsoft.com/en-us/azure/virtual-machine-scale-sets/virtual-machine-scale-sets-upgrade-scale-set*.

# Skill 2.7 Manage containers with Azure Container Services (ACS)

Azure Container Service (ACS) is used to provision and manage hosted container environments. ACS provides a cluster of virtual machines that are preconfigured to run the orchestrator of your choice: Docker Swarm, DC/OS, or Kubernetes. These orchestrators make the running of containerized applications at scale possible.

There are many different Azure resources that are deployed to make the cluster function. These include VMs, VM scale sets, load balancers, public IP addresses, VNets, and other supporting resources such as storage. By creating and connecting these resources ACS removes the need for previous container orchestration expertise required to run containers on Azure. This makes it very quick and easy to deploy and manage containerized applications.

ACS also removes the burden of operations and maintenance by provisioning, upgrading, and scaling resources on demand. Applications never need to go offline to scale up, down, or out.

This skill explores how to use ACS to provision, manage, and monitor your container deployments on Azure.

> **This skill covers how to:**
> - Configure for open-source tooling
> - Create and manage container images
> - Implement Azure Container Registry
> - Deploy a Kubernetes cluster in ACS
> - Manage containers with Azure Container Services (ACS)
> - Scale applications using Docker Swarm, DC/OS, or Kubernetes
> - Migrate container workloads to and from Azure
> - Monitor Kubernetes by using Microsoft Operations Management Suite (OMS)

## Configure for open-source tooling

Microsoft has put major effort into making sure that Azure is an open cloud. This is evident in the ability to use open-source tools with ACS. All ACS clusters can be provisioned and managed using the open-source tools either created by Microsoft or supported on the Azure platform.

For example, Microsoft exposes the standard Kubernetes API endpoints. By using these standard endpoints, you can leverage any software that can connect to a Kubernetes cluster. Also supported are tools such as kubectl, helm, or even the docker command from within the Azure portal using the Azure Cloud Shell, as seen in Figure 2-59.

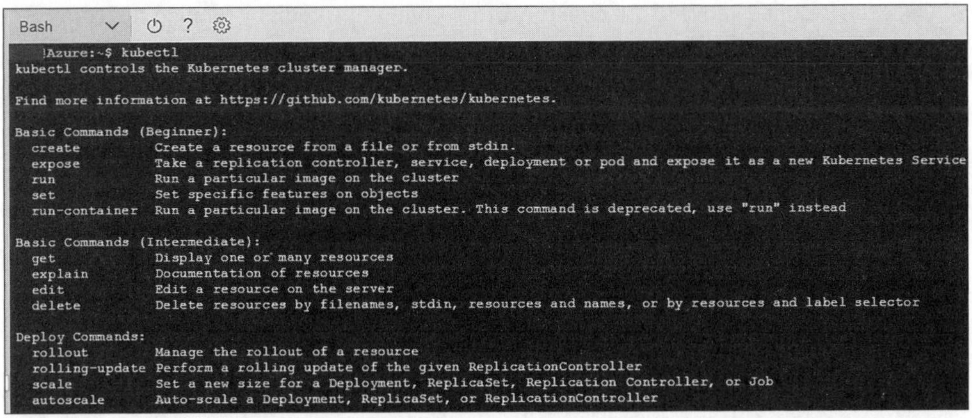

**FIGURE 2-59** Kubernetes kubectl command line tool running in the Azure Cloud Shell

# Create and manage container images

Container images are simply packages of applications and their components needed to run them. A container image is a stand-alone, executable package of an application that includes everything required to run. This could include the code, runtime (Java or .NET), system tools, system libraries, and settings.

When you start a container the first action that is taken is to locate the image. Images are always run locally, but often the image is in a container registry (see the topic on Implementing Azure Container Registry in this chapter).

> **MORE INFORMATION  CONTAINER IMAGES**
>
> To learn the basics of working with container images Microsoft recommends this tutorial from Docker at *https://docs.docker.com/get-started/*. To work with containers, you need both Git for source control management, and Docker installed on your PC. In this example, you will use a sample provided by the Azure team to work with Azure Container Service (ACS). You need to have also installed Git for source control management and Docker on your PC.

The process to create the container image follows three steps:

- Clone the application source from GitHub.
- Create a container image from the application source.
- Test the application with Docker locally.

To clone the application source provided by Microsoft, open your command line and run the following command.

```
git clone https://github.com/Azure-Samples/azure-voting-app-redis.git
```

Once this is cloned, move to the directory azure-voting-app-redis by running this command.

```
cd azure-voting-app-redis
```

Run the dir or ls command to see the files that located in the source code directory, as seen in Figure 2-60. Notice that there is a docker-compose.yaml file. This file has the required information that allows you to create the container.

```
posh~git ~ azure-voting-app-redis [master]
~\Documents\GitHub\azure-voting-app-redis [master ≡]> dir


    Directory: C:\Users\DanPatrick\Documents\GitHub\azure-voting-app-redis


Mode                LastWriteTime         Length Name
----                -------------         ------ ----
d-----       11/1/2017   9:30 AM                azure-vote
d-----       11/1/2017   9:30 AM                kubernetes-manifests
-a----       11/1/2017   9:30 AM           1258 .gitignore
-a----       11/1/2017   9:30 AM           1256 azure-vote-all-in-one-redis.yml
-a----       11/1/2017   9:30 AM            329 docker-compose.yml
-a----       11/1/2017   9:30 AM           1183 LICENSE
-a----       11/1/2017   9:30 AM           1564 README.md


~\Documents\GitHub\azure-voting-app-redis [master ≡]>
```

FIGURE 2-60 Azure Sample Source Code after being cloned

Next, use the docker-compose command to create the container image referencing the docker-compose.yaml file that is in the directory. Figure 2-60 shows this command after it has executed.

```
docker-compose up -d
```

```
posh~git ~ azure-voting-app-redis [master]
~\Documents\GitHub\azure-voting-app-redis [master ≡]> docker-compose up -d
Creating network "azurevotingappredis_default" with the default driver
Building azure-vote-front
Step 1/3 : FROM tiangolo/uwsgi-nginx-flask:python3.6
python3.6: Pulling from tiangolo/uwsgi-nginx-flask
ad74af05f5a2: Pull complete
2b032b8bbe8b: Pull complete
a9a5b35f6ead: Pull complete
3245b5a1c52c: Pull complete
032924b710ba: Pull complete
0d7cffe4bfd7: Pull complete
450f5ea3e7ea: Pull complete
b1dca9769b8b: Pull complete
00aad0154741: Pull complete
6fc86093db75: Pull complete
054414bb9937: Pull complete
0239199795ca: Pull complete
de0e522d4614: Pull complete
33ba099388b0: Pull complete
98510c3d47ba: Pull complete
c9a7fc2937a6: Pull complete
cd8c29bc2595: Pull complete
4b5168cda12b: Pull complete
0ab0573420d2: Pull complete
54001acad531: Pull complete
75affa92f259: Pull complete
e502ece37633: Pull complete
a880eefbb3e5: Pull complete
05751bf2b4a0: Pull complete
Digest: sha256:adff5f084beea00bc8c40e33eba5d8c6b7ed999d2a0de8299d8e5648a37a6f4b
Status: Downloaded newer image for tiangolo/uwsgi-nginx-flask:python3.6
```

FIGURE 2-61 Container created using the docker-compose command

> ***IMPORTANT*** **CREATING THE CONTAINER**
>
> **To create the container, you must have Docker installed and running on your machine. This is what is being used to create the container. If you are running Docker for Windows you must have it set to run Linux containers at the time of creating and running this image because it uses Linux.**

Once this command is completed, you can list the images that are now local to your PC by running this command. Figure 2-62 shows the images that are located on the PC.

```
docker images
```

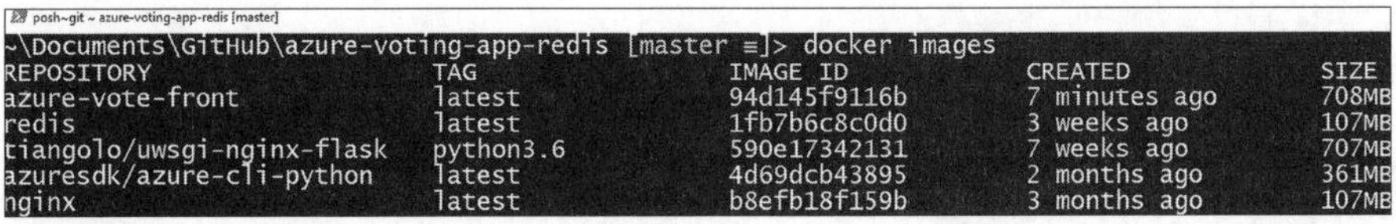
posh~git ~ azure-voting-app-redis [master]
~\Documents\GitHub\azure-voting-app-redis [master ≡]> docker images
REPOSITORY TAG IMAGE ID CREATED SIZE
azure-vote-front latest 94d145f9116b 7 minutes ago 708MB
redis latest 1fb7b6c8c0d0 3 weeks ago 107MB
tiangolo/uwsgi-nginx-flask python3.6 590e17342131 7 weeks ago 707MB
azuresdk/azure-cli-python latest 4d69dcb43895 2 months ago 361MB
nginx latest b8efb18f159b 3 months ago 107MB

**FIGURE 2-62** Local Docker images

To see the running containers, run the following command. In Figure 2-63, notice that the application is now running on your local machine on port 8080.

```
docker ps
```

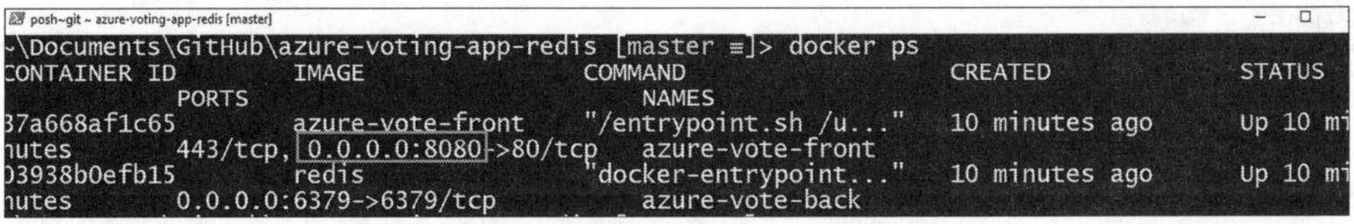
posh~git ~ azure-voting-app-redis [master]
~\Documents\GitHub\azure-voting-app-redis [master ≡]> docker ps
CONTAINER ID IMAGE COMMAND CREATED STATUS
PORTS NAMES
37a668af1c65 azure-vote-front "/entrypoint.sh /u..." 10 minutes ago Up 10 mi
nutes 443/tcp, 0.0.0.0:8080->80/tcp azure-vote-front
03938b0efb15 redis "docker-entrypoint..." 10 minutes ago Up 10 mi
nutes 0.0.0.0:6379->6379/tcp azure-vote-back

**FIGURE 2-63** Running containers listed using the docker ps command

As seen in Figure 2-64, open your local web browser and see the Azure voting application up and running using the container image that you just created. Make sure to reference the port 8080 where the container is running on your local PC.

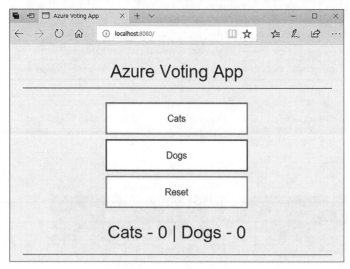

**FIGURE 2-64** Azure Voting App running locally as a Docker container

Once you have verified that applications functions using this container image you can stop it running the containers and remove them. You don't want to remove the image because this will be used again.

```
docker-compose stop
docker-compose down
```

## Implement Azure Container Registry

Azure Container Registry (ACR) is an Azure-based, private registry for Docker container images. A container registry is important for container deploys because you can store all the images for your applications in one location. These are the gold images for your application, so it is critical to leverage a registry. As containers are created, they are pulled from this location.

The steps required to upload your image to ACR include:

- Deploying an Azure Container Registry (ACR) instance
- Tagging a container image for ACR
- Uploading the image to ACR

Deploying and working with the ACR from your local PC requires that you use the Azure CLI 2.0. This must be installed and running on your PC. Once this is completed, use the following commands to work with ACR and your image.

Login to Azure using the Azure CLI using the following command.

```
az login
```

Open the Azure Cloud Shell and first create a Resource group.

```
az group create --name ContainersRG --location westus2
```

Next, create the Azure Container Registry located in the Resource group you just created.

```
az acr create --resource-group ContainersRG --name ExamRefRegistry --sku Basic
--admin-enabled true
```

After the ACR has been created you can then login to the registry using the `az acr login` command.

```
az acr login --name ExamRefRegistry --username ExamRefRegistry --password <password
 found in azure portal>
```

List the name of your ACR Server using the following command, as seen in Figure 2-65. Make note that this must be a globally unique name.

```
az acr list --resource-group ContainersRG --query "[].{acrLoginServer:loginServer}"
--output table
```

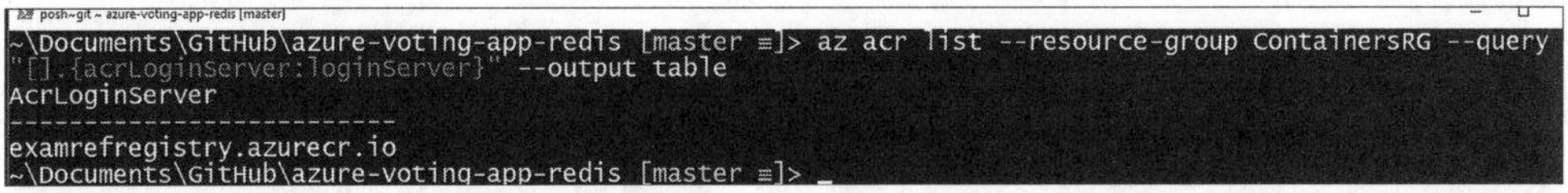

**FIGURE 2-65** The Azure Container Service Server

Run the following command to list the images that are local on your PC. These should be there based on the images you already created, as seen in Figure 2-66.

```
docker images
```

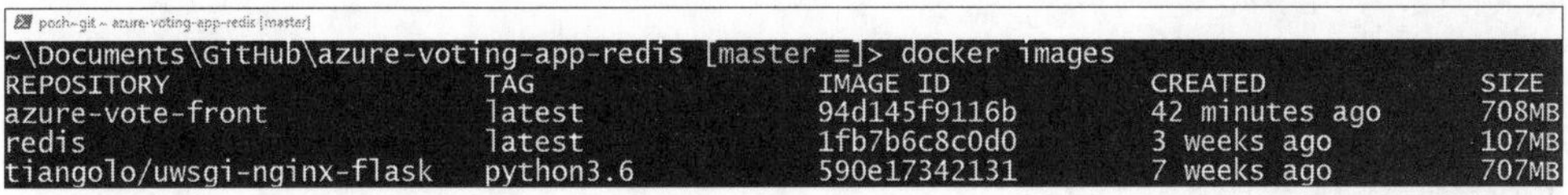

**FIGURE 2-66** Docker images command run on local PC

These images need to be tagged with the loginServer name of the registry. The tag is used for routing when pushing container images to the ACR. Run the following command to tag the azure-vote-front image referencing the ACR Server name. Notice that the v-1 is added to the end, which provides a version number. This is important for production deployments because it allows multiple versions of the same image to be stored and used.

```
docker tag azure-vote-front examrefregistry.azurecr.io/azure-vote-front:redis-v1
```

As seen in Figure 2-67, run the docker images command again and notice that a new image has been added with the TAG added.

```
X push-git - azure-voting-app-redis [master]
-\Documents\GitHub\azure-voting-app-redis [master ≡]> docker images
REPOSITORY                                    TAG          IMAGE ID       CREATED            SIZE
azure-vote-front                              latest       94d145f9116b   About an hour ago  708MB
examrefregistry.azurecr.io/azure-vote-front   redis-v1     94d145f9116b   About an hour ago  708MB
redis                                         latest       1fb7b6c8c0d0   3 weeks ago        107MB
tiangolo/uwsgi-nginx-flask                    python3.6    590e17342131   7 weeks ago        707MB
azuresdk/azure-cli-python                     latest       4d69dcb43895   2 months ago       361MB
nginx                                         latest       b8efb18f159b   3 months ago       107MB
```

**FIGURE 2-67** Tag added to azure-vote-front image

Now it's time to push this image up to the ACR. Use the following command, as seen in Figure 2-68, and make sure that the ACR server is correct.

```
docker push examrefregistry.azurecr.io/azure-vote-front:redis-v1
```

```
X push-git - azure-voting-app-redis [master]
-\Documents\GitHub\azure-voting-app-redis [master ≡]> docker push examrefregistry.azurecr.io/azure-vote-front:redis-v1
he push refs to a repository [examrefregistry.azurecr.io/azure-vote-front]
468a9c6b0c3: Pushed
8fcbe580aca: Pushed
75e51c5e84e: Pushed
889a339caa2: Pushed
ba5e66e1bc9: Pushed
1b3b1f0ab7b: Pushed
6ddad2c15b4: Pushed
```

**FIGURE 2-68** Image pushed to the Azure Container Service

When you push your image to the ACR it appears in the Azure portal as a Repository. Open the Azure Portal and locate your ACR, then move to the Repository section. In Figure 2-69, notice that azure-vote-front is the image that you created and is now in Azure.

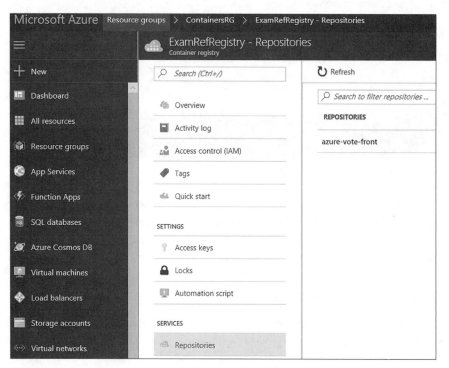

**FIGURE 2-69** Azure Container Services in the Azure Portal showing the image

If you click through the azure-vote-front you see the tag that you added as redis-v1, as seen in Figure 2-70.

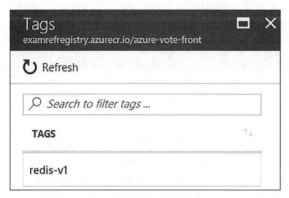

**FIGURE 2-70** Azure-vote-front Image Tag in the Azure portal

## Deploy a Kubernetes cluster in ACS

Deploying a Kubernetes cluster using ACS can be accomplished using either the Azure portal, PowerShell or the Azure CLI. The focus from Microsoft for these types of open source tools is on the command line, and as such that is the focus of this skill. The primary tools used for working with Kubernetes are the Azure CLI az command and the Kubernetes CLI kubectl command.

> **MORE INFORMATION** **AZURE CONTAINER SERVICES**
>
> Azure Container Services can be deployed using PowerShell using the New-AzureRMContainerService cmdlet. Review the following article to learn its usage: *https://docs.microsoft. com/en-us/powershell/module/azurerm.compute/?view=azurermps-5.0.0#container_service.*

To use the Azure CLI to create the Kubernetes cluster (K8s), you execute just one command. This command simplifies the entire creation of the cluster to only one line. Notice the agent count parameter; this is the number of nodes that will be available to your applications. This of course could be changed if you wish to have more than one node to your cluster. For this example, all the commands will be run from the Azure Cloud Shell.

```
az acs create --orchestrator-type kubernetes --resource-group ContainersRG
--name ExamRefK8sCluster --generate-ssh-keys --agent-count 1
```

Once the cluster has been created you need to gain access by issuing a command to get the credentials. This command configures the kubectl, which is the K8s cluster that was just created in ACS. This is done using the following command.

```
az acs kubernetes get-credentials --resource-group=ContainersRG --name=ExamRefK8sCluster
```

Verify your connection to the cluster by listing the nodes, as seen in Figure 2-71.

```
kubectl get nodes
```

```
@Azure:~$ kubectl get nodes
NAME                          STATUS    ROLES     AGE      VERSION
k8s-agentpool0-14583630-0     Ready     agent     10m      v1.7.7
k8s-master-14583630-0         Ready     master    10m      v1.7.7
```

FIGURE 2-71 Kubernetes clusters nodes running Azure

## Manage containers with Azure Container Services (ACS)

Once you have built a cluster, the next natural step is to deploy applications using your container images. Each of the components will now come together to provide an application experience for your users. The Azure Container Registry (ACR), where the image is stored will be accessed to download the image to the Kubernetes cluster running in Azure Container Services (ACS), which will provide the power and management to run the Azure voting sample application.

First you need to update a Docker compose file to reference your image that was uploaded to the ACR. From your local PC you need to use an editor to make a change to the image reference in the azure-vote-all-in-line-redis.yaml file in your git repo, as seen in Figure 2-72. The image should reference the server name of your ACR. To find the server name you can run the following command:

```
az acr list --resource-group ContainersRG --query "[].{acrLoginServer:loginServer}"
 --output table
```

```
spec:
  containers:
  - name: azure-vote-front
    image: examrefregistry.azurecr.io/azure-vote-front:redis-v1
    ports:
    - containerPort: 80
```

FIGURE 2-72 Azure Container Registry Server name updated

Once this file has been updated it should be pushed to the ACR again because this change is only found on your local PC currently. Use the following command to push the image to the registry.

```
docker push examrefregistry.azurecr.io/azure-vote-front:redis-v1
```

Next, you deploy the application to Kubernetes using the kubectl command from your local PC. First you need to install the kubectl command line. If you are using Windows this can be done by opening a cmd prompt as administrator and running the following command.

```
az acs kubernetes install-cli
```

Now that the kubectl is installed locally, you need to configure it to use your K8s Cluster in Azure. Run the following command to configure kubectl for this purpose. You need to reference your RSA key for this cluster, which can be found in the .ssh folder of your cloud shell.

```
az acs kubernetes get-credentials -n ExamRefK8sCluster -g ContainersRG
--ssh-key-file <name of private key file>
```

Once you have kubectl configured, a simple command starts the Azure voting application running on the K8s customer in Azure. Figure 2-73 shows the feedback from the command line after successfully starting the application on the K8s cluster.

```
kubectl create -f azure-vote-all-in-one-redis.yml
```

```
deployment "azure-vote-back" created
service "azure-vote-back" created
deployment "azure-vote-front" created
service "azure-vote-front" created
```

FIGURE 2-73 Azure voting application sample running on Kubernetes in Azure

Once the application has been started you can run the following command to watch because Kubernetes and Azure configure it for use. In Figure 2-74, notice how it moves from having a pending Public IP address to an address as shown.

```
Kubectl get service azure-vote-front --watch
```

| NAME | TYPE | CLUSTER-IP | EXTERNAL-IP | PORT(S) | AGE |
|------|------|------------|-------------|---------|-----|
| azure-vote-front | LoadBalancer | 10.0.111.189 | <pending> | 80:31199/TCP | 1m |
| azure-vote-front | LoadBalancer | 10.0.111.189 | 51.143.97.154 | 80:31199/TCP | 3m |

FIGURE 2-74 Kubectl watching the azure-vote-front application running in Azure

Once the application has moved to having an external IP this means that you can now connect to the application with a web browser, as seen in Figure 2-75.

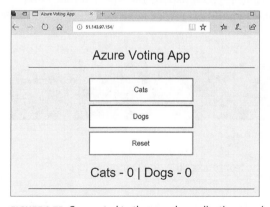

FIGURE 2-75 Connected to the sample application running on a Kubernetes cluster in Azure

# Scale applications using Docker Swarm, DC/OS, or Kubernetes

There are two methods for scaling applications running in Azure Container Services:

- Scaling the Azure infrastructure
- Leveraging the orchestrator for allocation of resources

Azure is unaware of your applications running on your cluster. It is only aware of the infrastructure that was provisioned for the orchestrator to provide the compute, storage, and networking. The Azure infrastructure that provides compute to the cluster is via virtual machine scale sets. These can scale up and down based on your needs. This can be done using the az command line tool or the Azure portal.

To scale a Kubernetes cluster, you would run a command, such as the following:

```
az acs scale --resource-group=ContainersRG --name= ExamRefK8sCluster --new-agent-count 3
```

After this command completes you can run the kubectl get nodes command again to see that the nodes have been added to the cluster, as seen in Figure 2-76.

```
dan@Azure:~$ kubectl get nodes
NAME                          STATUS    ROLES     AGE       VERSION
k8s-agentpool0-14583630-0     Ready     agent     22m       v1.7.7
k8s-agentpool0-14583630-1     Ready     agent     2m        v1.7.7
k8s-agentpool0-14583630-2     Ready     agent     3m        v1.7.7
k8s-master-14583630-0         Ready     master    22m       v1.7.7
```

FIGURE 2-76 Kubernetes clusters nodes running Azure

Within the orchestrator itself you can make a change to resources that are being leveraged for the service. In the case of Kubernetes, you might want to scale your pods. Pods are like instances of your application. To do this manually you would use the command line using kubectl. First run a command to see the number of pods, as seen in Figure 2-77.

```
kubectl get pods
```

```
@Azure:~$ kubectl get pods
NAME                                 READY     STATUS     RESTARTS     AGE
azure-vote-back-4149398501-mf6fs     1/1       Running    0            11m
azure-vote-front-439619988-mhf9q     1/1       Running    0            11m
```

FIGURE 2-77 Kubernetes pods hosting the sample application

Next, run the following command to scale the frontend of the application. Figure 2-78 shows the pods after they have been scaled.

```
kubectl scale --replicas=5 deployment/azure-vote-front
```

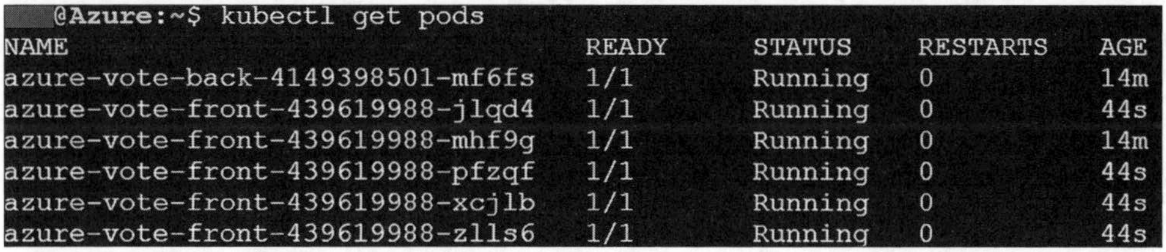

```
 @Azure:~$ kubectl get pods
NAME                                   READY    STATUS     RESTARTS    AGE
azure-vote-back-4149398501-mf6fs       1/1      Running    0           14m
azure-vote-front-439619988-jlqd4       1/1      Running    0           44s
azure-vote-front-439619988-mhf9g       1/1      Running    0           14m
azure-vote-front-439619988-pfzqf       1/1      Running    0           44s
azure-vote-front-439619988-xcjlb       1/1      Running    0           44s
azure-vote-front-439619988-zlls6       1/1      Running    0           44s
```

**FIGURE 2-78** Kubernetes pods scaled horizontally

Kubernetes also supports the ability to scale pods horizontally using auto-scaling. For example, you can configure based on the CPU utilization. Defining the limits in your deployment file does this. Here is an example of a command using kubectl to autoscale the azure-vote-front deployment.

```
kubectl autoscale deployment azure-vote-front --cpu-percent=50 --min=3 --max=10
```

## Migrate container workloads to and from Azure

The magic of containers is that they can be leveraged on almost any platform without any change to the application or the containers. Migrating container workloads is made easier by leveraging the Azure Container Registry (ACR). Moving images into or out of ACR is simple and provides the means for these migrations.

Once the containers are moved into Azure then it is more a function of starting the containers and managing them with an ACS cluster. The cluster manages the complexities of scaling and connecting the applications together by providing service discovery inside of the cluster.

Some code might be updated depending upon the service that is deployed and run in Azure. For example, if a large website would be migrated to Azure you may want to update the code to reference image and large data files in the HTML code as hosted in Azure Storage. This would offload the loading of images to the Azure Storage service rather than relying on those calls to come through to the containers. By doing this the containers focus on the logic of the application and heavy lifting of providing downloads can be service by the Azure platform.

## Monitor Kubernetes by using Microsoft Operations Management Suite (OMS)

The Containers Monitoring Solution makes monitoring Kubernetes on Azure possible, which is a part of Log Analytics. Figure 2-79 shows that the Container Monitoring Solution allows you to view and manage your container hosts from a single location.

**FIGURE 2-79** Container Management Solution running in the Azure portal

You can view which containers are running, what container image they're running, and where those containers are running. You can also view detailed audit information showing commands used with containers.

Troubleshooting containers can be complex because there are many of them. The Container Management Solution simplifies these tasks by allowing you to search centralized logs without having to remotely connect to hosts. You are also able to search the data as one pool of information rather than having those logs isolated on each machine.

Finding containers that may be using excess resources on a host is also easy. You can view centralized CPU, memory, storage, and network usage and performance information for containers. The solution supports the following container orchestrators:

- Docker Swarm
- DC/OS
- Kubernetes
- Service Fabric
- Red Hat OpenShift

---

***MORE INFORMATION*** **MONITOR A CLUSTER**

To monitor a cluster a manifest file is created and then started on the K8s cluster using the kubeclt command line tool. To learn how to create a monitoring manifest file to monitor a K8s cluster review *https://docs.microsoft.com/en-us/azure/acs/tutorial-kubernetes-monitor*.

---

# Though experiment

In this thought experiment, apply what you have learned about in this Chapter. You can find answers to these questions in the next section.

You are the IT administrator for Contoso and you are tasked with migrating an existing web farm and database to Microsoft Azure. The web application is written in PHP and is deployed across 20 physical servers running RedHat for the operating system and Apache for the web server. The backend consists of two physical servers running MySQL in an active/passive configuration.

The solution must provide the ability to scale to at least as many web servers as the existing solution and ideally the number of web server instances should automatically adjust based on the demand. All the servers must be reachable on the same network so the administrator can easily connect to them using SSH from a jump box to administer the VMs.

Answer the following questions for your manager:

1. Which compute option would be ideal for the web servers?
2. Should all of the servers be deployed into the same availability set, or should they be deployed in their own?
3. What would be the recommended storage configuration for the web servers? What about the database servers?
4. What feature could be used to ensure that traffic to the VMs only goes to the appropriate services (Apache, MySQL, and SSH)?

# Thought experiment answers

This section contains the answers to the thought experiment for this chapter.

1. The web servers are best served by deploying them into a virtual machine scale set (VMSS). Autoscale should be configured on the VMSS to address the requirement of automatically scaling up/down the number of instances based on the demand (CPU) used on the web servers.
2. No, the web servers should be deployed into their own availability set, which is provided by a VMSS, and the database tier should be deployed into its own scale set.
3. The web servers will likely not be I/O intensive so Standard storage may be appropriate. The database servers will likely be I/O intensive so Premium storage is the recommended approach. To minimize management overhead and to ensure that storage capacity planning is done correctly managed disks should be used in both cases.
4. Use Network Security Groups (NSGs) to ensure that only traffic destined for allowed services can communicate to the VMs.

# Chapter summary

This chapter covered a broad range of topics ranging from which workloads are supported in Azure VMs, to creating and configuring virtual machines and monitoring them. This chapter also discussed containers and using Azure Container Services to manage and monitor container based workloads. Here are some of the key takeaways from this chapter:

- Most workloads can run exceedingly well in Azure VMs; however, it is important to understand that there are some limitations such as not being able to run 32-bit operating systems, or low level network services such as hosting your own DHCP server.

- Each compute family is optimized for either general or specific workloads. You should optimize your VM by choosing the most appropriate size.

- You can create VMs from the portal, PowerShell, the CLI tools, and Azure Resource Manager templates. You should understand when to use which tool and how to configure the virtual machine resource during provisioning and after provisioning. For example, availability sets can only be set at provisioning time, but data disks can be added at any time.

- You can connect to Azure VMs using a public IP address or a private IP address with RDP, SSH, or even PowerShell. To connect to a VM using a private IP you must also enable connectivity such as site-to-site, point-to-site, or ExpressRoute.

- The Custom Script Extension is commonly used to execute scripts on Windows or Linux-based VMs. The PowerShell DSC extension is used to apply desired state configurations to Windows-based VMs.

- To troubleshoot a problem that only occurs when an application is deployed you can deploy a debug version of your app, and enable remote debugging on Windows-based VMs.

- VM storage comes in standard and Premium storage. For I/O intensive workloads or workloads that require low latency on storage you should use Premium storage.

- There are unmanaged and managed disks and images. The key difference between the two is with unmanaged disks or images it is up to you to manage the storage account. With managed disks, Azure takes care of this for you so it greatly simplifies managing images and disks.

- On Windows-based VMs you can enable the Azure Diagnostics Agent to capture performance data, files and folders, crash dumps, event logs, application logs, and events from ETW and have that data automatically transfer to an Azure Storage account. On Linux VMs you can only capture and transfer performance data.

- You can configure alerts based on metric alerts (captured from Azure Diagnostics) to Activity Log alerts that can notify by email, web hook, SMS, Logic Apps, or even an Azure Automation Runbook.

- Azure Fault Domains provide high availability at the data center level. Azure Availability Sets provide high availability within a data center, and a properly designed multi-region solution that takes advantage of regional pairing provides availability at the Azure region level.

- Managed disks provide additional availability over unmanaged disks by aligning with availability sets and providing storage in redundant storage units.
- Virtual Machine Scale Sets (VMSS), can scale up to 1000 instances. You need to ensure that you create the VMSS configured for large scale sets if you intend to go above 100 instances. There are several other limits to consider too. Using a custom image, you can only create up to 300 instances. To scale above 100 instances you must use the Standard SKU of the Azure Load Balancer or the Azure App Gateway.

# CHAPTER 3

# Design and implement a storage strategy

Implementing storage is one of the most important aspects of building or deploying a new solution using Azure. There are several services and features available for use, and each has their own place. Azure Storage is the underlying storage for most of the services in Azure. It provides service for storage and retrieval of files and also has services that are available for storing large volumes of data through tables, and a fast-reliable messaging service for application developers with queues. In this chapter we'll review how to design a storage strategy with an emphasis on Azure Storage blobs and files as well as introducing Azure Data Lake store, emphasizing how to protect the data you store in it.

## Skills covered in this chapter:

- Skill 3.1: Implement Azure Storage blobs and files
- Skill 3.2: Manage Access
- Skill 3.3: Configure diagnostics, monitoring, and analytics
- Skill 3.4: Implement storage encryption

## Skill 3.1: Implement Azure Storage blobs and files

Azure Storage accounts expose two services for storing files blobs and files. The blob storage service allows application developers and tools that use the Azure Storage API to store files directly in storage. The second service, Azure files, allows for file access through the Server Message Block (SMB) protocol. This allows you to access files in an Azure Storage account as you would a traditional file share through a mapped drive or a UNC path.

> **This skill covers how to:**
> - Manage blob storage
> - Use the async blob copy service
> - Manage SMB File Storage
> - Configure the Content Delivery Network (CDN)
> - Configure custom domains for storage and CDN

# Manage blob storage

Azure blob storage is a service for storing unstructured data such as text files, videos, or as we saw in Chapter 2, "Create and manage compute resources," virtual hard disk files for virtual machines. A storage account exposes multiple endpoints, one for each of the services it exposes:

- *https://[account name].blob.core.windows.net* (blob)
- *https://[account name].table.core.windows.net* (table)
- *https://[account name].queue.core.windows.net* (queue)
- *https://[account name].file.core.windows.net* (file)

> **NOTE   SSL JUST WORKS**
>
> Each Azure storage endpoint can be accessed via HTTP or HTTPS (SSL) by default. No additional configuration is needed to access blobs through the HTTPS endpoint.

Figure 3-1 shows some of the concepts of a storage account. Each blob storage account can have one or more containers and all blobs must be uploaded to a container. Containers are similar in concept to a folder on your computer, in that they are used to group blobs within a storage account. There can be a container at the base of the storage account, appropriately named root, and there can be containers one level down from the root container.

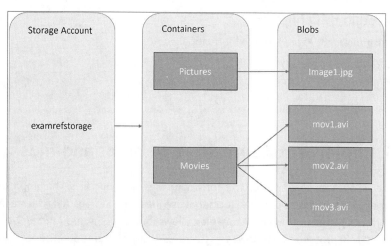

**FIGURE 3-1** Azure Storage account entities and hierarchy relationships

## The root container

To create a container at the root of the storage account, specify the special name $root for the container name. This allows you to store blobs in the root of the storage account and reference them with URLs such as: *https://[account name].blob.core.windows.net/fileinroot.txt*.

## Storage account types

A storage account can be created as a general purpose or a blob storage account. A general-purpose account can be created as standard or premium and supports all Azure Storage Services. The blob storage account is a specialized storage account used to store block blobs and append blobs. You can't store page blobs in these accounts, therefore you can't store VHD files. These accounts allow you to set an access tier to hot or cool; the tier can be changed at any time.

The hot access tier is used for files that are accessed frequently, so you pay a higher cost for storage, but the cost of accessing blobs is much lower. You pay a higher cost for accessing blobs stored in the cool access tier, but the cost of actual storage is much lower. Table 3-1 shows which services are supported with each type of storage account.

**TABLE 3-1** Storage account types and their supported blob types

| Storage account type | General-purpose Standard | General-purpose Premium | Blob storage, hot and cool access tiers |
|---|---|---|---|
| Services supported | Blob, File, Queue Services | Blob Service | Blob Service |
| Types of blobs supported | Block blobs, page blobs, and append blobs | Page blobs | Block blobs and append blobs |

## Understanding blob types

Blobs come in three types, and it is important to understand when each type of blob should be used and what the limitations are for each.

Page blobs are a collection of 512-byte pages optimized for random read and write operations. The maximum size for a page blob is eight terabytes TB. Virtual machine hard disks are created as page blobs, which can be stored in a standard or premium storage account.

Block blobs are designed for efficient uploading. Block blobs are comprised of blocks that can be written to and committed as a set. The maximum size for a block blob is slightly more than 4.75 TB. They are used for files such as videos, images, and text.

Append blobs are comprised of blocks and are optimized for append operations. This is useful for operations that only require writing to the end of the file such as a logging system. When you modify an append blob, blocks are added to the end of the blob only, using the append block operation. Updating or deleting existing blocks is not supported. Unlike a block blob, an append blob does not expose its block IDs.

### EXAM TIP

The type of the blob is set at creation and cannot be changed after the fact. A common problem that may show up on the exam is if a .vhd file was accidently uploaded as a block blob instead of a page blob. The blob would have to be deleted first and reuploaded as a page blob before it could be mounted as an OS or Data Disk to an Azure VM.

### MORE INFO    BLOB TYPES

You can learn more about the intricacies of each blob type here: *https://docs.microsoft.com/en-us/rest/api/storageservices/understanding-block-blobs--append-blobs--and-page-blobs.*

## Setting metadata with storage

Within Azure Storage, blobs and containers support setting additional metadata properties for both system and user purposes. For instance, a system purpose is the last modified date of an object, whereas a user-defined metadata property may be storing the name or IP address of the server that stored the blob for later lookup.

You can set and retrieve the metadata on both containers and blobs through the Azure SDK or the REST API. Azure Storage Explorer supports setting metadata at the blob level. Figure 3-2 shows using Storage Explorer to add a custom metadata property named Author with a value of Michael Washam.

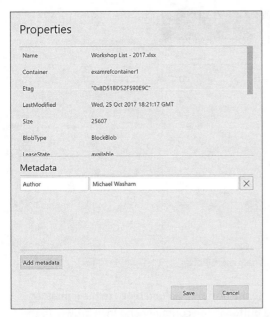

**FIGURE 3-2** Setting metadata on a blob using Azure Storage Explorer

**MORE INFO**   **AZURE STORAGE EXPLORER**

Azure Storage Explorer is a GUI based tool that runs on Windows, Mac and Linux. It provides capabilities to manage blobs and files as well as tables and queues on your storage account. You can download Azure Storage Explorer and learn more about its feature set here: *https:// azure.microsoft.com/en-us/features/storage-explorer/.*

**MORE INFO**   **SETTING CONTAINER METADATA**

There are currently no tools from Microsoft that allow you to set metadata directly on a container. There are REST APIs that support this, and you can also set them using the .NET SDK for Azure Storage. See the following for an example of setting metadata using the REST API: *https://docs.microsoft.com/en-us/rest/api/storageservices/set-container-metadata.*

## Managing blobs and containers (Azure Portal)

You can create a container through the Azure Management Portal, Azure Storage Explorer, third-party storage tools, or through the command line tools. To create a container in the Azure Management Portal, open a storage account by clicking Browse > Storage Accounts, and then type the name of your storage account. Within the storage account blade, click the Containers tile, and then click the + Container button, as shown in Figure 3-3. The access level can be changed later, and will be discussed in more detail in Skill 3.2.

**FIGURE 3-3** Creating a container using the Azure Management Portal

After a container is created, you can also use the portal to upload blobs to the container as demonstrated in Figure 3-4. Click the Upload button in the container and then browse to the blob to upload. If you click the Advanced button you can select the blob type (blob, page or append), the block size, and optionally a folder to upload the blob to.

**FIGURE 3-4** The Azure Management Portal uploads a blob to a storage account container

## Managing blobs and containers (PowerShell)

To create a container using the Azure PowerShell cmdlets, use the New-AzureStorageContainer cmdlet, as shown in the following example. This cmdlet uses a storage context object that contains the name of the storage account and the storage account key to authenticate to Azure. To specify the Private access type, specify the value Off to the `Permission` parameter. Blob and Container, other access types, are the same using PowerShell.

```
$storageAccount = "[storage account name]"
$resourceGroup = "[resource group name]"
$storageKey = Get-AzureRmStorageAccountKey -ResourceGroupName $resourceGroup `
                                      -StorageAccountName $storageAccount
$context = New-AzureStorageContext -StorageAccountName $storageAccount `
                                  -StorageAccountKey $storageKey.Value[0]
New-AzureStorageContainer -Context $context `
                          -Name "examrefcontainer1" `
                          -Permission Off
```

You can use the PowerShell cmdlets to upload a file as well using the Set-AzureStorageBlob-Content cmdlet as shown in the following example.

```
$containerName = "[storage account container]"$blobName = "[blob name]"
$localFileDirectory = "C:\SourceFolder"
$localFile = Join-Path $localFileDirectory $BlobName
Set-AzureStorageBlobContent -File $localFile `
                            -Container $ContainerName `
                            -Blob $blobName `
                            -Context $context
```

> **MORE INFO  MANAGING BLOB STORAGE WITH POWERSHELL**
>
> The Azure PowerShell cmdlets offer a rich set of capabilities for managing blobs in storage. You can learn more about their capabilities here: *https://docs.microsoft.com/en-us/azure/ storage/blobs/storage-how-to-use-blobs-powershell.*

## Managing blobs and containers (CLI)

The Azure CLI tools can also be used to create a storage account container with the az storage container create command. The `public-access` parameter is used to set the permissions. The supported values are off, blob, and container.

```
storageaccount = "[storage account name]"
containername = "[storage account container]"
az storage container create --account-name $storageaccount --name $containername
--public-access off
```

You can use the Azure CLI to upload a file as well using the az storage blob upload command as shown in the following example.

```
container_name="[storage account container]"
file_to_upload="C:\SourceFolder\[blob name]"
blob_name="[blob name]"
az storage blob upload --container-name $container_name --file $file_to_upload
--name $blob_name
```

## Managing blobs and containers (Storage Explorer)

Azure Storage Explorer is a cross platform application that allows you to manage storage accounts, including copying data between storage accounts and uploading and downloading data. It also allows you to create and manage permissions on a storage account container. To create a container, expand the Storage Accounts node, and expand the storage account you want to use, right-clicking on the Blob Containers node. This will open a new menu item where you can create a blob container as shown in Figure 3-5.

**FIGURE 3-5** Creating a container using the Azure Storage Explorer

Azure Storage Explorer provides the ability to upload a single file or multiple files at once. The Upload Folder feature provides the ability to upload all of the files and folders, recreating the hierarchy in the Azure Storage Account. Figure 3-6 shows the two upload options.

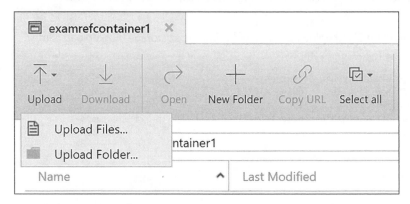

**FIGURE 3-6** Uploading files and folders using Azure Storage Explorer

## Managing blobs and containers (AzCopy)

AzCopy is a command line utility that can be used to copy data to and from blob, file, and table storage, and also provides support for copying data between storage accounts. AzCopy is designed for optimal performance, so it is commonly used to automate large transfers of files and folders. There are two versions of AzCopy: one for Windows and one for Linux.

The following example shows how you can use AzCopy to download a single blob from a container to a local folder. In this example, key would need to be replaced with the actual storage account key for the command to complete.

```
AzCopy /Source:https://[source storage].blob.core.windows.net/[source container]
 /Dest:C:\destFolder /SourceKey:key /Pattern:"Workshop List - 2017.xlsx"
```

This example shows how you can switch the /Dest and /Source parameters to upload the file instead.

```
AzCopy /Source:C:\sourceFolder /Dest:https://[dest storage].blob.core.windows.net/
[dest container] /DestKey:key /Pattern:"Workshop List - 2017.xlsx"
```

---

> *MORE INFO*   **AZCOPY EXAMPLES**
>
> AzCopy provides many capabilities beyond simple uploading and downloading of files. For more information see the following: *https://docs.microsoft.com/en-us/azure/storage/common/storage-use-azcopy.*

---

## Understanding storage account replication options

You can set an Azure Storage account to one of the types shown in Table 3-2.

**TABLE 3-2** Storage account replication options

| Account Type | Description |
| --- | --- |
| Standard_LRS (Locally redundant storage) | Makes three synchronous copies of your data within a single data center. Applicable to general purpose or blob storage accounts. |
| Standard_ZRS (Zone redundant storage) | Stores three copies of data across multiple datacenters within or across regions. For block blobs only. Applicable to general purpose storage accounts. |
| Standard_GRS (Geographically redundant storage) | Same as LRS (three copies local), plus three additional asynchronous copies to a second data center hundreds of miles away. Applicable to general purpose or blob storage accounts. |
| Standard_RAGRS (Read-access geographically redundant storage) | Same capabilities as GRS, plus you have read access to the data in the secondary data center. Applicable to general purpose or blob storage accounts. |
| Premium_LRS (Locally redundant storage) | Same as Standard_LRS, but is for a Premium storage account. This is currently the only replication option available for a Premium storage account and is only available on general purpose storage accounts. Only page blobs are supported in a Premium storage account. |

You can set the replication type for a storage account after it is created through the Azure portal by clicking the Configuration link on the storage account and selecting the replication type. It can also be set during the creation of a storage account as shown in Figure 3-8. A Premium storage account can only be set to Premium_LRS and a Zone Redundant Storage account can only be set to Standard_ZRS.

To set the value using the Azure PowerShell cmdlets, use the Type parameter of New-AzureStorageAccount (at creation) or the Set-AzureStorageAccount cmdlets (after creation), as shown in the following example.

```
$accountName = "[storage account name]"
$location    = "West US"
$type        = "Standard_LRS"
New-AzureStorageAccount -StorageAccountName $accountName `
                        -Location $location `
                        -Type $type
$type        = "Standard_RAGRS"
Set-AzureStorageAccount -StorageAccountName $accountName `
                        -Type $type
```

> **NOTE**  **STANDARD_ZRS AND BLOCK BLOBS**
>
> You cannot change the Standard ZRS (zone replicated) to any other storage account type and vice versa. Zone replicated storage accounts only support block blobs.

## Using the async blob copy service

The async blob copy service is a server-side based service that can copy files you specify from a source location to a destination in an Azure Storage account. The source blob can be located in another Azure Storage account, or it can even be outside of Azure, as long as the storage service can access the blob directly for it to copy. This service uses excess bandwidth and does not offer an SLA on when the copy will complete. There are several ways to initiate a blob copy using the async blob copy service.

### Async blob copy (PowerShell)

Use the Start-AzureStorageBlobCopy cmdlet to copy a file using PowerShell. This cmdlet accepts either the source URI (if it is external), or as the example below shows, the blob name, container, and storage context to access the source blob in an Azure Storage account. The destination requires the container name, blob name, and a storage context for the destination storage account.

```
$blobCopyState = Start-AzureStorageBlobCopy -SrcBlob $blobName `
                                            -SrcContainer $srcContainer `
                                            -Context $srcContext `
                                            -DestContainer $destContainer `
                                            -DestBlob $vhdName `
                                            -DestContext $destContext
```

Let's review the parameters in the preceding example:

- **SrcBlob** expects the file name of source file to start copying.
- **SrcContainer** is the container the source file resides in.
- **Context** accepts a context object created by the New-AzureStorageContext cmdlet. The context has the storage account name and key for the source storage account and is used for authentication.
- **DestContainer** is the destination container to copy the blob to. The call will fail if this container does not exist on the destination storage account.
- **DestBlob** is the filename of the blob on the destination storage account. The destination blob name does not have to be the same as the source.
- **DestContext** also accepts a context object created with the details of the destination storage account including the authentication key.

Here is a complete example of how to use the Start-AzureStorageBlob copy cmdlet to copy a blob between two storage accounts.

```
$blobName          = "[file name]"
$srcContainer      = "[source container]"
$destContainer     = "[destination container]"
$srcStorageAccount  = "[source storage]"
$destStorageAccount = "[dest storage]"
$sourceRGName      = "[source resource group name]"
$destRGName        = "[destination resource group name]"
$srcStorageKey = Get-AzureRmStorageAccountKey -ResourceGroupName $sourceRGName
-Name $srcStorageAccount
$destStorageKey = Get-AzureRmStorageAccountKey -ResourceGroupName $destRGName
 -Name $destStorageAccount
$srcContext = New-AzureStorageContext -StorageAccountName $srcStorageAccount `
                                -StorageAccountKey $srcStorageKey.Value[0]
$destContext = New-AzureStorageContext -StorageAccountName $destStorageAccount `
                                -StorageAccountKey $destStorageKey.Value[0]
New-AzureStorageContainer -Name $destContainer `
                        -Context $destContext
$copiedBlob = Start-AzureStorageBlobCopy -SrcBlob $blobName `
                                -SrcContainer $srcContainer `
                                -Context $srcContext `
                                -DestContainer $destContainer `
                                -DestBlob $blobName `
                                -DestContext $destContext
```

There are several cmdlets in this example. The Get-AzureRmStorageKey cmdlet accepts the name of a storage account and the resource group it resides in. The return value contains the storage account's primary and secondary authentication keys in the .Value array of the returned object. These values are passed to the New-AzureStorageContext cmdlet, including the storage account name, and the creation of the context object. The New-AzureStorage-Container cmdlet is used to create the storage container on the destination storage account. The cmdlet is passed the destination storage account's context object ($destContext) for authentication.

The final call in the example is the call to Start-AzureStorageBlobCopy. To initiate the copy this cmdlet uses the source (Context) and destination context objects (DestContext) for authentication. The return value is a reference to the new blob object on the destination storage account.

Pipe the copied blob information to the Get-AzureStorageBlobCopyState cmdlet to monitor the progress of the copy as shown in the following example.

```
$copiedBlob | Get-AzureStorageBlobCopyState
```

The return value of Get-AzureStorageBlobCopyState contains the CopyId, Status, Source, BytesCopied, CompletionTime, StatusDescription, and TotalBytes properties. Use these properties to write logic to monitor the status of the copy operation.

> **MORE INFO**   **MORE EXAMPLES WITH POWERSHELL**
>
> There are many variations for using the async copy service with PowerShell. For more information see the following: *https://docs.microsoft.com/en-us/powershell/module/azure. storage/start-azurestorageblobcopy.*

## Async blob copy (CLI)

The Azure CLI tools support copying data to storage accounts using the async blob copy service. The following example uses the az storage blob copy start command to copy a blob from one storage account to another. This example is very similar to the PowerShell example in the previous section. For authentication the command requires the storage account name and key for the source (if the blob is not available via public access) and the destination. The storage account key is retrieved using the az storage account keys list command.

```
blobName="[file name]"
srcContainer="[source container]"
destContainer="[destination container]"
srcStorageAccount="[source storage]"
destStorageAccount="[destination storage]"
az storage blob copy start \
   --account-name "$destStorageAccount" \
   --account-key "$destStorageKey" \
   --destination-blob "$blobName" \
   --destination-container "$destContainer" \
   --source-account-name "$srcStorageAccount" \
   --source-container "$srcContainer" \
   --source-blob "$blobName" \
     --source-account-key "$srcStorageKey"
```

After the copy is started, you can monitor the status using the az storage blob show command as shown in the following example.

```
az storage blob show \
   --account-name "$destStorageAccount" \
   --account-key "$destStorageKey" \
   --container-name "$destContainer"
    --name "$blobName"
```

> **MORE INFO**   **MORE EXAMPLES WITH CLI**
>
> There are many variations for using the async copy service with the Azure CLI. For more information see the following: *https://docs.microsoft.com/en-us/cli/azure/storage/blob/copy*.

## Async blob copy (AzCopy)

The AzCopy application can also be used to copy between storage accounts. The following example shows how to specify the source storage account using the /source parameter and /sourcekey, and the destination storage account and container using the /dest parameter and /DestKey.

```
AzCopy /Source:https://[source storage].blob.core.windows.net/[source container]/
 /Dest:https://[destination storage].blob.core.windows.net/[destination container]/
 /SourceKey:[source key] /DestKey:[destination key] /Pattern:*.vhd
```

AzCopy offers a feature to mitigate the lack of SLA with the async copy service. The /SyncCopy parameter ensures that the copy operation gets consistent speed during a copy. AzCopy performs the synchronous copy by downloading the blobs to copy from the specified source to local memory, and then uploading them to the Blob storage destination.

```
AzCopy /Source:https://[source storage].blob.core.windows.net/[source container]/
 /Dest:https://[destination storage].blob.core.windows.net/[destination container]/
 /SourceKey:[source key] /DestKey:[destination key] /Pattern:*.vhd /SyncCopy
```

## Async blob copy (Storage Explorer)

The Azure Storage Explorer application can also take advantage of the async blob copy service. To copy between storage accounts, navigate to the source storage account, select one or more files and click the copy button on the tool bar. Then navigate to the destination storage account, expand the container to copy to, and click Paste from the toolbar. In Figure 3-7, the Workshop List – 2017.xlsx blob was copied from examrefstorage\examrefcontainer1 to examrefstorage2\examrefdestation using this technique.

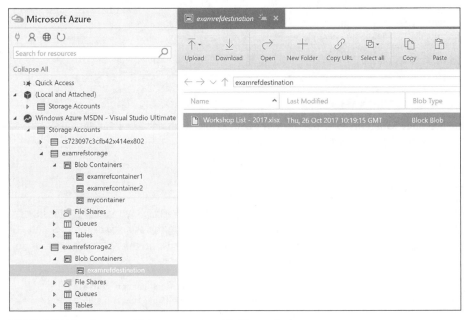

**FIGURE 3-7** Using the async blob copy service with StorageExplorer

## Manage SMB File Storage

The Microsoft Azure file service offers the ability to create file shares (up to 5 TB) that use the SMB version 3.0 protocol directly in an Azure Storage account. The shares can be accessed using regular file share methods, such as a mapped drive or file I/O APIs and commands. Figure 3-8 shows the hierarchy of files stored in Azure files.

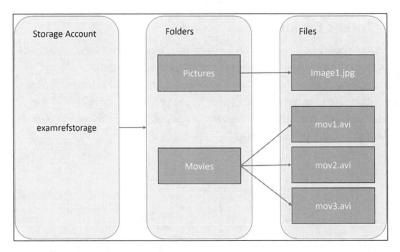

**FIGURE 3-8** Azure files entities and relationship hierarchy

There are several common use cases for using Azure files. A few examples include the following:

- Migration of existing applications that require a file share for storage.
- Shared storage of files such as web content, log files, application configuration files, or even installation media.

To create a new file share using the Azure portal, open the blade for a storage account, click the Files tile, and then click the + File Share button, as shown in Figure 3-9.

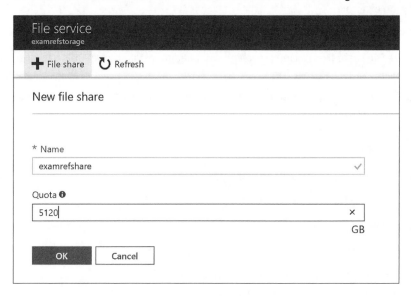

**FIGURE 3-9** Adding a new share with Azure files

To create a share using the Azure PowerShell cmdlets, use the following code:

```
$storageAccount = "[storage account]"
$rgName = "[resource group name]"
$shareName = "contosoweb"
$storageKey = Get-AzureRmStorageAccountKey -ResourceGroupName $rgName -Name
 $storageAccount
$ctx = New-AzureStorageContext -StorageAccountName $storageAccount `
                               -StorageAccountKey $storageKey.Value[0]
New-AzureStorageShare -Name $shareName -Context $ctx
```

The Azure CLI tools can also be used to create a file share as the following example demonstrates:

```
rgName="[resource group name]"
storageAccountName="[storage account]"
shareName="contosoweb"
constring=$(az storage account show-connection-string -n $storageAccountName -g
$rgName --query 'connectionString' -o tsv)
az storage share create --name $shareName --quota 2048 --connection-string $constring
```

To access a share created in Azure files from a Windows machine, you should store the storage account name and key using the Cmdkey.exe utility. This allows you to associate the credentials with the URI to the Azure files share. The syntax for using Cmdkey.exe is shown in the following example.

```
cmdkey.exe /add:[storage account name].file.core.windows.net /user:[storage account
 name] /pass:[storage account key]
```

After the credentials are stored, use the net use command to map a drive to the file share, as shown in the following example.

```
net use z: \\examrefstorage.file.core.windows.net\contosoweb
```

To access an Azure File share from a Linux machine you need to install the cifs-utils package from the Samba project.

On Ubuntu and Debian-based distributions, use the apt-get package manager to install the package as the following example shows:

```
sudo apt-get update
sudo apt-get install cifs-utils
```

On RHEL and CentOS, use the yum package manager:

```
sudo yum install samba-client samba-common cifs-utils
```

On openSUSE, use the zypper package manager:

```
sudo zypper install samba*
```

After the cifs-utils package is installed create a mount point for the share:

```
mkdir mymountpoint
```

Next, you will mount the Azure File Share to the mount point.

```
sudo mount -t cifs //[storage account name].file.core.windows.net/[share name]
 ./mymountpoint -o vers=2.1,username=[storage account name],password=
[storage account key],dir_mode=0777,file_mode=0777,serverino
```

> **MORE INFO**  **PORT 445**
>
> Azure files use the SMB protocol. SMB communicates over TCP port 445; check to see if your firewall is not blocking TCP ports 445 from a client machine or that your ISP doesn't block this port if you are trying to connect to the file share over the internet.

## Configuring the Content Delivery Network

Use the Azure Content Delivery Network (CDN) to deliver static content such as images, text, or media closer to your users. To store content in a CDN endpoint you first create a new CDN endpoint. To do this using the Azure portal click New, Web + Mobile, CDN and then provide a name for the CDN Profile, the name of the resource group, as well as the region and pricing tier. Figure 3-10 shows the creation dialog.

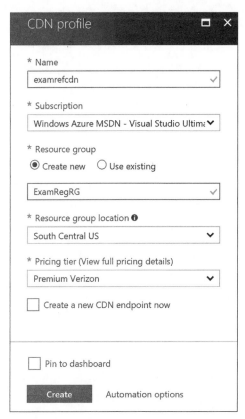

**FIGURE 3-10** Creating a CDN profile using the Azure portal

*MORE INFO* **AZURE CDN PRICING TIERS**

Currently, there are three pricing tiers: Standard Akamai, Standard Verizon, and Premium Verizon. The Azure CDN overview page has a comprehensive list of the different features and capabilities of the tiers: *https://docs.microsoft.com/en-us/azure/cdn/cdn-overview*.

After the CDN profile is created, you next add an endpoint to the profile. Add an Endpoint by opening the CDN profile in the portal and click the + Endpoint button. On the creation dialog, specify a unique name for the CDN endpoint, and the configuration for the origin such as the type (Storage, Web App, Cloud Service, or Custom), the host header and the origin port for HTTP and HTTPS), and then click the Add button. Figure 3-11 shows an endpoint using an Azure Storage account as the origin type.

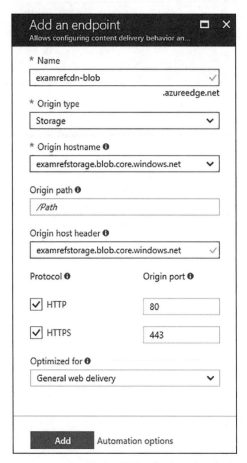

**FIGURE 3-11** Creating a CDN endpoint using the Azure portal

Blobs stored in public access enabled containers are replicated to the CDN edge endpoints. To access the content within the CDN, instead of your storage account, change the URL for the blob to reference the absolute path of the created CDN endpoint combined with the relative path of the original file, as shown in the following:

- Original URL within storage
  - *http://storageaccount.blob.core.windows.net/imgs/logo.png*
- New URL accessed through CDN
  - *http://examrefcdn-blob.azureedget.net/imgs/logo.png*

Figure 3-12 shows how this process works at a high level. For example, a file named Logo.png that was originally in the imgs public container in Azure Storage can be accessed through the created CDN endpoint. Figure 3-12 also shows the benefits of a user accessing the file from the United Kingdom to the storage account in the West US versus accessing the same file through a CDN endpoint, which will resolve much closer to the user.

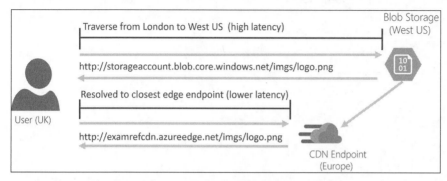

**FIGURE 3-12** Accessing content from a CDN instead of a storage account

The additional benefit of using a CDN goes beyond deploying your content closer to users. A typical public-facing web page contains several images and may contain additional media such as .pdf files. Each request that is served from the Azure CDN means it is not served from your website, which can remove a significant amount of load.

Managing how long content stays in the CDN is different depending on if your origin domain is from an Azure storage account, or an Azure cloud service, or an Azure web app.

For content served from a web site, set the CacheControl HTTP header. This setting can be set programmatically when serving up the content, or by setting the configuration of the web app.

Manage the content expiration through storage by setting the time-to-live (TTL) period of the blob itself. Figure 3-13 demonstrates how using Storage Explorer you can set the Cache-Control property on the blob files directly. You can also set the property using Windows PowerShell or the CLI tools when uploading to storage.

**FIGURE 3-13** Setting the CacheControl property of a blob using Azure Storage Explorer

*EXAM TIP*

You can control the expiration of blob data in the CDN by setting the CacheControl metadata property of blobs. If you do not explicitly set this property the default value is seven days before the data is refreshed or purged if the original content is deleted.

> *MORE INFO* **MANAGING THE TIME-TO-LIVE (TTL) OF CDN CONTENT**
>
> You can learn more about how to programmatically set the CacheControl HTTP header for web apps here: *https://docs.microsoft.com/en-us/azure/cdn/cdn-manage-expiration-of-cloud-service-content*. And learn about using PowerShell and the CLI tools here *https://docs.microsoft.com/en-us/azure/cdn/cdn-manage-expiration-of-blob-content*.

## Versioning assets with Azure CDN

To remove content from the CDN altogether, there are three approaches, depending on how the content has been added. If the content is stored in storage, you can set the container to private, or delete the content from the container, or even delete the container itself. If the content is in a cloud service or an Azure web app, you can modify the application to no longer serve the content. You can also purge the content directly from the CDN endpoint. Keep in mind that even if the content is deleted from storage, or no longer accessible from your web application, it will remain in the CDN endpoint until its TTL has expired. To immediately remove it from the CDN, you should purge the content as shown in Figure 3-14.

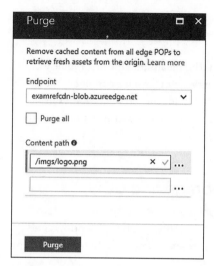

**FIGURE 3-14** Purging a file from the Azure CDN

**EXAM TIP**

The Content path of the CDN purge dialog supports specifying regular expressions and wildcards to purge multiple items at once. Purge all and Wildcard purge are not currently supported by Azure CDN from Akamai. You can see examples of expressions here: *https://docs.microsoft.com/en-us/azure/cdn/cdn-purge-endpoint*.

Using query strips is another technique for controlling information cached in the CDN. For instance, if your application hosted in Azure cloud services or Azure web apps has a page that generates content dynamically, such as: http://[CDN Endpoint].azureedge.net/chart.aspx. You can configure query string handling to cache multiple versions, depending on the query string passed in. The Azure CDN supports three different modes of query string caching configuration:

- **Ignore query strings** This is the default mode. The CDN edge node will pass the query string from the requestor to the origin on the first request and cache the asset. All subsequent requests for that asset that are served from the edge node will ignore the query string until the cached asset expires.

- **Bypass caching for URL with query strings** In this mode, requests with query strings are not cached at the CDN edge node. The edge node retrieves the asset directly from the origin and passes it to the requestor with each request.

- **Cache every unique URL**  This mode treats each request with a query string as a unique asset with its own cache. For example, the response from the origin for a request for foo.ashx?q=bar is cached at the edge node and returned for subsequent caches with that same query string. A request for foo.ashx?q=somethingelse is cached as a separate asset with its own time to live.

**EXAM TIP**

By default, assets are first cached as they are requested. This means that the first request from each region may take longer, since the edge servers will not have the content cached and will need to forward the request to the origin server. Pre-loading content avoids this first hit latency. If you are using Azure CDN from Verizon you can pre-load assets to mitigate this initial lag.

## Configuring custom domains for storage and CDN

Both an Azure storage account and an Azure CDN endpoint allow you to specify a custom domain for accessing blob content instead of using the Azure URLs (blob.core.windows.net and azureedge.net). To configure either service, you must create a new CNAME record with the DNS provider that is hosting your DNS records.

For example, to enable a custom domain for the blobs.contoso.com sub domain to an Azure storage account, create a CNAME record that points from blobs.contoso.com to the Azure storage account [storage account].blob.core.windows.net. Table 3-3 shows an example mapping in DNS.

**TABLE 3-3** Mapping a domain to an Azure Storage account in DNS

| CNAME RECORD | TARGET |
| --- | --- |
| blobs.contoso.com | contosoblobs.blob.core.windows.net |

Mapping a domain that is already in use within Azure may result in minor downtime as the domain is updated. If you have an application with an SLA, by using the domain you can avoid the downtime by using a second option to validate the domain. Essentially, you use an intermediary domain to validate to Azure that you own the domain by performing the same process as before, but instead you add an intermediary step of using the asverify subdomain. The asverify subdomain is a special subdomain recognized by Azure. By prepending asverify to your own subdomain, you permit Azure to recognize your custom domain without modifying the DNS record for the domain. After you modify the DNS record for the domain, it will be mapped to the blob endpoint with no downtime.

After the asverify records are verified in the Azure portal, you then add the correct DNS records. You can then delete the asverify records, because they are no longer used. Table 3-4 shows the example DNS records created when using the asverify method.

**TABLE 3-4** Mapping a domain to an Azure Storage account in DNS with the asverify intermediary domain

| CNAME RECORD | TARGET |
|---|---|
| asverify.blobs.contoso.com | asverify.contosoblobs.blob.core.windows.net |
| blobs.contoso.com | contosoblobs.blob.core.windows.net |

To enable a custom domain for an Azure CDN endpoint, the process is almost identical. Create a CNAME record that points from cdn.contoso.com to the Azure CDN endpoint [CDN endpoint].azureedge.net. Table 3-5 shows mapping a custom CNAME DNS record to the CDN endpoint.

**TABLE 3-5** Mapping a domain to an Azure CDN endpoint in DNS

| CNAME RECORD | TARGET |
|---|---|
| cdncontent.contoso.com | examrefcdn.azureedge.net |

The cdnverify intermediate domain can be used just like asverify for storage. Use this intermediate validation if you're already using the domain with an application because updating the DNS directly can result in downtime. Table 3-6 shows the CNAME DNS records needed for verifying your domain using the cdnverify subdomain.

**TABLE 3-6** Mapping a domain to an Azure CDN endpoint in DNS with the cdn intermediary domain

| CNAME RECORD | TARGET |
|---|---|
| cdnverify.cdncontent.contoso.com | cdnverify.examrefcdn.azureedge.net |
| cdncontent.contoso.com | examrefcdn.azureedge.net |

After the DNS records are created and verified you then associate the custom domain with your CDN endpoint or blob storage account.

**EXAM TIP**

Azure Storage does not yet natively support HTTPS with custom domains. You can currently use the Azure CDN to access blobs with custom domains over HTTPS.

**MORE INFO    CONFIGURING CUSTOM DOMAINS FOR STORAGE AND CDN**

You can learn more about configuring custom domains for storage here: *https://docs.microsoft.com/en-us/azure/storage/blobs/storage-custom-domain-name*. And you can learn more about the Azure CDN here: *https://docs.microsoft.com/en-us/azure/cdn/cdn-map-content-to-custom-domain*.

# Skill 3.2: Manage access

There are several techniques for controlling access to objects within an Azure storage account. Using the authentication key and storage account name is one technique. Granting access using a shared access signature or via a policy to allow granular access with an expiration is another technique. A new capability called Virtual Network Service Endpoints provides the ability to restrict access to storage accounts only from specific networks in your virtual network or from your on-premises network. In addition to granting access, understanding how to update (rollover) storage keys for security purposes and revoking access is of vital importance, and is the focus of Skill 3.2.

> **This skill covers how to:**
> - Manage storage account keys
> - Create and use shared access signatures
> - Use a stored access policy
> - Configure Virtual Network Service Endpoints

## Manage storage account keys

By default, every request to an Azure storage account requires authentication. The only exception was briefly mentioned in Skill 3.1, which discussed how by setting the security policy, you can optionally enable anonymous access at the container level for blob storage. The available options for this security policy are described in Table 3-7.

**TABLE 3-7** Container permissions and resulting access

| Access Type | Resulting access |
| --- | --- |
| Private/Off | No anonymous access (default) |
| Blob | Access blobs via anonymous requests |
| Container | List and access blobs via anonymous requests |

There are several options available for authenticating users, which provide various levels of access. The first type of authentication is by using the Azure storage account name and authentication key. With the storage account name and key, you have full access to everything within the storage account. You can create, read, update, and delete containers, blobs, tables, queues, and file shares. You have full administrative access to everything other than the storage account itself (you cannot delete the storage account or change settings on the storage account, such as its type).

To access the storage account name and key, open the storage account from within the Azure portal and click the Keys tile. Figure 3-15 shows the primary and secondary access keys for the Examrefstorage Storage Account. With this information, you can use storage management tools like Storage Explorer, or command-line tools like Windows PowerShell, CLI, and AzCopy.exe to manage content in the storage account.

**FIGURE 3-15** Access keys for an Azure storage account

Each storage account has a primary and a secondary key. The reason there are two keys is to allow you to modify applications to use the secondary key instead of the first, and then regenerate the first key using the Azure portal or the command line tools. In PowerShell, this is accomplished with the New-AzureRmStorageAccountKey cmdlet and for the Azure CLI you will use the az storage account keys renew command. This technique is known as key rolling, and it allows you to reset the primary key with no downtime for applications that access storage using the authentication key directly.

Applications will often use the storage account name and key for access to Azure storage. Sometimes this is to grant access by generating a Shared Access Signature token and sometimes for direct access with the name and key. It is important to protect these keys because they provide full access to the storage account.

Azure Key Vault helps safeguard cryptographic keys and secrets used by cloud applications and services. By using Key Vault, you can encrypt keys and secrets (such as authentication keys, storage account keys, data encryption keys, .PFX files, and passwords) by using keys that are protected by hardware security modules (HSMs).

The following example shows how to create an Azure Key Vault and then securely store the key in Azure Key Vault (software protected keys) using PowerShell.

```
$vaultName = "[key vault name]"
$rgName = "[resource group name]"
$location = "[location]"
$keyName = "[key name]"
$secretName = "[secret name]"
$storageAccount = "[storage account]"
# create the key vault
New-AzureRmKeyVault -VaultName $vaultName -ResourceGroupName $rgName -Location $location
# create a software managed key
$key = Add-AzureKeyVaultKey -VaultName $vaultName -Name $keyName -Destination 'Software'
# retrieve the storage account key (the secret)
$storageKey = Get-AzureRmStorageAccountKey -ResourceGroupName $rgName -Name
 $storageAccount

# convert the secret to a secure string
$secretvalue = ConvertTo-SecureString $storageKey[0].Value -AsPlainText -Force
```

```
# set the secret value
$secret = Set-AzureKeyVaultSecret -VaultName $vaultName -Name $secretName -SecretValue
 $secretvalue
The same capabilities exist with the Azure CLI tools.
vaultName="[key vault name]"
rgName="[resource group name]"
location="[location]"
keyName="[key name]"
secretName="[secret name]"
storageAccount="[storage account]"
secretValue="[storage account key]"

# create the key vault
azure keyvault create --vault-name "$vaultName" --resource-group "$rgName"
 --location "$location"

# create a software managed key
azure keyvault key create --vault-name "$vaultName" --key-name $keyName
 --destination software

# set the secret value
azure keyvault secret set --vault-name "$vaultName" --secret-name "$secretName"
 --value "$secretValue"
```

In addition to supporting software protected keys, for added assurance, when you use Azure Key Vault, you can import or generate keys in hardware security modules (HSMs) that never leave the HSM boundary. This scenario is often referred to as bring your own key, or BYOK. The HSMs are FIPS 140-2 Level 2 validated. Azure Key Vault uses Thales nShield family of HSMs to protect your keys.

> **MORE INFO**   **GENERATE AND TRANSFER HSM-PROTECTED KEYS FOR AZURE KEY VAULT**
>
> You can learn more about the bring your own key (BYOK) scenario here: *https://docs.micro-soft.com/en-us/azure/key-vault/key-vault-hsm-protected-keys.*

Accessing and unencrypting the stored keys is typically done by a developer, although keys from Key Vault can also be accessed from ARM templates during deployment.

> **MORE INFO**   **ACCESSING ENCRYPTED KEYS FROM AZURE KEY VAULT**
>
> You can learn more about how developers securely retrieve and use secrets from Azure Key Vault here: *https://docs.microsoft.com/en-us/azure/storage/blobs/storage-encrypt-decrypt-blobs-key-vault.*

## Creating, and using, shared access signatures

A Shared Access Signature (SAS) is a URI that grants access to specific containers, blob, queues, and tables. Use a SAS to grant access to a client that should not have access to the entire con-tents of the storage account, but that still require secure authentication. By distributing a SAS

URI to these clients, you can grant them access to a resource for a specified period of time, with a specified set of permissions.

You can create SAS tokens using Storage Explorer or the command line tools (or programmatically using the REST APIs/SDK. Figure 3-16 demonstrates how to create a SAS token using Azure Storage Explorer.

**FIGURE 3-16** Creating a Shared Access Signature using Azure Storage Explorer

The following example shows how to create a SAS URI using the Azure PowerShell cmdlets. The example creates a storage context using the storage account name and key that is used for authentication, and to specify the storage account to use. The context is passed the New-AzureStorageBlobSASToken cmdlet, which is also passed the container, blob, and permissions (read, write, and delete), along with the start and end time that the SAS URI is valid for.

```
$storageAccount = "[storage account]"
$rgName = "[resource group name]"
$container = "[storage container name]"
$storageKey = Get-AzureRmStorageAccountKey –ResourceGroupName $rgName
 -Name $storageAccount
$context = New-AzureStorageContext -StorageAccountName $storageAccount `
                              -StorageAccountKey $storageKey[0].Value
$startTime = Get-Date
$endTime = $startTime.AddHours(4)
New-AzureStorageBlobSASToken -Container $container `
                       -Blob "Workshop List - 2017.xlsx" `
                       -Permission "rwd" `
                       -StartTime $startTime `
                       -ExpiryTime $endTime `
                       -Context $context
```

Figure 3-17 shows the output of the script. After the script executes, notice the SAS token output to the screen.

```
?sv=2016-05-31&sr=b&sig=jFnSNYWvxt6Miy6Lc5xvT0Y1IOwerdWcFvwba065fws%3D&st=2017-10-26T14%3A55%3A44Z&se=2017-10-26T18%3A55%3A44Z&sp=rwd
```

**FIGURE 3-17** Creating a Shared Access Token

This is a query string that can be appended to the full URI of the blob or container the SAS URI was created with, and passed to a client (programmatically or manually). Use the SAS URI by combining the full URI to the secure blob or container and appending the generated SAS token. The following example shows the combination in more detail.

The full URI to the blob in storage.

```
https://examrefstorage.blob.core.windows.net/examrefcontainer1/Workshop%20
List%20-%202017.xlsx
```

The combined URI with the generated SAS token.

```
https://examrefstorage.blob.core.windows.net/examrefcontainer1/Workshop%20
List%20-%202017.xlsx?sv=2016-05-31&sr=b&sig=jFnSNYWvxt6
Miy6Lc5xvT0Y1IOwerdWcFvwba065fws%3D&st=2017-10-26T14%3A55%3A44Z&se=
2017-10-26T18%3A55%3A44Z&sp=rwd
```

The Azure CLI tools can also be used to create SAS tokens using the az storage blob generate-sas command.

```
storageAccount="[storage account name]"
container="[storage container name]"
storageAccountKey="[storage account key]"
blobName="[blob name]"
az storage blob generate-sas \
    --account-name "$storageAccount" \
    --account-key "$storageAccountKey" \
    --container-name "$container" \
    --name "$blobName" \
    --permissions r \
    --expiry "2018-05-31"
```

## Using a stored access policy

Creating a shared access signature is fine for many operations, but in some cases, you may want to create a SAS token based off of a predefined policy instead of creating the token using ad-hoc permissions and expiration periods. A stored access policy allows you to define the permissions, start, and end date for access to the container. Figure 3-18 shows using the Azure Storage Explorer to create two stored access policies.

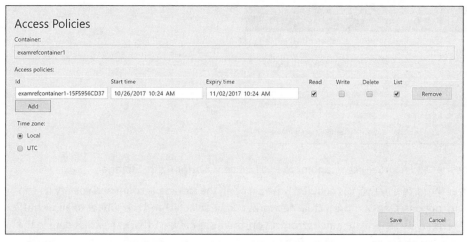

**FIGURE 3-18** Creating stored access policies using Azure Storage Explorer

To use the created policies, reference them by name during creation of a SAS token using storage explorer, or when creating a SAS token using PowerShell or the CLI tools.

# Virtual Network Service Endpoints

Configuring Virtual Network Service Endpoints (VSPE) for your Azure storage accounts allows you to remove access from the public internet, and allowing only traffic from your virtual network.

Another benefit of using VSPE is optimized routing. Without VSPE, any routes in your virtual network that force internet traffic to your premises and/or virtual appliances, known as forced-tunneling, also force Azure service traffic to take the same route as the internet traffic. Service endpoints provide optimal routing for Azure traffic. Endpoints always take service traffic directly from your virtual network to the service on the Microsoft Azure backbone network. Keeping traffic on the Azure backbone network allows you to continue auditing and monitoring outbound internet traffic from your virtual networks, through forced-tunneling, without impacting service traffic.

To configure a VSPE first enable the virtual network by specifying which services can connect to the virtual network. At the time of this writing only Azure SQL Database and Azure Storage are allowed as enabled for VSPE. Figure 3-19 shows enabling service endpoints for Azure Storage for the Apps subnet of a virtual network.

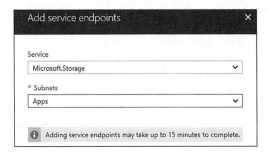

**FIGURE 3-19** Adding a Service endpoint to a virtual network for Azure Storage

After the virtual network is enabled, you can open the storage account and specify its connectivity options. One or more virtual networks can be selected and the subnet to allow traffic from. You can also specify IP ranges from an on-premises network that can access data in the storage account. Figure 3-20 shows how to enable Virtual Service Endpoints on a storage account.

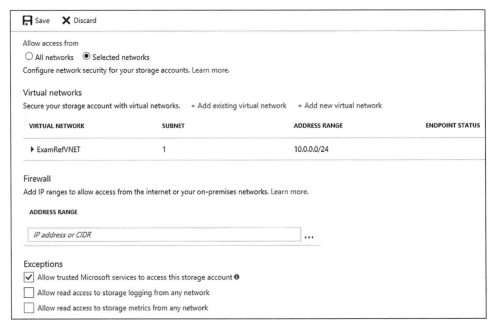

**FIGURE 3-20** Configuring a Storage account for virtual network service endpoint access

# Skill 3.3: Configure diagnostics, monitoring, and analytics

For any application that is deployed in the cloud that has a dependency on storage, under-standing how to enable Azure Storage Diagnostics is critical to ongoing operations. Azure Storage Diagnostics provides the ability to capture metrics and log data. You can use this information to analyze storage service usage, diagnose issues with requests made against the storage account, and to improve the performance of applications that use a service. Diagnos-tics also allows for a configurable retention period to automatically manage the storage of the data generated. Like other services in Azure, the Azure storage service also provides built-in monitoring and alerting capabilities to provide alerts on configurable thresholds.

> **This skill covers how to:**
> - Configure Azure Storage Diagnostics
> - Analyze diagnostic data
> - Enabling monitoring and alerts

## Configuring Azure Storage Diagnostics

The first step to enable diagnostics on an Azure Storage account is to open the storage account properties and click on the Diagnostics link on the left under monitoring. In the new blade that opens, set Status to On. From here, you can select the metrics you wish to capture, as well as the logging and retention settings. Figure 3-21 shows the Azure portal configuration for enabling storage diagnostics on the storage account.

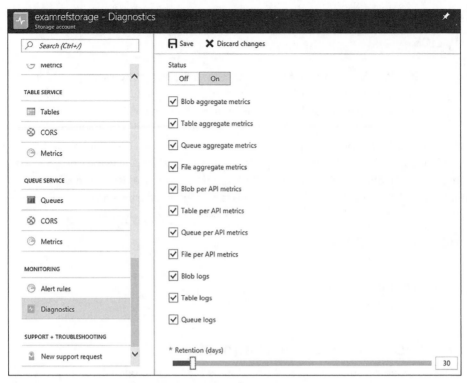

**FIGURE 3-21** Enabling diagnostics for an Azure Storage account

You can also enable and configure storage diagnostics by using the Set-AzureStorageServiceLoggingProperty and Set-AzureStorageServiceMetricsProperty Azure PowerShell cmdlets.

In the following example, the Set-AzureStorageMetricsProperty cmdlet enables hourly storage metrics on the blob service with a retention period of 30 days and at the ServiceAndApi level. The next call is to the Set-AzureStorageServiceLoggingProperty cmdlet, which is also configuring the blob service and a 30-day retention period but is only logging delete operations.

```
$storageAccount = "[storage account name]"
$rgName  = "[resource group name]"
$storageKey = Get-AzureRmStorageAccountKey -ResourceGroupName $rgName
 -Name $storageAccount
$context = New-AzureStorageContext -StorageAccountName $storageAccount `
                                   -StorageAccountKey $storageKey[0].Value
Set-AzureStorageServiceMetricsProperty -ServiceType Blob `
                                       -MetricsType Hour `
                                       -RetentionDays 30 `
                                       -MetricsLevel ServiceAndApi `
                                       -Context $context
Set-AzureStorageServiceLoggingProperty -ServiceType Blob `
                                       -RetentionDays 30 `
                                       -LoggingOperations Delete `
                                       -Context $context
```

Metrics data is recorded at the service level and at the service and API level. At the service level, a basic set of metrics such as ingress and egress, availability, latency, and success percentages, which are aggregated for the Blob, Table, and Queue services, is collected. At the service and API level, a full set of metrics that includes the same metrics for each storage API operation, in addition to the service-level metrics, is collected. Statistics are written to a table entity every minute or hourly depending on the value passed to the MetricsType parameter (the Azure portal only supports using hour).

Logging data is persisted to Azure blob storage. As part of configuration, you can specify which types of operations should be captured. The operations supported are: All, None, Read, Write, and Delete.

## Analyzing diagnostic data

After you have enabled and configured diagnostics for capture, the next step is to understand how to retrieve the data and understand what it means. Metrics data is captured in several tables in the storage account being monitored. Table 3-9 lists the names of the tables created, and where the data for hourly and minute metrics is created per service.

TABLE 3-9 Container permissions and resulting access

| Metrics type | Table names |
| --- | --- |
| Hourly | $MetricsHourPrimaryTransactionsBlob |
| Hourly | $MetricsHourPrimaryTransactionsTable |
| Hourly | $MetricsHourPrimaryTransactionsQueue |
| Minute | $MetricsMinutePrimaryTransactionsBlob |
| Minute | $MetricsMinutePrimaryTransactionsTable |
| Minute | $MetricsMinutePrimaryTransactionsQueue |
| Capacity | $MetricsCapacityBlob (blob service only) |

To view the data, you can programmatically access table storage, or use a tool such as Storage Explorer or Visual Studio as demonstrated in Figure 3-22.

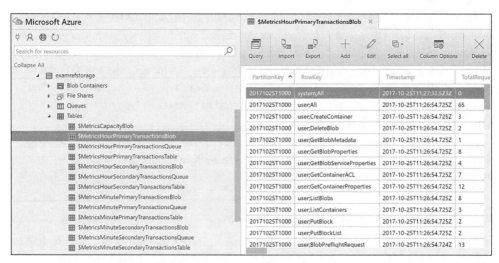

**FIGURE 3-22** Viewing Diagnostics Data using Azure Storage Explorer

*MORE INFO*  **AZURE STORAGE METRICS SCHEMA**

You can read the full schema for captured metrics here: *https://docs.microsoft.com/en-us/ rest/api/storageservices/Storage-Analytics-Metrics-Table-Schema*.

Logging data is stored in blob storage within the storage account in a container named $logs that is also accessible from Azure Storage Explorer. Each blob stored in the container starts with the service name (Blob, Table, and Queue). Each file within the container has a list of the operations performed on the storage account. The operation types logged depend on what setting was specified when configuring logging such as (All, Reads, Writes or Deletes).

*MORE INFO*  **STORAGE ANALYTICS LOG FORMAT**

For more details about the storage analytics log format see the following: *https://docs. microsoft.com/en-us/rest/api/storageservices/Storage-Analytics-Log-Format*.

# Enabling monitoring and alerts

Enabling monitoring on Azure Storage is a similar experience to other services such as virtual machines. The first step is to enable diagnostics to capture data that can be monitored. The second step is to configure charts in the Azure portal and enable alerts for the criteria you are interested in. Figure 3-23 shows some of the default metrics for the storage account. To enable other metrics, open the storage account properties in the Azure portal. Click one of the default monitoring metrics, such as Total requests, and then select a check mark by each metric you are interested in monitoring.

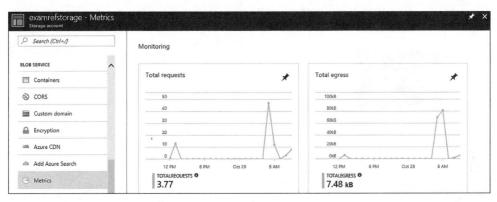

**FIGURE 3-23** Monitoring metrics for an Azure Storage account

Add an alert by clicking the Alerts Rules link on the storage account. Then click Add Alert. Figure 3-24 shows the Alert Rules page in the Azure portal, where you can select the Resource (blob, queue, or table), and specify the alert name and description, along with the actual metric to alert on. In this example, the value in the Metric drop-down is set to capacity and (not shown) is the threshold and condition. The Condition is set to Greater Than, and the Threshold is set to 5497558138880 (5 TB in bytes). Each alert can be configured to email members of the owners, contributors, and reader roles, or a specific email address.

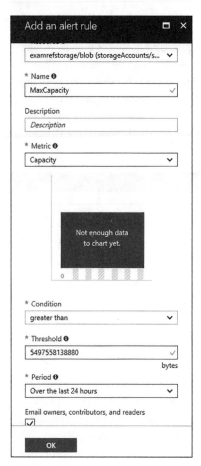

**FIGURE 3-24** Adding an alert rule in the Azure portal

# Skill 3.4: Implement storage encryption

In this skill, we'll discuss how to implement encryption of data using Azure Storage Service encryption as well as how to encrypt and protect data managed by Azure Data Lake Store.

> **This skill covers how to:**
>
> - Encrypt data using Azure Storage Service Encryption (SSE)
> - Implement encryption and role based access control with Azure Data Lake Store

# Encrypt data using Azure Storage Service Encryption (SSE)

Encrypting data is one of the most important aspects of any security strategy whether the data is in transit or at rest. There are many ways to encrypt data, such as programmatically encrypting it in your own application and storing the encryption keys in Azure Key Vault, encrypting VM disks, or in the case of Azure Storage taking advantage of the Azure Storage Service Encryption feature.

The Azure Storage Service encryption feature helps you protect and safeguard your data by automatically encrypting and decrypting data using 256-bit AES encryption as it is written in an Azure Storage Account for blobs and files. The service works with the following storage account configurations:

- Standard Storage: General purpose storage accounts for Blobs and File storage and Blob storage accounts
- Premium storage
- All redundancy levels (LRS, ZRS, GRS, RA-GRS)
- Azure Resource Manager storage accounts (but not classic)
- All regions

To enable SSE, open the storage account in the Azure portal, click on Encryption under Blobs or Files, and click Enabled under Storage service encryption and then click save. Figure 3-25 shows the option for enabling Storage service encryption.

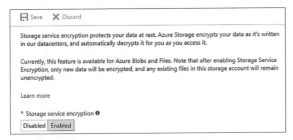

**FIGURE 3-25** Enabling encryption on Azure blob storage

### EXAM TIP

Storage service encryption only encrypts newly created data after encryption is enabled. For example, if you create a new Resource Manager storage account but don't turn on encryption, and then you upload blobs or archived VHDs to that storage account and then turn on SSE, those blobs will not be encrypted unless they are rewritten or copied.

# Implement encryption and role based access control with Azure Data Lake Store

Azure Data Lake is a data repository designed for big data analytic workloads. Azure Data Lake enables you to capture data of any size, type, and ingestion speed in one single place for operational and exploratory analytics. For this skill, it is important to understand how to encrypt the data in an Azure Data Lake as well as control access to it using role based access control (RBAC).

Azure Data Lake store supports encryption in transit and at rest. Data in transit is always encrypted and transmitted using HTTPS. For encryption at rest, you can enable transparent encryption that is on by default. When you create the data lake store you can choose to not enable encryption, or to enable encryption where the keys are managed by the Data Lake Store, or where the keys are managed by you in your own Azure Key Vault. Figure 3-26, shows the creation process where the encryption type is specified as key managed by Data Lake Store.

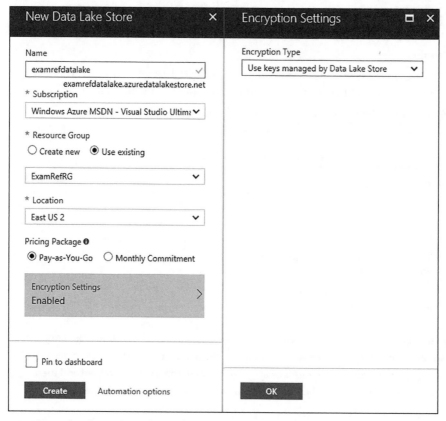

**FIGURE 3-26** Creating an Azure Data Lake Store and configuring encryption

Access to the Azure Data Lake store is over a public IP address. You can enable the firewall to only allow in certain source IP addresses such as a client application from in Azure or from on-premises. Figure 3-27 demonstrates how to configure the firewall rules to allow in one or more IP addresses by specifying the start IP and end IP range.

**FIGURE 3-27** Configuring the firewall rules for an Azure Data Lake Store

Azure Data Lake Store implements an access control model that derives from HDFS, which in turn derives from the POSIX access control model. This allows you to specify file and folder access control lists (ACLs) on data in your data lake using users or groups from your Azure AD tenant.

There are two kinds of access control lists (ACLs): Access ACLs and Default ACLs.

- **Access ACLs** These control access to an object. Files and folders both have Access ACLs.

- **Default ACLs** A "template" of ACLs associated with a folder that determine the Access ACLs for any child items that are created under that folder. Files do not have Default ACLs.

The permissions on a filesystem object are Read, Write, and Execute, and they can be used on files and folders as shown in Table 3-10.

**TABLE 3-10** File system permissions for Azure Data Lake Store

| Permission | File | File |
|---|---|---|
| Read (R) | Can read the contents of a file | Requires Read and Execute to list the contents of the folder |
| Write (W) | Can write or append to a file | Requires Write and Execute to create child items in a folder |
| Execute (X) | Does not mean anything in the context of Data Lake Store | Required to traverse the child items of a folder |

To configure permissions on a data item in your data lake, open the Data Lake Store in the Azure portal and click Data Lake Explorer. From there, right click the data file you wish to secure and click Access as shown in Figure 3-28.

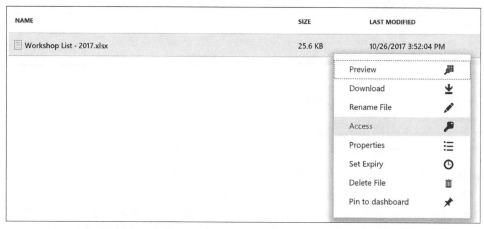

**FIGURE 3-28** Controlling access on data in an Azure Data Lake Store

The next screen will display the current users that have access to the file and what their permissions are. You can add additional users by clicking the Add button, then selecting the User or Group, and then specifying the permissions (Read, Write or Execute) as shown in Figure 3-29.

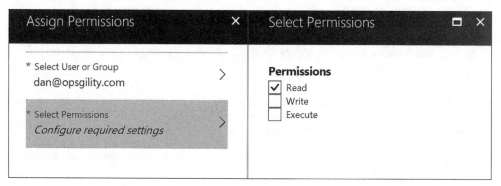

**FIGURE 3-29** Adding a new user to an Azure Data Lake Store file

There are several user and group concepts to understand at a basic level.

- **Super User**  A super-user has the most rights of all the users in the Data Lake Store. A super-user has the following permissions:
  - Has read, write, and execute permissions to all files and folders.

- Can change the permissions on any file or folder.
- Can change the owning user or owning group of any file or folder.

Everyone in theAzure Ownersrole (role based access control) for a Data Lake Store account is automatically a super-user for that account.

- **Owning User**   The user who created the item is automatically the owning user of the item. The owner of an item can do the following:
  - Change the permissions of a file that is owned.
  - Change the owning group of a file that is owned, if the owning user is also a member of the target group.

- **Owning Group**   Every user is associated with a "primary group." For example, user "alice" might belong to the "finance" group. Alice might also belong to multiple groups, but one group is always designated as her primary group. In POSIX, when Alice creates a file, the owning group of that file is set to her primary group, which in this case is "finance."

> *MORE INFO*   **SECURING DATA IN AZURE DATA LAKE**
>
> Going in-depth into POSIX security is beyond the scope of this chapter, but it is certainly a worthwhile task to read and understand to not only prepare you for the exam but to also ensure your data lake data is secure. You can learn more about securing data here: *https://docs.microsoft.com/en-us/azure/data-lake-store/data-lake-store-access-control*.

# Thought experiment

In this thought experiment, apply what you have learned about this objective. You can find answers to these questions in the "Answers" section at the end of this chapter.

You are the web administrator for www.contoso.com which is hosted in virtual machines in the West US Azure region. Several customers from England and China complain that the PDF files for your product brochures take too long time to download. Currently, the PDF files are served from the /brochures folder of your website.

1. What steps should you take to mitigate the download time for your PDFs?
2. What changes need to happen on the *www.contoso.com* web site?

# Thought experiment answers

This section contains the solution to the thought experiment for the chapter.

To mitigate this problem, move the PDF files closer to the customer locations. This can be solved by moving the PDF files to Azure Storage and then enabling them for CDN.

1. Create an Azure Storage account and move the pdf files to a container named brochures and enable public access (blob) on the container. Next, you should create a new CDN profile and an endpoint that originates from the blob storage account. From there, pre-load the PDF files into CDN to minimize the content being delayed when the first user requests it.

2. The website pages would will need to change to refer to the URL of the CDN endpoint. For example, if the PDF was previously referenced by *www.contoso.com/brochures/ product1.pdf* it would now be referenced by contosocdn.azureedge.net/brochures/ product1.pdf unless the CDN endpoint was configured for custom domains.

# Chapter summary

This chapter covered a broad range of topics focused on Azure Storage, CDN, and security related to Azure Data Lake Store.

Below are some of the key takeaways from this chapter:

- Azure storage can be managed through several tools directly from Microsoft. The Azure portal, PowerShell, CLI, Storage Explorer, and AzCopy. It's important to know when to use each tool.

- Access to blobs can be controlled using several techniques. Among them are: storage account name and key, shared access signature (SAS), public access level of the container they reside in, and using firewall/virtual network service endpoints.

- Use the async blob copy service to copy files between storage accounts or from outside publicly accessible locations to your Azure storage account.

- Storage accounts and CDN both support custom domains. Enabling SSL is only supported on custom domains when the blob is accessed via CDN.

- Enable diagnostics and alerts to monitor the status of your storage accounts.

- Storage Explorer and Visual Studio have capabilities for browsing blob and table storage to download and review diagnostic data.

- Storage service encryption automatically encrypts and decrypts data added or updated in your storage account. If the data already existed in the storage account prior to enabling SSE it will not be encrypted.

- Azure Data Lake store will be default support encryption at rest and always in transit.

- You can choose to have Azure Data Lake store manage your encryption keys, or reference keys out of an existing Azure Key Vault.

- The security for Azure Data Lake store is based on POSIX permissions. You can assign users / groups from Azure AD access with read, write, and execute permissions per item.

- Users that are in the role based access control Owners role will automatically be added as Super User.

# CHAPTER 4

# Implement Virtual Networks

A zure Virtual Networks (VNet) provide the infrastructure for deploying workloads that require an advanced network configuration. VNets provide support for hybrid network connectivity from Azure to either your on-premises network or to other VNets within Azure regions. The use of VMs in Azure is entirely dependent upon the VNets where deployed. These can be internet-facing applications that are deployed behind either the Azure load balancer for Layer 4 workloads, or the Azure Application Gateway, which can deploy more complex Layer 7 implementations. Azure VNets also provide support for deploying intranet or n-tier workloads using the internal load balancer. Workloads, such as Active Directory, are also enabled in the cloud using features only supported in VNets (such as subnets and static IP addresses). This chapter will focus on VNets as well as how to create and configure them. There is also a focus on key hybrid technologies.

## Skills covered in this chapter:

- Skill 4.1 Configure Virtual Networks
- Skill 4.2 Design and implement multi-site or hybrid network connectivity
- Skill 4.3 Configure ARM VM Networking
- Skill 4.4 Design and implement a communication strategy

## Skill 4.1: Configure Virtual Networks

Configuring an Azure VNet involves network design skills such as specifying the address spaces (IP network ranges), and dividing the network into subnets. Setting up name resolution with DNS at the Virtual Network level is critical when connecting multiple networks together, and VNet peering is one option for this that is covered here. Securing VNets by implementing network security groups, along with the ability to control the routing on VNets applying User Defined Routes, is also covered. These serve as the most important tasks for deployment of VMs into VNets to provide services for your cloud implementation. One such deployment of VMs will be the use of the Azure Application Gateway used for Layer 7 load balancing. Customization of these many services, along with designing the VNet itself, is covered in this skill.

> **This skill covers how to:**
> - Create a VNet
> - Design subnets
> - Setup DNS at the Virtual Network level
> - User Defined Routes (UDRs)
> - Connect VNets using VNet peering
> - Setup network security groups (NSGs)
> - Deploy a VM into a VNet
> - Implement Application Gateway

## Create a Virtual Network (VNet)

Azure VNets enable you to securely connect Azure VMs to each other and to extend your on-premises network to the Azure cloud. A VNet is a representation of your own network in the cloud and is a logical isolation of the Azure cloud dedicated to your subscription.

VNets are isolated from one another allowing you to create separate VNets for development, testing, and production. Although it's not recommended, you can even use the same Classless Inter-Domain Routing (CIDR) address blocks. The best plan is to create multiple VNets that use different CIDR address blocks. This allows you to connect these networks together if you wish. Each VNet can be segmented into multiple subnets. Azure provides internal name resolution for VMs and cloud service role instances connected to a VNet. You can optionally configure a VNet to use your own DNS servers instead of using Azure internal name resolution.

The following are some of the connectivity capabilities that you should understand about VNets:

- **internet connectivity**  All Azure Virtual Machines (VMs), connected to a VNet, have access to the internet by default. You can also enable inbound access to specific resources running in a VNet, such as a web server.

- **Azure resource connectivity**  Azure resources such as VMs can be connected to the same VNet. The VMs can connect to each other by using private IP addresses, even if they are in different subnets. Azure provides system routes between subnets, VNets, and on-premises networks, so you don't have to configure and manage routes.

- **VNet connectivity**  VNets can be connected together, enabling VMs connected to any VNet to communicate with any VM on any other VNet.  This can be accomplished by using VNet peering if they are in the same region or by using VPN Gateways if they are in different Azure regions.  Traffic from one VNet to another VNet is always secured and never egresses to the internet.

- **On-premises connectivity** VNets can be connected to on-premises networks through private network connections and Azure (ExpressRoute), or through an encrypted Site-to-Site VPN connection over the internet.

- **Traffic filtering (firewall)** VM network traffic can be filtered by using 5-tuple inbound and outbound by source IP address and port, destination IP address and port, and protocol.

- **Routing** You can optionally override Azure's default routing by configuring your own routes, or by using BGP routes through a VPN Gateway.

All VMs connected to a VNet have outbound connectivity to the internet by default. The resource's private IP address is source network address translated (SNAT), to a Public IP address by the Azure infrastructure. You can change the default connectivity by implementing custom routing and traffic filtering.

To communicate inbound to Azure resources from the internet, or to communicate outbound to the internet without SNAT, a resource must be assigned a Public IP address.

Azure VNets can be created by using the Azure portal, Azure PowerShell cmdlets, or the Azure CLI.

## Creating a Virtual Network using the Azure Portal

To create a new VNet by using the Azure portal, first click New and then select Networking. Next, click Virtual Network as shown in Figure 4-1.

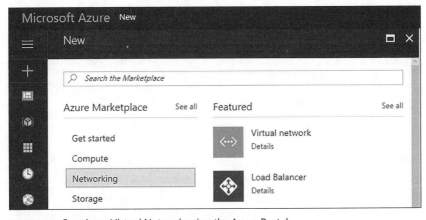

**FIGURE 4-1** Creating a Virtual Network using the Azure Portal

The Create Virtual Network blade opens. Here you can provide configuration information about the Virtual Network. This blade requires the following inputs, as shown in Figure 4-2:

- Name of the Virtual Network

- Address Space to be used for the VNet using CIDR notation

- Subscription in which the VNet is created

- The resource group where the VNet is created
- Location for VNet
- Subnet Name for the first subnet in the VNet
- The Address Range of the first Subnet

**FIGURE 4-2** Create Virtual Network Blade

The address space is the most critical configuration for a VNet in Azure. This is the IP range for the entire network that will be divided into subnets. The address space can almost be any IP range that you wish (public or private). You can add multiple address spaces to a VNet. To ensure this VNet can be connected to other networks, the address space should never overlap with any other networks in your environment. If a VNet has an address space that overlaps with another Azure VNet or on-premises network, the networks cannot be connected, as the routing of traffic will not work properly.

> **IMPORTANT** **ADDRESS RANGES**
>
> There are some address ranges that cannot be used for VNets.

These include the following:

- 224.0.0.0/4 (Multicast)
- 255.255.255.255/32 (Broadcast)
- 127.0.0.0/8 (Loopback)
- 169.254.0.0/16 (Link-local)
- 168.63.129.16/32 (Internal DNS)

> **MORE INFO  ADDRESS SPACE FROM IP RANGES**
>
> Whether you define your address space as public or private, the address space is only reachable from within that Virtual Network or any other network that you successfully connected to in the VNet. Typically, the address spaces are from IP ranges defined in RFC 1918. This RFC includes IP addresses in the following ranges:

- 10.0.0.0 - 10.255.255.255 (10.0.0.0/8)
- 172.16.0.0 - 172.31.255.255 (172.16.0.0/12)
- 192.168.0.0 - 192.168.255.255 (192.168.0.0/16)

Once the VNet has completed provisioning, you can review the settings using the Azure portal. Notice the Apps subnet has been created as part of the inputs you made as seen in Figure 4-3.

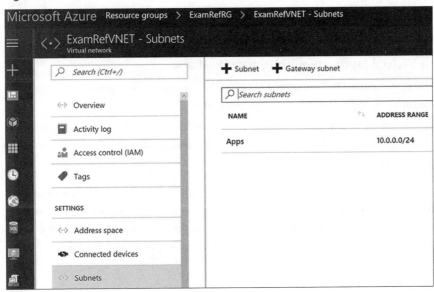

**FIGURE 4-3** Virtual Network created using the Azure portal

To create another subnet in the ExamRefVNET, click +Subnet on this blade and provide the following inputs, as shown in Figure 4-4:

- Name of the Subnet: Data.
- Address Range: This is the portion of the address space that is made available for the subnet. In the case, it is 10.0.1.0/24.

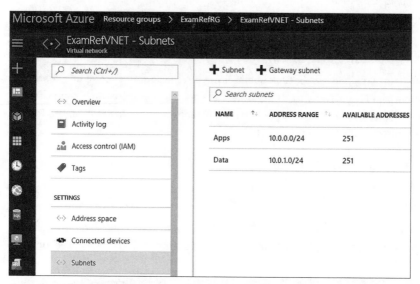

**FIGURE 4-4** Virtual Network created using the Azure Portal with two subnets Apps and Data

## Creating a Virtual Network with PowerShell

Using the Azure PowerShell cmdlets, you can create and configure VNets programmatically. Let's walk through how to create a VNet using PowerShell.

Before you can create or manage any resources in your Azure subscription by using the Azure PowerShell cmdlets, you must log in by executing the Login-AzureRmAccount cmdlet.

```
Login-AzureRmAccount
```

Once the PowerShell session is authenticated to Azure, the first thing needed will be a new resource group. Using the New-AzureRmResourceGroup cmdlet, you can create a new resource group. This cmdlet requires you to specify the resource group name as well as the name of the Azure region. These values are defined in the variables $rgName and $location.

```
$rgName    = "ExamRefRGPS"
$location  = "Central US"
New-AzureRmResourceGroup -Name $rgName -Location $location
```

If you wanted to use an existing resource group you can use the Get-AzureRmResource-Group cmdlet to see if the resource group. You can also use the Get-AzureRmLocation cmdlet to view the list of available regions.

In the code example below, the New-AzureRmVirtualNetworkSubnetConfig cmdlet is used to create two local objects that represent two subnets in the VNet. The VNet is subsequently created with the call to New-AzureRmVirtualNetwork. It is passed the address space of 10.0.0.0/16. You could also pass in multiple address spaces like how the subnets were passed in using an array. Notice how $subnets = @() creates an array and then the array is loaded with two different commands using the New-AzureRmVirtualNetworkSubnetConfig cmdlet. When the New-AzureRmVirtualNetwork cmdlet is called in the last command of the script, the two subnets are then populated by the array values that have been loaded in the $subnets.

```
$subnets = @()
$subnet1Name = "Apps"
$subnet2Name = "Data"
$subnet1AddressPrefix = "10.0.0.0/24"
$subnet2AddressPrefix = "10.0.1.0/24"
$vnetAddresssSpace = "10.0.0.0/16"
$VNETName = "ExamRefVNET-PS"
$rgName = "ExamRefRGPS"
$location = "Central US"
$subnets = New-AzureRmVirtualNetworkSubnetConfig -Name $subnet1Name `
                              -AddressPrefix $subnet1AddressPrefix
$subnets = New-AzureRmVirtualNetworkSubnetConfig -Name $subnet2Name `
                              -AddressPrefix $subnet2AddressPrefix
$vnet = New-AzureRmVirtualNetwork -Name $VNETName `
                      -ResourceGroupName $rgName `
                      -Location $location `
                      -AddressPrefix $vnetAddresssSpace `
                      -Subnet $subnets
```

Following the completion of the PowerShell script, there should be a new resource group and a new VNet provisioned. In Figure 4-5, you see the VNet ExamRefVNET-PS was created in the ExamRefRGPS resource group. You can now click on the subnets button to view the new App and Data subnets and their address ranges.

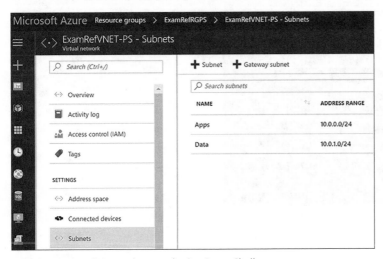

**FIGURE 4-5** Virtual Network created using PowerShell

## Creating a Virtual Network using the Azure CLI

By using the Azure CLI 2.0, you can create and configure VNets by using individual commands or as a part of a script to be run using a bash script or batch file depending upon the platform (bash is supported on Linux, macOS, or Windows Subsystem for Linux).

> **IMPORTANT AZURE CLI**
>
> The Azure CLI is available on many platforms including Windows, MAC, Linux and even as a Docker container. It is also available in the Azure portal and is called the Azure Cloud Shell. To learn more about installing the Azure CLI 2.0, read this article: *https://docs.microsoft. com/en-us/cli/azure/install-azure-cli?view=azure-cli-latest*.

> **NOTE AZURE CLOUD SHELL**
>
> For these examples, use the Azure Cloud Shell. If you are using the Azure CLI installed on your machine or from a Docker container, you first need to log in to Azure by using the az login command and follow the instructions to authenticate your session.

In this case here, let's walk through each command to create the VNet using the Azure CLI Cloud Shell. To initiate the Azure CLI Cloud Shell, open the Azure portal and then click the CLI symbol along the upper right-hand corner as seen in Figure 4-6.

**FIGURE 4-6** Azure CLI Cloud Shell

After a few moments, the Cloud Shell will be ready, and you will see an interactive bash prompt. In Figure 4-7, Azure Cloud Shell is ready to use with your subscription.

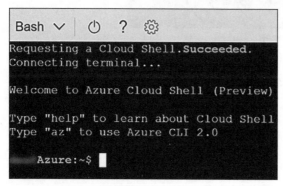

**FIGURE 4-7** Azure CLI Cloud Shell

The first step will be creating a new resource group for the VNet using the Azure CLI. This will be accomplished using the `az group create` command. You will need to specify a location for the resource group. To locate a list of regions that are available for your subscription, you can use the command `az account list-locations`.

```
az group create -n ExamRefRGCLI -l "centralus"
```

Next, you can create the new VNet using the az network vnet create command.

```
az network vnet create --resource-group ExamRefRGCLI -n ExamRefVNET-CLI
--address-prefixes 10.0.0.0/16 -l "centralus"
```

Then, following the creation of the VNet, create the App and Data subnets. This is accomplished using the az network vnet subnet create command. You will run these commands one at a time for each subnet.

```
az network vnet subnet create --resource-group ExamRefRGCLI --vnet-name
ExamRefVNET-CLI -n Apps --address-prefix 10.0.1.0/24
az network vnet subnet create --resource-group ExamRefRGCLI --vnet-name
ExamRefVNET-CLI -n Data --address-prefix 10.0.2.0/24
```

After running these commands there should be a new resource group named ExamRefRGCLI and the newly provisioned VNet named ExamRefVNET-CLI. In Figure 4-8, you see the ExamREFVNET-CLI, which was created in the ExamRefRGCLI resource group. If you click the Subnets button you will see the new App and Data subnets with the address ranges from the commands entered.

**FIGURE 4-8** Virtual Network created using the Azure CLI Cloud Shell

# Design subnets

A subnet is a child resource of a VNet, which defines segments of address spaces within a VNets. These are created using CIDR blocks of the address space that was defined for the VNet. NICs can be added to subnets and connected to VMs. This will provide connectivity for various workloads.

The name of a subnet must be unique within that VNet. You cannot change the subnet name subnet following its creation. During the creation of a VNet while using the Azure portal, the requirement is for you to define one subnet, even though a VNet isn't required to have any subnets. In the portal, you can define only one subnet when you create a VNet. You can add more subnets to the VNet later after it has been created. You can create a VNet that has multiple subnets by using Azure CLI or PowerShell.

When creating a subnet, the address range must be defined. The address range of the new subnet must be within the address space you assigned for the VNet. The range that is entered will determine the number of IP Addresses that are part of the subnet.

### EXAM TIP

Azure will hold back a total of 5 IP Addresses for every subnet that is created in a VNet. Azure reserves the first and last IP addresses in each subnet like standard IP networks with one for the network identification and the other for broadcast. Azure also holds three additional addresses for internal use starting from the first address in the subnet.  For example, if the CIDR range of a subnet has its first IP as .0 then the first useable IP would be .4. So, if the address range was 192.168.1.0/24 then 192.168.1.4 would be the first address assigned to a NIC.  Also, the smallest subnet on an Azure VNet would be a CIDR /29. This would provide 3 useable IP Addresses and 5 IP Addresses that Azure would use.

Subnets provide the ability to isolate network traffic between various types of workloads. These are often different types of servers or even tiers of applications. Examples of this could include separating traffic bound for web servers and database servers. These logical segmentations allow for clean separations, so they can be secured and managed. This allows for very precise application of rules securing data traffic as well as how traffic flows into and out of a given set of VMs.

In Azure, the security rules are applied using network security groups, and the traffic flows are controlled using route tables. Designing the subnets should be completed upfront and should be considered while determining the address space. Remember that for each subnet, Azure holds back 5 IP Addresses. If you create a VNet with 10 subnets, you are losing 50 IP addresses to Azure. Careful up-front planning is critical to not causing yourself a shortage of IPs later.

Changes to subnets and address ranges can only be made if there are no devices connected to the subnet. If you wish to make a change to a subnet's address range, you would first have to delete all the objects in that subnet. If the subnet is empty, you can change the range of addresses to any range that is within the address space of the VNet not assigned to any other subnets.

Subnets can be only be deleted from VNets if they are empty. Once a subnet is deleted, the addresses that were part of that address range would be released and available again for use within new subnets that you could create.

Subnets have the following properties:  Name, Location, Address range, Network security group, Route table and Users. Table 4-1 discusses each of these properties.

**TABLE 4-1** Properties of a Virtual Network Subnet

| Property | Description |
| --- | --- |
| Name | Subnet name up to 80 characters. May contain letters, numbers, underscores, periods, or hyphens. Must start with a letter or number. Must end with a letter, number, or underscore. |
| Location | Azure location must be the same as the Virtual Network. |
| Address Range | Single address prefix that makes up the subnet in CIDR notation. Must be a single CIDR block that is part of one of the VNets address spaces. |
| Network Security Group | NSGs are essentially firewall rules that can be associated to a subnet.  These rules are then applied to all NICs that are attached to that subnet. |
| Route Table | Route table applied to the subnet that would change the default system routes.  These are used to send traffic to destination networks that are different than the routes that Azure uses by default. |
| Users | Which users have access to use the subnet as a part of Role-Based Access Control. |

***EXAM TIP***

**Network security groups (NSGs) can be associated to subnets, individual NICs or both. NSGs associated with subnets will enforce their inbound or outbound rules to all NICs that are connected to the subnet. Inbound rules from a subnet NSG will apply first as packets entering the subnet prior to entering the NIC. Upon enforcement following the NSG in association with the subnet, any NSGs associated with NICs would then be enforced. The opposite is true for outbound rules with the NIC NSG being enforced followed by the subnet NSG, as the traffic is following in the reverse direction. For example, if a VM was running a web server on PORT 80, and it has a NSG associated to the NIC with an inbound Rule that allowed traffic on PORT 80, and the subnet did not, the packets would be discarded without ever reaching the VM. The reason is because the NSG at the subnet level is blocking the traffic on PORT 80 for all NICs.**

# Gateway subnets

The basis for deploying hybrid clouds is the connection of an on-premises network along with an Azure VNet. This configuration allows clients and servers deployed in Azure to communicate with those in your datacenter and network. To deploy this type of connection, a VPN Gateway needs to be created in Azure. All VPN Gateways must be placed into a special gateway subnet.

The gateway subnet contains the IP addresses the VPN Gateway VMs and services will use. When you create your VPN Gateway, special Azure managed VMs are deployed to the gateway subnet, and they are configured with the required VPN Gateway settings. Only the VPN Gateways should be deployed to the gateway subnet and its name must be "GatewaySubnet" to work properly.

When you create the gateway subnet, you are required to specify the number of IP addresses available using an address range. The IP addresses in the gateway subnet will be allocated to the gateway VMs and services. It's important to plan ahead because some configurations require more IP addresses than others. For example, if you plan on using ExpressRoute and a Site to Site VPN as a failover, you will need more than just two IPs. You can create a gateway subnet as small as /29, but it's Microsoft's recommendation to create a gateway subnet of /28 or larger (i.e., /28, /27, /26). That way, if you add functionality in the future, you won't have to tear down your gateway. Just delete and recreate the gateway subnet to allow for more IP addresses.

## Creating a GatewaySubnet using the Azure portal

The GatewaySubnet can be created using the Azure portal, PowerShell or CLI. Because these aren't created very often they are typically created using the Azure portal.

To create the GatewaySubnet, first open an existing VNet, and move to the subnets under settings. From here, the current subnets can be reviewed. Click +GatewaySubnet, and you will be required to enter the address range for the subnet as seen in Figure 4-9.

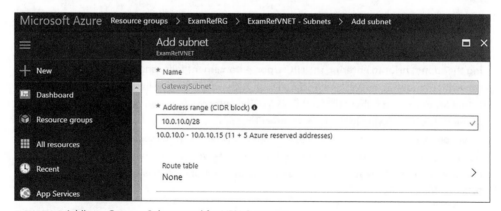

**FIGURE 4-9** Adding a GatewaySubnet used for VPN Gateways

Once the Gateway subnet is added, the VPN Gateway can be created and placed into this subnet. Many network administrators will create this address range much further away from their subnets in terms of the IP Addressing. Figure 4-10 shows, the GatewaySubnet created using a CIDR block of 10.0.100.0/28. The other subnets are using /24 CIDR blocks for Apps and Data. In this case the GatewaySubnet is 98 subnets away from the others. This is not required, as the GatewaySubnet could be any CIDR address range belonging to the address space of the VNet. This would provide for a continuation of the subnet scheme put in place if the admin wanted to build additional subnets. The next logical subnet would be in the 10.0.2.0/24 and so forth as more are created.

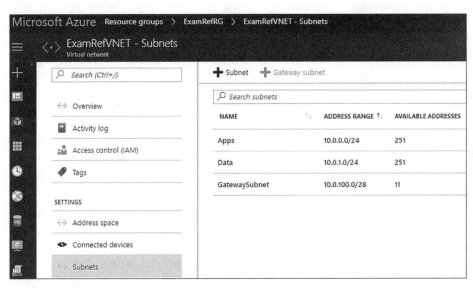

**FIGURE 4-10** GatewaySubnet after being created using the Azure Portal

## Setup DNS at the Virtual Network level

The Domain Naming Service (DNS) is critical on all modern networks, and VNets are no different. It is possible for all network communication to be completed by using IP addresses, but it is much simpler to use names that can easily be remembered and do not change. There are two options for providing DNS services to a VNet:

- **Azure Provided DNS**   Highly durable and scalable service
- **Customer Managed DNS**   Build and deploy your own DNS Servers

By default, Azure DNS is configured when creating a VNet. VMs connected to the VNet use this service for name resolution inside the VNet, as well as on the public internet. Along with resolution of public DNS names, Azure provides internal name resolution for VMs that reside within the same VNet. Within a VNet the DNS suffix is consistent, so the Fully Qualified Domain Name (FQDN), is not needed. This means that VMs on the same VNet using the Azure DNS Server can connect directly via their host names.

Although Azure-provided name resolution does not require any configuration, it is not the appropriate choice for all deployment scenarios. If your needs go beyond what Azure provided DNS can provide, you will need to implement your own Customer Managed DNS Servers. Table 4-2 captures the recommended DNS infrastructure based on various common requirements. Focus in on the scenarios that would require you to deploy your own DNS.

**TABLE 4-2** Determining a DNS strategy for an Azure Virtual Network

| Requirement | Recommended DNS infrastructure |
| --- | --- |
| Name resolution between role instances or VMs located in the same cloud service or VNet | Azure provided DNS |
| Name resolution between role instances or VMs located in different VNets | Customer managed DNS |
| Resolution of on-premises computer and service names from role instances or VMs in Azure | Customer managed DNS |
| Resolution of Azure hostnames from on-premises computers | Customer managed DNS |
| Reverse DNS for internal IPs | Customer managed DNS |

When using your own DNS servers, Azure provides the ability to specify multiple DNS servers per VNet. Once in place, this configuration will cause the Azure VMs in the VNet to use your DNS servers for name resolution services. You must restart the VMs for this configuration to update.

You can alter the DNS Servers configuration for a VNet using the Azure portal, PowerShell or Azure CLI.

### Configuring VNet Custom DNS Settings using the Azure portal

To configure the DNS Servers using the Azure portal, open the VNet that will be configured and click DNS Servers, as seen in Figure 4-11. Select Custom and then input the IP Addresses of your DNS Servers that have been configured and click Save.

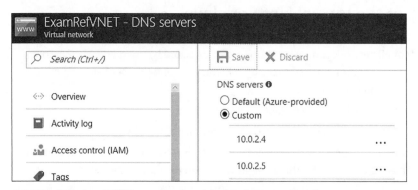

**FIGURE 4-11** Custom DNS Servers configured using the Azure Portal

## Configuring VNet Custom DNS Settings using PowerShell

When creating a new VNet, you can specify the customer DNS settings configuration using PowerShell. The New-AzureRmVirtualNetwork cmdlet with the -DNSServer (as a part of the command) will create a new VNet with the DNS Servers already specified. This command would assume that your resource group was already created.

```
$subnets = @()
$subnet1Name = "Apps"
$subnet2Name = "Data"
$subnet1AddressPrefix = "10.0.0.0/24"
$subnet2AddressPrefix = "10.0.1.0/24"
$vnetAddresssSpace = "10.0.0.0/16"
$VNETName = "ExamRefVNET-PS"
$rgName = "ExamRefRGPS"
$location = "Central US"

$subnets = New-AzureRmVirtualNetworkSubnetConfig -Name $subnet1Name `
                                 -AddressPrefix $subnet1AddressPrefix
$subnets = New-AzureRmVirtualNetworkSubnetConfig -Name $subnet2Name `
                                 -AddressPrefix $subnet2AddressPrefix
$vnet = New-AzureRmVirtualNetwork -Name $VNETName `
                                 -ResourceGroupName $rgName `
                                 -Location $location `
                                 -AddressPrefix $vnetAddresssSpace `
                                 -DNSServer 10.0.0.4,10.0.0.5 `
                                 -Subnet $subnet
```

## Configuring VNet Custom DNS settings using the Azure CLI

To create a VNet using the Azure CLI and specify custom DNS Servers, you will need to add the –dns-servers argument when using both az network vnet create commands.

```
az network vnet create --resource-group ExamRefRGCLI -n ExamRefVNET-CLI
--address-prefixes 10.0.0.0/16 --dns-servers 10.0.0.4 10.0.0.5 -l "centralus"
```

> **IMPORTANT  VNET SETTINGS**
>
> When you change your VNet settings to point to your Customer Managed DNS Servers, you will need to restart each of the VMs in that particular VNet. All IP addresses and settings in Azure are provided via the Azure DHCP Servers. The only way to make sure the change is picked up by the OS on the VMs is to reboot. When the VM reboots, it will re-acquire the IP Address and the new DNS Settings will be in place

Customer-managed DNS servers within a VNet can forward DNS queries to Azure's recursive resolvers to resolve hostnames within that VNet. For example, you could use a Domain Controller (DC), running in Azure to respond to DNS queries for its domains, and forward all other queries to Azure. This allows your VMs to see both on-premises resources (via the DC), and Azure-provided hostnames (via the forwarder). Access to Azure's recursive resolvers is provided via the virtual IP 168.63.129.16. If you promote a Domain Controller that is running as VM in Azure, it will automatically pick up the Azure DNS resolver as a Forwarder. In Figure 4-12, you see a Domain Controller deployed to an Azure VNet acting as a DNS Server for that VNet. The Forwarder is set to the address of the Azure recursive resolver.

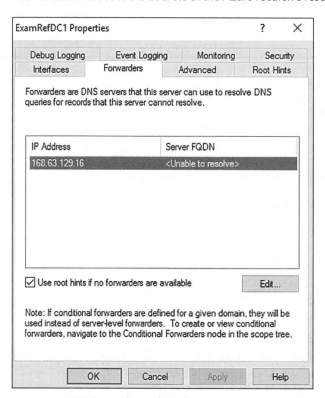

**FIGURE 4-12** DNS Forwarder configuration on a Domain Controller running in a Virtual Network

## User Defined Routes (UDRs)

Azure VMs that are added to a VNet can communicate with each other over the network automatically. Even if they are in different subnets or attempting to gain access to the internet, there are no configurations required by you as the administrator. Unlike typical networking, you will not need to specify a network gateway, even though the VMs are in different subnets. This is also the case for communication from the VMs to your on-premises network when a hybrid connection from Azure to your datacenter has been established.

This ease of setup is made possible by what is known as system routes. System routes define how IP traffic flows in Azure VNets. The following are the default system routes that Azure will use and provide for you:

- Within the same subnet
- Subnet to another subnet within a VNet
- VMs to the internet
- A VNet to another VNet through a VPN Gateway
- A VNet to another VNet through VNet peering (Service Chaining)
- A VNet to your on-premises network through a VPN Gateway

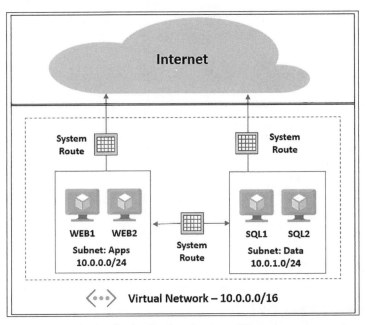

FIGURE 4-13 N-Tier Application Deployed to Azure VNet using system routes

Figure 4-13 shows an example of how these system routes make it easy to get up and running. System routes provide for most typical scenarios by default, but there are use cases where you will want to control the routing of packets.

One of the scenarios is when you want to send traffic through a virtual appliance such as a third-party load balancer, firewall or router deployed into your VNet from the Azure Marketplace.

To make this possible, you must create User Defined Routes (UDRs). These UDRs specify the next hop for packets flowing to a specific subnet through your appliance instead of following the system routes. As seen in Figure 4-14, by using the UDR, traffic will be routed through the device to the destination.

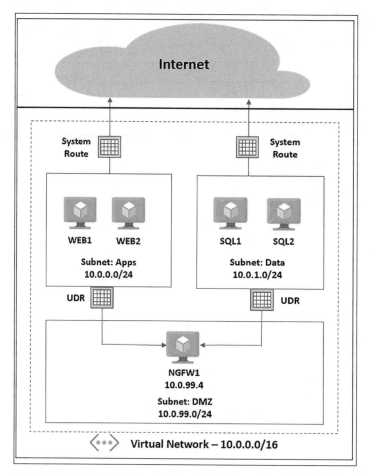

**FIGURE 4-14** N-Tier Application Deployed with a Firewall using User Defined Routes

Figure 4-15 shows a UDR that has been created to allow for traffic to be directed to a virtual appliance. In this case, it would be a Firewall running as a VM in Azure in the DMZ subnet.

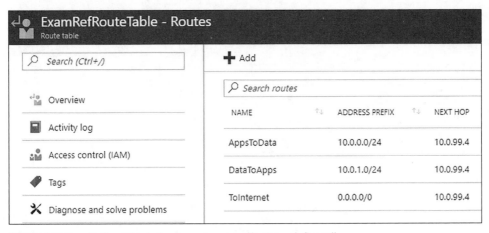

**FIGURE 4-15** User Defined Route forcing network traffic through firewall

## Connect VNets using VNet peering

VNet peering allows you to connect two Azure Resource Manager (ARM), VNets located in the same region together without complex integration. The peered VNets must have non-overlapping IP address spaces. The address spaces in either VNet cannot be added to or deleted from a VNet once a VNet is peered with another VNet.

Once peered, the VNets appear as one network and all VMs in the peered VNets can communicate with each other directly. The traffic between VMs is routed through the Microsoft backbone network in the same way that traffic is routed between the VM in the same VNet through private IP addresses.

You can create a VNet peering using the Azure portal, PowerShell or Azure CLI. Figure 4-16 shows VNETA and VNETB, and they are both in the North Central Azure region. These two VNets will be used to describe how to create VNet peerings.

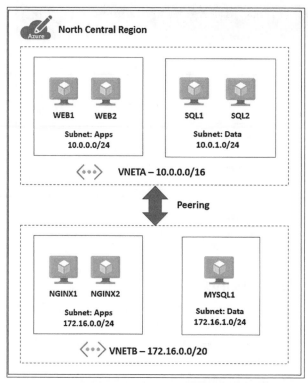

**FIGURE 4-16** VNet peering between two networks in the North Central Region

## Creating a VNet peering using the Azure portal

The VNets you wish to peer must already be created to establish a VNet peering. To create a new VNet peering from VNETA to VNETB as shown in Figure 4-17, connect to the Azure portal and locate VNETA. Once this is located under Settings, click peerings, and then select +Add. This will load the Add peering blade. Use the following inputs to connect a standard VNet peering:

- **Name**    VNETA-to-VNETB
- **Peer Details**    Resource Manager (leave the I Know My Resource ID unchecked)
- **Subscription**    Select the Subscription for VNETB
- **Virtual Network**    Choose VNETB
- **Configuration**    Enabled (leave the remaining three boxes unchecked for this simple VNet Peering)

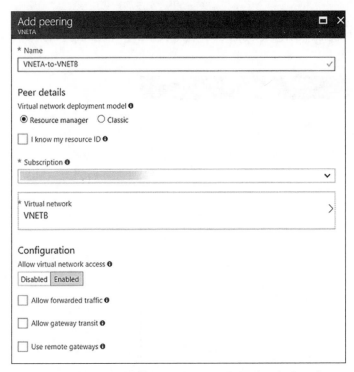

**FIGURE 4-17** Adding peering from VNETA to VNETB using the Portal

Once this process has been completed, the VNet peering will appear in the portal along with the initiation of peering status, as seen in Figure 4-18. To complete the VNet peering, you will follow the same steps on VNETB.

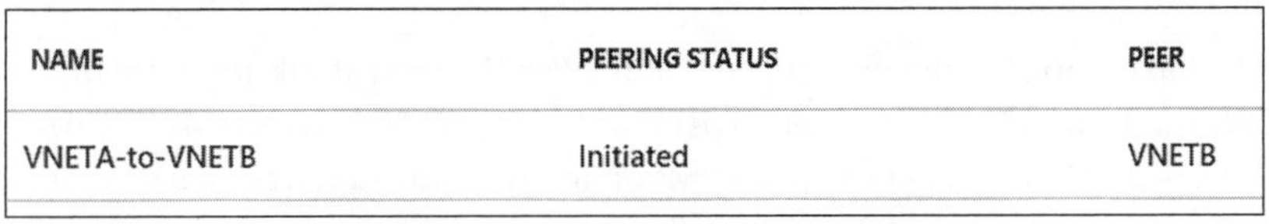

| NAME | PEERING STATUS | PEER |
|------|----------------|------|
| VNETA-to-VNETB | Initiated | VNETB |

**FIGURE 4-18** VNETA-to-VNETB Peering showing as Initiated in the Azure Portal

Now, in the portal, complete the same steps using VNETB. Open VNETB in the Azure portal and click peerings. Next, click +Add and complete the Add peering blade by using the following inputs, as shown in Figure 4-19:

- **Name**   VNETB-to-VNETA
- **Peer Details**   Resource Manager (Leave the I Know My Resource ID checkbox unchecked)
- **Subscription**   Select the Subscription for VNETA

- **Virtual Network**    Choose VNETA
- **Configuration**    Enabled (leave the other three boxes unchecked for this simple peering)

**FIGURE 4-19** Adding peering from VNETB to VNETA using the Portal

Once the portal has completed the provisioning of the VNet Peering, it will appear in the peering of VNETB and show as Connected with a peer of VNETA, as seen in Figure 4-20. Now the two VNets: VNETA and VNETB are peers, and VMs on these networks can see each other. They are accessible, as if this was one Virtual Network.

| NAME | PEERING STATUS | PEER |
| --- | --- | --- |
| VNETB-to-VNETA | Connected | VNETA |

**FIGURE 4-20** VNETB-to-VNETA Peering showing as Connected in the Azure Portal

In Figure 4-21, the peering blade of VNETA shows the peering status VNETA-to-VNETB is also as Connected to VNETB.

| NAME | PEERING STATUS | PEER |
|------|----------------|------|
| VNETA-to-VNETB | Connected | VNETB |

FIGURE 4-21 VNETA-to-VNETB Peering showing as Connected in the Azure Portal

## Creating a VNet peering using PowerShell

When creating a new VNet peering using PowerShell, you will first leverage the Get-AzureRm-VirtualNetwork cmdlet to assign information about the VNETA and VNETB into two variables. Using the Add-AzureRmVirtualNetworkPeering, create the VNet peerings on both VNets just as you did in the portal. Upon completion, the VNet peering will provision, and move to a connected peering status. You can use the Get-AzureRmVirtualNetworkPeering cmdlet to verify the peering status of the VNets.

```
# Load VNETA and VNETB into Variables
$vneta = Get-AzureRmVirtualNetwork `
-Name "VNETA" `
-ResourceGroupName "VNETARG"

$vnetb = Get-AzureRmVirtualNetwork `
-Name "VNETB" `
-ResourceGroupName "VNETBRG"

# Peer VNETA to VNETB.
Add-AzureRmVirtualNetworkPeering `
  -Name 'VNETA-to-VNETB' `
  -VirtualNetwork $vneta `
  -RemoteVirtualNetworkId $vnetb.Id

# Peer VNETB to VNETA.
Add-AzureRmVirtualNetworkPeering `
  -Name 'VNETA-to-VNETB' `
  -VirtualNetwork $vnetb `
  -RemoteVirtualNetworkId $vneta.Id

#Check on the Peering Status
  Get-AzureRmVirtualNetworkPeering `
  -ResourceGroupName VNETARG `
  -VirtualNetworkName VNETA `
  | Format-Table VirtualNetworkName, PeeringState
```

## Creating VNet Peering using the Azure CLI

To create a VNet peering using the Azure CLI, you will need to use the az network vnet show command to get the Resource ID of each VNet. Next, you will use the az network vnet peering create command to create each of the VNet peerings. Upon successfully running these commands, you can use the az network vnet peering list command to see the peering status as Connected.

```
# Get the Resource IDs for VNETA and VNETB.
az network vnet show --resource-group VNETAResourceGroupName --name VNETA
--query id --out tsv
az network vnet show --resource-group VNETBResourceGroupName --name VNETB
 --query id --out tsv

# Peer VNETB to VNET: the output from the Command to find the Resource ID
 for VNETA & VNETB is used with the --remote-vnet-id argument
az network vnet peering create --name VNETA-to-VNETB --resource-group VNETARG
 --vnet-name VNETA --allow-vnet-access --remote-vnet-id /subscriptions/
11111111-1111-1111-1111-111111111111/resourceGroups/VNETBRG/
providers/Microsoft.Network/virtualNetworks/VNETB

# Peer VNETB to VNETA. the output from the Command to find the Resource ID for
 VNETA is used with the --remote-vnet-id argument
az network vnet peering create --name VNETB-to-VNETA --resource-group
VNETBRG --vnet-name VNETB --allow-vnet-access --remote-vnet-id /subscriptions/
11111111-1111-1111-1111-111111111111/resourceGroups/VNETARG/providers/
Microsoft.Network/virtualNetworks/VNETA

#To See the Current State of the Peering
az network vnet peering list --resource-group VNETARG --vnet-name VNETA -o table
```

## Setup Network Security Groups (NSGs)

A network security group (NSG) is a networking filter (firewall) containing a list of security rules, which when applied allow or deny network traffic to resources connected to Azure VNets. These rules can manage both inbound and outbound traffic. NSGs can be associated to subnets and/or individual network interfaces attached to ARM VMs and to classic VMs. Each NSG has the following properties regardless of where it is associated:

- NSG Name
- Azure region where the NSG is located
- Resource group
- Rules that define whether inbound or outbound traffic is allowed or denied

***EXAM TIP***

**When an NSG is associated to a subnet, the rules apply to all resources connected to the subnet. Traffic can further be restricted by also associating an NSG to a VM or NIC. NSGs that are associated to subnets are said to be filtering "North/South" traffic, meaning packets flow into and out of a subnet. NSGs that are associated to network interfaces are said to be filtering "East/West" traffic, or how the VMs within the subnet connect to each other.**

## NSG Rules

NSG Rules are the mechanism defining traffic the administrator is looking to control. Table 4-3 captures the important information to understand about NSG Rules.

**TABLE 4-3** NSG properties

| PROPERTY | DESCRIPTION | CONSTRAINTS | CONSIDERATIONS |
|---|---|---|---|
| Name | Name of the rule | Must be unique within the region. Must end with a letter, number, or underscore. Cannot exceed 80 characters. | You can have several rules within an NSG, so make sure you follow a naming convention that allows you to identify the function of your rule. |
| Protocol | Protocol to match for the rule | TCP, UDP, or * | Using * as a protocol includes ICMP (East-West traffic only), as well as UDP and TCP, can reduce the number of rules you need. This is a very broad approach, so it's recommended that you only use when necessary. |
| Source port range | Source port range to match for the rule | Single port number from 1 to 65535, port range (example: 1-65535), or * (for all ports) | Source ports could be ephemeral. Unless your client program is using a specific port, use * in most cases. Try to use port ranges as much as possible to avoid the need for multiple rules. Multiple ports or port ranges cannot be grouped by a comma. |
| Destination port range | Destination port range to match for the rule | Single port number from 1 to 65535, port range (example: 1-65535), or * (for all ports) | Try to use port ranges as much as possible to avoid the need for multiple rules. Multiple ports or port ranges cannot be grouped by a comma. |
| Source address prefix | Source address prefix or tag to match for the rule | Single IP address (example: 10.10.10.10), IP subnet (example: 192.168.1.0/24), Tag or * (for all addresses) | Consider using ranges, default tags, and * to reduce the number of rules. |
| Destination address prefix | Destination address prefix or tag to match for the rule | Single IP address (example: 10.10.10.10), IP subnet (example: 192.168.1.0/24), Tag or * (for all addresses) | Consider using ranges, default tags, and * to reduce the number of rules. |
| Direction | Direction of traffic to match for the rule | Inbound or outbound | Inbound and outbound rules are processed separately, based on direction. |

| PROPERTY | DESCRIPTION | CONSTRAINTS | CONSIDERATIONS |
|----------|-------------|-------------|----------------|
| Priority | Rules are checked in the order of priority. Once a rule applies, no more rules are tested for matching. | Unique Number between 100 and 4096. Uniqueness is only within this NSG. | Consider creating rules jumping priorities by 100 for each rule to leave space for new rules you might create in the future. |
| Access | Type of access to apply if the rule matches | Allow or deny | Keep in mind that if an allow rule is not found for a packet, the packet is dropped. |

## Default Rules

All NSGs have a set of default rules, as shown in Table 4-5 and Table 4-6. These default rules cannot be deleted, but since they have the lowest possible priority, they can be overridden by the rules that you create. The lower the number, the sooner it will take precedence.

The default rules allow and disallow traffic as follows:

- **Virtual network**   Traffic originating and ending in a Virtual Network is allowed both in inbound and outbound directions.
- **internet**   **O**utbound traffic is allowed, but inbound traffic is blocked.
- **Load balancer**   Allow Azure's load balancer to probe the health of your VMs and role instances. If you are not using a load balanced set, you can override this rule.

**TABLE 4-5** Default Inbound Rules

| Name | Priority | Source IP | Source Port | Destination IP | Protocol | Access |
|------|----------|-----------|-------------|----------------|----------|--------|
| AllowVNetInBound | 65000 | VirtualNetwork | * | VirtualNetwork | * | Allow |
| AllowAzureLoad BalancerInBound | 65001 | AzureLoadBalancer | * | * | * | Allow |
| DenyAllInBound | 65500 | * | * | * | * | Deny |

**TABLE 4-6** Default Outbound Rules

| Name | Priority | Source IP | Source Port | Destination IP | Protocol | Access |
|------|----------|-----------|-------------|----------------|----------|--------|
| AllowVNetOutBound | 65000 | VirtualNetwork | * | VirtualNetwork | * | Allow |
| AllowinternetOutBound | 65001 | * | * | internet | * | Allow |
| DenyAllOutBound | 65500 | * | * | * | * | Deny |

**EXAM TIP**

NSG Rules are enforced based on their Priority. Priority values start from 100 and go to 4096. Rules will be read and enforced starting with 100 then 101, 102 etc., until all rules have been evaluated in this order. Rules with the priority "closest" to 100 will be enforced first. For example, if you had an inbound rule that allowed TCP traffic on Port 80 with a priority of 250 and another that denied TCP traffic on Port 80 with a priority of 125, the NSG rule of deny would be put in place. This is because the "deny rule", with a priority of 125 is closer to 100 than the "allow rule", containing a priority of 250.

## Default Tags

Default tags are system-provided identifiers to address a category of IP addresses. You can use default tags in the source address prefix and destination address prefix properties of any rule.

There are three default tags you can use:

- **VirtualNetwork (Resource Manager) (VIRTUAL_NETWORK for classic)** This tag includes the Virtual Network address space (CIDR ranges defined in Azure) all connected on-premises address spaces and connected Azure VNets (local networks).

- **AzureLoadBalancer (Resource Manager) (AZURE_LOADBALANCER for classic)** This tag denotes Azure's infrastructure load balancer. The tag translates to an Azure datacenter IP where Azure's health probes originate.

- **internet (Resource Manager) (INTERNET for classic)** This tag denotes the IP address space that is outside the Virtual Network and reachable by public internet. The range includes the Azure owned public IP space.

> **MORE INFORMATION  MICROSOFT AZURE DATACENTER IP RANGES**
>
> The Microsoft Azure Datacenter IP Ranges can be downloaded at this link: *https://www.microsoft.com/en-us/download/details.aspx?id=41653*. This file contains the IP address ranges (including compute, SQL, and storage ranges) used in the Microsoft Azure datacenters. An updated file is posted weekly that reflects the currently deployed ranges and any upcoming changes to the IP ranges. New ranges appearing in the file are not used in the datacenters for at least one week. By downloading this file once a week, network admins have an updated method to correctly identify services running in Azure. This is often used to whitelist Azure services on corporate firewalls.

## Associating NSGs

NSGs are used to define the rules of how traffic is filtered for your IaaS deployments in Azure. NSGs by themselves are not implemented until they are "associated", with a resource in Azure. NSGs can be associated to ARM network interfaces (NIC), which are associated to the VMs, or subnets.

For NICs associated to VMs, the rules are applied to all traffic to/from that Network Interface where it is associated. It is possible to have a multi-NIC VM, and you can associate the same or different NSG to each Network Interface. When NSGs are applied to subnets, rules are applied to traffic to/from all resources connect to that subnet.

**EXAM TIP**

Understanding the effective rules of NSGs is critical for the exam. Security rules are applied to the traffic by priority in each NSG in the following order:

- **NSG applied to subnet** If a subnet NSG has a matching rule to deny traffic, the packet is dropped.
- **NSG applied to NIC** If VM\NIC NSG has a matching rule that denies traffic, packets are dropped at the VM\NIC, even if a subnet NSG has a matching rule that allows traffic.

Outbound traffic:

- **NSG applied to NIC** If a VM\NIC NSG has a matching rule that denies traffic, packets are dropped.
- **NSG applied to subnet** If a subnet NSG has a matching rule that denies traffic, packets are dropped, even if a VM\NIC NSG has a matching rule that allows traffic.

## Configuring and Associating NSGs with Subnets

NSGs are a bit different than other types of resources in Azure given they are first created. You must add rules to them (inbound or outbound), and they must be associated to have the desired effect of filtering traffic based on those rules. Remember that NSGs with no rules will have the six default rules covered earlier in this section.

NSGs can be configured and associated with subnets using the Azure portal, PowerShell or the Azure CLI.

## Creating an NSG and associating with a subnet using the Azure portal

To create a NSG using the portal, first click New, then Networking, and select network security group. Once the Create Network Security Group blade loads you will need to provide a Name, the Subscription where your resources are located, the resource group for the NSG and the Location (this must be the same as the resources you wish to apply the NSG). In Figure 4-22, the NSG will be created to allow HTTP traffic into the Apps subnet and be named AppsNSG.

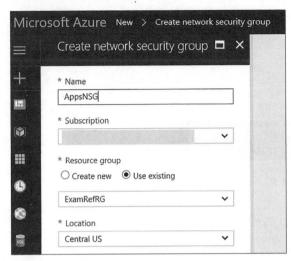

**FIGURE 4-22** Creating a Network Security Group using the Azure Portal

After AppsNSG is created, the portal opens the Overview blade. Here, you see that the NSG has been created, but there are no inbound or outbound security rules beyond the default rules. In Figure 4-23, the Inbound Security Rules blade of the AppsNSG is shown.

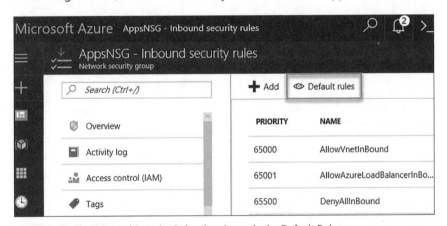

**FIGURE 4-23** The Inbound Security Rules showing only the Default Rules

The next step is to create the inbound rule for HTTP. Under the settings area, click on Inbound Security Rules link. The next step will be to click +Add to allow HTTP traffic on Port 80 into the Apps subnet. In the Add inbound security rule blade, configure the following items, and click OK as seen in Figure 4-24.

- **Source** Any
- **Source** Port Ranges *
- **Destination** IP Addresses
- **Destination IP Addresses/CIDR Ranges** The Apps Subnet: 10.0.0.0/24

- **Destination Port Ranges**  80
- **Protocol**  TCP
- **Action**  Allow
- **Priority**  100
- **Name**  Port 80_HTTP

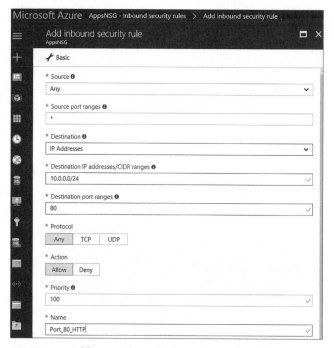

**FIGURE 4-24**  Adding an Inbound Rule to allow HTTP traffic

Once the portal is saved the inbound rule, it will appear in the portal. Review your rule to ensure it has been created correctly. This NSG with its default rules and the newly created inbound rule named Port_80_HTTP are not filtering any traffic. It has yet to be associated with a subnet or a Network Interface, so the rules are currently not in effect. The next task will be to associate it with the Apps subnet. In the Azure portal / Settings, click subnets button, and click +Associate. The portal will ask for two configurations: "Name of the Virtual Network" and the "Name of the subnet". In Figure 4-25, the VNet ExamRefVNET and subnet Apps has been selected.

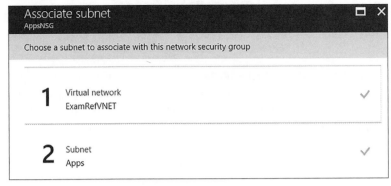

**Associate subnet**
AppsNSG

Choose a subnet to associate with this network security group

**1** Virtual network
ExamRefVNET                                          ✓

**2** Subnet
Apps                                                 ✓

**FIGURE 4-25** The AppsNSG has been associated with the Apps Subnet

After being saved, the rules of the NSG are now being enforced for all network interfaces that are associated with this subnet. This means that TCP traffic on Port 80 is allowed for all VMs that are connected to this subnet. Of course, you need to have a webserver VM configured and listening on Port 80 to respond, but with this NSG, you have opened the ability for Port 80 traffic to flow to the VMs in this subnet from any other subnet in the world.

> **IMPORTANT NSGS**
>
> Remember that NSGs can be associated with network interfaces as well as subnets. For example, if a webserver is connected to this Apps subnet and it didn't have an NSG associated with its network interface, the traffic would be allowed. If the VM had an NSG associated to its network interface, an inbound rule configured exactly like the PORT_80_HTTP rule created here would be required to allow the traffic through. To learn how to work with NSGs associated to network interfaces in Skill 4.3 Configure ARM VM Networking.

## Creating an NSG and associating with a subnet using PowerShell

To create an NSG and configure the rules by using PowerShell, you need to use the New-AzureRmNetworkSecurityRuleConfig and New-AzureRmNetworkSecurityGroup PowerShell cmdlets together. In this example, it's assumed that you have run the Login-AzureRmAccount command and have already created a resource group and the Vnet (created from the earlier example of creating a Vnet by using PowerShell).

```
#Build a new Inbound Rule to Allow TCP Traffic on Port 80 to the Subnet
$rule1 = New-AzureRmNetworkSecurityRuleConfig -Name PORT_HTTP_80 `
                                    -Description "Allow HTTP" `
                                    -Access Allow `
                                    -Protocol Tcp `
                                    -Direction Inbound `
                                    -Priority 100 `
                                    -SourceAddressPrefix * `
                                    -SourcePortRange * `
                                    -DestinationAddressPrefix 10.0.0.0/24 `
                                    -DestinationPortRange 80
```

```
$nsg = New-AzureRmNetworkSecurityGroup -ResourceGroupName ExamRefRGPS `
                                       -Location centralus `
                                       -Name "AppsNSG" `
                                       -SecurityRules $rule1
```

After the NSG has been created along with the inbound rule, next you need to associate this with the subnet to control the flow of network traffic using this filter. To achieve this goal, you need to use Get-AzureRmVirtualNetwork and the Set-AzureRmVirtualNetworkSubnetConfig. After the configuration on the subnet has been set, use Set-AzureRmVirtualNetwork to save the configuration in Azure.

```
#Associate the Rule with the Subnet Apps in the Virtual Network ExamRefVNET-PS
$vnet = Get-AzureRmVirtualNetwork -ResourceGroupName ExamRefRGPS -Name ExamRefVNET-PS

Set-AzureRmVirtualNetworkSubnetConfig -VirtualNetwork $vnet `
                                      -Name Apps `
                                      -AddressPrefix 10.0.0.0/24 `
                                      -NetworkSecurityGroup $nsg
Set-AzureRmVirtualNetwork -VirtualNetwork $vnet
```

## Creating an NSG and associating with a subnet using the Azure CLI

Creating a NSG using the CLI is a multi-step process just as it was with the portal and Power-Shell. The az network nsg create command will first be used to create the NSG. Upon creation of the NSG, will be the rule where we will again allow Port 80 to the subnet. This is created using the az network nsg rule create command. Upon creation, this will be associated with the Apps subnet on the VNet using the az network vnet subnet update command.

```
# Create the NSG

az network nsg create --resource-group ExamRefRGCLI --name AppsNSG

# Create the NSG Inbound Rule allowing TCP traffic on Port 80

az network nsg rule create --resource-group ExamRefRGCLI --name PORT_HTTP_80
--nsg-name AppsNSG --direction Inbound --priority 100 --access Allow
--source-address-prefix "*" --source-port-range "*" --destination-address-prefix "*"
 --destination-port-range "80" --description "Allow HTTP" --protocol TCP

# Associate the NSG with the ExamRefVNET-CLI Apps Subnet

az network vnet subnet update --resource-group ExamRefRGCLI
--vnet-name ExamRefVNET-CLI --name Apps --network-security-group AppsNSG
```

## Deploy a VM into a Virtual Network

VMs can only be deployed into Virtual Networks. VNets provide the networking capabilities that make it possible to benefit from the services of the VM you deploy. The Azure portal allows you to create a VM in an existing Virtual Network, requiring you to specify the subnet. Another option is to create a new VNet while you are creating the new VM.

After a VM is deployed into a VNet, it cannot be moved to another VNet (without deleting it and re-creating), so it is important to consider carefully which VNet the VM should be deployed to during creation.

When creating a VM using the Azure portal, the VNets available to you are filtered to only those in the same subscription and region where you are creating the VM. As seen in Figure 4-26, the selection of the VNet is on Step 3 of creating a VM in the portal after the Basics such as the Name, Location and resource group are selected along with the Size of the VM in Step 2.

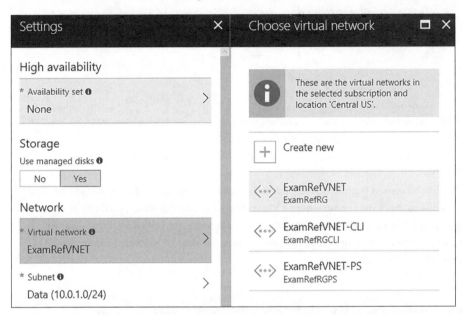

**FIGURE 4-26** The Virtual Network is selected from a list of those in the same subscription and Azure Region.

**EXAM TIP**

Availability sets are used to inform the Azure fabric that two or more of your VMs are providing the same workload and thus should not be susceptible to the same fault or update domains. If you select an availability set during the creation of a VM in the portal, you can only deploy your VM to the VNet where the other VMs are deployed and the option to create a new VNet is removed.

After you select the VNet where the VM is connected, you are required to specify the subnet. In Figure 4-27, the subnet choices are only those that are within the VNet that was selected previously.

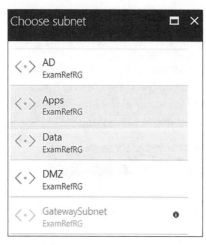

**FIGURE 4-27** A subnet is required to be selected when provisioning a VM into a VNet

***EXAM TIP***

VMs cannot be moved from one VNet to another without deleting and recreating them, but it is possible to move the subnet where a VM is located within the same VNet. This is done by changing the IP configuration of the NIC. If the VM has a static IP address this must be changed to dynamic prior to the move. This is due to the static IP address being outside the address range of the new subnet.

***MORE INFORMATION*** **DEPLOYING VMS TO VIRTUAL NETWORKS**

To learn more about how to deploy VMs to Virtual Networks, refer to Skill 2.1 Deploy Workloads on Azure Resource Manager Virtual Machines.

## Implement Application Gateway

Microsoft Azure Application Gateway (App Gateway), is a feature rich dedicated virtual appliance providing application delivery controller (ADC) as a service. This service allows for different types of layer 7 load balancing. App Gateway assists you in optimizing a web farm by offloading CPU intensive SSL termination. It can also provide layer 7 routing capabilities including round robin distribution of incoming traffic, cookie-based session affinity and URL path-based routing.

The App Gateway can host up to 20 websites at the same time, and can be configured as internet facing gateway, internal only gateway, or a combination of both. It also supports the use of Azure services as a backend such as Azure Web Apps and API Gateways.

App Gateway provides health monitoring of backend resources and custom probes to monitor for more specific scenarios. These are used by the App Gateway to know what servers are online and ready for server traffic. This is critical in providing the high-availability required by administrators.

---

**EXAM TIP**

App Gateway performs load balancing using a round robin scheme and its Load balancing is accomplished at Layer 7. This means it only handles HTTP(S) and WebSocket traffic. This is different from the Azure load balancer which works at Layer 4 for many different types of TCP and UDP traffic. It can offload SSL Traffic, handle cookie-based session affinity and act as a Web Application Firewall (WAF).

---

## Web Application Firewall (WAF)

A key capability of App Gateway is acting as a web application firewall (WAF). When enabled, the WAF provides protection to web applications from common web vulnerabilities and exploits. These include common web-based attacks such as cross-site scripting, SQL injection attacks and session hijacking.

## Cookie-based session affinity

The cookie-based session affinity is a common requirement of many web applications. It is required when your application needs to maintain a user session on the same back-end server. By using gateway-managed cookies, App Gateway will direct all traffic from a user session to the same back-end for processing.

## Secure Sockets Layer (SSL) offload

Security is critical for all web applications, and one of the key tasks of web servers is dealing with the overhead of decrypting HTTPS traffic. The App Gateway will take this burden off your web servers by terminating the SSL connection at the Application Gateway and forwarding the request to the server unencrypted. This doesn't mean that the site is now open to hackers as App Gateway will re-encrypt the response before sending it back to the client. It will still be critical to ensure that NSGs are used extensively on the subnets of the VNet where the App Gateway and Web Servers are deployed. This is to ensure the unencrypted traffic can't be seen by others.

## End to End SSL

App Gateway supports end to end encryption of traffic. It does this by terminating the SSL connection at the App Gateway and applying routing rules to the traffic. It re-encrypts the packet, and forwards it to the appropriate backend based on the routing rules defined. All responses from the web server go through the same process back to the end user.

## URL-based content routing

URL routing allows for directing traffic to different back-end servers based on the content being requested by the user. Typical load balancers will just "spread" the traffic across servers. But with URL routing, you can determine based on the traffic being requested which servers are leveraged. For example, traffic for a folder called /images could be sent to one farm of servers and traffic for folder called /video could be sent to a CDN. This capability reduces the unneeded load on backends that don't serve specific content.

> **MORE INFORMATION  AZURE APPLICATION GATEWAY**
>
> To read more about the Azure Application Gateway follow this link: *https://docs.microsoft.com/en-us/azure/application-gateway/application-gateway-introduction*.

## Application Gateway Sizes

There are three sizes of deployable App Gateways: Small, Medium, and Large. You can create up to 50 application gateways per subscription, and each application gateway can have up to 10 instances each. Each application gateway can consist of 20 http listeners. Table 4-7 shows an average performance throughput for each application gateway instance with SSL offload enabled.

**TABLE 4-7** Performance throughput of the App Gateway

| Back-end page response | Small | Medium | Large |
|---|---|---|---|
| 6K | 7.5 Mbps | 13 Mbps | 50 Mbps |
| 100K | 35 Mbps | 100 Mbps | 200 Mbps |

## Deployment into Virtual Networks

Application Gateway requires its own subnet. When creating your VNets, ensure you leave enough address space to incorporate one for the App Gateway. The dedicated subnet for your App Gateway will need to be provisioned before creating the App Gateway. Given there is a limit of 50 App Gateways per subscription, this VNet doesn't need to be larger than a /26 CIDR, as this will provide 59 usable Addresses. Also, once an App Gateway is deployed to this subnet, only other App Gateway can be added to it.

## Creating an App Gateway using the Azure Portal

This is a three-step process. First is the addition of the dedicated subnet to your VNet. In the example, this subnet was already added and named AppGateway with an address space of 10.0.98.0/26.

Secondly, create the App Gateway using open the Azure portal. As seen in Figure 4-28, New. Then, select Networking followed by Application Gateway.

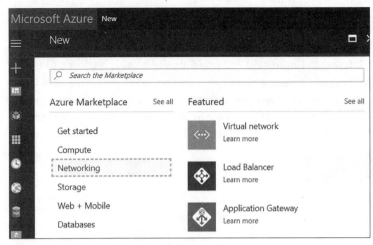

**FIGURE 4-28** Creating a New Application Gateway using the Azure Portal

The Create Application Gateway blade opens. Next complete the basics, such as the name, tier (Standard or WAF), size of the App Gateway, and number of instances of the App Gateway, among others, as shown in Figure 4-29.

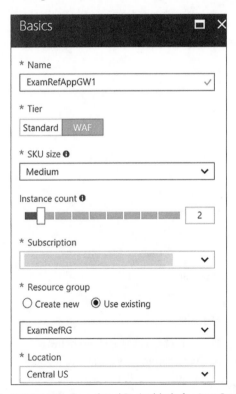

**FIGURE 4-29** Completed Basics blade for App Gateway

The third step is the Settings blade where critical information is collected in regards to how the App Gateway will be deployed. The first selection is the Virtual Network where it will be deployed. A subnet will be selected next. Remember, the subnet will already have to be created before creating the App Gateway. In Figure 4-30, the App Gateway is being deployed to the ExamRefVNET into a subnet called AppGateway using a /26. Next will be the Frontend IP Configuration (this is important if this App Gateway will be made available to the internet or only the Intranet). Here you can select Public and then create a New Public IP Address. Additional selections will be the Protocol, Port, and WAF configurations.

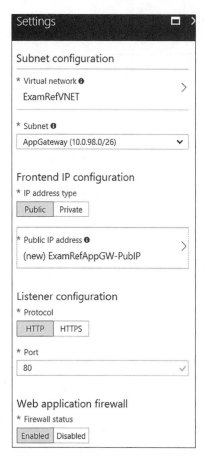

FIGURE 4-30 Completed Settings blade for an internet facing App Gateway

## Creating an App Gateway using the PowerShell

Creating an App Gateway using PowerShell is somewhat complex because there are many configurations that are required for this Virtual Appliance. These commands assume that your resource group was already created along with the VNet ExamRefVNET-PS that was created in earlier examples. You can walk through each part of the code to get an idea of how this created.

First you will create a new subnet in the VNet for the App Gateway instances. Remember, this subnet is only to be used by the App Gateway. This code will use the Get-AzureRMVirtualNetwork, Add-AzureRmVirtualNetworksubnetConfig and Set-AzureRmVirtualNetwork cmdlets.

```
# Create a subnet in the ExamRefVNET-PS VNet with the Address Range of 10.0.98.0/26
$vnet = Get-AzureRmVirtualNetwork -ResourceGroupName ExamRefRGPS `
                                  -Name ExamRefVNET-PS
Add-AzureRmVirtualNetworkSubnetConfig -Name AppGateway `
                                      -AddressPrefix "10.0.98.0/26" `
                                      -VirtualNetwork $vnet
Set-AzureRmVirtualNetwork -VirtualNetwork $vnet
```

The next step is to create the Public IP Address that will be used by the App Gateway. This code uses the New-AzureRMPublicIpAddress cmdlet. It is important to note that you can't use a Static IP Address with the App Gateway.

```
# Create a Public IP address that is used to connect to the application gateway.
$publicip = New-AzureRmPublicIpAddress -ResourceGroupName ExamRefRGPS `
                                       -Name ExamRefAppGW-PubIP `
                                       -Location "Central US" `
                                       -AllocationMethod Dynamic
```

The following commands then used to create the various configurations for the App Gateway. Each of these commands use different cmdlets to load these configurations into variables that are ultimately passed to the New-AzureRmApplicationGateway cmdlet. Upon completion of the App Gateway, the last command will set the WAF configuration.

```
# Create a gateway IP configuration. The gateway picks up an IP address from the
 configured subnet

$vnet = Get-AzureRmvirtualNetwork -Name "ExamRefVNET-PS" -ResourceGroupName
 "ExamRefRGPS"
$subnet = Get-AzureRmVirtualNetworkSubnetConfig -Name "AppGateway" -VirtualNetwork
 $vnet
$gipconfig = New-AzureRmApplicationGatewayIPConfiguration -Name "AppGwSubnet01"
 -Subnet $subnet

# Configure a backend pool with the addresses of your web servers. You could add
 pool members here as well.
$pool = New-AzureRmApplicationGatewayBackendAddressPool -Name "appGatewayBackendPool"

# Configure backend http settings to determine the protocol and port that is used
 when sending traffic to the backend servers.
$poolSetting = New-AzureRmApplicationGatewayBackendHttpSettings -Name
                "appGatewayBackendHttpSettings" `
                -Port 80 `
Protocol Http `
 -CookieBasedAffinity Disabled `
 -RequestTimeout 30

# Configure a frontend port that is used to connect to the application gateway
 through the Public IP address
```

```
$fp = New-AzureRmApplicationGatewayFrontendPort -Name frontendport01 `
                                    -Port 80
# Configure the frontend IP configuration with the Public IP address created earlier.
$fipconfig = New-AzureRmApplicationGatewayFrontendIPConfig -Name fipconfig01 `
 -PublicIPAddress $publicip


# Configure the listener.  The listener is a combination of the front-end IP
configuration, protocol, and port
$listener = New-AzureRmApplicationGatewayHttpListener -Name listener01 `
                                        -Protocol Http `
                                        -FrontendIPConfiguration $fipconfig `
                                        -FrontendPort $fp


# Configure a basic rule that is used to route traffic to the backend servers.
$rule = New-AzureRmApplicationGatewayRequestRoutingRule -Name rule1 `
                                        -RuleType Basic `
                                        -BackendHttpSettings
$poolSetting `

                                        -HttpListener $listener `
                                        -BackendAddressPool $pool


# Configure the SKU for the application gateway, this determines the size and
 whether WAF is used.
$sku = New-AzureRmApplicationGatewaySku -Name "WAF_Medium" `
                                -Tier "WAF" `
                                -Capacity 2
# Create the application gateway
New-AzureRmApplicationGateway -Name ExamRefAppGWPS `
                            -ResourceGroupName ExamRefRGPS `
                            -Location "Central US" `
                            -BackendAddressPools $pool `
                            -BackendHttpSettingsCollection $poolSetting `
                            -FrontendIpConfigurations $fipconfig `
                            -GatewayIpConfigurations $gipconfig `
                            -FrontendPorts $fp `
                            -HttpListeners $listener `
                            -RequestRoutingRules $rule `
                            -Sku $sku `
                            -WebApplicationFirewallConfiguration


# Set WAF Configuration to Enabled
$AppGw = Get-AzureRmApplicationGateway -Name ExamRefAppGWPS -ResourceGroupName
 ExamRefRGPS
Set-AzureRmApplicationGatewayWebApplicationFirewallConfiguration -ApplicationGateway
 $AppGw `
                                                -Enabled $True `
                                                -FirewallMode "Detection" `
                                                -RuleSetType "OWASP" `
                                                -RuleSetVersion "3.0"
```

## Creating the App Gateway using the Azure CLI

You will use the az network command with different arguments. The first step will be to create the AppGateway subnet. Next is the Public IP Address followed by the App Gateway Virtual Appliance. The command to create the App Gateway is quite large, but this is common when using the CLI. After the App Gateway has been provisioned, you will then enable the WAF using the az network application gateway command.

```
# Create a subnet for the App Gateway in the ExamRefVNET-CLI VNet with the Address
 Range of 10.0.98.0/26
az network vnet subnet create -g ExamRefRGCLI --vnet-name ExamRefVNET-CLI
               -n AppGateway --address-prefix 10.0.98.0/26

# Create a Public IP address that is used to connect to the application gateway.
az network public-ip create -g ExamRefRGCLI -n ExamRefAppGW-PubIP

# Create the App gateway named ExamRefAppGWCLI
az network application-gateway create -n "ExamRefAppGWCLI" -g "ExamRefRGCLI"
--vnet-name "ExamRefVNET-CLI" --subnet "AppGateway" --capacity 2 --sku WAF_Medium
 --http-settings-cookie-based-affinity Disabled --http-settings-protocol Http
--frontend-port 80 --routing-rule-type Basic --http-settings-port 80
--public-ip-address "ExamRefAppGW-PubIP"

# Enable the WAF
az network application-gateway waf-config set -g "ExamRefRGCLI" -n "ExamRefAppGWCLI"
 --enabled true --rule-set-type OWASP --rule-set-version 3.0
```

# Skill 4.2: Design and implement multi-site or hybrid network connectivity

The term hybrid cloud is used in many ways across the IT industry. Typically, hybrid cloud means to connect your local datacenters to the cloud and run workloads in both locations. This section covers connecting VNets to other VNets, as well as options for connecting your on-premises network to the Azure cloud. There are a range of connection types that can be leveraged for the many scenarios that you as a cloud administrator could face on the exam.

> **This skill covers how to:**
> - Choose the appropriate solution between ExpressRoute, Site-to-Site, and Point-to-Site
> - Choose the appropriate gateway
> - Identity supported devices and software VPN solutions
> - Identify network prerequisites
> - Configure Virtual Networks and multi-site Virtual Networks
> - Implement Virtual Network peering and service chaining

# Choose the appropriate solution between ExpressRoute, Site-to-Site and Point-to-Site

When connecting your on-premises network to a VNet, there are three options that provide connectivity for various use cases. These include Point-to-Site virtual private network (VPN), Site-to-Site VPN, and Azure ExpressRoute.

## Point-to-Site (P2S) virtual private network (VPN)

This connection type is between a single PC connected to your network and Azure VPN Gateway running over the internet. Sometimes referred to as a "VPN Tunnel," this on-demand connection is initiated by the user and secured by using a certificate. The connection uses the SSTP protocol on port 443 to provide encrypted communication over the internet between the PC and the VNet. The P2S connection is very easy to setup because it requires little or no change to your existing network. The latency for a point-to-site VPN is unpredictable because the traffic traverses the internet.

P2S connections are useful for remote employees or those that only want to establish connectivity when they need it and can disconnect from the Azure VNet when they are finished with their tasks. In Figure 4-31, depicts an example of developers or testers that only need to connect to the Azure VNet when they are writing code or performing tests on their applications.

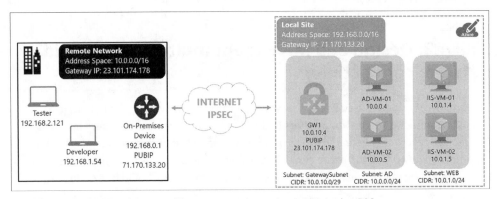

**FIGURE 4-31** Remote Developers and Tester connecting to Azure VNet using P2S

## Site-to-Site (S2S) VPN

S2S connections are durable methods for building cross-premises and hybrid configurations. S2S connections are established between your VPN on-premises device and an Azure VPN Gateway. This connection type enables any on-premises devices you authorize to access VMs and services that are running in an Azure VNet. The connection is known as an IPSec VPN that provides encrypted network traffic crossing over the internet between your on-premises VPN device and the Azure VPN Gateway. The secure encryption method used for these VPN tunnels is IKEv2. Just as with P2S VPNs, the latency for S2S VPNs is unpredictable because the network connection is an internet connection. The on-premises VPN device is required to have a static Public IP address assigned to it and it cannot be located behind a NAT. An example of a S2S VPN is shown in Figure 4-32.

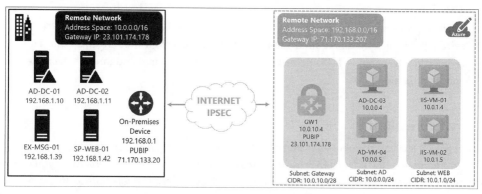

**FIGURE 4-32** S2S VPN connection between Azure and On-Premises

There is a variation of this S2S network where you create more than one VPN connection from your VPN Gateway typically connecting to multiple on-premises sites. This is known as a Multi-Site S2S connection. When working with multiple connections, you must use a route-based VPN type. Because each VNet can only have one VPN Gateway, all connections through the gateway share the available bandwidth. In Figure 4-33, you see an example of a network with three sites and two VNets in different Azure regions.

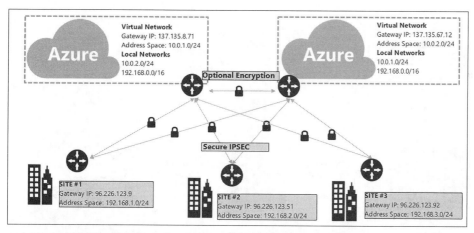

**FIGURE 4-33** Multi-Site S2S Network with three locations and two Azure VNets

S2S VPNs should be used for connecting to Azure on a semi-permanent or permanent basis based on your plans for the cloud. These connections are always on and reliable (only as much as your internet connection though). If there are issues with your internet provider or on the public internet infrastructure, your VPN tunnel could go down or run slowly from time to time. Mission critical workloads running in Azure in a hybrid-cloud configuration should use ExpressRoute with a S2S as a backup.

**EXAM TIP**

**P2S connections do not require an on-premises static, public-facing IP address or a VPN device. S2S connections do required a static Public IP address to ensure zero downtime and they must not be behind a NAT. P2S and S2S connections can be initiated through the same Azure VPN Gateway.**

## Azure ExpressRoute

ExpressRoute lets you connect your on-premises networks into the Microsoft cloud over a private connection hosted by a Microsoft ExpressRoute provider. With ExpressRoute, you can establish connections to Microsoft cloud services, such as Microsoft Azure, Office 365, and Dynamics 365.

ExpressRoute is a secure and reliable private connection. Network traffic does not egress to the internet. The latency for an ExpressRoute circuit is predictable because traffic stays on your provider's network and never touches the internet.

Connectivity can be from a Multiprotocol Label Switching (MPLS), any-to-any IPVPN network, a point-to-point ethernet network, or a virtual cross-connection through a connectivity provider at a co-location facility. Figure 4-34 shows the options for connecting to ExpressRoute.

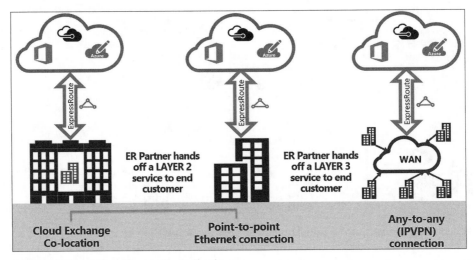

**FIGURE 4-34** Examples of ExpressRoute Circuits

ExpressRoute is only available in certain cities throughout the world, so it is important to check with a provider to determine its availability.

**MORE INFORMATION** **EXPRESSROUTE**

To locate the cities where ExpressRoute can be used and the providers that support the connection review the following article: *https://docs.microsoft.com/en-us/azure/expressroute/expressroute-locations*.

An ExpressRoute connection does not use a VPN Gateway, although it does use a Virtual Network gateway as part of its required configuration. In an ExpressRoute connection, the Virtual Network gateway is configured with the gateway type 'ExpressRoute,' rather than 'VPN'

To connect to Azure using ExpressRoute, set up and manage the routing or contract with a service provider to manage the connection. ExpressRoute uses the BGP routing protocol to facilitate the connections between the routers on the network. There is support for the use of private and public Autonomous System Numbers (ASN), and public or private IPs depending upon which part of the Microsoft cloud that you are connecting to with ExpressRoute.

**EXAM TIP**

BGP Routing is supported on S2S VPNs and ExpressRoute. BPG is the routing protocol that the routers use to track each other's networks and helps to facilitate the movement of network traffic from one network to another. Public Autonomous System Numbers (ASN), are globally unique numbers on the internet just like Public IP addresses. They are managed by groups around the world, such as the American Registry for internet Names (ARIN) in the US and others like it.

Each ExpressRoute circuit has two connections to two Microsoft edge routers from your network edge. Microsoft requires dual BGP connections from your edge to each Microsoft edge router. You can choose not to deploy redundant devices or ethernet circuits at your end; however, connectivity providers use redundant devices to ensure that your connections are handed off to Microsoft in a redundant manner. Figure 4-35 shows a redundant connectivity configuration.

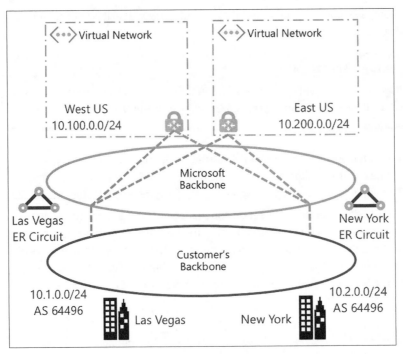

**FIGURE 4-35** Multiple Cities Connected to ExpressRoute in Two Azure Regions

As seen in Figure 4-36, ExpressRoute has three routing domains: Azure Public, Azure Private, and Microsoft. They are configured as an active-active load sharing configuration. Azure Services are assigned categories based on what they provide and have different IP Address schemes within the Azure regions.

- **Azure Private Peering** Azure compute services, namely virtual machines (IaaS) and cloud services (PaaS), that are deployed within a Virtual Network can be connected through the private peering domain. The private peering domain is a trusted extension of your core network into Microsoft Azure.

- **Azure Public Peering** Services such as Azure Storage, SQL databases, and websites are offered on Public IP addresses. You can privately connect to services hosted on Public IP addresses, including VIPs of your cloud services, through the public peering routing domain.

- **Microsoft Peering** ExpressRoute provides private network connectivity to Microsoft cloud services. Software as a Service offerings, like Office 365 and Dynamics 365, were created to be accessed securely and reliably via the internet.

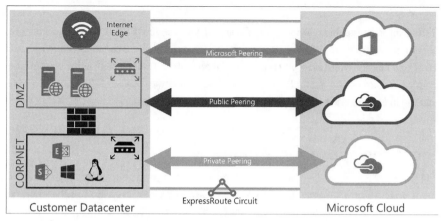

**FIGURE 4-36** ExpressRoute Routing Domains

ExpressRoute can be purchased in different speeds and in one of two modes: Metered or Unlimited.

- **Metered**   All inbound data transfer is free of charge, and all outbound data transfer is charged based on a pre-determined rate. Users are also charged a fixed monthly port fee (based on high availability dual ports).

- **Unlimited**   All inbound and outbound data transfer is free of charge. Users are charged a single fixed monthly port fee (based on high availability dual ports).

### EXAM TIP

ExpressRoute supports the following speeds:  50 Mbps, 100 Mbps, 200 Mbps, 500 Mbps, 1 Gbps, 2 Gbps, 5 Gbps, and 10 Gbps.

There is also a premium add-on that can be enabled if your network is global enterprise in nature. The following features are added to your ExpressRoute circuit when the premium add-on is enabled:

- Increased routing table limit from 4000 routes to 10,000 routes for private peering.

- More than 10 VNets can be connected to the ExpressRoute circuit.

- Connectivity to Office 365 and Dynamics 365.

- Global connectivity over the Microsoft core network. You can now link a VNet in one geopolitical region with an ExpressRoute circuit in another region.

**EXAM TIP**

If the ExpressRoute Premium Add-on is enabled, you can link a VNet created in a different part of the world to your ExpressRoute circuit. For example, you can link a VNet in Europe West to an ExpressRoute circuit created in Silicon Valley. This is also true for your public peering resources. An example of this would be connecting to your SQL Azure database located in Europe West from a circuit in New York.

## Choose the appropriate gateway

A VPN Gateway is a type of Virtual Network gateway that sends encrypted traffic over a public connection to an on-premises location. You can also use VPN Gateways to send encrypted traffic between Azure VNets over the Azure Backbone network. To send encrypted network traffic between your Azure VNET and an on-premises datacenter, you must create a VPN Gateway for your VNet.

Each VNet can only have one VPN Gateway. However, you can create multiple connections to the same VPN Gateway. An example of this is a multi-site connection configuration. When you create multiple connections to the same VPN Gateway, all VPN tunnels, including Point-to-Site VPNs, share the bandwidth that is available for the gateway.

A Virtual Network gateway is composed of two or more VMs that are deployed to a specific subnet called the GatewaySubnet. The VMs that are in the GatewaySubnet are created upon creation of the VPN Gateway. VPN Gateway VMs are configured to contain routing tables and gateway services specific to that VPN Gateway. You can't directly configure the VMs that are part of the VPN Gateway, and you should never deploy additional resources to the Gateway-Subnet.

When you create a VNet gateway using the gateway type **vpn**, it creates a specific type of VPN Gateway that encrypts traffic. The Gateway SKU that you select determines how powerful the provisioned VMs will be to handle the amount of aggregate throughput (network traffic for all devices sending and received through). It is important to note the Basic VPN Gateway is only recommended for very small networks with only a few users. The VPN options are captured in Table 4-8.

**TABLE 4-8** VPN Gateway options

| SKU | S2S/VNet-to-VNet Tunnels (Maximum) | P2S Connections (Maximum) | Aggregate Throughput Benchmark |
| --- | --- | --- | --- |
| VpnGw1 | 30 | 128 | 650 Mbps |
| VpnGw2 | 30 | 128 | 1 Gbps |
| VpnGw3 | 30 | 128 | 1.25 Gbps |
| Basic | 10 | 128 | 100 Mbps |

## Identify support devices and software VPN solutions

To facilitate a Site-to-Site (S2S), cross-premises VPN connection using a VPN Gateway, a VPN device is required to configured on-premises. These S2S connections can be used to create a hybrid solution, or whenever you want to secure connections between your on-premises networks and your VNets.

In partnership with device vendors, Microsoft has a validated a set of standard VPN devices proven to be compatible. These devices range from routers and firewalls to software that can be run on Linux or Windows servers. All of the devices in the device guide should work with the Azure VPN Gateways. If you have a device that is not listed, there is guidance from Microsoft on the standards that are supported and by using this information, it is possible to connect to the Azure network.

> **MORE INFORMATION  APPROVED LIST OF DEVICES**
>
> To locate the approved list of devices and configuration guides, read the following article: *https://docs.microsoft.com/en-us/azure/vpn-gateway/vpn-gateway-about-vpn-devices*.

# Identify network prerequisites

Connecting to the Azure cloud does require proper planning, and there are some very important steps to look at prior to configuring VNets and hybrid connections to Azure.

Here are some considerations that you should start with when determining how to connect your network to Azure:

- **IP address spaces**  It is critical that your IP address spaces don't overlap with existing networks or those that you are planning for in the future.  This is complicated even further when considering that you are most likely building more than one VNet in Azure. It is best to use an offline IP Address Management (IPAM), tool to ensure that all your networks are accounted for before you build anything.

- **Public IP addresses & AS numbers**  If you plan on using S2S or ExpressRoute connections to Azure, it is important to have public registered IP addresses.  If you are using ExpressRoute or BGP with S2S connections having a registered AS number for your company is the proper way to configure the network.

- **VPN devices**  Making sure that you have an approved VPN device is the best bet for creating VPN connections to Azure.  You should test these devices by creating a VPN to a test network to ensure that it works properly as a part of your Azure pilot project.

- **Estimated network throughput** It is important to understand the amount of network traffic that goes from your site to Azure over the VPN Gateway. You need this information to select the VPN Gateway SKU to provision. This is also useful for deciding on the size of the ExpressRoute circuit if you chose to go with this type of configuration.

- **Subscriptions** It is also important to consider the number of subscriptions that you have and if they have the same Azure AD Tenet associated with them. This impacts your network design because there are limits to the various configurations and the number of possible connections, depending upon how you configured the subscriptions for your company.

## Implement Virtual Network peering service chaining

VNet peering allows you to connect two Azure Resource Manager (ARM), VNets located in the same region together without complex integration. The peered VNets must have non-overlapping IP address spaces. The address spaces in either VNet cannot be added to or deleted from a VNet once a VNet is peered with another VNet.

Once they are peered, the VNets appear as one network and the VM in the peered VNets can communicate with each other directly. The traffic between VMs is routed through the Microsoft backbone network in the same way that traffic is routed between VM in the same VNet through private IP addresses.

You can peer VNets that exist in two different subscriptions, if a privileged user of both subscriptions authorizes the peering, and the subscriptions are associated to the same Azure Active Directory tenant. There is also a limit of 50 VNet peerings per subscription.

Figure 4-37 shows two VNets in the North Central region peered together. Notice their IP address spaces do not overlap as this would make the peering impossible.

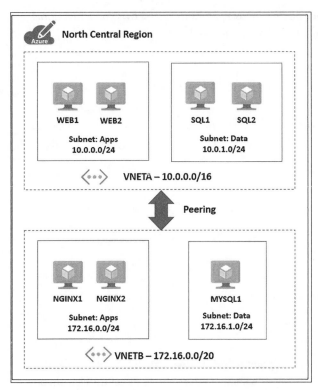

**FIGURE 4-37** VNet peering between two networks in the North Central Region

Network Traffic flowing through VNet peerings is private, as it never touches any gateways or the internet. This connection is low-latency and high-bandwidth between resources in different VNets. The same speed considerations for VMs on the local VNet apply (based on the VM size). Once Vnet peering is enabled, VMs on each VNet will have the ability to use resources in one VNet from another.

**EXAM TIP**

It is possible to peer Virtual Networks created through the Azure Resource Manager to a Virtual Network created using the Azure classic deployment model. Two Azure classic VNets cannot be peered together.

**IMPORTANT** AZURE VNET PEERING

Azure VNet peering between VNets in different Azure regions is in Public Preview.

It is important to understand that VNet peering is between two Virtual Networks. There is no derived transitive relationship across the peerings. If you peer VNetA to VNetB and then peer VNetB with VNetC, VNetA is not peered to VNetC. Figure 4-38 shows you a functional architecture of this and describes how VNetA is not peered to VNetC.

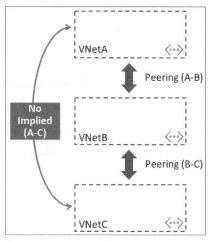

**FIGURE 4-38** Vnet Peerings do not have a transitive relationship

## Service Chaining

You can configure user-defined routes that point to VMs in peered VNets as the "next hop," IP address to enable service chaining. Service chaining enables you to direct traffic from one VNet to a virtual appliance in a peered Virtual Network through user-defined routes. Figure 4-39 provides a view of a network where service chaining is implemented.

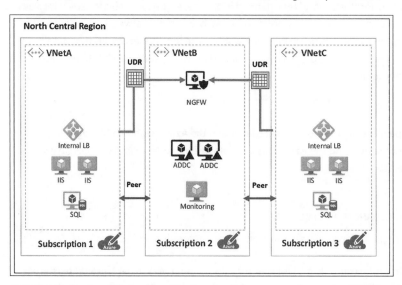

**FIGURE 4-39** Service chaining allows for the use of common services across VNet Peerings

# Configure Virtual Network and Multi-Site Virtual Networks

You can connect VNets to each other, enabling resources connected to either VNet to communicate with each other across VNets. You can use either or both of the following options to connect VNets to each other:

- **Peering**   Enables resources connected to different Azure VNets within the same Azure region to communicate with each other. The bandwidth and latency across the VNets is the same as if the resources were connected to the same VNet.

- **VNet-to-VNet connection**   Enables resources connected to different Azure VNets within the same, or different Azure regions. Unlike peering, bandwidth is limited between VNets because traffic must flow through an Azure VPN Gateway.

Using VNet-to-VNet connections allows for connecting Azure regions to each other via the Microsoft backbone. This configuration allows for always on connections between the Azure datacenters.

Peering and VNet-to-VNet connections can be used together to enable all networks to see each other. Peering would be setup between one or more VNets within the same Azure regions and then one of these networks would have a VNet-to-VNet VPN setup. The Allow Gateway Transit must be turned on for these packets to be leveraged.

## Creating a VNet-to-VNet connection across Azure Regions using a VPN Gateway using the Azure Portal

Figure 4-40 shows a diagram of what you should create. VNETA and VNETB are peered in the North Central Azure regions. Another VNet, VNETC, should be deployed to the North Europe region and then connected to VNETB via a S2S VPN.

The following steps capture the basic process of connecting these networks together:

- Create gateway subnets on each VNETB and VNETC
- Provision virtual network gateways on VNETB and VNETC
- Create connections between the two networks
- Configure VNETA to VNET B peering to Use Remote Gateway
- Configure VNETB to VNETA peering to Allow Gateway Transit

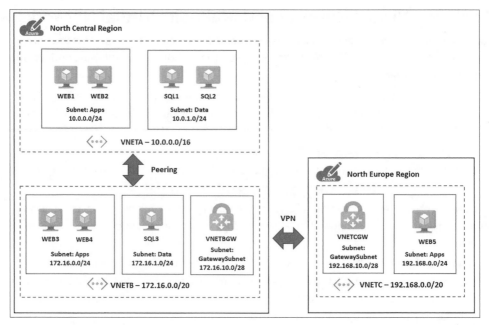

**FIGURE 4-40** Multi-Region VNet deployment using Peering in and VPN Gateway over the Microsoft Backbone

## Create GatewaySubnets on each VNETB and VNETC

Using the portal, navigate to each of the VNets, and click the subnets link under settings. From the subnets blade select the +Gateway subnet and assign an address space using a /28 CIDR, as seen in Figure 4-41 and Figure 4-42.

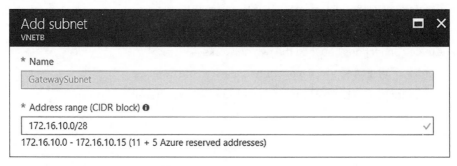

**FIGURE 4-41** Adding a GatewaySubnet to VNETB

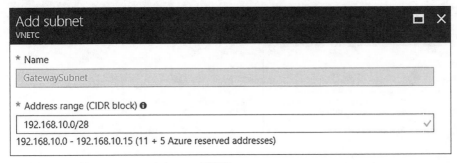

**FIGURE 4-42** Adding a GatewaySubnet to VNETC

## Provision Virtual Network Gateways on VNETB and VNETC

As shown in Figure 4-43 and Figure 4-44, provision the VPN Gateways by using the Azure portal. Click New, Networking, and then select Virtual Network Gateway.

Complete the following information for VNETB:

- **Name**   VNETBGW
- **Gateway type**   VPN
- **VPN Type**   Route-based
- **SKU**   VpnGw1
- **Virtual Network**   VNETB
- **First IP Configuration**   Create New, VNETBGW-PUBIP
- **Location**   North Central US

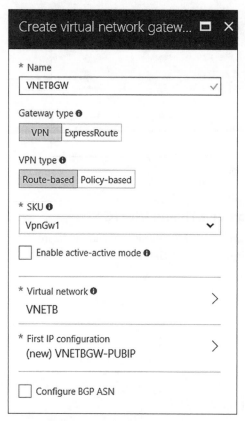

**FIGURE 4-43** Creating the Azure VPN Gateway for VNETB

Complete the following information for VNETC:

- **Name** VNETCGW
- **Gateway type** VPN
- **VPN Type** Route-based
- **SKU** VpnGw1
- **Virtual Network** VNETC
- **First IP Configuration** Create New, VNETCGW-PUBIP
- **Location** North Europe US

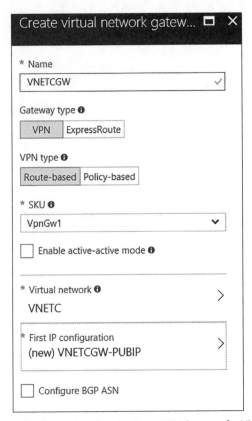

**FIGURE 4-44** Creating the Azure VPN Gateway for VNETC

## Create Connections between the two Networks

After you provision the VPN Gateways, create two connections in Azure to bring up the VPN tunnel. To create this object, open VNETB in the Azure portal, as shown in Figure 4-45. Under Settings, locate Connections and click it to open. When the Connections blade opens, click +Add.

Complete the VNETB Add connection blade by using the following inputs:

- **Name**    VNETB-VNETC-Conn1
- **Connections**    Vnet-to-Vnet
- **Second Virtual Network Gatewa**    VNETCGW
- **Shared Key**    A1B2C3D4E5 (any unique value matching on both sides)

**FIGURE 4-45** Creating the Connection between VNETB to VNETC

This process needs to be repeated for VNETC. Open VNETC in the Azure portal, as shown in Figure 4-46. Under Settings, locate Connections and click it to open. When the Connections blade opens, click +Add.

Complete the VNETC Add connection blade by using the following inputs:

- **Name**   VNETC-VNETB-Conn1
- **Connections**   Vnet-to-Vnet
- **Second Virtual Network Gateway**   VNETBGW
- **Shared Key**   A1B2C3D4E5 (any unique value matching on both sides)

**FIGURE 4-46** Creating the Connection between VNETC to VNETB

## Configure VNETA to VNETB Peering to Use Remote Gateway

To allow packets from VNETA to cross the VPN Gateway configured on VNETB, reach VNETC, you must make a change to the VNETA-to-VNETB peering by opening VNETA in the portal to locate the peerings link. Then open the VNETA-to-VNETB, and select Use Remote Gateways in the Configuration section, as seen in Figure 4-47.

**FIGURE 4-47** Enabling the Use remote gateways option for the VNETA-to-VNETB Peering

## Configure VNETB to VNETA Peering to Allow Gateway Transit

To allow packets from VNETA to VNETC you must make a configuration change to the VNETB-to-VNETA peering. To do so, open the VNETB in the portal and locate the peerings blade. Select the VNEB-to-VNETA connection followed by the Allow Gateway Transit option in the Configuration section, as seen in Figure 4-48.

**FIGURE 4-48** Enabling the Allow gateway transit option for the VNETB-to-VNETA peering

After the connection objects are created, it might take a few minutes for the connection to come up. Figure 4-49 shows the status of the connection object by looking on the Overview blade of VNETB-VNETC-Conn1.

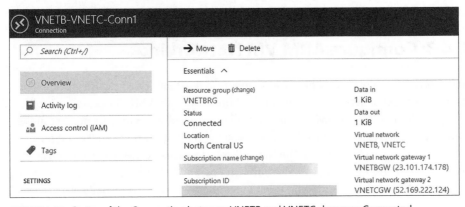

**FIGURE 4-49** Status of the Connection between VNETB and VNETC shown as Connected

## Gateways and On-premises Connectivity

Any VNet can have its own VPN Gateway and use it to connect to an on-premises network. When VNets are peered, this doesn't change. You can also configure VNet- -VNet connections using VPN Gateways. Even the VNet(s) are peered to other VNet(s).

When both options for VNet interconnectivity are configured, the traffic between the VNets flows through the peering configuration (that is, through the Azure backbone).

When VNets are peered in the same region, you can configure the VPN Gateway in the peered VNet as a method to point traffic to an on-premises network. In this case, the VNet using a re-mote gateway unfortunately cannot have its own gateway. A VNet can have only one gateway. The gateway can either be a local or remote gateway. In Figure 4-50, you see VNetA and VNetB located in the West Europe region peered together with VNetA providing VPN services to both networks. In this configuration, all three networks can reach each other.

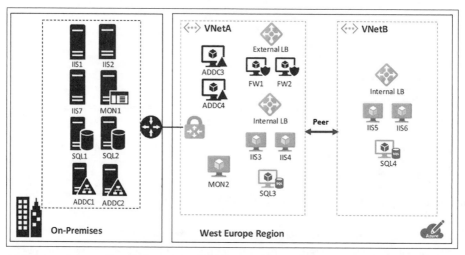

**FIGURE 4-50** Gateway Transit allows peered VNets to connect with networks that are across a VPN Gate-way

# Skill 4.3: Configure ARM VM Networking

Arguably, VMs are the most widely deployed compute in the Public cloud. Azure provides a very deep and rich set of networking configuration possibilities for VMs. These are important to understand from the perspective of the VM, as many configurations that are possible at the VNet level are also possible at the VM level. In this skill, you will study these configurations. Many configurations are performed at the Network Interface level of VMs including public IP Addresses, private IP Addresses, network security groups, and DNS settings. Others focus more on the use of VMs as Web Servers integrate with VMs along with the Azure load balancer and the App Gateway.

**This skill covers how to:**

- Configure Private Static IP addresses
- Public IPs
- DNS at the network interface level
- Network Security Groups (NSGs)
- User Defined Routes (UDRs) with IP Forwarding
- External and Internal Load Balancing with HTTP and TCP Health probes
- Direct Server Return
- Design and Implement Application Gateway

# Configure Private Static IP Addresses

VMs in Azure use TCP/IP to communicate with services in Azure, other VMs you have deployed in Azure, on-premises networks, and the internet.

There are two types of IP addresses you can use in Azure:

- **Public IP addresses**   Used for communication with the internet
- **Private IP addresses**   Used for communication within an Azure virtual network (Vnet), and your on-premises network when you use a VPN Gateway to build a hybrid network

Private IP addresses allow Azure resources to communicate with other resources in a virtual network or an on-premises network through a VPN Gateway or ExpressRoute circuit, without using an internet-reachable IP address.

Using the Azure Resource Manager, a private IP address is associated to the following types of Azure resources:

- VM network interfaces
- Internal load balancers (ILBs)
- Application gateways

Private IP addresses are created with an IPv4 or IPv6 address. VMs cannot communicate between private IPv6 addresses on a Vnet, but can communicate inbound to a private IPv6 address from the internet when using an internet-facing load balancer.

There are two methods used to assign private IP addresses: dynamic or static. The default allocation method is dynamic, where the IP address is automatically allocated from the resource's subnet (using an Azure DHCP server). This IP address can change when you stop and start the resource.

**EXAM TIP**

**IPv4 address assignments can be either dynamic or static.  Private IPv6 addresses can only be assigned dynamically.**

A private IP address is allocated from the subnet's address range that the network interface is attached to. The address range of the subnet itself is a part of the Virtual Network's address space.

You can set the allocation method to static to ensure the IP address remains the same. When you specify static, you specify a valid IP address that is part of the resource's subnet.

Static private IP addresses are commonly used for:

- Virtual machines that act as domain controllers or DNS servers
- Resources that require firewall rules using IP addresses
- Resources accessed by other apps/resources through an IP address

All VMs on a Vnet are assigned a private IP address. If the VM has multiple NICs, a private IP address is assigned to each one. You can specify the allocation method as either dynamic or static for a NIC.

All Azure VMs are assigned Azure Managed DNS servers by default, unless custom DNS servers are assigned. These DNS servers provide internal name resolution for VMs within the same Vnet.

When you create a VM, a mapping for the hostname to its private IP address is added to the Azure DNS servers. If a VM has multiple network interfaces, the hostname is mapped to the private IP address of each NIC. VMs assigned Azure DNS servers can resolve the hostnames of all VMs within the same Vnet to their private IP addresses.

> **MORE INFORMATION** **DNS SERVERS TO NICS**
>
> To learn more about assigning custom DNS servers to NICs, see the DNS at the network interface (NIC) level in Skill 4.3.

## Internal load balancers (ILB) & Application Gateways

Private IP addresses can be assigned to the front-end configuration of an internal load balancer (ILB), or an App Gateway. This IP becomes the internal endpoint, accessible only to the resources within the Vnet, and any remote networks that are connected with the proper network routing in place. You can assign either a dynamic or static private IP address to the front-end configuration.

In Table 4-9, the various resources, their associations, and the type of IP allocation methods (dynamic or static) are captured.

**TABLE 4-9** IP allocation methods

| Resource | Association | Supports Dynamic | Support Static |
|---|---|---|---|
| Virtual Machine | Network Interface | Yes | Yes |
| Internal load balancer | Front-End Config | Yes | Yes |
| App Gateway | Front-End Config | Yes | Yes |

## Enabling static private IP addresses on VMs with the Azure portal

The Network Interface of a VM holds the configurations of the private IP address. This is known as IP Configuration. You can either add new IP Configurations to a NIC or update it from dynamic to static. Using the portal, locate the NIC for the VM that you wish to have a Static IP Address. Once the blade loads for the NIC, click on IP Configurations, then select the IP Configuration you wish to update, as seen in Figure 4-51. Here, you can update the private IP address settings Assignment to be Static, and assign the IP Address. This Address must be within the address range of the subnet where the NIC is located and not currently in use unless you are going to use the address the NIC is already assigned to.

FIGURE 4-51  Assigning a Static Private IP Address to a NIC

## Enabling static private IP addresses on VMs with PowerShell

When updating an existing NIC to use a static IP address, use two PowerShell cmdlets: Get-AzureRmNetworkInterface and Set-AzureRmNetworkInterface. First, use the Get-AzureRm-NetworkInterface to locate the NIC that should be assigned the static IP followed by updating the configuration to be static with its IP address. To save this to Azure, use the Set-AzureRm-NetworkInterface cmdlet.

```
# Update existing NIC to use a Static IP Address and set the IP
$nic=Get-AzureRmNetworkInterface -Name examrefwebvm1892 -ResourceGroupName ExamRefRGPS
```

```
$nic.IpConfigurations[0].PrivateIpAllocationMethod = "Static"
$nic.IpConfigurations[0].PrivateIpAddress = "10.0.0.5"
Set-AzureRmNetworkInterface -NetworkInterface $nic
```

### Enabling static private IP addresses on VMs with the Azure CLI

By using the Azure CLI to update a NIC to a static private IP address, use one simple command, az network NIC ip-config with the update argument. Again, the name of the NIC and the resource group are required along with the IP configuration. Remember you are updating the IP configuration properties of the NIC resource.

```
# Update existing nic to use a Static IP Address and set the IP
az network nic ip-config update --name ipconfig1 --nic-name examrefwebvm1400 --resource-
group ExamRefRGCLI --private-ip-address 10.0.1.5
```

# Public IP Address

Public IP addresses allow Azure resources to communicate with internet and public-facing Azure services. Public IP addresses can be created with an IPv4 or IPv6 address. Only internet-facing load balancers can be assigned a Public IPv6 address.

A Public IP address is an Azure Resource that has its own properties, in the same way a VM or VNet is a Resource. Some of the resources you can associate a Public IP address resource with include:

- Virtual machine via network interfaces
- internet-facing load balancers
- VPN Gateways
- Application gateways

Like private IP addresses, there are two methods an IP address is allocated to an Azure Public IP address resource: dynamic or static. The default allocation method is dynamic. In fact, an IP address is not allocated at the time the Public IP address resource is created by the Azure fabric.

***EXAM TIP***

Dynamic Public IP addresses are released when you stop (or delete) the resource. After being released from the resource, the IP address will be assigned to a different resource by Azure. If the IP address is assigned to a different resource while your resource is stopped, once you restart the resource, a different IP address will be assigned. If you wish to retain the IP address, the Public IP address should be changed to static, and that is assigned immediately and never changed.

If you change the allocation method to static, you as the administrator cannot specify the actual IP address assigned to the Public IP address resource. Azure assigns the IP address from a pool of IP addresses in the Azure region where the resource is located.

Static Public IP addresses are commonly used in the following scenarios:

- When you must update firewall rules to communicate with your Azure resources.
- DNS name resolution, where a change in IP address would require updating host or A records.
- Your Azure resources communicate with other apps or services that use an IP address-based security model.
- You use SSL certificates linked to an IP address.

One unique property of the Public IP address is the DNS domain name label. This allows you to create a mapping for a configured, fully qualified domain name (FQDN) to your Public IP address. You must provide an Azure globally unique host name that consists of 3-24 alpha-numeric characters, and then Azure adds the domains, creating a FQDN.

**EXAM TIP**

When you add a DNS Name to your Public IP address, the name will follow this pattern: hostname.region.cloudapp.azure.com. For example, if you create a public IP resource with contosowebvm1 as a DNS Name, and the VM was deployed to a VNet in the Central US region, the fully-qualified domain name (FQDN) of the VM would be: contosowebvm1.centralus.cloudapp.azure.com. This DNS name would resolve on the public internet as well as your VNet to the Public IP address of the resource. You could then use the FQDN to create a custom domain CNAME record pointing to the Public IP address in Azure. If you owned the contoso.com domain, you could create a CNAME record of www.contoso.com to resolve to contosowebvm1.centralus.cloudapp.azure.com. That DNS name would resolve to your Public IP Address assigned by Azure. The client traffic would be directed to the public IP Address associated with that name.

Table 4-10, shows the specific property through which a Public IP address can be associated to a top-level resource and the possible allocation methods (dynamic or static) that can be used.

**TABLE 4-10** Public IP Address associations

| Top-level resource | IP Address association | Dynamic | Static |
|---|---|---|---|
| Virtual machine | Network interface | Yes | Yes |
| internet-facing load balancer | Front-end configuration | Yes | Yes |
| VPN Gateway | Gateway IP configuration | Yes | No |
| Application gateway | Front-end configuration | Yes | No |

## Virtual machines

You can associate a Public IP address with any VM by associating it to its NIC. Public IP addresses, by default, are set to dynamic allocation, but this can be changed to static.

> **IMPORTANT  VM AND PUBLIC IP ADDRESSES**
>
> When a VM is assigned a public IP Address, it is exposed to the public internet. The only protection from attackers would include network security groups (NSGs) associated with the NIC or the subnet where the VM resides. The administrator of the VM could implement OS based Firewalling techniques providing additional security.

## internet-facing Load Balancers

Public IP addresses (either a dynamic or static) can be associated with an Azure load balancer by assigning it to the front-end configuration. The Public IP address then becomes the load balancer's virtual IP address (VIP). It is possible to assign multiple Public IP addresses to a load balancer front end which enables multi-VIP scenarios like a multi-site environment with SSL-based websites.

## VPN Gateways

An Azure VPN Gateway connects an Azure VNet to other Azure VNets or to an on-premises network. A Public IP address is required to be assigned to the VPN Gateway to enable it to communicate with the remote network. You can only assign a dynamic Public IP address to a VPN Gateway.

## Application gateways

You can associate a Public IP address with an Azure App Gateway by assigning it to the gateway's frontend configuration. This Public IP address serves as a load-balanced VIP. You can only assign a dynamic Public IP address to an application gateway frontend configuration.

## Creating a Public IP Address using the Azure Portal

Creating a new Public IP Address is a simple process when using the portal. Click New, and then search for Public IP Address in the Marketplace. Like all resources in Azure, some details will be required including the Name of the resource, IP Version, assignment or allocation method, DNS name label, subscription, resource group and location/region. The location is critical, as an IP Address must be in the same location/region as the resource where you want to assign it. Figure 4-52 shows the Azure Create Public IP Address Blade.

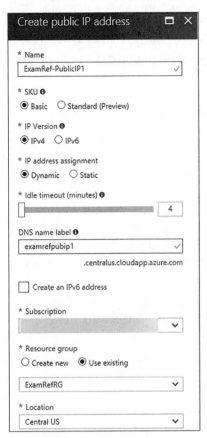

**FIGURE 4-52** Creating a Public IP Address in the Azure Portal

## Creating a Public IP Address using the PowerShell

When creating a new Public IP address by using PowerShell, the New-AzureRmPublicIpAddress cmdlet is employed. In this script, variables are created for reuse of the code. This command assumes that your resource group is already created.

```
# Creating a Public IP Address
# Set Variables
$publicIpName = "ExamRef-PublicIP1-PS"
$rgName = "ExamRefRGPS"
$dnsPrefix = "examrefpubip1ps"
$location = "centralus"

# Create the Public IP
New-AzureRmPublicIpAddress -Name $publicIpName `
                           -ResourceGroupName $rgName `
                           -AllocationMethod Static `
                           -DomainNameLabel $dnsPrefix `
                           -Location $location
```

## Creating a Public IP Address using the Azure CLI

When creating a new Public IP address by using the Azure CLI, only one command is required. The command, az network public-ip with the create argument. You need to provide details with respect to the name, resource group, DNS lab, and where it is dynamic or static.

```
# Creating a Public IP Address
az network public-ip create -g ExamRefRGCLI -n ExamRef-PublicIP1-CLI --dns-name
examrefpubip1cli --allocation-method Static
```

# DNS at the Network Interface (NIC) Level

By default, Azure DNS is configured when creating a VM. VMs that are connected to the VNet use this service for name resolution inside the VNet and on the public internet. Along with the resolution of public DNS names, Azure provides internal name resolution for VMs that reside within the same VNet. Within a VNet, the DNS suffix is consistent, so the FQDN is not needed. This means that VMs on the same VNet using the Azure DNS Server can connect directly via their host names.

Just as it is possible to configure your own Customer Managed DNS Servers for a VNet, this configuration is also possible at the NIC level. When using your own DNS servers, Azure provides the ability to specify multiple DNS servers per NIC.

The DNS Servers configuration for a Network Interface on a VM can be completed using the Azure portal, PowerShell or Azure CLI.

### Configure DNS Settings on Network Interfaces using the Azure Portal

To configure the DNS Servers on a Network Interface using the Azure portal, open the NIC associated with the VM requiring the custom settings, as seen in Figure 4-53. Next, click on the DNS Servers link in the Settings menu. You can then enter the DNS Servers you wish for this VM to use. In the example, the two DNS Servers are well known, and they are publicly available on the internet but different than the VNet.

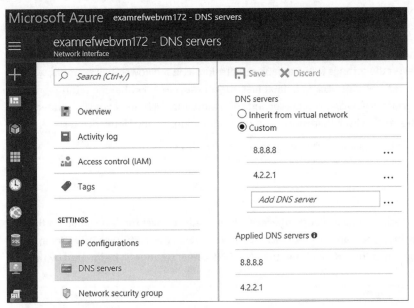

FIGURE 4-53 Custom DNS Servers for Network Interface configured using the Portal

## Configure DNS Settings on Network Interfaces using the PowerShell

When creating a new VNet, you can specify the DNS Configure the DNS Servers using Power-Shell. The Set-AzureRmNetworkInterface along with the Get-AzureRmNetworkInterface cmd-lets will be used together to make the change to an existing Network Interface. The first line of PowerShell will get the existing interface and its configurations followed by using the Clear and Add Methods that will update the PowerShell pipeline with new configuration that will be passed to the Set-AzureRmNetworkInterface to update and save to the Network Interface. The DnsSettings.DnsServers.Clear() method is first used to clear out the current configuration no matter what is there. Then the DnsSettings.DnsServers.Add ("dns-server-ip-address") will be used to input the IPs that should be used by the Network Interface.

```
$nic = Get-AzureRmNetworkInterface `
        -ResourceGroupName "ExamRefRG" `
        -Name "examrefwebvm172"
$nic.DnsSettings.DnsServers.Clear()
$nic.DnsSettings.DnsServers.Add("8.8.8.8")
$nic.DnsSettings.DnsServers.Add("4.2.2.1")
$nic | Set-AzureRmNetworkInterface
```

### EXAM TIP

When you change your VNet settings to point to your customer provided DNS servers on its network interfaces, you must restart VMs for the new settings to be assigned to the VM's operating system. When the VM reboots it re-acquires its IP address and the new DNS settings are in place.

### Configure DNS Settings on Network Interfaces using the Azure CLI

To update an existing a Network Interface using the Azure CLI as well as specify custom DNS Servers add the --dns-servers argument when using the az network nic update command. The first command will revert the settings to the default servers. Just as in the PowerShell example, we want to remove the current settings back to default first, so you know exactly what the settings are on the Network Interface. If you only run the second command, your DNS Servers will be added to the bottom of the existing list if there are already custom settings on the Network Interface.

```
az network nic update -g ExamRefRG -n examrefwebvm172 --dns-servers ""
az network nic update -g ExamRefRG -n examrefwebvm172 --dns-servers 8.8.8.8 4.2.2.1
```

**EXAM TIP**

DNS Servers specified for a Network Interface take precedence over those specified for the VNet. This means if you want specific machines on your VNet, use a different DNS Server, you can assign this at the NIC level, and the VNet DNS Server setting will be ignored by that VM.

## Network Security Groups (NSGs)

A network security group (NSG) is a networking filter containing a list of security rules that when applied will allow or deny network traffic to resources connected to Azure VNets. These rules can manage both inbound and outbound Traffic. NSGs can be associated to subnets, individual Network Interfaces attached to ARM VMs, and Classic VMs.

In this section, you will learn how to configure NSGs on Network Interfaces and are associated with VMs in Azure Resource Manager. The process of filtering network traffic via a NSG on a NIC is multi-step. First, the network security group must be created. Next, the desired rules would need to be created in that NSG. Once these two steps are completed it will then be associated with the NIC.

**EXAM TIP**

NSGs that are associated to network interfaces are said to be filtering "East/West" traffic.

### Creating an NSG and Associating with a NIC using the Azure Portal

To create a NSG to be associated with a NIC in the portal click New, followed by Networking and then, select network security group. Once the Create network security group blade loads, provide a Name, the Subscription where your resources are located, the resource group for the NSG and the Location (this must be the same as the resources you wish to apply to the NSG).

In Figure 4-54, the NSG will be created to allow HTTP traffic on Port 80 into a NIC of a VM named ExamRefWEBVM1. The name of the NSG is ExamRefWEBVM1-nsg located in the same resource group ExamRefRG.

**FIGURE 4-54** Creating an NSG that is associated with a VM NIC

Once the ExamRefWEBVM1-nsg has been created, the portal will open the Overview blade. Here, you will see the NSG has been created, but there are no inbound or outbound security rules beyond the default rules.

To create the inbound rule to allow port 80 select Inbound Security Rules followed by +Add. For the Add inbound security rule, update using the following details, as seen in Figure 4-55:

- **Source** Any
- **Source port ranges** *
- **Destination** Any
- **Destinations port ranges** 80
- **Protocol** Any
- **Action** Allow
- **Priority** 100
- **Name** PORT_HTTP_80
- **Description** All HTTP

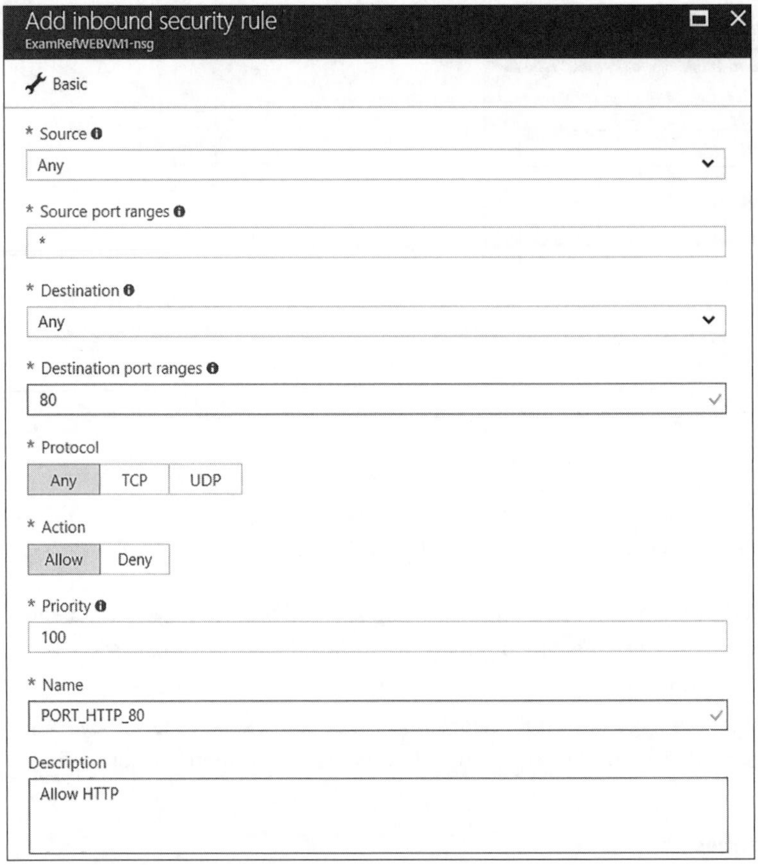

**FIGURE 4-55** An Inbound Rule to Allow traffic on Port 80 is created

Once the portal has configured the inbound rule, it will appear in the portal. Review your rule to ensure it has been created correctly. Now, this NSG with its default rules and newly created inbound rule named Port_80_HTTP is currently not filtering any traffic since it has yet to be associated with NIC. In Figure 4-56, you see the NIC of ExamRefWEBVM1 being selected after selecting Network Interfaces under Settings, followed by selecting +Associate. The portal will ask you to select the NIC name associated with ExamRefWEBVM1. The NSG will immediately start filtering traffic.

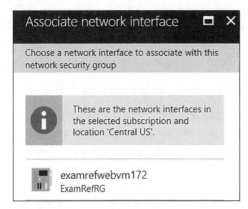

**FIGURE 4-56** Associating the NSG with the NIC of the VM

Upon association of the NSG with the NIC, TCP traffic on Port 80 will be allowed to this VM. Of course, you would need to have a webserver VM configured and listening on Port 80 to respond, but with this NSG, the ability is now opened for that traffic to flow to the VMs.

## Creating an NSG and Associating with a Subnet using PowerShell

To create a NSG and configure the rules using PowerShell, use the New-AzureRmNetworkSecurityRuleConfig and New-AzureRmNetworkSecurityGroup PowerShell cmdlets together. In this example, it's assumed you have run the Login-AzureRmAccount command as well as created a resource group and the VNet from the earlier example using PowerShell. The NSG will be created to allow HTTP traffic on Port 80 into a NIC of a VM named ExamRefWEBVM1. The name of the NSG is ExamRefWEBVM1-nsg located in the same resource group ExamRefRGPS.

```
#Build a new Inbound Rule to Allow TCP Traffic on Port 80 to the Subnet
$rule1 = New-AzureRmNetworkSecurityRuleConfig -Name PORT_HTTP_80 `
                                  -Description "Allow HTTP" `
                                  -Access Allow `
                                  -Protocol Tcp `
                                  -Direction Inbound `
                                  -Priority 100 `
                                  -SourceAddressPrefix * `
                                  -SourcePortRange * `
                                  -DestinationAddressPrefix 10.0.0.0/24 `
                                  -DestinationPortRange 80

#Create a new Network Security Group and add the HTTP Rule
$nsg = New-AzureRmNetworkSecurityGroup -ResourceGroupName ExamRefRGPS `
                                  -Location centralus `
                                  -Name "ExamRefWEBVM1-nsg" `
                                  -SecurityRules $rule1
```

After the NSG is created, along with the inbound rule, next you need to associate this with the NIC to control the flow of network traffic by using this filter. To achieve this goal, use Get-AzureRmNetworkInterface. After the configuration on the NIC has been set, use Set-AzureRmNetworkInterface to save the configuration to the NIC.

```
#Associate the Rule with the NIC from ExamRefWEBVM1
$nic = Get-AzureRmNetworkInterface -ResourceGroupName ExamRefRGPS -Name examrefwebvm1892
$nic.NetworkSecurityGroup = $nsg
Set-AzureRmNetworkInterface -NetworkInterface $nic
```

### Creating an NSG and Associating with a NIC using the Azure CLI

Creating an NSG by using the CLI is a multi-step process, just as it is with the portal and Pow-erShell. The `az network nsg create` command is first used to create the NSG. After the NSG is created, next create the rule to allow Port 80 to the subnet. This is created by using the `az network nsg rule create` command. After the rule has been created, this is associated with the NIC of a VM named ExamRefWEBVM1 by using the `az network nic update` command. The name of the NSG is ExamRefWEBVM1-nsg, located in the same resource group ExamRefRGCLI.

```
# Create the NSG
az network nsg create --resource-group ExamRefRGCLI --name ExamRefWEBVM1-nsg

# Create the NSG Inbound Rule allowing TCP traffic on Port 80
az network nsg rule create --resource-group ExamRefRGCLI --name PORT_HTTP_80
--nsg-name ExamRefWEBVM1-nsg --direction Inbound --priority 100 --access Allow
--source-address-prefix "*" --source-port-range "*" --destination-address-prefix
"*" --destination-port-range "80" --description "Allow HTTP" --protocol TCP

# Associate the NSG with the NIC from ExamRefWEBVM1
az network nic update --resource-group ExamRefRGCLI --name examrefwebvm1400
 --network-security-group ExamRefWEBVM1-nsg
```

# User Defined Routes (UDR) with IP Forwarding

User Defined Routes (UDR) allow for changing the default system routes that Azure creates for you in an Azure VNet. The UDRs forward traffic to a virtual appliance such as a firewall. For that traffic to be allowed to pass to that virtual appliance, you must enable IP forwarding on the network interface of the VM.

A virtual appliance is nothing more than a VM that runs an application used to handle network traffic in some way. By default, VMs in Azure do not have the ability to forward packets that are intended for a different destination, so this configuration allows those packets to flow through the device. Of course, the firewall device would have to be configured as well by using its internal tools to pass this traffic. This configuration doesn't typically involve any changes to the Azure UDR or VNet.

IP forwarding can be enabled on a network interface by using the Azure portal, PowerShell, or the Azure CLI. In Figure 4-57, you see that the network interface of the NGFW1 VM has the IP forwarding set as Enabled. This VM is now able to accept and send packets that were not originally intended for this VM.

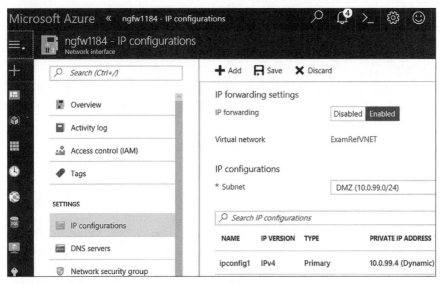

**FIGURE 4-57** IP Forwarding Enabled on a Virtual Appliance

# External and Internal load balancing with HTTP and TCP health probes

The Azure load balancer provides the means for you to deliver highly available and high per-forming web based applications using your VMs running in a VNet. This is a Layer 4 (TCP, UDP) load balancer that distributes inbound traffic among healthy instances of services defined in a load-balanced set.

The load balancer can run in three different configurations:

- Load balance incoming internet traffic to VMs. This configuration is known as internet-facing load balancing.

- Traffic between virtual machines in a VNet is also supported.  These can be between virtual machines in cloud services, or between on-premises computers and virtual ma-chines in a cross-premises Virtual Network.  This is known as internal load balancing.

- Forward external traffic to a specific virtual machine, which is a means of using Network Address Translation (NAT).

The load balancer uses a hash-based distribution algorithm. Like most load balancers, it uses a 5-tuple hash composed of source IP, source port, destination IP, destination port, and protocol type to map traffic to available servers, by default. This provides stickiness within a transport session, meaning that packets in the same TCP or UDP session are directed to the same instance behind the load-balanced endpoint. If, or when, the client closes and reopens the connection or starts a new session from the same source IP, the source port changes.

You have control over how inbound communication comes into your endpoints, known as the input endpoint. An input endpoint listens on a public port and forwards traffic to an internal port. You can map the same ports for an internal or external endpoint or use a different port for them.

For example, you can have a web server configured to listen to port 81 while the public endpoint mapping is port 80. The creation of a public endpoint triggers the creation of a load balancer instance.

## Health Probes

At its core, the purpose of a load balancer is twofold: to spread traffic across a farm of VMs that are providing a service so you don't overload them and to ensure that the VMs are healthy and ready to accept traffic.

The Azure load balancer can probe the health of your VMs deployed into a VNet. When a VM probe experiences a failure, this means that the VM is no longer able to provide the service, therefore the load balancer marks it as an unhealthy instance and stops sending new connections to the VM. Existing connections are not impacted by being removed from the pool of healthy instances, but users could experience failures if they have current open connections to that VM.

The Azure load balancer supports two types of probes for virtual machines:

- **TCP Probe**   This probe relies on a successful TCP session establishment to a defined probe port.  If the VM responds to the request to establish a simple TCP connection on the port defined when creating the probe, the VM is marked as healthy.  For example, a TCP probe could be created connecting to portal 80.  If the machine is active and allows connections on port 80, the load balancer would be able to connect and the machine would pass the probe.  If for some reason the machine was stopped or the load balancer could no longer connect to port 80, it would be marked as unhealthy.

- **HTTP Probe**   This probe is used to determine if a VM is serving webpages without issues by using the HTTP protocol.  When a webpage loads successfully, there is an HTTP error code that is given: 200.  This error code means that the page loaded successfully.  One of the configurations on the HTTP probe is the path to the file used for the probe which by default, is marked a "/".  This tells the Azure load balancer to load the default webpage from the VM.  Often this would be default.aspx or index.html, but you can configure this if you want to create your own page to check the health of a site. Just returning the default page with 200 doesn't provide deeper insight as to the true functionally of your site, so using some custom logic to determine the health of the site could make sense.  A developer would create a custom page and then you would configure the load balancer to load that page.  If it loads correctly, the 200 is provided and the VM is put into the pool of available VMs to service client requests.

For both TCP and HTTP probes you can configure the interval and the unhealthy threshold. The interval is the amount of time between the probe attempts, or in other words how often Azure uses this probe. Unhealthy threshold is the number of consecutive failures that must occur before the VM is considered unhealthy.

## Creating the Azure load balancer using the Azure portal

To use the Azure load balancer, the administrator must first provision the resource including the Frontend IP configuration. After this step has been completed then you will need to create the backend pool, heath probes, and load balancing rules.

To create the load balancer in the portal, select New, followed by Networking and locate the load balancer. As seen in Figure 4-58, supply a name for the load balancer, assign a type of Public or Internal, select a public or private IP Address, along with the subscription, resource group, and location. In the case of the example, an internet facing load balancer will be created with a public IP Address, and it will point to two Web Servers named ExamRefWEBVM1 and ExamRefWEBVM2 that are part of an Availability Set called ExamRefWebAVSet. Both VMs have one NIC that is connected to the Apps subnet of the ExamRefVNET VNet.

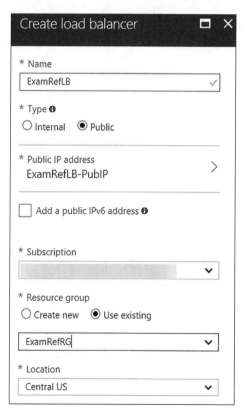

**FIGURE 4-58** Creating a Load Balancer with the Azure portal

After the load balancer has been created, execute the next steps to integrate your VMs with the load balancer:

- Backend Pool
- Health Probe HTTP
- Load Balancing Rule

Figure 4-59 shows the portal to add a backend pool. To create the backend pool, open the load balancer in the portal and then in the Settings section, click Backend pools. Next click +Add Provide a Name for the Backend Pool, leave the IPv4 section for the IP Version and move to the Associated to drop-down. Select Availability Set and another drop-down appears. Select ExamRefWebAVSet from the drop-down list. Next click the +Add a target network IP configuration. Next a Target virtual machine drop-down appears and you can select ExamRefWEBVM1 along with its network IP configuration. Click +Add a target network IP configuration again and follow this same procedure to select ExamRefWEBVM2. After you complete adding both VMs, click OK.

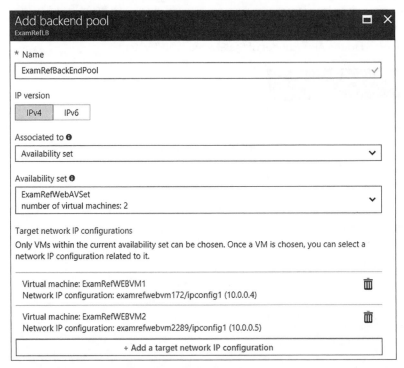

**FIGURE 4-59** Creating the Backend pool which exposes the VMs

To ensure your Web Servers are ready, you will need to add the HTTP Probe. To begin configuring the HTTP probe, select the Health probe link in Settings and then +Add. As seen in Figure 4-60, provide a Name, select the HTTP protocol, and accept the defaults of Port 80, Interval of 5 and Unhealth threshold of 2. Then click OK. Notice that there is an additional item named path which is the location of a file or folder on the web server for the load balancer to connect.

FIGURE 4-60 Creating a HTTP Health Probe

Now that you have created the backend pool telling the load balancer which machines are to be used, and you have configured the probes to help determine which ones are healthy, you will now put it all together with the load balancing rules. These rules help to bring these configurations together connecting the Frontend to the Backend. To create the rule, click the load balancing rules link under settings, and then select +Add. Complete the following configurations, as seen in Figure 4-61:

- **Name**    ExamRefLBRule
- **IP Version**    IPv4
- **Frontend IP Address**    Select the Public IP Address
- **Protocol**    TCP
- **Port**    80
- **Backend port**    80
- **Backend pool**    Select the Pool you created
- **Heath Probe**    Select the TCP Rule
- **Session**    Persistence None
- **Idle Timeout**    4 minutes
- **Floating IP**    Disabled

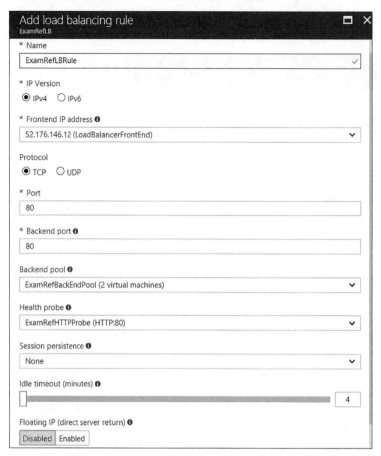

**FIGURE 4-61** Creating the Load Balancing Rule using the Backend Pool and Health Probe

After this is put in the place, if the VMs added to the backend pool are configured with a web server and there are no network security groups or other firewalls blocking port 80, you should be able to connect to the Public IP address of the load balancer and see the webpage.

## Creating the Azure Load Balancer using PowerShell

When creating a new load balancer by using PowerShell, there are quite a few steps involved. The script must first create a Public IP address, the front IP configuration, backend pool, and the HTTP probe. Then, the load balancer rule is followed by the load balancer resource where these other configurations will be put in place. After you create the load balancer, update the backend pool referencing the NICs of the VMs that are serving the website. The PowerShell cmdlets used for this script include:

```
New-AzureRmPublicIpAddress
New-AzureRmLoadBalancerFrontendIpConfig
New-AzureRmLoadBalancerBackendAddressPoolConfig
New-AzureRmLoadBalancerProbeConfig
New-AzureRmLoadBalancer
Get-AzureRmVirtualNetwork
Get-AzureRmVirtualNetworkSubnetConfig
Get-AzureRmNetworkInterface
Set-AzureRmNetworkInterfaceIpConfig
Set-AzureRmNetworkInterface
```

In this example, an internet facing load balancer will be created with a public IP Address, and it will point to two Web Servers named ExamRefWEBVM1 and ExamRefWEBVM2, and they are part of an Availability Set called ExamRefWebAVSet. Both VMs have one NIC connected to the Apps subnet of the ExamRefVNET-PS VNet created in earlier steps.

```
# Set Variables
$publicIpName = "ExamRefLB-PublicIP-PS"
$rgName = "ExamRefRGPS"
$dnsPrefix = "examreflbps"
$location = "centralus"
$lbname = "ExamRefLBPS"
$vnetName = "ExamRefVNET-PS"

# Create the Public IP
$publicIP = New-AzureRmPublicIpAddress -Name $publicIpName `
                          -ResourceGroupName $rgName `
                          -AllocationMethod Static `
                          -DomainNameLabel $dnsPrefix `
                          -Location $location

#Create Frontend IP Configuration
$frontendIP = New-AzureRmLoadBalancerFrontendIpConfig -Name ExamRefFrontEndPS `
                                       -PublicIpAddress $publicIP

# Create Backend Pool
$beAddressPool = New-AzureRmLoadBalancerBackendAddressPoolConfig -Name
ExamRefBackEndPoolPS

#Create HTTP Probe
$healthProbe = New-AzureRmLoadBalancerProbeConfig -Name HealthProbe `
                                       -RequestPath '/' `
                                       -Protocol http `
                                       -Port 80 `
                                       -IntervalInSeconds 5 `
                                       -ProbeCount 2

#Create Load Balancer Rule
$lbrule = New-AzureRmLoadBalancerRuleConfig -Name ExamRefRuleHTTPPS `
                                    -FrontendIpConfiguration $frontendIP `
                                    -BackendAddressPool  $beAddressPool `
                                    -Probe $healthProbe `
```

```
                                        -Protocol Tcp `
                                        -FrontendPort 80 `
                                        -BackendPort 80

#Create Load Balancer
New-AzureRmLoadBalancer -ResourceGroupName $rgName `
                        -Name $lbName `
                        -Location $location `
                        -FrontendIpConfiguration $frontendIP `
                        -LoadBalancingRule $lbrule `
                        -BackendAddressPool $beAddressPool `
                        -Probe $healthProbe

# Add the Web Servers to the Backend Pool
$vnet = Get-AzureRmVirtualNetwork -Name $vnetName `
                                  -ResourceGroupName $rgName
$subnet = Get-AzureRmVirtualNetworkSubnetConfig -Name Apps `
                                                -VirtualNetwork $vnet
$nic1 = Get-AzureRmNetworkInterface -Name examrefwebvm1480 `
                                    -ResourceGroupName $rgName
$nic1 | Set-AzureRmNetworkInterfaceIpConfig -Name ipconfig1 `
                                            -LoadBalancerBackendAddressPool
                                            $beAddressPool `
                                            -Subnet $subnet
$nic1 | Set-AzureRmNetworkInterface

$nic2 = Get-AzureRmNetworkInterface -Name examrefwebvm2217 `
                                    -ResourceGroupName $rgName
$nic2 | Set-AzureRmNetworkInterfaceIpConfig -Name ipconfig1 `
                                            -LoadBalancerBackendAddressPool
                                            $beAddressPool `
                                            -Subnet $subnet
$nic2 | Set-AzureRmNetworkInterface
```

## Creating the Azure load balancer using the Azure CLI

The same configurations are required when creating a load balancer by using the Azure CLI as
they are when creating load balancers in the portal or PowerShell. The process using CLI is not
quite as intricate as the process using PowerShell though. You can leverage the az network lb
command with a few different arguments along with the az network public-ip to create the
Public IP address.

```
# Creating a Public IP Address
az network public-ip create -g ExamRefRGCLI -n ExamRefLB-PublicIP-CLI --dns-name
 examreflbcli --allocation-method Static

#Create Load Balancer
az network lb create -n ExamRefLBCLI -g ExamRefRGCLI -l centralus --backend-pool-name
 ExamRefBackEndPoolCLI --frontend-ip-name ExamRefFrontEndCLI --public-ip-address
 ExamRefLB-PublicIP-CLI

#Create HTTP Probe
az network lb probe create -n HealthProbe -g ExamRefRGCLI --lb-name ExamRefLBCLI
--protocol http --port 80 --path / --interval 5 --threshold 2

#Create Load Balancer Rule
az network lb rule create -n ExamRefRuleHTTPCLI -g ExamRefRGCLI --lb-name
ExamRefLBCLI --protocol Tcp --frontend-port 80 --backend-port 80
--frontend-ip-name ExamRefFrontEndCLI --backend-pool-name ExamRefBackEndPoolCLI
 --probe-name HealthProbe

# Add the Web Servers to the Backend Pool
az network nic ip-config address-pool add --address-pool ExamRefBackEndPoolCLI
 --lb-name ExamRefLBCLI -g ExamRefRGCLI --nic-name examrefwebvm160 --ip-config-name
 ipconfig1
az network nic ip-config address-pool add --address-pool ExamRefBackEndPoolCLI
--lb-name ExamRefLBCLI -g ExamRefRGCLI --nic-name examrefwebvm2139 --ip-config-name
 ipconfig1
```

# Direct Server Return

Some application scenarios require the same port to be used on the frontend configuration and the backend on the VMs. Common examples of port reuse include clustering for high availability, network virtual appliances, and exposing multiple TLS endpoints without re-encryption.

If you want to reuse the backend port across multiple rules, you must enable Floating IP in the load balancer rule definition. Floating IP is a portion of what is known as Direct Server Return (DSR). In Azure, this ability is typically only used for deploying SQL Server Always On Availability Groups. This is a clustering technology for providing highly available databases using Azure VMs. Microsoft recommends only using this feature when configuring SQL Always On Availability Groups Listener. This can only be configured with creating a load balancing rule and the frontend port must match the backend port. Figure 4-62 shows a SQL Always on Listener with the direct server return set to Enabled.

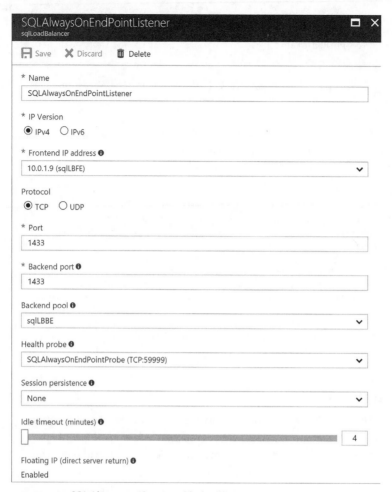

**FIGURE 4-62** SQL Always on Listener with the Direct Server Return Enabled

This functionality should only be used if the VM that is responding as a part of the backend pool is connecting directly to a VM within the VNet or networks that are connected to the VNet. It is not supported to use direct server return with clients that are on the internet. This is due to the server talking back directly to the client rather than its traffic going through the load balancer back to the client.

> **MORE INFORMATION  SQL SERVER ALWAYS ON AVAILABILIT GROUPS IN AZURE**
>
> To learn more about running SQL Server Always On Availability Groups in Azure review the following article: *https://docs.microsoft.com/en-us/azure/virtual-machines/windows/sql/virtual-machines-windows-portal-sql-alwayson-int-listener.*

# Design and Implement Application Gateway (App Gateway)

The Application Gateway can be deployed as a Layer 7 load balancer into a VNet. VMs that are a part of the VNet can then be added as the backend pool of an App Gateway. These VMs host the application, much like the Azure load balancer being added to the backend pool is a part of the NIC IP configuration. This can be accomplished by using the Azure portal, PowerShell, and the Azure CLI.

> **MORE INFORMATION** APPLICATION GATEWAY
>
> To learn about how to Implement the Application Gateway refer to Skill 4.1 Configure Virtual Networks.

## Configure VMs as Backend Pool for App Gateway using the Azure Portal

To configure the VMs as part of the Backend pool using the Azure portal open the App Gateway and then select backend pools under the Settings section. Next, click on the name of the Backend pool created when the App Gateway was provisioned. Then, select +Add target followed by VM. From there, you can select the first VM and its IP Configuration. In the case of this example, the ExamRefWEBVM1 and ExamRefWEBVM2 have been selected with ipconfig1 from each VM. Notice their private IP address is listed, as this is the IP Address the App Gateway will use when directing traffic to the VMs. Once they have been added click Save and the App Gateway will update. Figure 4-63 shows the appGatewayBackendPool with the VMs configurations added.

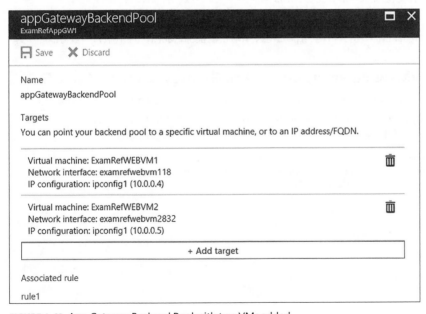

**FIGURE 4-63** App Gateway Backend Pool with two VMs added

After the portal reports that the App Gateway update is complete, you can connect to the Public IP address of the App Gateway by using your web browser. It does take a few minutes for the sites to come online, so be patient.

## Configure VMs as Backend Pool for App Gateway using the PowerShell

To update the backend pool of the App Gateway with the VMs you will use a combination of the Get-AzureRmApplicationGateway cmdlet along with the with the Get-AzureRmApplicationGatewayBackendAddressPool and Get-AzureRmNetworkInterface. These cmdlets will be used to load information about the various resources into variables that can then be used with the Set-AzureRmApplicationGatewayBackendAddressPool cmdlet to configure the backend pool with the addresses of your web servers. These backend pool members are all validated to be healthy by probes, whether they are basic probes or custom probes. Traffic is then routed to them when requests come into the application gateway. Backend pools can be used by multiple rules within the application gateway. This means one backend pool could be used for multiple web applications that reside on the same host.

```
# Add VM IP Addresses to the Backend Pool of App Gateway
$appGw = Get-AzureRmApplicationGateway -Name "ExamRefAppGWPS" -ResourceGroupName
 "ExamRefRGPS"
$backendPool = Get-AzureRmApplicationGatewayBackendAddressPool -Name
 "appGatewayBackendPool" -ApplicationGateway $AppGw
$nic01 = Get-AzureRmNetworkInterface -Name "examrefwebvm1480" -ResourceGroupName
"ExamRefRGPS"
$nic02 = Get-AzureRmNetworkInterface -Name "examrefwebvm2217" -ResourceGroupName
"ExamRefRGPS"
Set-AzureRmApplicationGatewayBackendAddressPool -ApplicationGateway $appGw `
                        -Name $backendPool `
                        -BackendIPAddresses
$nic01.IpConfigurations[0].PrivateIpAddress,$nic02.IpConfigurations[0].PrivateIpAddress
```

## Configure VMs as Backend Pool for App Gateway using the Azure CLI

Only one command is required to update the backend pool of the App Gateway using the Azure CLI. The az network application-gateway address-pool is used, but you must know the IP Addresses of the VM's IP Configurations to make this work properly.

```
# Add VM IP Addresses to the Backend Pool of App Gateway
az network application-gateway address-pool update -n appGatewayBackendPool
--gateway-name ExamRefAppGWCLI -g ExamRefRGCLI --servers 10.0.0.6 10.0.0.7
```

# Skill 4.4: Design and implement a communication strategy

This section focuses on the various methods and connectivity choices to securely extend your on-premises network into the Microsoft cloud. There are two types of connections for connecting to the MS cloud covered in this section: the S2S VPN and an Azure resource known as Azure App Hybrid Connections for exposing services inside your network without a VPN.

> **This skill covers how to:**
> - Leverage Site-to-Site (S2S) VPN to connect to an on-premises infrastructure
> - Implement Hybrid Connections to access data sources on-premises

## Leverage Site-to-Site (S2S) VPN to connect to an on-premises infrastructure

S2S connections are used for building hybrid configurations. Once established between your VPN on-premises device and an Azure VPN Gateway, this connection type allows your on-premises users and VMs to VMs and services that are running in an Azure VNet.

Running workloads in the cloud and on-premises is very common and as such, these connections make this possible. In the case of adding a VPN connection to Azure you are essentially just adding another datacenter to your network; it just happens to be the public Azure cloud.

Figure 4-64 shows a VNET that has been connected to an on-premises datacenter by using ExpressRoute. There is an intranet SharePoint farm deployed along with its data tier and domain controllers. Notice the use of the multiple load balancers to facilitate the deployment requirement of the application. This entire Virtual Network, application, data, and identity is available and functional for the clients that are on the other side of the ExpressRoute circuit.

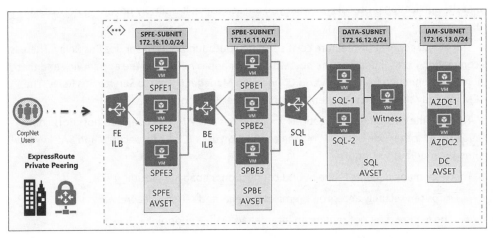

**FIGURE 4-64** Virtual Network and Services connected to On-premises using ExpressRoute

# Implement Hybrid Connections to access data sources on-premises

Within the Azure App Service, hybrid connections can be used to access application resources in other networks. This connection provides access FROM your application running in Azure TO an application endpoint hosted in your datacenter. It does this is such a way that there is not a requirement to build out a complex full S2S or hybrid cloud infrastructure.

In many scenarios, this type of connection solves the problem customers have if that want to build an application in the cloud, but the data is "locked," in their datacenter. By using the hybrid connection in Azure, the App Service can connect to that data. Figure 4-65 shows a functional diagram of this type of hybrid connection.

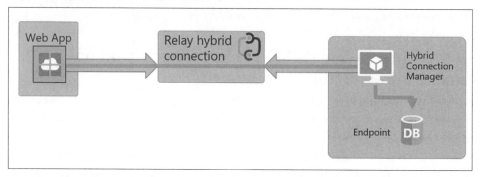

**FIGURE 4-65** Hybrid Connection from App Services to an On-premises Database

When these connections are created it only allows the Web App to talk to the datacenter. It does not enable full communication between the local server and the Web App running in Azure. Each hybrid connection correlates to a single TCP host and port combination. This means that the hybrid connection endpoint can be on any operating system and any application, provided you are hitting a TCP listening port. Hybrid connections do not know or care what the application protocol is or what you are accessing. It is simply providing network access.

The hybrid connections feature consists of two outbound calls to Service Bus Relay. There is a connection from a library on the host where your app is running in the app service and then there is a connection from the Hybrid Connection Manager (HCM) to Service Bus Relay. The HCM is a relay service that you deploy within the network hosting.

Through the two joined connections your app has a TCP tunnel to a fixed host:port combination on the other side of the HCM. The connection uses TLS 1.2 for security and SAS keys for authentication/authorization.

There are many benefits to the hybrid connections capability including:

- Apps can securely access on premises systems and services securely
- The feature does not require an internet accessible endpoint

- Each hybrid connection matches to a single host:port combination, which is an excellent security aspect

- It normally does not require firewall holes as the connections are all outbound over standard web ports

- The feature is running at the network level, so it is agnostic to the language used by your app and the technology used by the endpoint

# Thought experiment

In this thought experiment, apply what you have learned about virtual networks in this chapter. You can find answers to these questions in the Answers section at the end of this chapter.

Your management team has named you as the lead architect to implement the first cloud deployment in Contoso's history. There is a new web based application that runs on IIS Server using a SQL database that they want implemented in Azure.

During a meeting with the application vendor and your manager, you have gained a better understanding of the implementation needs and Contoso's requirements. The application must run on Azure VMs and the SQL server needs to be implemented as an Always on Availability Group cluster. The vendor has told you that the application supports multiple web front ends for high-availability. Your manager has mentioned multiple times how important security is given this is the first cloud installation. During the conversation, she made it clear that the Azure implementation should be secured using a multi-layered approach using firewall rules, and that it must be deployed using a web application firewall (WAF).

At the end of the meeting your manager also mentioned that as a part of this project you should implement a permanent low latency connection between your primary datacenter and Azure, as there are many follow-on projects after this one. It is also important to have all servers be able to communicate using their host names and not IP addresses as well because it must support authentications to your Active Directory domain controllers. The onsite network is a class A 10.0.0.0/16 Network, but you do have access to 8 class C public addresses provided by your network service provider and registered in your company's name with the ARIN.

1. Given that the solution required VMs, the configuration will require a VNet. What should you consider with respect to the address space of the VNet? What address space will you use? Also, what subnets should you create to support the requirements? What are the CIDR ranges for these subnets?

2. Where would each tier of the application be deployed using the subnets that you have defined? How will you secure these subnets and VMs?

3. What type of connection will be created between your on-premises datacenter and Azure? How will DNS Services be implemented?

4. What is the basic architecture for the application?

# Thought experiment answers

This section contains the solution to the thought experiment for the chapter.

1. The VNet should have an address space that has an ample number of IP addresses (for future growth), but it cannot overlap the current network space, so a class B private network at 172.16.0.0/20 will be implemented. The following subnets will be created:

   - **Apps**  172.16.0.0/24
   - **Data**  172.16.1.0/24
   - **Identity**  172.16.2.0/24
   - **AppGateway**  172.16.99.0/24
   - **GatewaySubnet**  172.16.100.0/28

2. The different subnets will contain various VMs to meet the requirements. There will be network security groups on each subnet and each VMs NIC. Inbound rules will be created to allow the least privileged access for traffic into a subnet and then into the NIC.

   - **Apps**  IIS VMs hosting the application
   - **Data**  SQL Server VMs providing the databases
   - **Identity**  AD Domain Controllers/DNS
   - **AppGateway**  App Gateway VMs
   - **GatewaySubnet**  ExpressRoute VPN Gateways

3. An ExpressRoute connection between Azure and the on-premises datacenter will be created. The Public IP addresses will be configured as the endpoint for the ExpressRoute circuit. The AD domain controllers will be setup as DNS servers by configuring the VNet to point to those servers.

4. The Azure Application Gateway will be used to publish the IIS VMs as a Backend Pool. These VMs which will be installed into the Apps subnet. The App Gateway will also be configured as a web application firewall (WAF). The SQL Server Always On cluster will be installed into the Data subnet behind an internal load balancer that will be configured using Direct Server Return. The domain controllers will be installed into the Identity subnet and configured to provide DNS services, including the configuration on the VNet to point to these servers for DNS.

# Chapter summary

This chapter covered the many topics that make up Virtual Networks in Azure. These topics range from designing and implementing Virtual Networks, to connecting Virtual Networks to other Virtual Networks. Configuring Azure VMs for use with Virtual Networks was also covered including how to secure them using network security groups which are essentially firewalls. You also reviewed deploying web applications, both internet and Intranet facing, by using the

Azure load balancer and the Azure Application Gateway. This chapter also discussed the different options for connecting on-premises networks to Azure, including Site-to-Site VPNs and ExpressRoute.

Below are some of the key takeaways from this chapter:

- Azure Virtual Networks are isolated cloud networks using the IP address space and are required for deploying virtual machines in Azure.

- Subnets allow you to isolate workloads and can be used with network security groups to create firewall rules.

- The GatewaySubnet is a special subnet that is only used for VPN Gateways.

- Azure provides DNS services, but a customer can implement their own DNS servers. The DNS servers can be configured either at the VNet or the network interface level.

- The Azure Application Gateway is a Layer 7 load balancer that can offload SSL traffic, provide web application firewall services, and URL based routing.

- Azure VNets can be connected to each other either by using peering or VPN tunnels.

- VNet peering allows VMs to see each other as one network, but their relationships are non-transitive. If VNETA and VNETB are peered and VNETB and VNETC are peered VNETA and VNETC are not peered.

- There are three types of hybrid connections with Azure Point to Site, Site-to-Site and ExpressRoute.

- VPN Gateways make hybrid connections possible and choosing the correct one should be based on the throughput that is required and the type of connection, but most connections are route-based.

- BGP Routing is used for ExpressRoute and Multi-Site VPN connections.

- ExpressRoute is only available in certain cities around the world and has a premium add-on to support large global networks.

- Public and private IP addresses have two allocation methods: dynamic or static.

- Public IPs can be assigned to VMs, VPN Gateways, internet-facing load balancers or Application Gateways.

- User Defined Routes change the default behavior of subnets allowing you to direct the traffic to other locations. Typically, traffic is sent through a virtual appliance such as a firewall. If traffic is sent to a virtual appliance, IP forwarding must be enabled on the NIC of the VM.

- The Azure load balancer can be used for internet or intranet workloads providing web based applications in a highly available configuration. Health probes are used to ensure the VMs are ready to accept traffic.

- Direct Server Return is an Azure load balancer configuration that is used with SQL Server Always On Availability group clusters deployed on VMs in an Azure VNet.

- Hybrid connections in Azure are a specific type of connection that allows for Azure Applications Apps to connect to on-premises resources such as databases without the need for a VPN. These are different than the hybrid cloud connections that are created by using S2S VPNs.

CHAPTER 5

# Design and deploy ARM templates

The Azure Resource Manager (ARM) provides a central control plane whereby Azure resources can be provisioned and managed. When you use the Azure portal to create and configure resources, you are using ARM. Likewise, if you use command line tools such as Azure PowerShell or the CLI, you are using ARM because these tools are simply invoking what the API's ARM exposes.

The Azure Resource Manager enables IT professionals and developers to describe an infrastructure in a declarative way using JSON documents, known as ARM templates, and then send those documents to ARM to provision the resources described in the template. This is a significant advancement from the approach of invoking a sequence of imperative commands to provision an infrastructure. The declarative model for provisioning resources is arguably what ARM is best known for. However, ARM is much more than a means for provisioning complex infrastructures. It is also the control plane through which access to resources, permissions, and policies are configured.

This chapter covers the Azure Resource Manager through the lens of an IT professional responsible for implementing infrastructures on Azure, configuring access to resources, and implementing built-in and custom policies to govern the environment.

## Skills covered in this chapter:

- Skill 5.1: Implement ARM templates
- Skill 5.2: Control access
- Skill 5.3: Design role-based access control (RBAC)

# Skill 5.1: Implement ARM templates

When you author an ARM template to describe an Azure infrastructure to be implemented, you have at least one JSON file that contains the definitions of the resources you want ARM to deploy. However, in most situations, your infrastructure is complex enough that you need several files to describe your infrastructure and parameterize deployments to support different environments, such as development, test, UAT, and production. If you have heard the term "infrastructure as code," that's exactly what ARM templates are. It is code (JSON files and scripts) that define the infrastructure and deploy it.

> **This skill covers how to:**
> - Author ARM templates
> - Deploy an ARM template

## Author ARM templates

In the simplest of cases, an infrastructure described as code includes the following types of files:

- **ARM template file**   This is a JSON file where the resources (virtual machines, virtual networks, etc.) for your infrastructure are described.  You may have one or multiple files used to describe your infrastructure.  For example, you may have one file that describes core infrastructure such as a virtual network, jumpbox server, and a virtual appliance. You may have another file that describes workload specific infrastructure, such as a cluster of web server virtual machines, availability set, load balancer, and database server cluster. This file is required.

- **ARM template parameter file**   This is a JSON file that provides parameter values for parameters defined in the ARM template file. For example, if you have a virtual machine resource defined in your ARM template file, it is common to have the size of the virtual machine parameterized so that you can deploy different sized virtual machines for different environments. This file is optional but almost always necessary for even a simple infrastructure. You may also have multiple files used to define parameter values.  Generally speaking, for each ARM template file you have an ARM template parameter file.

- **Deployment script file**   This can be a PowerShell script or a Bash script that is used to deploy the infrastructure described in the ARM template file using parameter values from an ARM template parameter file. If you are working solely in a Windows environment, a PowerShell script may be all you need. If you are working in a Windows, Linux, or Mac environment, authoring a Bash script with CLI commands would be necessary. It's common to have both a PowerShell script and a Bash script so the IT professional can use the scripting environment they are most comfortable with. This file is optional but always should be present. Without a deployment script, you would have to use the Azure portal to deploy your ARM template and specify parameter values, which is error prone and inefficient.

- **Artifact files**   These are files that augment your infrastructure deployment by configuring the internals of a resource. For example, if your ARM template file describes a Windows Server 2016 virtual machine resource, this is an ARM provision.  However, if you need the virtual machine to be an IIS web server, or Active Directory server, or file server, this configuration must be done *inside* the virtual machine instance. A common approach for Windows virtual machines is to use Desired State Configuration (DSC) to describe the desired state the virtual machine should be in *after* it has been provisioned. DSC requires PowerShell scripts, modules, and optionally other files to configure the virtual machine instance. These files are examples of artifact files that would be part of your infrastructure-as-code.  Artifact files are optional.

To author the ARM template files, parameter files, and deployment scripts, you want an editor that can provide a rich authoring experience for each of these types of files. While any text editor works, a couple of options that delivers a rich authoring experience with IntelliSense support are described below. Both can be downloaded from *https://www.visualstudio.com/downloads/*.

- **Visual Studio Code**   A code editor that runs on Windows, Linux, and Mac.  For authoring ARM templates and deployment scripts, install the following extensions: *Azure Resource Manager Tools*, *Azure CLI Tools*, and *PowerShell*.
- **Visual Studio Community 2017**   A full-fledged integrated development environment (IDE) that runs on Windows and Mac. For authoring ARM templates and deployment scripts, install the following extensions: Azure Resource Manager Tools and PowerShell tools.

The first line in an ARM template file is a $schema property that defines the schema for the document. This document specifies the types of elements that can be defined in the document, what their properties are, whether they are optional or required, and references to additional schema files for specific resource types. At the time of this writing, the value you should use for the $schema property and what you find references to in the ARM template documentation is at *http://schema.management.azure.com/schemas/2015-01-01/deploymentTemplate.json*.

---

*MORE INFORMATION*  **ARM TEMPLATE SCHEMAS**

The schemas for ARM template files and parameter files are open-sourced on GitHub at *https://github.com/Azure/azure-resource-manager-schemas*. Here, you can dig deeper into the schema definitions, follow the development of schema files, raise issues, and even contribute to the repository.

---

The schema file referenced in the $schema property defines five additional elements for an ARM template file as described here:

- **contentVersion**   A four-part version number for the document, such as 1.0.0.0. This is required.
- **variables**   An object containing variable definitions used in the document. This is optional.

- **parameters**   An object containing parameter values that can be passed in when deploying the ARM template. This is optional.

- **resources**   An array containing resource definitions. This is required.

- **outputs**   An object containing values resulting from the deployment of an ARM template. For example, if a deployment organizes a public facing load balancer, you may choose to output the IP address of the load balancer. This is optional.

The JSON code below is an example of a valid ARM template with all the required and optional elements. You can name the ARM template file anything you want. However, a common naming convention is to name it azuredeploy.json and is the filename that is used in this text.

```
{
    "$schema": "http://schema.management.azure.com/schemas/2015-01
-01/deploymentTemplate.json#",
    "contentVersion": "1.0.0.0",
    "parameters": {  },
    "variables": {  },
    "resources": [  ],
    "outputs": {  }
}
```

In the following sections, we add resources to the azuredeploy.json file to provision a Windows Server virtual machine with two network interface cards (NICs).

## Define a virtual network resource

Every resource in Azure is unique. So, the definition of a resource, and its properties and values, varies from one resource to the next. The schema that defines the structure of the ARM template file includes the schema that defines the shape of a resource. If you are ever unsure about how to define a resource, you can always refer to the resource schema if you need to. Also, Visual Studio Code and Visual Studio 2017 provide IntelliSense to help you author the resource definitions.

> *MORE INFORMATION* **RESOURCE SCHEMAS**
>
> A useful trick discovering the schema for a resource is to deploy the resource using the Azure portal first. Then, open the Resource Group blade for where the resource is deployed in, and click Automation Script to see the resource template.
>
> Azure Quickstart Templates are another source of community contributed ARM templates and scripts to deploy simple and complex infrastructures. This is also a good learning resource. You can access the Azure Quickstart Templates at *https://azure.microsoft.com/en-us/ resources/templates/.*

The code in Listing 5-1 below shows how a virtual network resource could be defined in the azuredeploy.json file. The brief narrative of the code added to define the virtual network is as follows:

- A parameter was added to allow for the name of the virtual network to be parameterized for each deployment. The name of the parameter, vnetName, is how the parameter value is referenced later in the resources array. The parameter is of type string, with a default value of vnet. In the resources array, the value of the parameter is accessed using the parameters() function.

- A few variables were added. The first is the vnetPrefix, which is referenced in the resources section to define the address space for the virtual network. The vnetAppsSubnetName and vnetAppsSubnetPrefix variables provide a name and address space for a subnet named Apps. Following are similar variables for a subnet named Data. In the resources array, the value of these variables are accessed using the variables() function.

- The actual definition of the virtual network resource is added to the resources array. The first four elements in the virtual network resource definition are common to all resources. Their values are different, but every resource must provide the following:

    - **name**  The name of the resource, which can be any value. In this scenario, the value is passed in as a parameter during template deployment.

    - **type**  The type of the resource is always in the format of <provider namespace>/<resource type>. For the virtual network resource, the provider namespace is Microsoft.Network and the resource type is virtualNetwork.

    - **apiVersion**  A resource type is defined in a resource provider. A resource provider exposes the APIs and schema for the resource types it contains. A resource provider takes on a new version number when resource types are added, changed, deleted, and when there are schema changes. As a result, resource providers usually have multiple API versions. So, when defining a resource in an ARM template, you must specify the version of the resource provider you wish to use.

    - **location**  The location refers to the region to deploy the resource in, such as East US, West US, West Europe, etc. It is common convention for a resource to be located in the same region as the resource group it is contained in. The resourceGroup() function exposes a location property for this purpose.

Next is the properties element, where resource-specific properties can be set. The properties element is present for most resources in Azure. However, its shape (i.e. properties inside) varies for each resource type. For the virtual network resource, the properties element provides settings for the address space of the virtual network and its subnets.

**LISTING 5-1** The azuredeploy.json file after adding a virtual network resource

```json
{
  "$schema": "https://schema.management.azure.com/schemas/2015-01
-01/deploymentTemplate.json#",
  "contentVersion": "1.0.0.0",
  "parameters": {
    "vnetName": {
      "type": "string",
      "defaultValue": "vnet"
    }
  },
  "variables": {
    "vnetPrefix": "10.0.0.0/16",
    "vnetAppsSubnetName": "Apps",
    "vnetAppsSubnetPrefix": "10.0.0.0/24",
    "vnetDataSubnetName": "Data",
    "vnetDataSubnetPrefix": "10.0.1.0/24"
  },
  "resources": [
    {
      "name": "[parameters('vnetName')]",
      "type": "Microsoft.Network/virtualNetworks",
      "apiVersion": "2016-03-30",
      "location": "[resourceGroup().location]",
      "properties": {
        "addressSpace": {
          "addressPrefixes": [
            "[variables('vnetPrefix')]"
          ]
        },
        "subnets": [
          {
            "name": "[variables('vnetAppsSubnetName')]",
            "properties": {
              "addressPrefix": "[variables('vnetAppsSubnetPrefix')]"
            }
          },
          {
            "name": "[variables('vnetDataSubnetName')]",
            "properties": {
              "addressPrefix": "[variables('vnetDataSubnetPrefix')]"
            }
          }
        ]
      }
    }
  ]
}
```

The Azure platform provides hundreds of resource types that can be used to define an infrastructure. As you learned in this section, a resource type is made available through a resource provider. You can get a list of all the resource providers using the Get-AzureRmResourceProvider Azure PowerShell cmdlet or by using the az `provider list` CLI command. For each of the providers returned, you can see the namespace, resource types, and API versions it supports.

## Define a pair of NIC resources

The NIC resource binds a virtual machine to a virtual network. Like a physical machine, a virtual machine can have multiple NICs to bind the virtual machine to multiple subnets, such as a public facing subnet and a non-public facing backend subnet. ARM provides a looping construct that is useful in scenarios such as this where you need to define multiple copies of a resource. Without it, you would have to explicitly define each copy of the resource plus any variables and parameters used to define the resource. This would result in very large template files with a large number of parameters and variables, which is important because there are limits to how large a template file can be and how many parameters and variables can be defined.

The code in Listing 5-2 shows the azuredeploy.json file with a pair of NIC resources added using ARM's looping construct. A brief narrative of the code added is as follows:

- A parameter was added to allow for the name of the NIC to be parameterized for each deployment.

- A few variables were added. The vnetID uses the resourceId() function to construct a string representing the unique resource ID of the virtual network resource. The vnetID is then referenced in the definition of variables nicAppsSubnetRef and nicDataSubnetRef, which uses the concat() function to construct a reference to the two subnets. These two variables are then placed into an array variable called nicSubnetRefs that are referenced by index in the NIC resource definition. The nicCount is used to indicate the number of NICs to be created.

- The NIC resource definition is added after the virtual network resource definition. In this resource definition, the dependsOn array is added with a reference to the vnetID variable. The dependsOn element provides a way to order the provisioning of resources defined in an ARM template. By default, ARM attempts to provision resources in parallel. This results in efficient deployment times. However, some resource types depend on the presence of another resource type as part of their definition, which is the case for the NIC resource. The NIC resource definition must specify the subnet in the virtual network it will be bound to, which requires that the virtual network resource already be provisioned. If you don't indicate this dependency in the dependsOn array, ARM will try to provision the NIC at the same time it provisions the virtual network, resulting in a failed deployment. ARM evaluates all the dependencies in an ARM template and then provisions the resources according to the dependency graph.

The looping mechanism for creating multiple resources of this type is provided by the copy element, where you need to provide only a name for the copy operation and a count value, which is provided by the `nicCount` variable. When ARM sees the copy element, it goes into a loop and provisions a new resource in each of the iterations. In this scenario, there are two iterations. A unique name must be provided for every resource, which can be problematic when using this looping mechanism. To resolve this conflict, the name makes use of the `copyIndex()` function to append the iteration number of the resource being provisioned. In other words, the `copyIndex()` returns the iteration number of the resource type being provisioned in the loop. The `copyIndex()` function can only be used in a resource definition if the copy object is also provided. The complete name for each NIC is constructed using the `concat()` function to concatenate the name provided as a parameter and then a number which is the iteration number from `copyIndex()`. The ARM looping mechanism is zero-based, which means `copyIndex()` will return 0 in the first iteration of the loop. The '1' passed to `copyIndex()` is used to increment the zero-based iteration number by 1 so that the number added to the end of the name begins with 1 instead of 0.

The copyIndex() function is also used to index back into the nicSubnetRefs array variable. This results in the first NIC being bound to the Apps subnet and the second NIC being bound to the Data subnet.

**LISTING 5-2** The azuredeploy.json file after adding a pair NIC resources

```
{
  "$schema": "https://schema.management.azure.com/schemas/2015-01-01/deploymentTemplate.
json#",
  "contentVersion": "1.0.0.0",
  "parameters": {
    "vnetName": {
      "type": "string",
      "defaultValue": "vnet"
    },
    "nicName": {
      "type": "string",
      "defaultValue": "nic"
    }
  },
  "variables": {
    "vnetPrefix": "10.0.0.0/16",
    "vnetAppsSubnetName": "Apps",
    "vnetAppsSubnetPrefix": "10.0.0.0/24",
    "vnetDataSubnetName": "Data",
    "vnetDataSubnetPrefix": "10.0.1.0/24",
    "vnetID": "[resourceId('Microsoft.Network/virtualNetworks',
parameters('vnetName'))]",
    "nicAppsSubnetRef": "[concat(variables('vnetID'), '/subnets/', variables('vnetAppsSu
```

```
bnetName'))]",
    "nicDataSubnetRef": "[concat(variables('vnetID'), '/subnets/', variables('vnetDataSu
bnetName'))]",
    "nicSubnetRefs": [ "[variables('nicAppsSubNetRef')]", "[variables('nicDataSubnetR
ef')]" ],
    "nicCount": 2
  },
  "resources": [
    {
      "name": "[parameters('vnetName')]",
      "type": "Microsoft.Network/virtualNetworks",
      "apiVersion": "2016-03-30",
      "location": "[resourceGroup().location]",
      "properties": {
        "addressSpace": {
          "addressPrefixes": [
            "[variables('vnetPrefix')]"
          ]
        },
        "subnets": [
          {
            "name": "[variables('vnetAppsSubnetName')]",
            "properties": {
              "addressPrefix": "[variables('vnetAppsSubnetPrefix')]"
            }
          },
          {
            "name": "[variables('vnetDataSubnetName')]",
            "properties": {
              "addressPrefix": "[variables('vnetDataSubnetPrefix')]"
            }
          }
        ]
      }
    },
    {
      "name": "[concat(parameters('nicName'), copyIndex(1))]",
      "type": "Microsoft.Network/networkInterfaces",
      "apiVersion": "2016-03-30",
      "location": "[resourceGroup().location]",
      "dependsOn": [
        "[variables('vnetID')]"
      ],
      "copy": {
        "name": "nicCopy",
        "count": "[variables('nicCount')]"
      },
      "properties": {
        "ipConfigurations": [
          {
            "name": "ipConfig",
            "properties": {
              "privateIPAllocationMethod": "Dynamic",
              "subnet": {
                "id": "[variables('nicSubnetRefs')[copyIndex()]]"
```

```
            }
          }
        }
      ]
    }
  }
]
}
```

## Define a virtual machine resource

The virtual machine resource definition, as shown in Listing 5-3, leverages the same ARM template authoring concepts discussed previously. Therefore, it is not necessary to narrate all the changes that were made to the template file to define the virtual machine resource. It is, however, worth pointing out the adminUser and adminPassword parameters that were added. These parameters do not provide a default value, which is recommend for secure information such as credentials. However, these parameters are required because the minLength property was included in the parameter definition. Because these parameters are strings, the minLength indicates the length of the string value must be at least 1 for the adminUser and 12 for the adminPassword. Similarily, the maxLength property can be included to limit the length of the parameter value if desired.

It is common to see examples where the credentials for a virtual machine resource, and other resource types that require credentials, are passed in as parameters. It's convenient to do so. However, for security reasons, it is not recommended to do this. Instead, it is recommended to store your credentials in Azure Key Vault and create template parameters to pass in the required Key Vault settings so that ARM can pull the credentials from Key Vault when provisioning the virtual machine. An example demonstrating how to use Key Vault to pass secure values into an ARM template during deployment is available at *https://docs.microsoft.com/en-us/ azure/azure-resource-manager/resource-manager-keyvault-parameter.*

LISTING 5-3 The azuredeploy.json file after adding the virtual machine resource

```
{
  "$schema": "https://schema.management.azure.com/schemas/2015-01-01/deploymentTemplate.
json#",
  "contentVersion": "1.0.0.0",
  "parameters": {
    "vnetName": {
      "type": "string",
      "defaultValue": "vnet"
    },
    "nicName": {
      "type": "string",
      "defaultValue": "nic"
    },
    "vmName": {
      "type": "string",
      "defaultValue": "vm"
    },
```

```json
      "vmSize": {
        "type": "string",
        "defaultValue": "Standard_DS2_v2"
      },
      "adminUser": {
        "type": "string",
        "minLength": 1
      },
      "adminPassword": {
        "type": "securestring",
        "minLength": 12
      }
    },
    "variables": {
      "vnetPrefix": "10.0.0.0/16",
      "vnetAppsSubnetName": "Apps",
      "vnetAppsSubnetPrefix": "10.0.0.0/24",
      "vnetDataSubnetName": "Data",
      "vnetDataSubnetPrefix": "10.0.1.0/24",
      "vnetID": "[resourceId('Microsoft.Network/virtualNetworks',
parameters('vnetName'))]",
      "nicAppsSubnetRef": "[concat(variables('vnetID'), '/subnets/', variables('vnetAppsSu
bnetName'))]",
      "nicDataSubnetRef": "[concat(variables('vnetID'), '/subnets/', variables('vnetDataSu
bnetName'))]",
      "nicSubnetRefs": [ "[variables('nicAppsSubNetRef')]", "[variables('nicDataSubnetR
ef')]" ],
      "nicCount": 2
    },
    "resources": [
      {
        "name": "[parameters('vnetName')]",
        "type": "Microsoft.Network/virtualNetworks",
        "apiVersion": "2016-03-30",
        "location": "[resourceGroup().location]",
        "properties": {
          "addressSpace": {
            "addressPrefixes": [
              "[variables('vnetPrefix')]"
            ]
          },
          "subnets": [
            {
              "name": "[variables('vnetAppsSubnetName')]",
              "properties": {
                "addressPrefix": "[variables('vnetAppsSubnetPrefix')]"
              }
            },
            {
              "name": "[variables('vnetDataSubnetName')]",
              "properties": {
                "addressPrefix": "[variables('vnetDataSubnetPrefix')]"
              }
            }
          ]
```

```
              }
          },
          {
            "name": "[concat(parameters('nicName'), copyIndex(1))]",
            "type": "Microsoft.Network/networkInterfaces",
            "apiVersion": "2016-03-30",
            "location": "[resourceGroup().location]",
            "dependsOn": [
              "[variables('vnetID')]"
            ],
            "copy": {
              "name": "nicCopy",
              "count": "[variables('nicCount')]"
            },
            "properties": {
              "ipConfigurations": [
                {
                  "name": "ipConfig",
                  "properties": {
                    "privateIPAllocationMethod": "Dynamic",
                    "subnet": {
                      "id": "[variables('nicSubnetRefs')[copyIndex()]]"
                    }
                  }
                }
              ]
            }
          },
          {
            "name": "[parameters('vmName')]",
            "type": "Microsoft.Compute/virtualMachines",
            "apiVersion": "2017-03-30",
            "location": "[resourceGroup().location]",
            "dependsOn": [ "nicCopy" ],
            "properties": {
              "hardwareProfile": {
                "vmSize": "[parameters('vmSize')]"
              },
              "osProfile": {
                "computerName": "[parameters('vmName')]",
                "adminUsername": "[parameters('adminUser')]",
                "adminPassword": "[parameters('adminPassword')]"
              },
              "storageProfile": {
                "imageReference": {
                  "offer": "WindowsServer",
                  "publisher": "MicrosoftWindowsServer",
                  "sku": "2016-Datacenter",
                  "version": "latest"
                },
                "osDisk": {
                  "createOption": "FromImage"
                }
              },
              "networkProfile": {
```

```
        "networkInterfaces": [
          {
            "id": "[resourceId('Microsoft.Network/networkInterfaces',
concat(parameters('nicName'), '1'))]",
            "properties": {
              "primary": true
            }
          },
          {
            "id": "[resourceId('Microsoft.Network/networkInterfaces',
concat(parameters('nicName'), '2'))]",
            "properties": {
              "primary": false
            }
          }
        ]
      }
    }
  }
]
}
```

Because most ARM templates define parameters to parameterize the deployment it is common to author an ARM template parameter file to provide the parameter values. You may even have multiple template parameter files for a single template. For example, consider the scenario where you need to deploy the same infrastructure for a line-of-business application in different environments, such as a testing environment and a production environment. To deploy the template to the testing environment, you may use fewer virtual machines and with fewer cores and less memory because you just need to test functionality of the application. To deploy the template to the production environment, you may require more virtual machines, each with more cores and memory to meet real production demand. To support this scenario, it is common to create separate template parameter files for each environment.

The first line in an ARM template parameter file is a $schema property that defines the schema for the document. It serves the same purpose as the $schema property you learned about for the template file. At the time of this writing, the value you should use for the $schema property and what you will find references to in documentation is at *http://schema.management.azure.com/schemas/2015-01-01/deploymentParameters.json*.

The schema file referenced in the $schema property defines two additional elements for an ARM template parameter file as described here:

- **contentVersion**   A four-part version number for the document, such as 1.0.0.0.  This is required.  This enables you to version your parameter file just like you would version the template file.

- **parameters**   An object containing the values for the parameters defined in the ARM template.  This is required.

The JSON code below is an example of a valid ARM template parameter file for the template created earlier in the text. You can name the ARM template parameter file anything you want.

However, a common naming convention is to name it azuredeploy.parameters.json, which is the filename used in this text.

```
{
  "$schema": "https://schema.management.azure.com/schemas/2015-01-01/
deploymentParameters.json#",
  "contentVersion": "1.0.0.0",
  "parameters": {
    "vmSize": {
      "value": "Standard_A2"
    },
    "adminUser": {
      "value": "adminuser"
    }
  }
}
```

Recall that some of the parameters defined in the template file included default values. So, it's only required to provide a parameter value for a parameter if you want a different value or if a default value is not provided and the parameter is required. In this case, a different value for the vmSize is provided and the adminUser value is provided since it is required. If a parameter is defined in a template that is required and you don't provide a value for the parameter in a template parameters file, you are prompted to enter the value at the time you deploy the template. This is another way to address the same security concern mentioned previously regarding the passing of credentials through a template parameter. Just don't store the password in the template parameter file because it results in the user being prompted to enter it at the time of deployment.

> ***MORE INFORMATION*** **DEPLOY ARM TEMPLATES TO EXISTING RESOURCE GROUPS**
>
> We cover the basic concepts necessary to author a simple ARM template. When you are defining templates for more complex architectures, it is a best practice to create a main template file that defines nested template resources. Each nested template resource can then reference a separate set of ARM template files to deploy that portion of the infrastructure. This technique enables you to break down a complex infrastructure into smaller and easier to manage parts. It also helps avoid exceeding the ARM template limits and quotas. The nested templates can also be re-used in other main templates. For example, you could have a nested template that defines a SQL Server and SQL Database. That nested template could be used by other templates anytime a SQL Server and SQL Database are required. For a deeper discussion on this technique and other ARM template authoring best practices, see *https://docs.microsoft.com/en-us/azure/azure-resource-manager/resource-manager-template-best-practices.*

As an ARM template's complexity increases, so does the number of parameters you must define to allow for parametrized deployments. A common practice in complex templates is to define a parameter as an object type. This enables you to pass in a JSON structure with multiple properties in a single object. In the example used in this text to create a virtual machine there were just a few parameters defined. You would probably have more though to parameterize things like the number of data disks you want, which operating system, and so on. Rather than creating a new parameter for each, you could create a single object parameter in the template file as shown here.

```
"parameters": {
  "vnetName": {
    "type": "string",
    "defaultValue": "vnet"
  },
  "nicName": {
    "type": "string",
    "defaultValue": "nic"
  },
  "vmSettings": {
    "type": "object"
  },
  "adminUser": {
    "type": "string",
    "minLength": 1
  },
  "adminPassword": {
    "type": "securestring",
    "minLength": 12
  }
},
```

Then, in the template parameter file, define the settings for the virtual machine as shown here.

```
"parameters": {
  "adminUser": {
    "value": "adminuser"
  },
  "vmSettings": {
    "value": {
      "vmName": "vm",
      "vmSize": "Standard_A2"
    }
  }
}
```

In the ARM template file, you can then reference these parameter values using the parameters() function and object notation as shown here.

```
"name": "[parameters('vmSettings').vmName]",
"type": "Microsoft.Compute/virtualMachines",
"apiVersion": "2017-03-30",
"location": "[resourceGroup().location]",
"dependsOn": [ "nicCopy" ],
"properties": {
  "hardwareProfile": {
    "vmSize": "[parameters('vmSettings').vmSize]"
  },
```

For further details on this technique and examples on how to use objects as parameters in ARM templates see *https://docs.microsoft.com/en-us/azure/architecture/building-blocks/extending-templates/objects-as-parameters*.

# Deploy an ARM template

There are two steps required to deploy an ARM template.

1. Create a resource group for the resources in the ARM template to be provisioned in.
2. Create a resource group deployment. This is the step where you send your template file and template parameter file to Azure Resource Manager. After the files are received, Azure Resource Manager evaluates the template to insure it is syntactically correct, determines resource dependencies, and then begins provisioning the resources into the resource group.

> **MORE INFORMATION  ARM TEMPLATES**
>
> It is possible to deploy an ARM template to an existing resource group rather than create a new resource group each time. This is often done when you are re-deploying an ARM template because it failed to deploy previously or perhaps you have added new resources to the template. By default, ARM template deployments are incremental, meaning that Azure Resource Manager will not try to redeploy resources from the template that already exist in the resource group. Instead, it will deploy resources in the template that don't already exist in the resource group. For more details on the incremental and complete modes that ARM supports and examples on how ARM behaves in these two modes, see *https://docs.microsoft.com/en-us/azure/azure-resource-manager/resource-group-template-deploy#incremental-and-complete-deployments*.

## Deploy an ARM template using Azure PowerShell

Use the New-AzureRmResourceGroup and New-AzureRmResourceGroupDeployment cmdlets to deploy an ARM template as shown here:

```
$resourceGroupName = "contoso"
$location = "westus"
$deploymentName = "contoso-deployment-01"

# Create the resource group
$rg = New-AzureRmResourceGroup -Name $resourceGroupName -Location $location -Force

# Deploy the ARM template
New-AzureRmResourceGroupDeployment -ResourceGroupName $rg.ResourceGroupName -Name
$deploymentName '
    -TemplateFile ".\azuredeploy.json" -TemplateParameterFile ".\azuredeploy.parameters.
json"
```

## Deploy an ARM template using CLI

Use the az `group create` and az `group deployment create` commands to deploy an ARM template as shown here:

```
#!/bin/bash

resourceGroupName="contoso"
location="westus"
deploymentName = "contoso-deployment-01"

# Create the resource group
az group create --name $resourceGroupName -- location $location

# Deploy the ARM template
az group deployment create --resource-group $resourceGroupName --name $deploymentName \
    --template-file "./azuredeploy.json" --parameters "./azuredeploy.parameters.json"
```

## Deploy an ARM template using the Azure portal

The Azure portal provides an interface whereby you can upload an ARM template file, provide parameter values, and even edit the template in your browser. To deploy an ARM template using this technique, search the Marketplace for Template Deployment. In the Template Deployment blade, click Create to begin a custom deployment, and then click the link To Build Your Own Template In The Editor. In the template editor blade, click the Load File link in the toolbar near the top of the blade, select your template file (ie: azuredeploy.json), and then click Save. In the Custom deployment blade, fill in the values for the parameters and click Purchase, as shown in Figure 5-1.

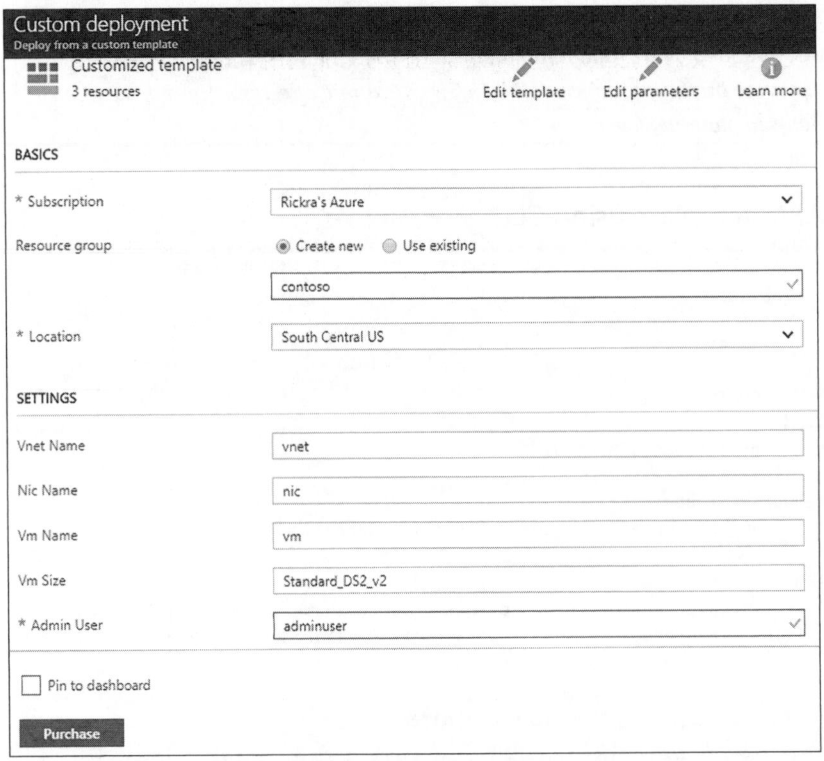

**FIGURE 5-1** Custom deployment of ARM template file using the Azure portal

# Skill 5.2: Control access

A challenge for many organizations adopting a cloud platform is how to implement controls, policies, and procedures to govern their cloud environments such that the benefits of the cloud can be realized while respecting the business's security, compliance, and operational requirements. While the concepts for managing access to resources in the cloud is like those for on-premises environments, the techniques for implementing these concepts are different. The global presence of cloud environments and the increasing number of services available in the cloud introduces new challenges for IT. Things like data sovereignty requirements that may not have been a concern for a company operating in Europe or the United States prior to adopting the cloud, suddenly become real. Managing the types of resources available to the organization and being able to identify those resources for things like cost chargebacks is another example.

# Leverage service principals with ARM authentication

When you sign-in to your Azure subscription you must authenticate to Azure Active Directory (AD). After successfully authenticating, you can manage resources within the subscription to the extent your permissions and the subscription policies allow you to. The permissions you have are tied to your identity in Azure AD. As an IT professional, such as an IT administrator, your permissions are generally less restrictive. Others in the organization may have permissions that allow them to do their job, such as being able to access several line-of-business applications, but nothing more. These identities and the permissions associated with them exist for the people in the organization. However, an identity (or directory object) does not always represent a person. There are many scenarios where an application or service needs to authenticate to Azure AD and perform functions to the extent it has permissions to do so. Identities such as this are called service principals, and the permissions associated with them are restricted to a very specific set of permissions.

Consider a scenario where an application needs access to a database, which requires a connection string to connect to the database. For added security, the connection string is stored and maintained in an Azure key vault. To read a secret in the key vault, the identity of the caller (in this case the application) must be authenticated and have permission to read the secret. To achieve this, a service principal is created for the application and given only the permission to read the secret from key vault. This very restrictive set of permissions, which is to read a secret from key vault, is all the application needs to function in this scenario. We use this scenario as context for the next few sections.

## Register an application in Azure AD

The first thing you need to do is register the application with Azure Active Directory. The application registration tells Azure AD the type of application (or client) that will be authenticating to Azure AD, and hence the OAuth2 protocol flow that occurs when the application needs to authenticate to Azure AD. There are two types of applications you can choose from when registering an application in Azure AD, which are Web App / API and Native. In the context of service principals, the only option that is applicable is the Web App / API application type.

When you register an application with Azure AD using command-line tools such as PowerShell or the CLI, the Web App / API application type is used. It's only when you're using the Azure portal that you see an option for the Native application type.

**MORE INFORMATION AZURE AD AUTHENTICATION SCENARIOS**

**You may be asking yourself if the Web App / API is the only option that applies, why are Native application types mentioned? The answer is that in this section, we're talking about a very specific use case of an application authenticating to Azure AD using a service principal. However, application registrations in Azure AD are typically the result of configuring an application to be protected by Azure AD, which requires users of the application to first authenticate to Azure AD before they can use the application. Those "user applications" can be web-based applications or native.**

A web-based application is exactly that, an application typically accessed through a browser using HTTPS, whereas a native application is an application running on a device, such as a desktop, phone, or tablet. The OAuth2 protocol flow that plays out when a user is authenticating to the application is different for each of these application types. For a detailed description of the different types of authentication scenarios using these types of applications see *https://docs.microsoft.com/en-us/azure/active-directory/develop/active-directory-authentication-scenarios*. Using the CLI, you can use the `az ad app create` command to create a new application registration with Azure AD as shown here:

```
#!/bin/bash

# Define properties for the AD app registration
adAppName="contos0"
adAppIdUris="https://contos0-app"

# Create a new app registration in Azure AD
az ad app create --display-name $adAppName --homepage $adAppIdUris --identifier-uris
$adAppIdUris
```

After the application registration is complete, you see the properties for the application registration, as shown in Figure 5-2.


```
{
  "appId": "380e2543-1441-4484-950c-6cebebe5b97c",
  "appPermissions": null,
  "availableToOtherTenants": false,
  "displayName": "contos0",
  "homepage": "https://contos0-app",
  "identifierUris": [
    "https://contos0-app"
  ],
  "objectId": "35608b3c-b294-4b74-983a-cfbcba89aeb0",
  "objectType": "Application",
  "replyUrls": []
}
```


**FIGURE 5-2** Azure AD application registration properties

Using Azure PowerShell, you can use the New-AzureRmADApplication cmdlet to create a new application registration with Azure AD as shown here:

```
# Define properties for the AD app registration
$adAppName="contos0"
$adAppIdUris="https://contos0-app"

# Create a new app registration in Azure AD
$app = New-AzureRmADApplication -DisplayName $adAppName -IdentifierUris $adAppIdUris
```

Using the Azure portal, you can create a new application registration from the Azure Active Directory blade. In the Azure AD blade, click App Registrations. In the App Registrations blade, click New Application Registration in the toolbar. Provide a name, select the application type, and provide a sign-on URL, which can be any unique URL in your Azure AD tenant, as shown in Figure 5-3.

**FIGURE 5-3**  Azure AD application registration using the Azure portal

When you create a new application registration using the Azure portal, an associated service principal is created automatically for you. If you use the command-line tools, you must explicitly create a service principal for your application, which is covered in the next section.

## Create a service principal in Azure AD

Using the CLI, you can use the az ad sp create command to create a new service principal for the application registered in the previous section. When creating the service principal, you need to provide the object ID of the application registration as a parameter.

```
#!/bin/bash

# The object ID of the application registered with Azure AD
adAppId="35608b3c-b294-4b74-983a-cfbcba89aeb0"

# Create a new service principal for the application
az ad sp create --id $adAppId
```

After the service principal is created, you see the properties for the service principal as shown in Figure 5-4.

```
{
  "appId": "380e2543-1441-4484-950c-6cebebe5b97c",
  "displayName": "contos0",
  "objectId": "1f18cd2e-adbf-42c2-9cfd-5eca8632c0ec",
  "objectType": "ServicePrincipal",
  "servicePrincipalNames": [
    "380e2543-1441-4484-950c-6cebebe5b97c",
    "https://contos0-app"
  ]
}
```

FIGURE 5-4 Azure AD service principal properties

> **MORE INFORMATION** **SERVICE PRINCIPAL USING CLI**
>
> For a deeper discussion and examples on creating a service principal using the CLI, managing roles, and updating the service principal credentials see *https://docs.microsoft.com/en-us/cli/azure/create-an-azure-service-principal-azure-cli*. Using Azure PowerShell, you can use the New-AzureRmADServicePrincipal cmdlet to create a new service principal for the application as shown here:

```
# Define properties for the AD app registration
$adAppName="contos0"
$adAppIdUris="https://contos0-app"

# Create a new app registration in Azure AD
$app = New-AzureRmADApplication -DisplayName $adAppName -IdentifierUris $adAppIdUris

# Create a new service principal for the application
$sp = New-AzureRmADServicePrincipal -ApplicationId $app.ApplicationId
```

For the application to authenticate to Azure AD, you need to create a key. In some documentation, this is referred to as the client secret. Either way, an application such as a web application in this scenario needs to provide an application ID and a key (client secret) when attempting to authenticate to Azure AD. This key could be created using the command-line tool during application registration. Or, you can create it afterward using the Azure portal. To create a key using the Azure portal, open the application registration blade for the application registered in Azure AD and click Keys. Specify a name for the key, the duration, and click Save. The key (or client secret) is displayed, as shown in Figure 5-5.

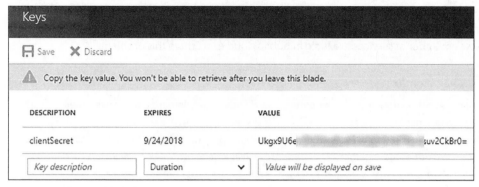

**FIGURE 5-5** The Keys blade for an application registered with Azure AD

Now you have all the pieces required for an application to authenticate itself with Azure AD using the service principal. The permissions for the service principal, such as being allowed to access the key vault, are configured with the key vault instance. The application, such as the web application, authenticates to Azure AD using the Application ID from the application registration and the Key (client secret).

There is a significant number of developer-related tasks needed to complete this scenario. Because this text is targeting the IT professional, those tasks are not covered here. Instead, only the tasks that most IT professionals would complete are covered. For a complete end-to-end description of all the tasks required to complete this, including assigning permissions to the key vault for the service principal see *https://docs.microsoft.com/en-us/azure/key-vault/key-vault-use-from-web-application*.

> **MORE INFORMATION** **APPLICATIONS AND SERVICE PRINCIPALS**
>
> It should be clear that there is a subtle, but very distinct, difference between an application registration in Azure AD and a service principal. In some documentation, these are sometimes referred to as one in the same. But, understanding the differences will aid the IT professional in creating robust service principal to application registration configurations. For more details on the differences between applications and service principals see *https://docs.microsoft.com/en-us/azure/active-directory/develop/active-directory-application-objects*.

# Set management policies

Organizations adopting public cloud quickly realize the need to govern their cloud environments to adhere to their business and operational requirements. Where an organization does business, the geographies where data can be stored, legal requirements for data protection, auditing user activity, and controlling costs are just a few examples of things an organization must consider.

It's easy for anyone in an organization to obtain an Azure subscription and start deploying solutions and building applications, resulting in shadow IT systems that could potentially put the organization at risk. Shadow IT is not unique to cloud because these same behaviors often occur in on-premises environments. However, the global footprint of public cloud and the massive number of services available in public cloud exacerbate this problem.

> **MORE INFORMATION** **ENTERPRISE GUIDANCE**
>
> Microsoft provides guidance for enterprises on how to implement and manage their Azure subscriptions. The concept is referred to as the enterprise Azure scaffold. It identifies patterns for provisioning subscriptions, defining and applying policies, and other best practices for subscription governance. The guidance is available at *https://docs.microsoft.com/en-us/ azure/azure-resource-manager/resource-manager-subscription-governance.*

Azure resource policies provide a mechanism for an organization to apply some governance to Azure resources used by the organization. Resource policies can be scoped to a subscription or to a resource group and are essential to implementing governance in Azure.

## Azure resource policy

An Azure resource policy, as its name implies, enforces policy on a resource at the time a resource is deployed. When you initiate a deployment for a resource using an ARM template, script, or REST API, ARM first validates the request before proceeding to provision the resource. As part of that validation, ARM checks for any policies that have been assigned and then validates the resource against those policies. If there is a conflict because of policy the deployment is aborted. For example, suppose you have a policy assigned to your subscription that says you can only deploy A-series virtual machines. If you tried to deploy a DS11 v2 virtual machine using the Azure portal, you would see an error message similar to that shown in figure 5-6.

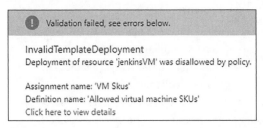

**FIGURE 5-6** Validation error in Azure port as a result of a resource policy conflict

Azure provides many *built-in* resource policies for common governance needs. You can also create your own custom policies if needed. Some of the built-in policies include, but are not limited to, the following:

- **Allowed locations**   Used to enforce geo-location requirements by restricting which regions resources can be deployed in.

- **Allowed virtual machine SKUs**   Restricts the virtual machines sizes/SKUs that can be deployed to a predefined set of SKUs. Useful for controlling costs of virtual machine resources.

- **Enforce tag and its value** Requires resources to be tagged. This is useful for tracking resource costs for purposes of department chargebacks.
- **Not allowed resource types** Identifies resource types that cannot be deployed. For example, you may want to prevent a costly HDInsight cluster deployment if you know your group would never need it.

You can discover all the built-in policies available by going to the Subscription blade in the Azure portal, and clicking Policies. In the Policies blade, click the Policies tab at the top of the page. This displays both built-in and any custom policies that may be defined, as shown in figure 5-7.

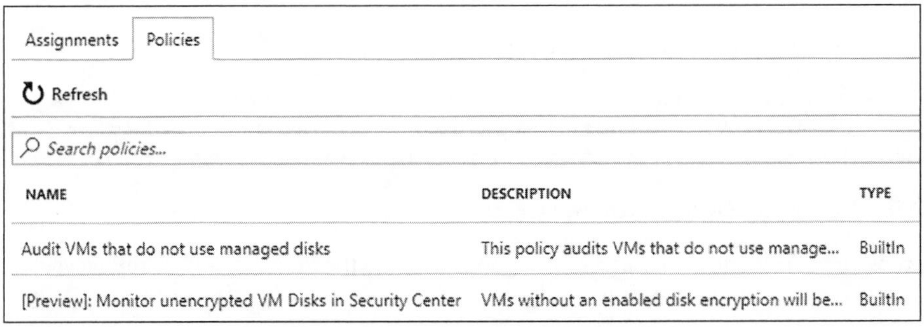

| Assignments | Policies | | |
|---|---|---|---|
| ↻ Refresh | | | |
| 🔍 Search policies... | | | |
| **NAME** | | **DESCRIPTION** | **TYPE** |
| Audit VMs that do not use managed disks | | This policy audits VMs that do not use manage... | BuiltIn |
| [Preview]: Monitor unencrypted VM Disks in Security Center | | VMs without an enabled disk encryption will be... | BuiltIn |

**FIGURE 5-7** Resource policies listed in the Subscription Policies blade in the Azure portal

## Custom resource policy

If you need to enforce something that is not covered by a built-in policy, then you can create a custom policy. A policy definition is described using JSON and includes a policy rule, which is an if/then construct. As an example, consider a policy that denies a storage account from being created unless the storage encryption service is enabled. The following JSON illustrates such a policy rule.

```
{
    "if": {
        "allOf": [
            {
                "field": "type",
                "equals": "Microsoft.Storage/storageAccounts"
            },
            {
                "field": "Microsoft.Storage/storageAccounts/enableBlobEncryption",
                "equals": "false"
            }
        ]
    },
    "then": {
        "effect": "deny"
    }
}
```

In the if section, there are two conditions defined. The first condition states that the type field for a resource must match the namespace Microsoft.Storage/storageAccounts. In other words, this policy rule only applies to storage accounts. The second condition states that the storage account field, enableBlobEncryption, be set to false. The allOf array states that all of the conditions described in the array must match.

In the then section, the effect property tells Azure Resource Manager to deny the request to provision the storage account.

To create a custom resource policy using Azure PowerShell, use the New-AzureRmPolicyDefinition cmdlet as shown in the following code (this assumes the JSON above was saved to a JSON file):

```
$policyName = "denyStorageAccountWithoutEncryption"

# Create a new policy definition
$policyDef = New-AzureRmPolicyDefinition -Name $policyName -DisplayName $policyName '
    -Description "Require storage accounts to have the storage encryption service
enabled" '
    -Policy ".\denyStorageWithoutEncryption.json"
```

To remove a policy definition using Azure PowerShell, use the Remove-AzureRmPolicyDefinition cmdlet as shown in the following code:

```
# Remove a policy definition
Remove-AzureRmPolicyDefinition -Name $policyDef.Name
```

> **MORE INFORMATION    ARM CUSTOM POLICIES**
>
> For more information on how to create a custom policy using other logical operators, resource fields, and different effects, see *https://docs.microsoft.com/en-us/azure/azure-resource-manager/resource-manager-policy*.

## Resource policy assignment

The previous sections discussed built-in and custom resource policy definitions. However, for a policy to be evaluated during resource deployment, it must be assigned. Resource policies can be assigned at the subscription and resource group level.

To assign a resource policy, open the Subscriptions blade in the Azure portal, and click Policies. In the Assignments tab, click the Add Assignment button near the top of the page. The Add Assignment blade provides an interface for you to select a policy definition, specify the scope (subscription or select a resource group), and provide other properties necessary to complete the assignment. Figure 5-8 shows a resource policy assignment of the custom policy definition created in the previous section. The scope is set to the resource group named contoso-app. After completing this assignment, if anyone tries to create a storage account in the contoso-app resource group without enabling the storage encryption service, the request is denied.

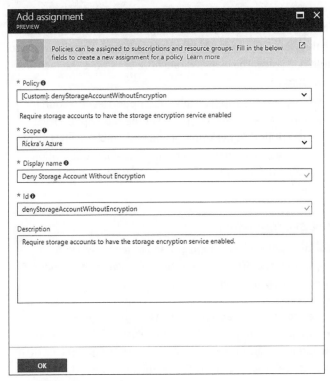

**FIGURE 5-8** Assigning a custom policy to a resource group using the Azure portal

To create a resource policy assignment at the subscription level for the custom policy defini-tion from the previous section using the CLI, use the az `policy assignment create` command, as shown in the following code:

```
#!/bin/bash
policyName = "denyStorageAccountWithoutEncryption"

# Create a new resource policy assignment at the subscription level
az policy assignment create --policy $policyName
```

## Lock resources

For some infrastructure resources, such as a virtual network, express route circuit, or network virtual appliance, it is often desired to lock down resources to mitigate the risks of accidental deletion or modification of resources. In Azure, resource locks provide this capability and are available at two levels:

- **CanNotDelete**  This lock level indicates that a resource can be read and modified, but it cannot be deleted.
- **ReadOnly**  This lock level indicates that a resource can be read, but it cannot be modi-fied or deleted.

Users assigned the Owner or User Access Administrator built-in role can create and remove locks. Users in these roles are not excluded from the lock. For example, if an owner creates a ReadOnly lock on a resource and then later tries to modify the resource, the operation will not be allowed because of the lock that is in place. The owner would have to remove the lock first, and then proceed to modify the resource.

The scope of a resource lock can vary. It can be applied at a subscription level, resource group, or as granular as a single resource. A resource lock applied at the subscription level would apply to all resources in the subscription. For example, if you have implemented a hub and spoke network topology where the resources in the hub are in a separate subscription from the spokes, you may want to apply a ReadOnly lock at the subscription level to protect against accidental modification or deletion.

> **MORE INFORMATION** **HUB AND SPOKE NETWORK**
>
> For more information on the hub and spoke network topology and to see a reference architecture detailing this pattern, see *https://docs.microsoft.com/en-us/azure/architecture/ reference-architectures/hybrid-networking/hub-spoke.*

If a lock is scoped at the resource group level, it applies to all resources in the resource group for which the lock has been applied. Resources in the resource group inherit the resource group lock. If a resource is added to a resource group where resource group lock of CanNotDelete is already present, that new resource inherits the CanNotDelete lock.

## Create a resource lock

Using the Azure portal, you can manage locks for any resource by clicking *Locks* in the resource blade. Figure 5-9 illustrates creating a CanNotDelete, resource group level lock.

**FIGURE 5-9** Creating a resource group level lock using the Azure portal

The Locks blade is where you can view and manage locks at a resource group level or resource level. If you need to manage locks at a subscription level, open the subscription blade and click Resource Locks, as shown in Figure 5-10.

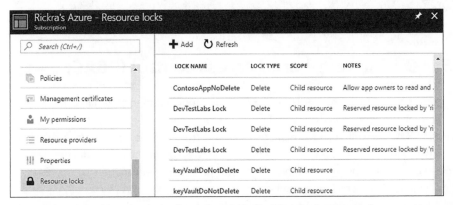

**FIGURE 5-10** Managing subscription level resource locks using the Azure portal

Using the CLI, you can use the az lock create command to create a new resource lock. The code below creates a resource lock on a virtual machine resource.

```
#!/bin/bash

# Resource lock properties
lockName="vmNoDeleteLock"
resourceGroupName="Dev"
resourceName="jenkinsVM"
resourceType="Microsoft.Compute/virtualMachines"

# Create a CanNotDelete resource lock for a virtual machine
az lock create --name $lockName --lockType CanNotDelete \
    --resource-group $resourceGroupName --resource-name $resourceName \
    --resource-type $resourceType
```

Using Azure PowerShell, you can use the New-AzureRmResourceLock cmdlet to create a new resource lock. The code below creates a resource lock on a resource group.

```
# Resource lock properties
$lockName = "devGroupNoDeleteLock"
$resourceGroupName = "Dev"

# Create a CanNotDelete resource lock for the resource group (ie: all resources in the
resource group)
New-AzureRmResourceLock -LockName $lockName -LockLevel CanNotDelete '
    -ResourceGroupName $resourceGroupName
```

Resource locks are proper resources just like any other resource you may already be familiar with. A difference is that a lock is specific to a resource unless it is scoped to the subscription.

# Skill 5.3: Design role-based access control (RBAC)

Managing access to resources in Azure is a critical part to implementing an organization's security and compliance requirements. Azure Resource Manager provides support for role-based access control (RBAC), enabling you to manage who has access to a resource and control what they can do with the resource. RBAC is tightly integrated with Azure Active Directory where the identity of users, user groups, applications, and service principals are managed. Using RBAC, you can implement a least-privilege model for resource access and control by scoping access and control to individual resources, resource groups, or subscriptions.

> This skill covers how to:
> - Implement Azure RBAC standard roles
> - Design Azure RBAC custom roles

## Implement Azure RBAC standard roles

Azure provides many built-in roles for common scenarios. Every role definition includes an actions and notactions property that controls what entities assigned to the role can do. The actions property lists the actions that are allowed, while the notactions property lists the actions that are not allowed. A role definition also includes an assignableScopes property, which scopes the permissions described in the actions and notactions. For example, a role may be scoped to a certain subscription, resource group, or resource.

To better understand these properties, we'll look at three of the most basic built-in roles in the following sections, which are the Owner, Contributor, and Reader roles. There are many more built-in roles than this, but most are a derivation of one of these three roles with actions and notactions specific to a specific resource type, such as the Virtual Machine Contributor built-in role. To get a list of all the built-in roles using Azure CLI, use the `az role definition list` command, as shown in Figure 5-11 (output abbreviated).

```
C:\>az role definition list --query "[?contains(properties.type,'BuiltInRole')].{RoleNam
e: properties.roleName }" --out table
RoleName
-------------------------------------------------
API Management Service Contributor
API Management Service Operator Role
API Management Service Reader Role
Application Insights Component Contributor
Application Insights Snapshot Debugger
Automation Job Operator
Automation Operator
Automation Runbook Operator
Backup Contributor
Backup Operator
Backup Reader
```

**FIGURE 5-11** Getting a list of built-in roles using Azure CLI

You can also get a list of roles (custom and built-in) using the Azure portal. Open the Subscription blade, or a Resource Group blade, or an individual resource blade, and click Access Control (IAM) in the left navigation. Next, click Roles in the toolbar at the top of the blade. This lists the roles that are available, and the number of users and groups already assigned to each role. For example, Figure 5-12 shows an abbreviated list of roles available for a resource group named "contoso-app."

| Roles contoso-app | | |
|---|---|---|
| **NAME** | **USERS** | **GROUPS** |
| Owner | 0 | 1 |
| Contributor | 2 | 0 |
| Reader | 0 | 0 |
| API Management Service Contributor | 0 | 0 |
| API Management Service Operator Role | 0 | 0 |

**FIGURE 5-12** Getting a list of built-in roles using the Azure portal

> **MORE INFORMATION** **BUILT-IN ROLES**
>
> At the time of writing, the number of built-in roles is increasing so documentation may not be current. However, you can always see what roles are available using the Azure CLI or PowerShell. For more information on how to manage roles using Azure CLI, see *https://docs.microsoft.com/en-us/azure/active-directory/role-based-access-control-manage-access-azure-cli*. For more information on how to manage roles using Azure PowerShell, see *https://docs.microsoft.com/en-us/azure/active-directory/role-based-access-control-manage-access-powershell*.

## Owner built-in role

The Azure CLI tools provide an easy way to view a role's definition using the `az role defini-tion` command, as shown in Figure 5-13 where the Owner built-in role definition is displayed.

```
C:\>az role definition list --name Owner
[
  {
    "id": "/subscriptions/9a2bc976-60a5-41f6-afa5-37510596c52b/providers/Microsoft.Autho
rization/roleDefinitions/8e3af657-a8ff-443c-a75c-2fe8c4bcb635",
    "name": "8e3af657-a8ff-443c-a75c-2fe8c4bcb635",
    "properties": {
      "assignableScopes": [
        "/"
      ],
      "description": "Lets you manage everything, including access to resources.",
      "permissions": [
        {
          "actions": [
            "*"
          ],
          "notActions": []
        }
      ],
      "roleName": "Owner",
      "type": "BuiltInRole"
    },
    "type": "Microsoft.Authorization/roleDefinitions"
  }
]
```

**FIGURE 5-13**  The role definition for the Owner built-in role

The actions allowed by the Owner role are defined as '*', which means any entity assigned to the Owner role for a resource has unrestricted permissions to perform any action within the assigned scopes. The assigned scopes are defined as '/', which means this role is available to any subscription, resource group, and resource.

The actions not allowed by the Owner role are defined as an empty array, meaning there are not any actions the Owner is not allowed to perform.

## Contributor built-in role

The Contributor built-in role is similar to the Owner role in that the actions allowed are defined as '*'. However, there are three actions the Contributor is not allowed to perform, as shown in Figure 5-14.

```
C:\>az role definition list --name "Contributor"
[
  {
    "id": "/subscriptions/9a2bc976-60a5-41f6-afa5-37510596c52b/providers/Microsoft.Autho
rization/roleDefinitions/b24988ac-6180-42a0-ab88-20f7382dd24c",
    "name": "b24988ac-6180-42a0-ab88-20f7382dd24c",
    "properties": {
      "assignableScopes": [
        "/"
      ],
      "description": "Lets you manage everything except access to resources.",
      "permissions": [
        {
          "actions": [
            "*"
          ],
          "notActions": [
            "Microsoft.Authorization/*/Delete",
            "Microsoft.Authorization/*/Write",
            "Microsoft.Authorization/elevateAccess/Action"
          ]
        }
      ],
      "roleName": "Contributor",
      "type": "BuiltInRole"
    },
    "type": "Microsoft.Authorization/roleDefinitions"
  }
]
```

**FIGURE 5-14** The role definition for the Contributor built-in role

The three actions not allowed by the Contributor role are defined as:

- Microsoft.Authorization/*/Delete
- Microsoft.Authorization/*/Write
- Microsoft.Authorization/elevateAccess/Action

These actions are all part of the Microsoft.Authorization namespace. In the first action, which is Microsoft.Authorization/*/Delete, the wildcard notation indicates that this role cannot perform any delete operations on any resource type in the Microsoft.Authorization namespace. To find all the delete operations in the Microsoft.Authorization namespace, use the az provider operation show command, as shown in Figure 5-15.

```
C:\>az provider operation show --namespace "Microsoft.Authorization" --query "[resourceT
ypes[].operations[?name.ends_with(@, 'delete')].name[]]"
[
  [
    "Microsoft.Authorization/classicAdministrators/delete",
    "Microsoft.Authorization/locks/delete",
    "Microsoft.Authorization/policyAssignments/delete",
    "Microsoft.Authorization/roleDefinitions/delete",
    "Microsoft.Authorization/policyDefinitions/delete",
    "Microsoft.Authorization/roleAssignments/delete",
    "Microsoft.Authorization/policySetDefinitions/delete"
  ]
]
```

**FIGURE 5-15** All Delete operations in the Microsoft.Authorization namespace

In the second action, which is Microsoft.Authorization/*/Write, the write operations that this role cannot perform are shown in Figure 5-16.

```
C:\>az provider operation show --namespace "Microsoft.Authorization" --query "[resourceT
ypes[].operations[?name.ends_with(@, 'write')].name[]]"
[
  [
    "Microsoft.Authorization/classicAdministrators/write",
    "Microsoft.Authorization/locks/write",
    "Microsoft.Authorization/policyAssignments/write",
    "Microsoft.Authorization/roleDefinitions/write",
    "Microsoft.Authorization/policyDefinitions/write",
    "Microsoft.Authorization/roleAssignments/write",
    "Microsoft.Authorization/policySetDefinitions/write"
  ]
]
```

**FIGURE 5-16**  All Write operations in the Microsoft.Authorization namespace

The third action, which is Microsoft.Authorization/elevateAccess/Action, does not include the wildcard notation. Instead, this is a specific action to elevate access as a tenant admin in the Azure Active Directory. In other words, the Contributor cannot manage other user's access to resources. To learn more about this specific action, see https://docs.microsoft.com/en-us/azure/active-directory/role-based-access-control-tenant-admin-access.

To summarize the Contributor built-in role, users assigned to this role can do any except the following:

- Create, modify, or delete classic administrators
- Create, modify, or delete locks
- Create, modify, or delete policy definitions, sets of policy definitions, or role definitions
- Create, modify, or delete policy assignments or role assignments
- Elevate access as an Azure AD tenant administrator (i.e. manage access for others)

## Reader built-in role

The Reader built-in role definition, as shown below in Figure 5-17, indicates that users assigned to this role can read any resource within the assigned scope, which is '/'.

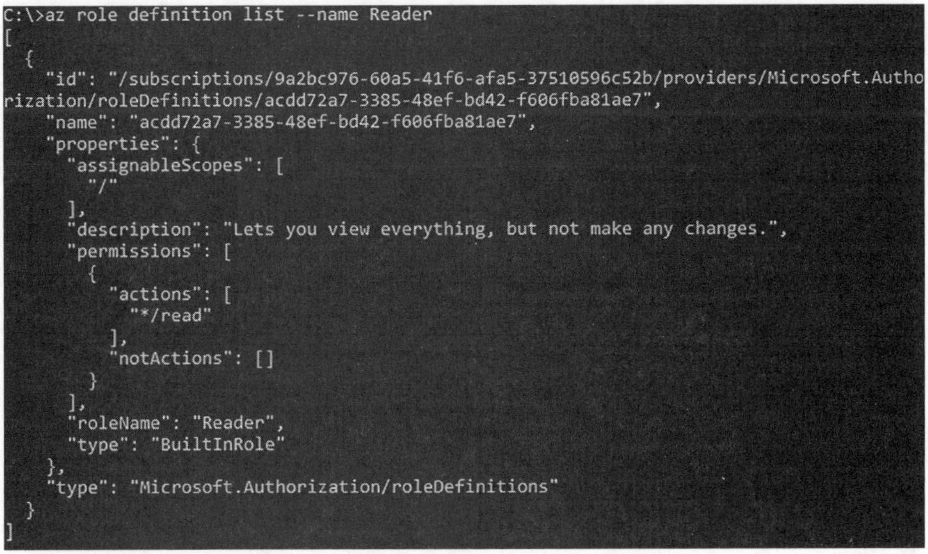

```
C:\>az role definition list --name Reader
[
  {
    "id": "/subscriptions/9a2bc976-60a5-41f6-afa5-37510596c52b/providers/Microsoft.Autho
rization/roleDefinitions/acdd72a7-3385-48ef-bd42-f606fba81ae7",
    "name": "acdd72a7-3385-48ef-bd42-f606fba81ae7",
    "properties": {
      "assignableScopes": [
        "/"
      ],
      "description": "Lets you view everything, but not make any changes.",
      "permissions": [
        {
          "actions": [
            "*/read"
          ],
          "notActions": []
        }
      ],
      "roleName": "Reader",
      "type": "BuiltInRole"
    },
    "type": "Microsoft.Authorization/roleDefinitions"
  }
]
```

**FIGURE 5-17** The role definition for the Reader built-in role

## Implement role assignment

A role definition by itself does not enforce any kind of role-based access control. To implement role-based access control, you must assign a role to a user, user group, or application. Furthermore, assignment of the role must be scoped to a subscription, resource group, or an individual resource.

The Azure portal provides a rich user interface for implementing role assignments. For example, to grant a user Contributor permission for all resources in a resource group, open the Resource Group blade, click Access Control (IAM) in the left navigation, and click +Add in the toolbar at the top of the blade. This opens the Add permissions blade where you can select the role (built-in or custom), the type of entity you want to assign the permissions to (user, user group, or application), and the name or email address of the entity you want to assign the role to. Figure 5-18 illustrates assigning the Contributor role to a user.

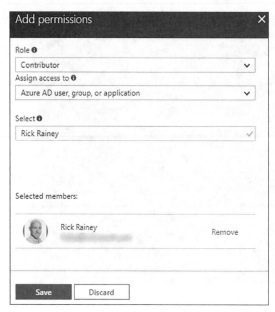

**FIGURE 5-18** Adding a Contributor role assignment to a resource in the Azure portal

The same role assignment scoped to a resource group using the Azure CLI could be implemented as follows:

```
#!/bin/bash

# Role assignment properties
roleName="Contributor"
assigneeName="johndoe@contoso.com"
resourceGroupName="contoso-app"

# Create a new role assignment
az role assignment create --role $roleName --assignee $assigneeName --resource-group
$resourceGroupName
```

Or, using Azure PowerShell, the same assignment could be implemented as follows:

```
$roleName = "Contributor"
$assigneeName = "cawatson@microsoft.com"
$resourceGroupName = "contoso-app"

New-AzureRmRoleAssignment -RoleDefinitionName $roleName -SignInName $assigneeName '
    -ResourceGroupName $resourceGroupName
```

## Design Azure RBAC custom roles

You can create custom role definitions if the built-in roles don't meet your requirements. For example, a member of a SysOps group may require permissions to manage multiple resource types, such as storage account, virtual networks, virtual machines, key vaults, and others.

A role definition is described using JSON and includes the properties you learned about earlier, such as the actions, notactions, and assignableScopes properties. The following JSON is an example of a custom role definition.

```
{
    "Name": "contoso-SysOps",
    "Description": "Manages spoke resources in a hub and spoke configuration.",
    "AssignableScopes": [
        "/subscriptions/ bfaf8b92-925c-4629-8333-137a0a64429c"
    ],
    "Actions": [
        "Microsoft.Storage/*",
        "Microsoft.Network/*",
        "Microsoft.Compute/*/read",
        "Microsoft.Authorization/*/read",
        "Microsoft.Resources/subscriptions/resourceGroups/*",
        "Microsoft.Insights/alertRules/*",
        "Microsoft.Insights/diagnosticSettings/*",
        "Microsoft.Support/*",
        "Microsoft.KeyVault/vaults/deploy/action"
    ],
    "NotActions": []
}
```

The custom role definition above sets the assignable scope to a specific subscription in the AssignableScopes array. This limits the role's availability to just this subscription. If you have a situation where you need to make the role available to several subscriptions, you can simply add additional subscription Ids to the scope.

The Actions array identifies names spaces and operations/actions that this role can perform. This list can be whatever you need it to be, as long as it is syntactically correct. The actions listed are an example of a SysOps role for users needing to manage spokes in a hub and spoke configuration.

To create a custom role definition using Azure CLI, use the `az role definition create` command as shown in the following code (this assumes the JSON above was saved to a JSON file named sysops.json):

```
az role definition create --role-definition "./sysops.json"
```

To create the same role definition using Azure PowerShell, use the New-AzureRmRoleDefinition cmdlet as shown in the following code:

```
New-AzureRmRoleDefinition -InputFile .\sysops.json
```

> **MORE INFORMATION    CUSTOM RBAC ROLES**
>
> Additional information on how to implement custom RBAC roles is available at *https://docs. microsoft.com/en-us/azure/active-directory/role-based-access-control-custom-roles*.

# Thought experiment

In this thought experiment, demonstrate your skills and knowledge of the topics covered in this chapter. You can find answer to this thought experiment in the next section.

You are the IT Administrator for Contoso and need to provision an environment in Azure to run a new line-of-business application. The application is a web application that internal users will access using their browsers. The application will be protected by Azure AD and Contos's Azure AD tenant is already synced with their on-premises Server Active Directory. The application will use SQL Database (PaaS) for data. The logical SQL Server that will host the SQL Database for this application will also need to host SQL Databases for other applications. Contoso has a strict policy stating keys and secrets must be stored in Azure Key Vault. Furthermore, all services and data storage must reside in the U.S. You need to implement ARM templates and scripts to deploy this environment. You also need to implement controls to insure the SQL Server is not accidentally deleted.

1. What kind of resources will you deploy to support the web application?

2. How many resource groups would you use, and which resources would exist in each?

3. How will you handle the requirement to protect the SQL Server from accidental deletion?

4. What will you need to do to support the requirement that all passwords and secrets be stored in Azure Key Vault?

5. How will you ensure data and services exist only in the U.S?

# Thought experiment answers

This section contains the solution to the thought experiment for this chapter.

1. The web application can be run in an Azure App Service Web App. Alternatively, you could run the application in virtual machines, but this introduces additional maintenance and security concerns that the business would have to manage. So, a web app would be the best option. Therefore, the resources needed to support the application would include the following:

   - App Service Web App

   - App Service Plan

   - SQL Server (PaaS)

   - SQL Database (PaaS)

   - Key Vault

2. You can put all of the resources in a single resource group. However, the SQL server will host your SQL Database and potentially the SQL Databases of other application owners. This suggests that the resource management lifecycle for the databases (and servers) is

going to be different. Therefore, it would be better for the SQL Server and SQL Database to be in a separate resources group.

3. You can use a resource lock to protect the SQL Server from accidental deletion. The lock can be added as a child resource of the SQL Server resource in the ARM template. An example of how this may be implemented in the ARM template is shown here:

```
{
    "name": "[concat(variables('contoso-srvName'),
 '/Microsoft.Authorization/SQLServerNoDelete')]",
        "type": "Microsoft.Sql/servers/providers/locks",
        "apiVersion": "2015-01-01",
        "properties": {
          "level": "CannotDelete"
        },
        "dependsOn": [
          "[resourceId('Microsoft.Sql/servers', variables('contoso-srvName'))]"
        ]
}
```

4. Because the application is using a SQL Database, it needs a connection string to connect to the database, which should be protected. The connection string can be stored in Azure Key Vault. To support this, you need to first create an application registration in Azure AD and then create a service principal for the application. The permissions for the key vault need to be updated to allow the web app to read the secret from Azure Key Vault. The client ID, client Secret, and secret URI for the connection string stored in Key Vault should be stored as app settings in the web app.

5. To ensure data and services stay in the U.S., you should assign the *Allowed Locations* resource policy and specify only US regions.

# Chapter summary

- Infrastructure described as code includes ARM template files, ARM template parameter files, artifacts such as custom scripts and DSC, and deployment scripts.

- The elements of an ARM template file are $schema, contentVersion, parameters, variables, resource, and outputs.

- The elements of an ARM template parameter file are $schema, contentVersion, and parameters.

- Every resource defined in an ARM template file must include the name, type, apiVersion, and location. The type is used to describe the resource type you want to implement, and is of the form < resource provider namespace >/< resource type >.

- Every resource in Azure is made available through a resource provider. The resource provider may define more than one resource type. For example, the resource provider for the Microsoft.Network namespace defines many resource types, such as virtualNetworks, loadBalancers, publicIPAddresses, routeTables, and more.

- The dependsOn element in an ARM template is used to inform Azure Resource Manager of resource dependencies for the resource.

- The copy element in an ARM template is used to create multiple instances of a resource type. When the copy element is used, the `copyIndex()` function can be used to return the current iteration ARM is in when provisioning the resource. The iteration value returned from `copyIndex()` is zero-based.

- There are two steps to deploy an ARM template. First, you must create a resource group if one doesn't already exist. Second, invoke a resource group deployment, where you pass your ARM template files to Azure Resource Manager to provision the resources described in the ARM template.

- When implementing complex architectures using ARM templates, you should de-compose the architecture into reusable nested templates that are invoked from the main template.

- A service principal can be created to use a password or certificate to authenticate with Azure AD. The latter is recommended when the service principal is used to run unattended code or script.

- An app registration must first be created in Azure AD before you can create a service principal. The service principal requires the application ID from the app registration.

- To create a new app registration using PowerShell, use the New-AzureRmADApplication cmdlet.

- To create a new app registration using CLI, use the `az ad app create` command.

- To create a new service principal using PowerShell, use the New-AzureRmADServicePrincipal cmdlet.

- To create a new service principal using CLI, use the `az ad sp create` command.

- Resource policies are comprised of policy definitions and policy assignments.

- Resource policies are evaluated against resource properties at the time of deployment.

- A policy rule is what ARM evaluates during a deployment. The policy rule is described in JSON and uses an `if/then` programming construct.

- To create a policy definition using PowerShell, use the New-AzureRmPolicyDefinition cmdlet.

- To create a policy definition using CLI, use `az policy definition create` command.

- To create a policy assignment using PowerShell, use the New-AzureRmPolicyAssignment cmdlet.

- To create a policy assignment using CLI, use the `az policy assignment create` command.

- A policy assignment can be scoped to an Azure subscription or to a resource group.

- The two types of resource locks are ReadOnly and CanNotDelete. Both types protect a resource from deletion and allow the resource to be read. The CanNotDelete also allows the resource to be modified.

- To create lock using PowerShell, use the New-AzureRmResourceLock cmdlet.

- To create lock using CLI, use the `az lock create` command.

- The three most basic built-in roles are Owner, Contributor, and Reader. Many of the other built-in roles are a derivation of these, but scoped to a specific resource type.

- Role-based Access Control (RBAC) is comprised of role definitions and role assignments.

- RBAC is evaluated against user actions on a resource at different scopes.

- A role assignment can be scoped to an Azure subscription, resource group, or resource. The entity for which a role can be assigned can be a user, user group, or application.

- The permissions property of a role definition includes an actions array and a notactions array. The actions array defines the actions/operations a member of the role can perform, while the notactions array defines the actions/operations a member of the role is not allowed to perform. The actions and notactions that are defined are scoped according to the scopes in the assignableScopes property.

- To create a role definition using PowerShell, use the New-AzureRmRoleDefinition cmdlet.

- To create a role definition using CLI, use `az role definition create` command.

- To create a role assignment using PowerShell, use the New-AzureRmRoleAssignment cmdlet.

- To create a role assignment using CLI, use the `az role assignment create` command.

# CHAPTER 6

# Manage Azure Security and Recovery Services

M icrosoft Azure provides many features that help customers secure their deployments as
well as protect and recover their data or services should the need arise. The first section
of this chapter focuses on security and reviews several related capabilities, including the use
of Key Vault to securely store cryptographic keys and other secrets, Azure Security Center to
help prevent, detect, and respond to threats, and several others. Even with proper precau-
tions taken, the need eventually arises to recover data or a critical workload. The second
section covers recovery-related services, including the use of snapshots and platform replication, and Azure Backup and Site Recovery to quickly restore access to data and services.

## Skills covered in this chapter:

- Skill 6.1: Manage data protection and security compliance
- Skill 6.2: Implement recovery services

## Skill 6.1: Manage data protection and security compliance

The unfortunate reality of the IT landscape is there are many threats to every organization's
digital assets. Many are of a malicious nature, but others come in the form of human error or
impersonal, catastrophic forces, such as hurricanes, earthquakes, or other natural disasters.
Regardless of where an organization's digital assets are deployed, one of the first planning
steps must be to determine how to protect these assets. To assist in this planning, this section
reviews the data protection and security compliance capabilities of the Azure platform.

**This skill covers how to:**

- Create and import encryption keys with Key Vault
- Automate tasks for SSL/TLS certificates
- Prevent and respond to security threats with Azure Security Center
- Configure single sign-on with SaaS applications using federation and password based
- Add users and groups to applications
- Revoke access to SaaS applications
- Configure federation with public consumer identity providers such as Facebook and Google

# Create and import encryption keys with Key Vault

Azure Key Vault allows for the secure storage of cryptographic keys and other secrets, using FIPS 140-2 Level 2 validated hardware security modules (HSMs). These keys and secrets can then be accessed by Azure Active Directory authenticated requests so that developers do not need to store credentials in their source code. Key Vault is available in two pricing tiers, as shown in Figure 6-1:

- A1 Standard
- P1 Premium

**EXAM TIP**

The key difference between the A1 and P1 pricing tiers is the A1 tier only allows for software-protected keys, whereas the P1 tier allows for keys to be protected by Hardware Security Modules (HSMs). If the workload requires keys be stored in HSMs, be sure to select the Premium tier.

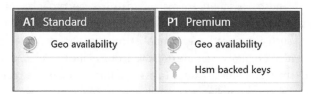

| A1  Standard | P1  Premium |
|---|---|
| 🌐 Geo availability | 🌐 Geo availability |
| | 🔑 Hsm backed keys |

**FIGURE 6-1** Pricing tier options for Key Vault as shown in the Azure portal

To begin using Key Vault, create a vault by using the Azure portal, PowerShell, or the Azure CLI.

1. **Create a Key Vault (Azure portal)**   In the Azure portal, search the Marketplace for Key Vault and open the Create key vault blade. Specify the name, resource group, location, and pricing tier (shown in Figure 6-2). Note that the name must be unique and follow these rules:

   ▪ Must only contain alphanumeric characters and hyphens

   ▪ Must start with a letter and end with a letter or digit

   ▪ Must be between 3-24 characters in length

   ▪ Cannot contain consecutive hyphens

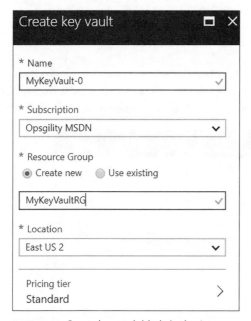

**FIGURE 6-2**  Create key vault blade in the Azure portal

This blade also allows the creator to specify an Azure Active Directory user or group and the permissions they have. These are defined within an Access policy, and the permissions apply to the data within the key vault, such as keys, secrets, and certificates, as shown in Figure 6-3.

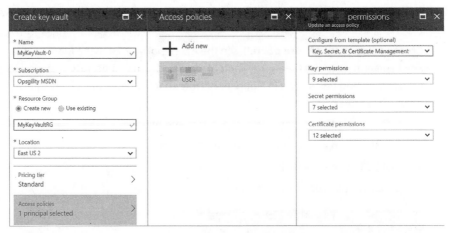

**FIGURE 6-3** Define the initial Access policy

Finally, this creation blade allows you to set advanced access policies, which govern the access of Azure resources (virtual machines, Resource Manager template deployments, and disk encryption) to retrieve key vault data (shown in Figure 6-4).

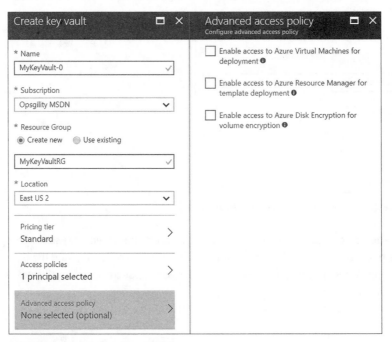

**FIGURE 6-4** Set Advanced access policy

2. **Create a Key Vault (PowerShell)** To create an Azure key vault with PowerShell, begin by creating a resource group. Use the New-AzureRmResourceGroup cmdlet for this task.

```
$rg = New-AzureRmResourceGroup -Name "MyKeyVaultRG" -Location "South Central US"
```

Next, use the New-AzureRmKeyVault to create the vault.

```
New-AzureRmKeyVault -VaultName "MyKeyVault-0" -ResourceGroupName $rg.
ResourceGroupName -Location "South Central US"
```

3.  **Create a Key Vault (CLI)**   To create an Azure key vault with the CLI, begin by creating a resource group.

```
az group create --name "MyKeyVaultRG" --location "South Central US"
```

Next, create the key vault.

```
az keyvault create --name "MyKeyVault-0" --resource-group "MyKeyVaultRG" --location "South Central US"
```

Once the key vault is created, it is ready to securely store keys, secrets and certificates. This section shows how to create keys using the Azure portal, PowerShell and the CLI.

4.  **Create a Key (Azure portal)**   After the key vault is created, you can create keys used for encrypting and decrypting data within the vault. Also, secrets such as passwords can be added to the key vault. Lastly, you can create or import certificates (*.PFX or *.PEM file format) into the vault. Once a key, secret or certificate exists in the vault, it can be referenced by URI, and each URI request is authenticated by Azure AD.

To create a key in the Azure portal, open the Key Vault created in the previous section and under Settings, click Keys (shown in Figure 6-5).

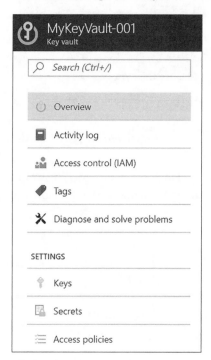

**FIGURE 6-5** CREATE A NEW KEY IN THE AZURE PORTAL

Next, select Add, and enter in a name. If this is a P1 Premium key vault, an HSM protected key can be selected. Otherwise it is software-protected. The key can also be given activation and expiration dates in this interface. These options are shown in Figure 6-6.

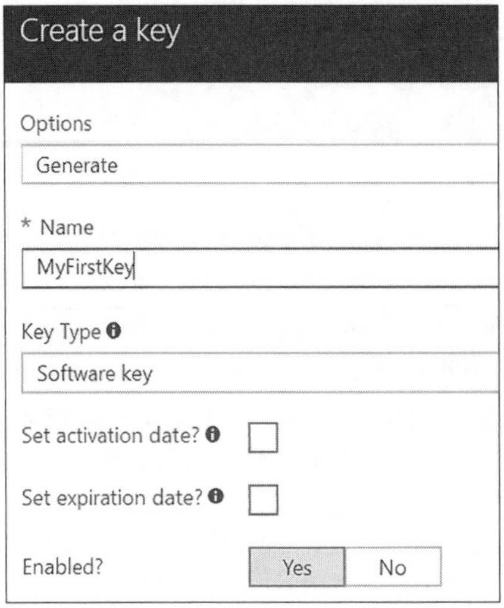

**FIGURE 6-6** Specify the parameters for creating a new key

5. **Create a Key (PowerShell)**   To create a key with PowerShell, use the Add-AzureKeyVaultKey cmdlet.

```
Add-AzureKeyVaultKey -VaultName "MyKeyVault-001" -Name "MyFirstKey" -Destination
"Software"
```

6. **Create a Key (CLI)**   To create a key with the CLI, use this syntax.

```
az keyvault key create --vault-name 'MyKeyVault-001' --name 'MyThirdKey'
--protection 'software'
```

This section demonstrates the process to create secrets using the Azure portal, PowerShell and the CLI.

1. **Add a Secret (Azure portal)**   To create a secret in the vault such as a password, from within the Azure portal, click Secrets under Settings, and then click Add (shown in Figure 6-7).

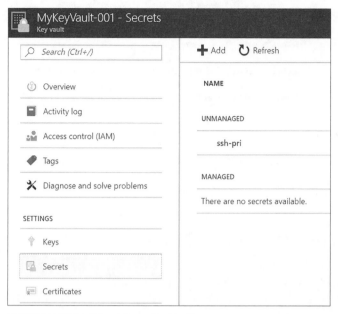

**FIGURE 6-7** Dialog for adding a Key Vault secret

Set the Upload options to Manual, and enter the secret name and value. You can add a Content type (optionally), which is a good place to store a password reminder. You can also enter an activation and expiration date as well. Finally, the secret can either be enabled (meaning it is useable) or not enabled. These options are shown in Figure 6-8.

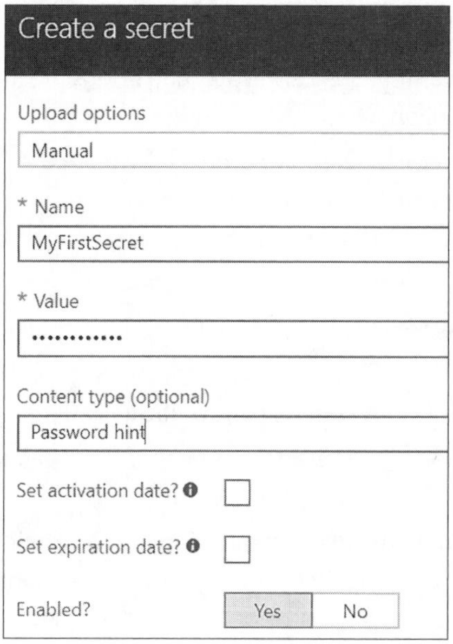

### Create a secret

Upload options

Manual

\* Name

MyFirstSecret

\* Value

••••••••••••

Content type (optional)

Password hint

Set activation date? ❶  ☐

Set expiration date? ❶  ☐

Enabled?          Yes    No

**FIGURE 6-8** COMPLETE THE CREATION OF THE SECRET

2. **Add a Secret (PowerShell)**   To create a secret with PowerShell, first convert the secret to a secure string with the ConvertTo-SecureString cmdlet, and store the output in a variable.

```
$mySecret = ConvertTo-SecureString -String 'P@ssword1233' -Force -AsPlainText
```

Next, add the secret to the vault by using the Set-AzureKeyVaultSecret cmdlet.

```
Set-AzureKeyVaultSecret -VaultName 'MyKeyVault-001' -Name 'MyFirstSecret'
-SecretValue $mySecret
```

3. **Add a Secret (CLI)**   Use this syntax to add a secret to the key vault with the CLI.

```
az keyvault secret set --vault-name 'MyKeyVault-001' --name 'MySecondSecret'
--value 'P@ssword321'
```

# Automate tasks for SSL/TLS Certificates

A foundational capability enabling data protection and security compliance is data encryption. Encrypting data at rest and in transit keeps sensitive information private, helping to prevent data leakage. In modern websites and applications, utilizing Transport Layer Security (TLS) has become the baseline in the industry to protect data in transit. TLS utilizes certificates to encrypt and decrypt data. Certificates are resources that have a lifecycle that must be managed. Managing this lifecycle can be manual and error-prone, making organizations vulnerable to customer-impacting issues. Fortunately, Azure has technologies that can assist in the lifecycle management of SSL/TLS certificates. This section covers the certificate management features of Azure Key Vault, along with another Azure solution called App Service Certificate.

## Azure Key Vault Certificate Management

Azure Key Vault provides management capabilities for x509 certificates and brings the following features to the task of certificate lifecycle management:

- Segregation of duties, so that a certificate owner (a user or group in Azure Active Directory) can handle the secure storage and management of x509 certificates without allowing application owners to access private key material
- The use of policies that dictate the life-cycle management of certificates
- Setting of contacts to be notified when certificate life-cycle events occur, including expiration or renewals
- Automatic enrollment and renewal of certificates with certain certificate issuers

The first certificate management activity to cover is importing certificates. The creating certificates will be considered.

1. **Importing Certificates**   Currently, it is not possible to create or import a certificate to the key vault in the Azure portal, although this capability is likely to be added soon. To import a certificate with PowerShell, it must be in the .PFX or .PEM format. These steps

assume you have exported your certificate with the password-protected private key to your hard drive. First, convert the private key password to a secure string.

```
$CertPwd = ConvertTo-SecureString -String "demo@pass123" -Force -AsPlainText
```

Next, use the Import-AzureKeyVaultCertificate cmdlet to import the certificate.

```
Import-AzureKeyVaultCertificate -VaultName 'MyKeyVault-001' -Name 'MyFirstCert'
-FilePath 'C:\ssh\MyCert.pfx' -Password $CertPwd
```

If you look in the Azure portal after this operation, notice that in addition to the certificate, a managed key and secret are added to the vault. The certificate and its corresponding key and secret together represent the certificate in key vault.

2. **Creating Certificates** To create a certificate with Key Vault, start by defining a Key Vault certificate policy. This is defined with the New-AzureKeyVaultCertificatePolicy cmdlet. Note, this cmdlet creates an in-memory structure, rather than a permanent policy. Populate a variable with this structure and pass this variable during certificate creation. This command defines a policy that is used to create a self-signed certificate.

```
$Policy = New-AzureKeyVaultCertificatePolicy -SecretContentType "application/x-
pkcs12" -SubjectN ame "CN=steverlabs.com" -IssuerName "Self" -ValidityInMonths
6 -ReuseKeyOnRenewal
```

Now, create the certificate.

```
Add-AzureKeyVaultCertificate -VaultName 'MyKeyVault-001' -Name "TestCert01"
-CertificatePolicy $ Policy
```

Creating a certificate in this way submits a job, and the status of this job can be checked with the Get-AzureKeyVaultCertificateOperation cmdlet, passing the Key Vault name and the certificate name.

```
Get-AzureKeyVaultCertificateOperation -VaultName 'MyKeyVault-001' -Name
"TestCert01"
```

It is also possible to enroll a certificate from a public certificate authority (CA). Currently, DigiCert and GlobalSign are the only supported CAs. The requestor must already have an account created with the CA and must already have proven ownership of the domains they are generating a certificate for. More details for leveraging DigiCert can be found here: *https://www.digicert.com/azure-key-vault*.

The following PowerShell instructions assume the Key Vault is already created. Start by creating an organization with the New-AzureKeyVaultCertificateOrganizationDetails cmdlet.

```
$org = New-AzureKeyVaultCertificateOrganizationDetails -Id
<OrganizationIDfromDigiCertAccount>
```

Next, store the DigiCert API Key in a variable as a secure string.

```
$secureApiKey = ConvertTo-SecureString <DigiCertCertCentralAPIKey> -AsPlainText -
Force
```

Next, create an issuer.

```
$accountId = "<DigiCertCertCentralAccountID>"
$issuerName = "digiCert01"
```

Now, set the Key Vault certificate issuer with the Set-AzureKeyVaultCertificateIssuer cmdlet, passing the variables you previously populated.

```
Set-AzureKeyVaultCertificateIssuer -VaultName 'MyKeyVault-001' -IssuerName
$issuerName -IssuerProvider DigiCert -AccountId $accountId -ApiKey $secureApiKey
-OrganizationDetails $org
```

Next, create the in-memory policy to be used in certificate creation.

```
$certificatePolicy = New-AzureKeyVaultCertificatePolicy -SecretContentType
application/x-pkcs12 -SubjectName "CN=myCommonName.com" -ValidityInMonths 12
-IssuerName $issuerName -RenewAtNumberOfDaysBeforeExpiry 60
```

Notice the -RenewAtNumberOfDaysDeforeExpiry parameter. When this is set, Key Vault automatically renews the certificate that is requested by using this policy. This automatic renewal feature of Key Vault prevents the certificate from expiring and relieves administrators from the tedious burden of manual renewals.

Finally, submit the certificate creation request.

```
Add-AzureKeyVaultCertificate -VaultName 'MyKeyVault-001' -CertificateName
'MyDigiCertCertificate' -CertificatePolicy $certificatePolicy
```

Remember that this command submits a job. To review the status, use the Get-AzureKeyVaultCertificateOperation cmdlet, passing the vault name and the certificate name.

```
Get-AzureKeyVaultCertificateOperation -VaultName 'MyKeyVault-001' -CertificateName
'MyDigiCertCertificate'
```

## Azure App Service Certificate

Another solution in Azure that helps organizations manage their SSL/TLS certificates is App Service Certificate. This service is specifically for use with App Service options, such as Web Apps, and it offloads much of the complexity for obtaining and managing SSL/TLS certificates. It utilizes Azure Key Vault for certificate storage. There are two certificate SKUs to choose from. The S1 Standard procures a certificate that allows SSL bindings for the root and www subdomain. If you need to create SSL bindings for the root domain and any first level subdomain, choose the W1 Wildcard option. These choices are shown in Figure 6-9.

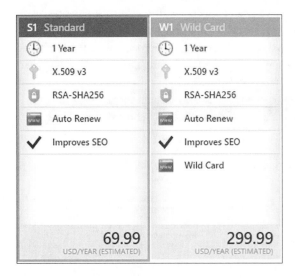

| S1 Standard | | W1 Wild Card | |
|---|---|---|---|
| 🕐 | 1 Year | 🕐 | 1 Year |
| 🔑 | X.509 v3 | 🔑 | X.509 v3 |
| 🛡 | RSA-SHA256 | 🛡 | RSA-SHA256 |
| www | Auto Renew | www | Auto Renew |
| ✓ | Improves SEO | ✓ | Improves SEO |
| | | www | Wild Card |
| **69.99** | | **299.99** | |
| USD/YEAR (ESTIMATED) | | USD/YEAR (ESTIMATED) | |

**FIGURE 6-9** Certificate options with Azure App Service Certificate

After creating the App Service Certificate, the first configuration step is to select an existing Key Vault or to create one for use with this service. Next, you must verify ownership for the domain that you entered during the service creation. After you verify ownership, the certificate can be imported into an App Service. These choices are shown in Figure 6-10.

**FIGURE 6-10** Importing an App Service Certificate into a Web App

With the App Service Certificate solution, you can easily rekey the certificate with one click and sync this update with the services that use the certificate. This feature eliminates human error and reduces the time normally required to accomplish this task manually. The certificate can also be configured to automatically renew, relieving administrators from another task that sometimes is forgotten. These settings are shown in Figure 6-11.

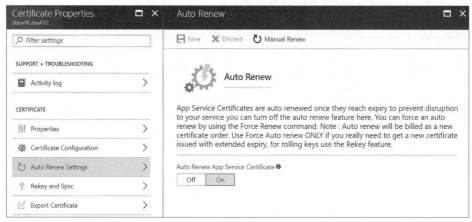

**FIGURE 6-11** App Service Certificate Auto Renew settings

# Prevent and respond to security threats with Azure Security Center

As organizations begin to deploy workloads into Azure, or any public cloud environment, a common challenge they face is to minimize threats by ensuring security best practices are followed. This is a difficult obstacle because of the learning curve required to understand these best practices. Azure Security Center (ASC) is a tremendous help in this situation because it evaluates deployments and offers recommendations for hardening existing configurations. In many cases, recommendations can be accomplished within the context of ASC. This ASC capability represents the prevention aspect of the solution. ASC also provides active monitoring of Azure deployments and surfacing of potentially malicious activity, which enables organizations to respond to threats.

## Enabling Azure Security Center

Azure Security Center's Free tier is enabled by default on all Azure subscriptions. Within the Azure portal, ASC is pinned by default to the services menu on the far left, as shown in Figure 6-12.

**FIGURE 6-12** Selecting the Azure Security Center service

Opening Azure Security Center reveals four sections of tiles including Overview, Prevention, Detection, and Advanced cloud defense. To configure ASC, begin by clicking the Security policy menu item followed by the subscription name (Figure 6-13).

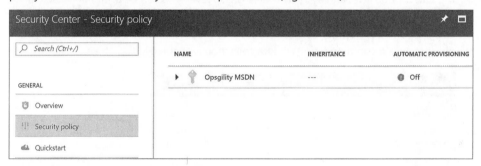

**FIGURE 6-13** Opening the Azure Security Center Security policy

This reveals the four sections of the security policy, namely Data collection, Security policy, Email notifications, and Pricing tier.

1. **Data Collection**   Azure Security Center can deduce many valuable security findings from your Azure deployments without collecting data from any virtual machines. However, the advanced features of ASC, including daily security monitoring and event analysis with threat detection, are not possible without this data collection. It is recommended that data collection be enabled, which involves an automatic installation of the Microsoft Monitoring Agent. This agent can be configured to collect and store data in a default Azure Log Analytics workspace, automatically created by ASC, or you can choose an existing workspace. Be sure to save any changes made in this dialog box, as shown in Figure 6-14. Note that data collection is enabled or disabled at the subscription level.

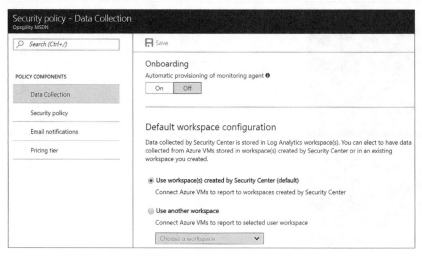

**FIGURE 6-14** Enabling data collection

2. **Security Policy**   The security policy allows users to choose the specific recommendations that ASC surfaces, shown below in Figure 6-15. These settings can be adjusted at
   the subscription level and at the resource group level. This can be useful because an
   organization might not want to see certain recommendations on resources that are
   designated as development or test. Notice that the first three options in this dialog box
   only produce recommendations if data collection is enabled.

**FIGURE 6-15** Setting the Azure Security Center security policy

3. **Email Notifications** The email notifications dialog box allows administrators to specify what email address and/or phone number should be used for notifications in the case where a compromise is detected. By default, the subscription owner's email address is populated here, but it is a good idea to change this to an email distribution list so that multiple people can be notified. It is also possible to opt in to emails about alerts and to send emails to all subscriptions owners. These options are shown in Figure 6-16.

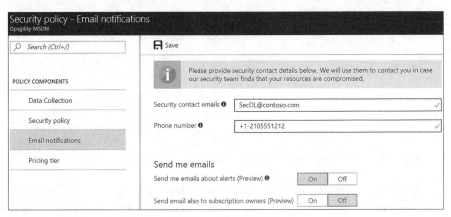

**FIGURE 6-16** Setting the Azure Security Center email notifications

4. **Pricing Tier** The last section of the security policy is the pricing tier, as shown in Figure 6-17. There are two pricing tiers available for ASC. The free tier is enabled by default and offers continuous security assessment and actionable recommendations for Azure deployments. The standard tier brings many other capabilities to bear, such as advanced threat detection and extended security monitoring to resources on-premises and in other clouds. The pricing tier can be set at the subscription level, which is then inherited by all resource groups in that subscription, or it can be set per resource group. This enables an organization to lower costs by only enabling the standard pricing tier on selected resources.

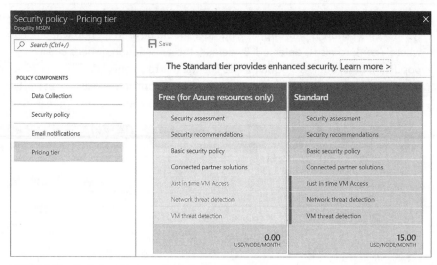

**FIGURE 6-17**  Choosing the Azure Security Center pricing tier

5. **Enabling protection for non-Azure Computers**  If using the standard tier of ASC, organizations can also add non-Azure machines to their ASC workspace for security monitoring. These can be machines on-premises or in other public clouds. This means that ASC is truly a hybrid security solution. To enable protection for other machines, a manual installation of the Microsoft Monitoring Agent must be performed, with the subsequent configuration of that agent to report in to the ASC workspace. To do this, under the General heading, click Onboarding to advanced security. From there, click Do you want to add non-Azure computers? Finally, click Add computers to download the Windows or Linux agent installation (see Figure 6-18). Be certain to take note of the Workspace ID and Key. These are provided during agent installation and are required to allow the agent to authenticate and report in to the ASC workspace.

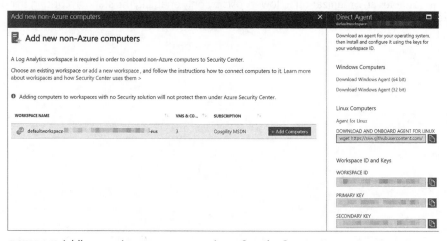

**FIGURE 6-18** Adding non-Azure computers to Azure Security Center

## Preventing Security Threats with Azure Security Center

One of the key pillars of Azure Security Center is helping organizations prevent security threats from happening in the first place. ASC accomplishes this goal by scanning your Azure deployments for sub-optimal security configurations, and then surfacing recommendations on how to remediate those problematic configurations. In many cases, these recommendations can be implemented within the ASC interface and many of the potential mitigations are from Microsoft partners. This integration with partner-provided solutions is another key value of ASC. If the recommendations made by Azure Security Center are all followed, the exposure to security threats is greatly minimized (Figure 6-19).

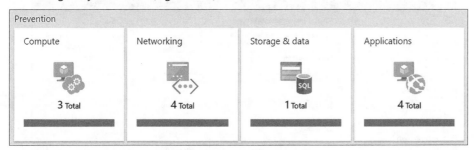

FIGURE 6-19 Azure Security Center's prevention tiles

There are four areas of recommendations available, including Compute, Networking, Storage and Data, and Applications, as shown in Figure 6-19.

1.  **Compute** Azure Security Center can monitor the configuration of both Infrastructure as a Service (IaaS) virtual machines and Cloud services. Within the compute blade, you can review a high-level view of findings. Examples of configuration items that are reviewed include endpoint protection and disk encryption status. Clicking a recommendation gives additional information and in many cases, allows for the remediation of the finding within the Azure Security Center dialog box. In the following example (Figure 6-20), three virtual machines are missing endpoint protection. By clicking this recommendation, you can install endpoint protection on all of them at once. This recommendation is one that is integrated with partner-provided security solutions. Trend Micro's Deep Security Agent is one of the antimalware solutions available to install automatically and within the recommendation context.

FIGURE 6-20 Remediating a security recommendation from Azure Security Center

An additional capability in Azure Security Center that relates to prevention is called Just in time (JIT) VM access. Enabling JIT VM access on one more VMs blocks inbound network traffic by default, using a network security group. When a person with write access for the VM requests access, the request is allowed temporarily based on the access policy in ASC. To enable Just in time VM access, click this option under the Advanced Cloud Defense section of ASC's menu options. Under Virtual machines, click the Recommended tab. Next, click the checkbox beside the VM that JIT should be enabled for and click Enable JIT on 1 VM. These selections are shown in Figure 6-21.

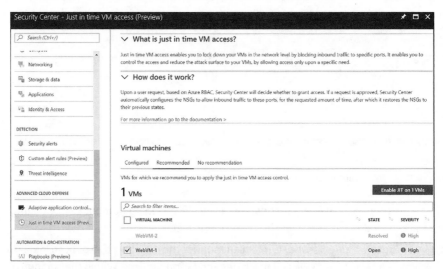

**FIGURE 6-21** Enable Just in time VM access on a single VM

This opens the JIT VM access configuration blade, where any ports not required can be deleted and any ports not pre-configured can be added. Also the maximum request time is set here, which defaults to three hours. These configurations are shown in Figure 6-22.

## JIT VM access configuration
WebVM-1 - PREVIEW

+ Add    🖫 Save    ✕ Discard

Configure the ports for which the just in time VM access will be applicable.

| PORT | PROT... | ALLOWED SOUR... | IP RANGE | TIME RANGE | |
|------|---------|-----------------|----------|------------|---|
| 22 *(Recommended)* | Any | Per request | N/A | 3 hours | |
| 3389 *(Recommended)* | Any | Per request | N/A | 3 hours | Delete |
| 5985 *(Recommended)* | Any | Per request | N/A | 3 hours | ... |
| 5986 *(Recommended)* | Any | Per request | N/A | 3 hours | ... |

**FIGURE 6-22** Adding or removing ports

Temporary network access is granted from the Just in time VM access interface on the Configured tab. Click the checkbox near the VM that access should be enabled for, and then click Request Access. In the Request Access blade, click On for each port that should be opened and then click Open ports (Figure 6-23).

**FIGURE 6-23** Requesting network access

2. **Networking** The networking node of Azure Security Center evaluates the accessibility of external facing resources (those with public IP addresses) and the use of traffic blocking/inspection technologies, such as network security groups (NSGs), network firewalls, and web application firewalls. Many types of recommendations are made, such as to further restrict traffic flow on existing network security groups, or to highlight VMs that are not protected at all by network security groups. As with the compute node, recommendations in the network node are actionable. They can be remediated from within the ASC interface. In the following example (Figure 6-24), the NSG protecting a subnet has a rule that is potentially too liberal. The rule allows RDP access from the source address of INTERNET, which is a tag that means any address on the public internet. It is likely that this should be constrained to only the source IP addresses where administration of the VM is likely to come from. The NSG rule can be edited by clicking Edit inbound rule within the recommendation.

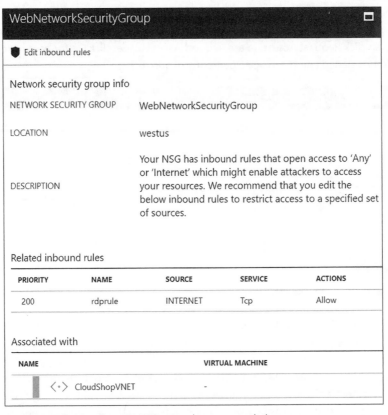

**FIGURE 6-24** Responding to a ASC network recommendation

3.  **Storage and data**   The Storage and Data node expands outside of pure IaaS, to surface recommendations surrounding platform as a service (PaaS) offerings. Azure Storage is Azure's robust cloud storage service, providing blob, disk, file, queue, and table storage types. Azure SQL database is Azure's database as a service (DBaaS) offering providing SQL databases without the server to manage. Example recommendations under storage and data include enabling encryption for Azure Storage (using Storage Service Encryption) and enabling transparent data encryption on SQL databases, as shown in Figure 6-25.

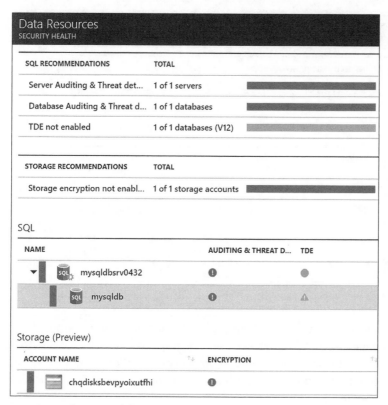

**FIGURE 6-25** Storage and data recommendations

4. **Applications** The applications node within Azure Security Center evaluates public-facing services, such as websites, and makes recommendations, such as using a web application firewall (WAF) in front of web applications. This recommendation is another example of tight partner integration. Web application firewalls from several partners are available for automatic deployment, including Barracuda, F5, and Fortinet.

Figure 6-26 shows a cloudshopip web application that does not have a WAF deployed in front of it. 'In front' of the application implies all inbound network traffic should be directed to the WAF so that it can be inspected for known attack patterns.

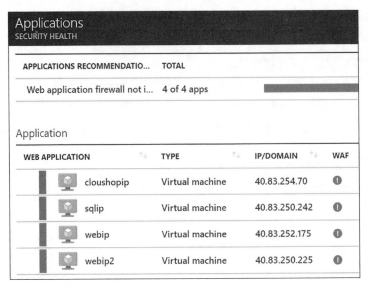

FIGURE 6-26  Web applications without Web Application Firewall protection

To implement a WAF to protect cloudshopip, click the web application and then click the recommendation Add a web application firewall. Either click Create New to begin the process of creating a new WAF, or choose an existing WAF. If you are creating a new WAF, choose the Microsoft or partner-provided option you want. These selections are shown in Figure 6-27.

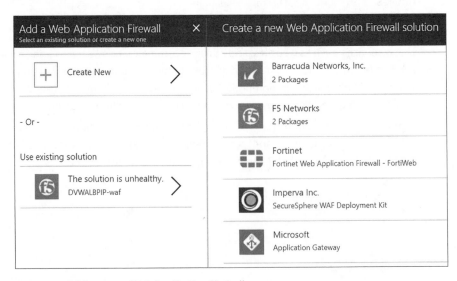

FIGURE 6-27  Adding a new Web Application Firewall

Walk through the guided steps to deploy the WAF. Most of the partner-provided options are automatically provisioned with no additional configuration required. Also, the WAF is a new source of security telemetry, which Azure Security Center evaluates and surfaces where appropriate.

Another prevention capability related to applications is called Adaptive application controls. This feature of ASC allows administrators to whitelist applications that are allowed to run on Windows machines running in Azure. By only allowing approved applications to run, protected machines are prevented from executing malware or other unwanted applications. Traditionally it has been difficult to determine which applications to include in a whitelist approach, because leaving any off the list can mean a non-functional application or machine. ASC helps solve this problem by analyzing the applications running on each server and helping the administrator develop an accurate whitelist.

To configure Adaptive application controls, click this option under Advanced Cloud Defense within the ASC menu options. Under Resource groups, click the Recommended tab. Select a resource group, which opens the Create application control rules dialog box, as shown in Figure 6-28.

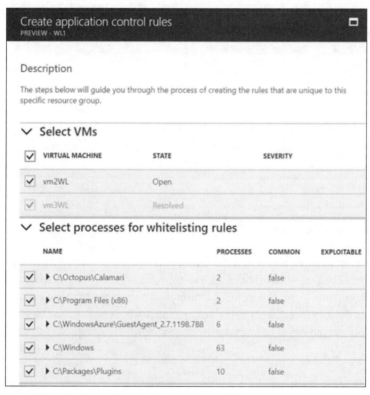

**FIGURE 6-28** Create application control rules dialog box

Select the VMs that application control should apply to. This reveals a list of processes that can be added or removed from application control.

> **NOTE EXPLOITABLE PROCESSES**
>
> Any processes marked as exploitable should be reviewed carefully. These processes likely represent malware.

After you select the processes, click Create. Application control is enabled in audit mode. After you validate that the whitelist does not adversely affect the workload, Application control can be changed to enforce mode. At this point, only approved processes are allowed to execute.

5. **Other Prevention Areas** The Recommendations blade, accessed from the tile of the same name, is one place to view all the recommendations that ASC suggests. The recommendations are ordered by severity, with the highest severity at the top. Clicking any recommendation gives you more information and in many cases, allows immediate remediation. It is also possible to dismiss recommendations, as shown in Figure 6-29, which can be useful when an organization decides to not act upon certain findings.

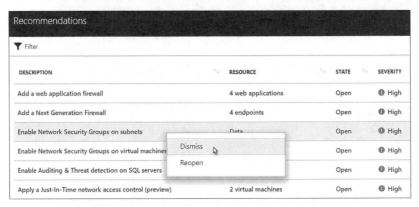

**FIGURE 6-29** Dismiss recommendations

Another prevention area with ASC is the Identity and Access solution. Within this solution, customers can see visualizations created from the security logging that is collected from monitored machines. This includes information about logons that are occurring (both successful and failed), a list of the accounts that are being used to attempt logons, and accounts with changed or reset passwords, as shown in Figure 6-30.

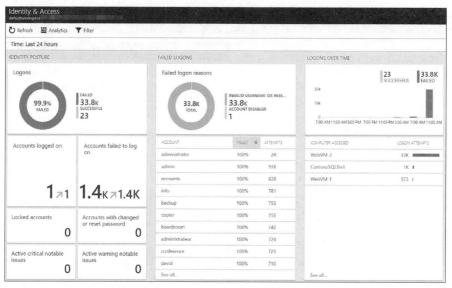

**FIGURE 6-30** The Identity and Access tiles within Azure Security Center

## Responding to security threats with Azure Security Center

Beyond prevention, Azure Security Center also detects probable malicious activity and gives actionable guidance on how to respond to threats. ASC accomplishes this by collecting and analyzing security data from a customer's Azure deployments, their virtual networks, and from any partner solutions they have deployed, such as anti-malware or web application firewalls. This security information is analyzed and correlated with global threat intelligence, by using machine learning models, to detect threats that would be impossible to identify with traditional, manual approaches. The best part of this approach for customers is that all of this platform-provided data analysis and correlation enables them to benefit without requiring them to maintain vast teams of data scientists and security experts within their company.

The detection tiles include the Security alerts and Most attached resources. Security alerts show events that are deemed as potentially malicious. In the following example, a remote desktop protocol (RDP) brute-force attack is underway against an Azure virtual machine. Clicking the alert gives a wealth of information, including the source IP address and how many logon attempts have failed as shown in Figure 6-31.

**FIGURE 6-31** Security Alert in Azure Security Center

It is also possible to create custom alerts. This feature is in preview as of this writing. To do so, select Custom alert rules under the Detection heading. Then, select New custom alert rule and complete the form. When custom alerts are triggered, they are shown on the Security alerts tile, as shown in Figure 6-32.

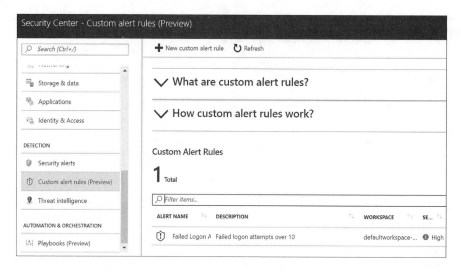

**FIGURE 6-32** Creating a custom alert in Azure Security Center

The following query finds failed logon attempts on Windows computers.

```
SecurityEvent | where EventID == 4625 and AccountType == 'User' | extend
LowerAccount=tolower(Account) | summarize Failed = count() by LowerAccount
```

> **NOTE   LOG ANALYTICS QUERY LANGUAGE**
>
> The above query is written using the new Log Analytics query language. Log Analytics workspaces created prior to October 2017 may still use the older query language, but all workspaces will be migrated to the new language by the end of 2017. See the article describing the new query language here: *https://docs.microsoft.com/en-us/azure/log-analytics/log-analytics-log-search-upgrade*
>
> Using this query in conjunction with the settings in a custom alert, allows an organization to be alerted when this condition occurs over a certain number of times. The configuration of the custom alert is shown in Figure 6-33.

**Edit custom alert rule**

\* Name ❶

Failed Logon Attempts

Description

Failed logon attempts over 10

Severity ❶

High

**Sources**

Subscription
Opsgility MSDN

Workspace
defaultworkspace

**Criteria**

\* Search Query ❶

SecurityEvent | where EventID == 4625 and AccountType == 'User' | extend LowerAccount=tolower(Account) | summarize Failed = count() by LowerAccount

Execute your search query now

Period ❶

Over the last 1 hours

**Evaluation**

Evaluation Frequency

Every 1 hours

**Generate alert based on**

Number of results

Greater than

\* Threshold

10

☑ Suppress Alerts ❶
\* Suppress alerts for (in minutes)

120

**FIGURE 6-33** Creating a custom alert in Azure Security Center

Finally, there is the Threat intelligence detection capability, which is also dependent on the standard tier of ASC. Threat intelligence is presented as a dashboard with four types of tracked information: Threat types, which gives a summary of the types of detected threats; Origin country, which shows an aggregate of malicious traffic by source country; Threat location, which shows both incoming and outgoing malicious traffic on a map of the world; Threat details, which gives additional information. These information sections are shown in Figure 6-34.

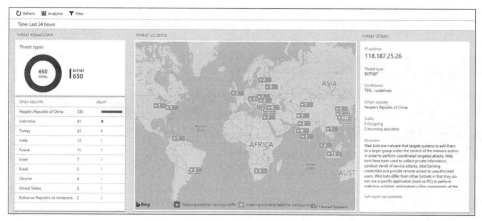

**FIGURE 6-34** Azure Security Center Threat intelligence dashboard

# Configure single sign-on with SaaS applications using federation and password based

One of the most compelling features of Azure Active Directory (Azure AD) is the ability to solve the problem of authenticating to software as a service (SaaS) applications. Organizations are using an ever-increasing number of SaaS applications to accomplish their core business. However today, users must remember a separate username and password for each application used. Azure AD allows users to sign in with their corporate account, called an organizational account, and they access the SaaS applications with a consistent logon experience. The actual logon is federated, or password-based. These logon types and the steps to configure them are discussed further in the following sections.

## Federated Single Sign-On

With Federation-based single sign-on (SSO), SaaS applications redirect authentication requests to Azure AD, rather than prompting the user for credentials that the application maintains. Within the application, the authenticated user must have an account that designates the permissions they have within the application (authorization). Accounts with SaaS applications can either be automatically provisioned through integration with Azure AD, or manually provisioned. Federated SSO is available for applications that support SAML 2.0, WS-Federation, or OpenID Connect protocols.

**EXAM TIP**

Be certain to know the protocols that are supported for use with federated single sign-on, namely SAML 2.0, WS-Federation, or OpenID Connect

The first step in configuring federated single sign-on is to add the application in Azure Active Directory. To do this within the Azure AD blade, click Enterprise applications, and then click New application, as shown in Figure 6-35.

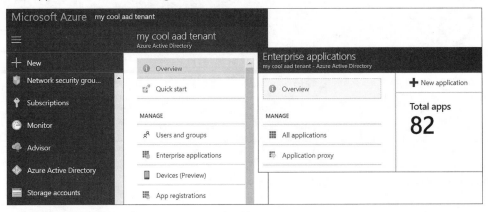

**FIGURE 6-35** Adding an application to Azure Active Directory

Within the search dialog box enter the application name to add one from the gallery. There are over 2,800 SaaS applications listed there. Click the application you want and select Add. After the application is added, select it to open its properties, and then select Single sign-on. Next, set the Single Sign-on Mode to SAML-based Sign-On. In the following example (figure 6-36), the SaaS application Aha! has been added. This application supports SAML 2.0 and is pre-integrated with Azure Active Directory.

**FIGURE 6-36** Enabling SAML-based Single Sign-on

There are several sections to complete to finish enabling SAML-based sign-on. The first is the SaaS application's sign-on and identifier URLs. These represent the sign on URLs for the application and are provided by the application provider. There is also the user attributes section where the user identifier attribute is specified. This is the attribute the SaaS application expects when linking a user defined in its user database with an Azure AD user. These two sections with example answers are shown in Figure 6-37.

Aha! Domain and URLs
Input the URLs and other details about your Aha! tenant into Azure AD.

* Sign on URL ❶     https://steverlabs.aha.io/session/new          ✓

* Identifier ❶      https://steverlabs.aha.io/                    ✓

☐ Show advanced URL settings

User Attributes   Learn more

Edit the user information sent in the SAML token when user sign in to Aha!.

User Identifier ❶    user.userprincipalname ⌄
☐ View and edit all other user attributes

**FIGURE 6-37** Application Sign-on URLs and User Attributes

The remaining configuration section is for the SAML signing certificate. Azure AD generates this certificate and it is used to sign the SAML token used in authentication. The metadata file from this certificate can be downloaded as a file and used to set up the SAML configuration within supported SaaS applications. Alternately, you can manually enter this information to configure the application. Figure 6-38 shows the SAML signing certificate dialog for the Aha! application.

SAML Signing Certificate   Learn more

Manage the certificate used by Azure AD to sign SAML tokens issued to Aha!.

| STATUS | EXPIRATION | THUMBPRINT | DOWNLOAD |
|--------|-----------|-----------|----------|
| Active | 9/28/2020 | A0EB14 | Metadata XML |

Create new certificate

☐ Show advanced certificate signing settings   Learn more

* Notification Email ❶    steve@opsgility.com

**FIGURE 6-38** SAML Signing Certificate information

With this information in place, click Save at the top of the page. This completes the federated single sign-on configuration on the Azure side. Now the SaaS application must be configured to use Azure AD as the SAML identity provider. This can be as simple as uploading the certificate metadata file previously discussed, or the certificate and other information might need to be entered manually. The steps to enable each application vary, so Microsoft has provided tutorials for hundreds of SaaS applications at this URL: *https://docs.microsoft.com/en-us/azure/active-directory/active-directory-saas-tutorial-list*. In the case of the application Aha!, which is used as an example here, the configuration involves uploading the metadata XML file. This populates all the required fields to configure Azure AD as the SAML identity provider, as shown in Figure 6-39.

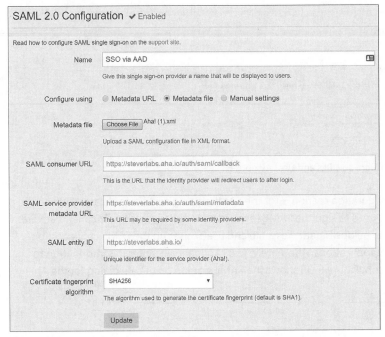

**FIGURE 6-39** Aha! SaaS application SAML identity provider configuration

## Password-based Single Sign-on

Some SaaS applications require the use of their own identity and present an HTML-based sign in page. Azure AD can also enable single sign-on for these applications through password-based single sign-on. This feature works by securely storing user account information and password and presenting these on behalf of the user. This occurs when the user accesses the application from the access panel (*https://myapps.microsoft.com*).

There are two methods of configuring password-based SSO. The first involves an administrator managing the credentials for access. In this case, an administrator enters a set of credentials when the application is added within Azure Active Directory. After users are granted access to this application, they open it and are authenticated automatically without knowing the sign on credentials. This can be useful in scenarios such as granting marketing resources access to a corporation's Twitter account. They can tweet on behalf of the corporation, but their access can be revoked at any time and they never have access to the credentials. The second method of enabling password-based SSO is where the user manages the credentials. This method works by allowing the user to enter their credentials upon first accessing the application from the access panel. The credentials are stored securely and are presented on behalf of the user during subsequent application accesses.

To configure password-based SSO, add an application within Azure AD by using the same process previously described. Figure 6-40 shows Twitter being added.

FIGURE 6-40 Adding Twitter to Azure AD

After the application is added, click Single sign-on, choose Password-based Sign-on as the Single Sign-on Mode, and click Save (shown in Figure 6-41).

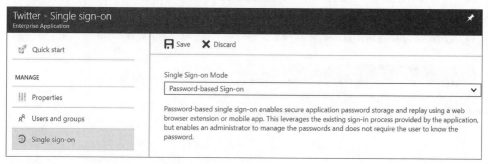

FIGURE 6-41 Configuring the Single Sign-on Mode

When you assign a user to this application, choose whether to use administrator managed or user managed credentials. To use administrator managed credentials, choose Yes at the prompt, Assign credentials on behalf of the user. If the user manages the credentials, choose No at this prompt. As shown in Figure 6-42, the administrator has entered credentials on behalf of the user.

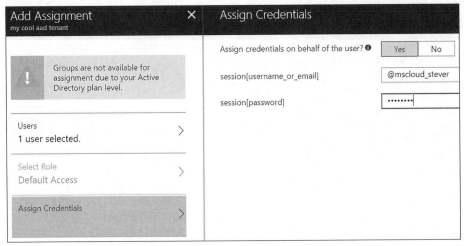

**FIGURE 6-42** Choosing administrator or user managed credentials

It's important to note that password-based SSO requires the installation of a web browser extension or plugin. It is this extension that securely accesses the credentials from Azure AD and passes them to the application on behalf of the user. Upon first access of the application from the access panel, the extension downloads and the user installs it. This operation only occurs once. Figure 6-43 shows the extension installation dialog.

**FIGURE 6-43** Installing the access panel extension

# Add users and groups to applications

After you add applications to Azure Active Directory, you can grant access to these applications to either users or groups. Note that granting access to applications via group membership requires Azure Active Directory Premium (at least the P1 edition). Table 6-1 provides a non-exhaustive list of the differences between the Azure Active Directory Editions.

**TABLE 6-1** Comparing Azure Active Directory Editions

| Features | Free | Basic | Premium P1 | Premium P2 |
| --- | --- | --- | --- | --- |
| Directory Objects | 500k | No Limit | No Limit | No Limit |
| Self-Service Password Change for cloud users | Included | Included | Included | Included |
| Company Branding (Logon Pages/ Access Panel customization) | Not Included | Included | Included | Included |
| Group-based access management/ provisioning | Not Included | Included | Included | Included |
| Multi-Factor Authentication | Not Included | Not Included | Included | Included |
| Identity Protection | Not Included | Not Included | Not Included | Included |
| Privileged Identity Management | Included | Included | Included | Included |

> **NOTE  USING GROUPS FOR APPLICATION ACCESS**
>
> Groups can be used for granting access to applications *only when Azure AD Basic or Premium (P1 or P2) is licensed.*

To grant access to an application, navigate to Enterprise applications within the Azure AD blade and click All applications. Here you see a list of the applications that are integrated with Azure Active Directory, as shown in Figure 6-44.

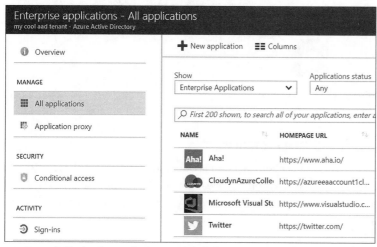

**FIGURE 6-44** Navigating to the integrated applications

Click the application you want to grant access to, and then click Users and groups. Next, click Add user, which allows either users or groups to be assigned to an application. Clearly, assigning individual users is not feasible at scale, so group-based assignment is preferred in this case. As shown in Figure 6-45, a group and a user have been granted access to the Aha! SaaS application.

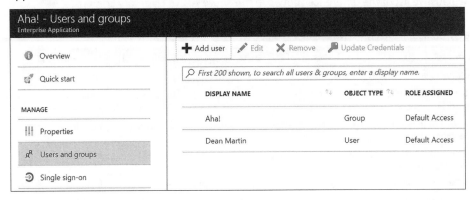

**FIGURE 6-45** A group and user provided with access to Aha!

After a user or a group of users has been assigned an application, they gain access to it via the access panel, also called the MyApps portal. This portal is an SSL-encrypted site that allows users defined in Azure AD to see and alter their information, such as phone number, and to see the applications that they have been provisioned access for, as shown in Figure 6-46.

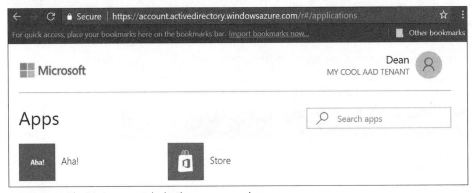

**FIGURE 6-46** The MyApps portal, aka the access panel

## Revoke access to SaaS applications

Revoking access to assigned SaaS applications is a simple operation. At scale, the best way to accomplish this is to remove a user from a group that was assigned an application. This use case does not involve the Enterprise applications section of Azure Active Directory. It is simply removing a user from a group.

To revoke access to an individual user, navigate to Enterprise applications within the Azure AD blade. From there, click All applications, and then click the specific application you want to adjust access to. Next, click Users and groups. This shows you the users and groups that have been assigned access to the application. Click the name of the user you want to remove and then click Remove, as shown in Figure 6-47.

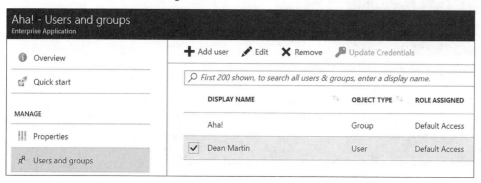

**FIGURE 6-47** Steps for un-assigning a user from an application

To remove access for a user in a group that was granted access to an application, remove the user from the group at the source of authority. If the group is sourced from Azure AD (meaning it was created and is managed there), remove the user from within Azure Active Directory. If the group is sourced from an on-premises Active Directory, make the membership change there.

# Configure federation with public consumer identity providers such as Facebook and Google

When web or mobile application developers are creating the next big app, a very common feature to add is authentication. However, building in authentication can be difficult and if not done well, can result in the application being exploited. This is where Azure AD B2C (business to consumer) fits in. Azure AD B2C allows developers to provide a reliable, scalable authentication experience that allows users to sign in with their existing social accounts (Facebook, Google, and others) or with their personal email address. The first step in enabling these features is to create an Azure AD B2C tenant.

Click New and in the search dialog box, enter Azure AD B2C. Click the returned result, as shown in Figure 6-48.

**FIGURE 6-48** Searching the Azure Marketplace for Azure AD B2C

On the marketplace page, click Create. Choose whether to create a new tenant or link a tenant to an existing Azure subscription. As shown in Figure 6-49, a new tenant is being created.

**FIGURE 6-49** Creating a new Azure AD B2C Tenant

Next enter the Organization name, Initial domain name, and choose the Country or region (Figure 6-50) and then click Create.

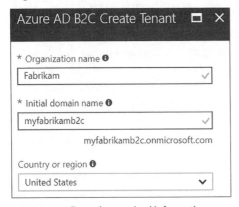

**FIGURE 6-50** Enter the required information

After the Azure AD B2C tenant is created, it must be linked to an Azure subscription. To do this, go through the same steps you used to create the B2C tenant up to the point where you are asked whether you want to create a new tenant or link an existing tenant to your subscription. This time, choose Link an existing Azure AD B2C Tenant to my Azure subscription. You need to complete the information in the Azure AD B2C Resource blade, shown in Figure 6-51, and then click Create.

FIGURE 6-51  Linking the Azure AD B2C tenant to your subscription

After the operation is complete, the resource that represents the B2C tenant can be viewed in the resource group chosen during the linking step, as shown in Figure 6-52.

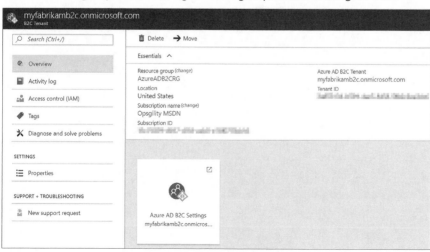

FIGURE 6-52  Azure AD B2C Resource in the linked subscription

Clicking the tile opens a new browser tab focused on the Azure AD B2C tenant. Within the B2C tenant, you can register the applications you want so that they can use the tenant for authentication. As mentioned earlier, Azure AD B2C can be used with several types of applications, including web, mobile, and API apps. For example purposes, the next section focuses on web applications to demonstrate how to register an application.

## Registering a web application

To register a web application, while focused on the Azure AD B2C tenant, click Azure AD B2C, Applications, and finally, click Add, as shown in Figure 6-53.

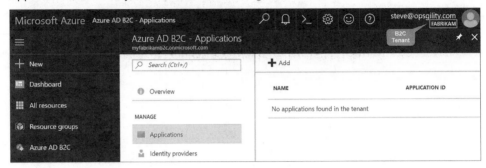

**FIGURE 6-53** Registering an application with Azure AD B2C

Next, enter the name of the application and select yes to indicate it is a web application. Also select Yes under 'Allow implicit flow' if the application uses Open ID Connect for sign-in. Next enter the reply URL, which represents endpoints where Azure AD B2C returns any authentication tokens the application requests. Finally, click Create. These configuration options are displayed in Figure 6-54.

**FIGURE 6-54** Entering the information to register an application

The application is displayed after the creation process completes. Click the application to display its properties. Take special note of the Application ID because this is a globally unique representation of the application within Azure AD B2C. This is used in the web application code during authentication operations.

The web application being referred in this example might also need to make calls to a web API secured by Azure AD B2C. If this is the case, the web application needs a client secret. The secret functions as a security credential, and therefore should be secured appropriately. To create the web app client secret, while within the properties blade of the newly created web application, click Keys. Next, click Generate key and then click Save to view the key. This key value is used as the application secret in the web application's code.

## Configuring Social Identity Providers

After the web application has been registered in Azure AD B2C, identity providers can be added. These can include local identities, where a user logs on with their email address and a password they set, or social identity providers, such as Facebook, Google, Amazon, or LinkedIn. There are two sets of steps needed to enable authentication with an identity provider. The first is to configure the Identity provider side. This process varies for each provider, but generally involves:

1. Creating a representation of the application within their system

2. Providing the web application ID and secret, created earlier in this section

3. Providing the login URL, which is where the authentication request is sent.

The process for adding the identity provider side is beyond the scope of this book, but the process for adding the Facebook identity provider within Azure AD B2C is explained in the next section.

### ADDING FACEBOOK AS AN IDENTITY PROVIDER

After the Identity provider side (Facebook, in this example) is configured, the next step is to add the Identity provider in the Azure AD B2C tenant. While focused on the web application that was added earlier in this section, click Identity providers, and then click Add. Supply a descriptive name for the provider, select the identity provider, and click OK. These configurations are shown in Figure 6-55.

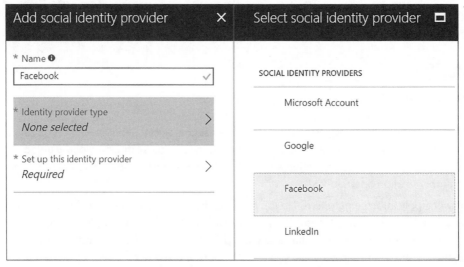

**FIGURE 6-55** Selecting the identity provider

Next, click Set up this identity provider, and enter the Client ID and Client Secret that were provided when the Facebook identity provider configuration was accomplished. Next, click OK and then click Create on the Add social identity provider blade, as shown in Figure 6-56.

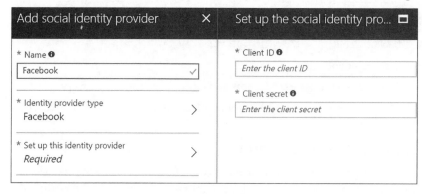

**FIGURE 6-56** Entering the social identity provider client ID and secret

> **NOTE  ENTER THE CORRECT CLIENT ID AND SECRET**
>
> The client ID and Secret being asked for in this step is NOT the Application ID and Secret provided during the initial registration of the web application within Azure AD B2C. Supply instead the Client ID and secret that were provided during the configuration of the identity provider side (in this case, Facebook).

Assuming all is configured properly within the web application, on the social identity provider, and within Azure AD B2C, the web application now allows users to authenticate via their existing Facebook credentials.

> **NOTE  AZURE AD BUSINESS TO BUSINESS (B2B)**
>
> Azure Active Directory also can allow users within an Azure AD tenant to grant access to documents, resources, and applications to users from another organization. External users (partners) are invited to access resources from the source Azure AD tenant, which means the inviting organization does not need to manage any partner identities. The inviting organization can terminate this access at any time. These features are enabled through Azure AD B2B.

# Skill 6.2: Implement recovery services

> **This skill covers how to:**
> - Create a backup vault
> - Deploy a backup agent
> - Backup and restore data, use of snapshots and Geo-replication for recovery
> - Implement DR as a service, Deploy ASR agent, ASR configuration and best practices

## Create a Recovery Services vault

Within Azure, a single resource is provisioned for either Azure Backup or Azure Site Recovery. This resource is called a Recovery Services vault. It is also the resource that is used for configuration and management of both Backup and Site Recovery.

### Create a Recovery Services vault (Azure Portal)

To create a Recovery Services vault from the Azure portal, click New, and in the marketplace search dialog box enter Backup and Site Recovery, and click the Backup and Site Recovery (OMS) option, as shown in Figure 6-57.

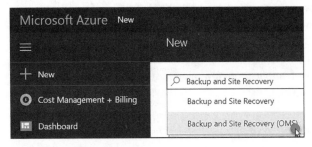

**FIGURE 6-57** Creating a Recovery Services vault

Within the marketplace page for Backup and Site Recovery (OMS), click Create. Enter the name of the vault and choose or create the resource group where it resides. Next, choose the region where you want to create the resource, and click Create (see Figure 6-58).

> **NOTE  OPERATIONS MANAGEMENT SUITE (OMS)**
>
> Operations Management Suite is a collection of features that are licensed together as a unit, including Azure Monitoring and Log Analytics, Azure Automation, Azure Security Center, Azure Backup and Azure Site Recovery.

**FIGURE 6-58** Completing the creation of the vault

## Create a Recovery Services vault (PowerShell)

To create a Recovery Services vault with PowerShell, start by creating the resource group it should reside in.

```
New-AzureRmResourceGroup -Name 'RSVaultRG' -Location 'South Central US'
```

Next, create the vault.

```
New-AzureRmRecoveryServicesVault -Name 'MyRSVault' -ResourceGroupName 'RSVaultRG'
-Location 'South Central US'
```

The storage redundancy type should be set at this point. The options are Locally Redundant Storage or Geo Redundant Storage. It is a good idea to use Geo Redundant Storage when protecting IaaS virtual machines. This is because the vault must be in the same region as the VM being backed up. Having the only backup copy in the same region as the item being protected is not wise, so Geo Redundant storage gives you three additional copies of the backed-up data in the sister (paired) region.

```
$vault1 = Get-AzureRmRecoveryServicesVault -Name 'MyRSVault'
Set-AzureRmRecoveryServicesBackupProperties -Vault $vault1 -BackupStorageRedundancy
 GeoRedundant
```

## Deploy a Backup Agent

There are different types of backup agents you can use with Azure Backup. There is the Micro-soft Azure Recovery Services (MARS) agent, which is a stand-alone agent used to protect files and folders. There is also the DPM protection agent that is used with Microsoft Azure Backup Server and with System Center Data Protection Manager. Finally, there is the VMSnapshot extension that is installed on Azure VMs to allow snapshots to be taken for full VM backups. The deployment of the DPM protection agent can be automated with either the use of System Center Data Protection Manager or Azure Backup Server. The VMSnapshot or VMSnapshot-Linux extensions are also automatically deployed by the Azure fabric controller. The remainder of this section focuses on deploying the MARS agent.

The MARS agent is available for install from within the Recovery Services vault. Click Backup under Getting Started. Under the Where Is Your Workload Running drop-down menu, select On-Premises, and under What Do You Want To Backup, choose Files And Folders. Next, click Prepare Infrastructure, and the Recovery Services agent is made available, as shown in Figure 6-59.

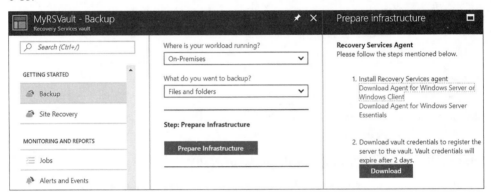

**FIGURE 6-59** Downloading the MARS agent

Notice there is only a Windows agent because the backup of files and folders is only sup-ported on Windows computers. Click the link to download the agent. Before initiating the installation of the MARS agent, also download the vault credentials file, which is right under the download links for the Recovery Services agent. The vault credentials file is needed during the installation of the MARS agent.

> **NOTE   VAULT CREDENTIALS EXPIRATION**
>
> The vault credentials are only valid for 48 hours from the time of download, so be sure to obtain them only when you are ready to install the MARS agent.
>
> During the MARS agent installation, a cache location must be specified. There must be free disk space within this cache location that is equal to or greater than five percent of the total amount of data to be protected. These configuration options are shown in Figure 6-60.

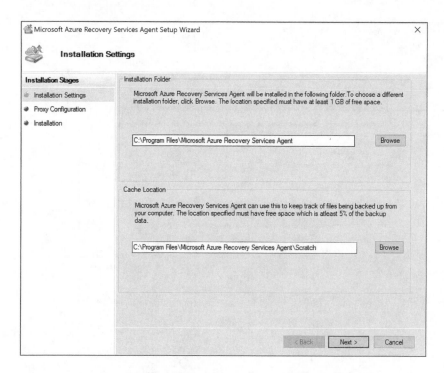

**FIGURE 6-60** Installing the MARS agent

The agent needs to communicate to the Azure Backup service on the internet, so on the next setup screen, configure any required proxy settings. On the last installation screen, any required Windows features are added to the system where the agent is being installed. After it is complete, the installation prompts you to Proceed to Registration, as shown in Figure 6-61.

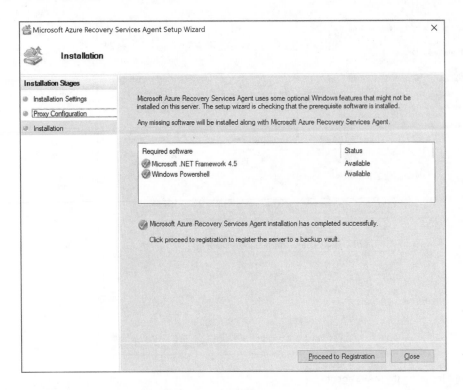

**FIGURE 6-61** Final screen of the MARS agent installation

Click Proceed to Registration to open the agent registration dialog box. Within this dialog box the vault credentials must be provided by browsing to the path of the downloaded file. The next dialog box is one of the most important ones. On the Encryption Settings screen, either specify a passphrase or allow the installation program to generate one. Enter this in twice, and then specify where the passphrase file should be saved. The passphrase file is a text file that contains the passphrase, so stored this file securely.

> **NOTE**  **AZURE BACKUP ENCRYPTION PASSPHRASE**
>
> Data protected by Azure Backup is encrypted using the supplied passphrase. If the passphrase is lost or forgotten, any data protected by Azure Backup is not able to be recovered and is lost.
>
> After the agent is registered with the Azure Backup service, it can then be configured to begin protecting data.

# Backup and restore data

In the last section, the MARS agent was installed and registered with the Azure Backup vault. Before data can be protected with the agent, it must be configured with settings such as, when the backups occur, how often they occur, how long the data is retained, and what data is protected. Within the MARS agent interface, click Schedule Backup to begin this configuration process.

Click to move past the Getting Started screen, and click Add items to add files and folders. Exclusions can also be set so that certain file types are not protected, as shown in Figure 6-62.

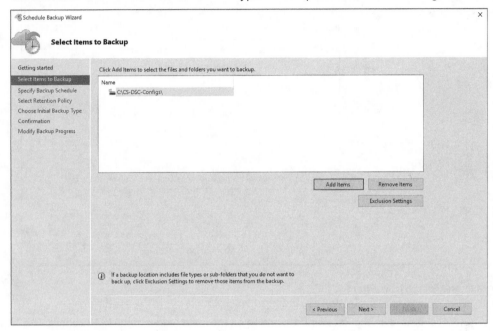

**FIGURE 6-62** Configuring the MARS agent to protect data

Next, schedule how often backups should occur. The agent can be configured to back up daily or weekly, with a maximum of three backups taken per day. Specify the retention you want, and the initial backup type (Over the network or Offline). Confirm the settings to complete the wizard. Backups are now scheduled to occur, but they can also be initiated at any time by clicking Back up now on the main screen of the agent. The dialog showing an active backup is shown in Figure 6-63.

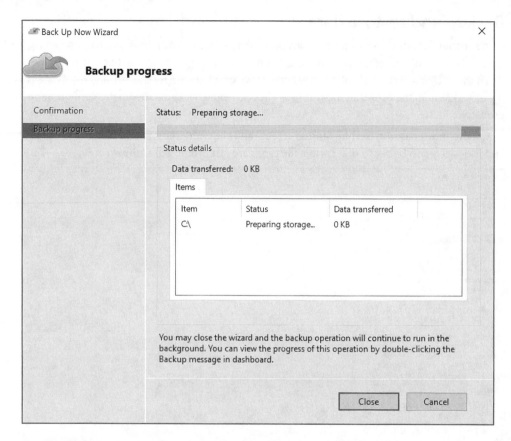

**FIGURE 6-63** Backup Now Wizard

To recover data, click the Recover Data option on the main screen of the MARS agent. This initiates the Recover Data Wizard. Choose which computer to restore the data to. Generally, this is the same computer the data was backed up from. Next, choose the data to recover, the date on which the backup took place, and the time the backup occurred. These choices comprise the recovery point to restore. Click Mount to mount the selected recovery point as a volume, and then choose the location to recover the data. Confirm the options selected and the recovery begins.

In addition to the MARS agent and protecting files and folders with Azure Backup, it is also possible to back up IaaS virtual machines in Azure. This solution provides a way to restore an entire virtual machine, or individual files from the virtual machine, and it is quite easy to set up. To back up an IaaS VM in Azure with Azure backup, navigate to the Recovery Service vault and under Getting Started, click Backup. Select Azure as the location where the workload is running, and Virtual machine as the workload to backup and click Backup, as shown in Figure 6-64.

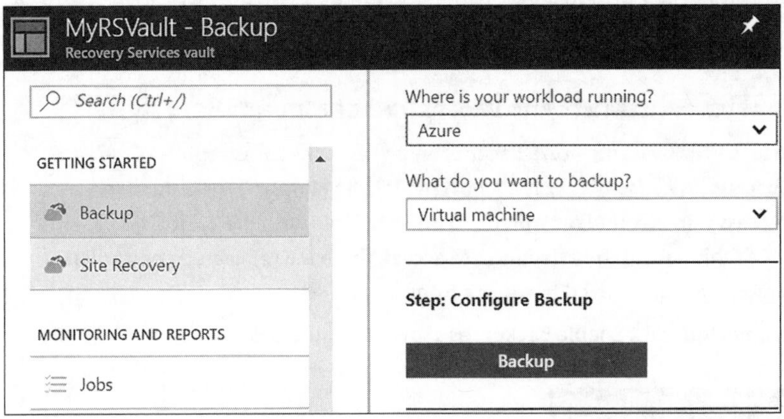

**FIGURE 6-64** Configuring Azure Backup to protect IaaS VMs

The next item to configure is the Backup policy. This policy defines how often backups occur and how long the backups are retained. The default policy accomplishes a daily backup at 06:00am and retains backups for 30 days. It is also possible to configure custom Backup policies. In this example, a custom Backup policy is configured that includes daily, weekly, monthly, and yearly backups, each with their own retention values. Figure 6-65 shows the creation of a custom backup policy.

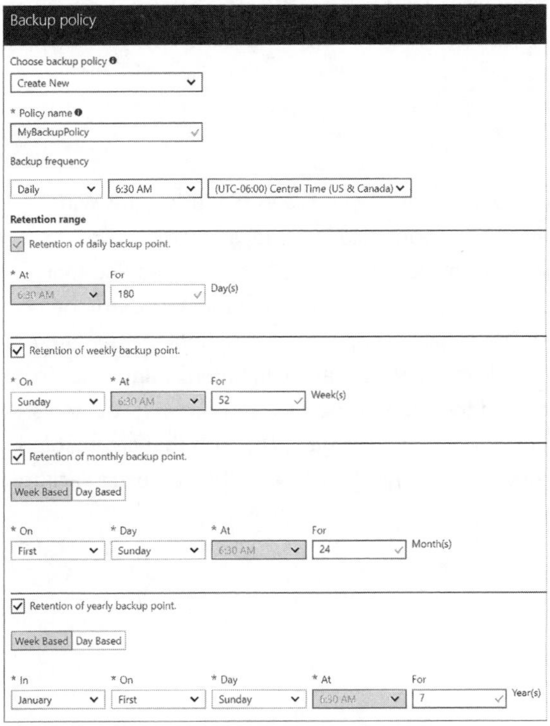

**FIGURE 6-65** Configuring a custom backup policy

Next, choose the VMs to back up. Only VMs within the same region as the Recovery Services vault are available for backup.

> **NOTE  AZURE IAAS VM PROTECTION AND VAULT STORAGE REDUNDANCY TYPE**
>
> When protecting IaaS VMs by using Azure Backup, only VMs in the same region as the vault are available for backup. Because of this, it is a best practice to choose Geo-Redundant storage or Read Access Geo-Redundant storage to be associated with the vault. This ensures that, in the case of a regional outage affecting VM access, there is a replicated copy of backups in another region that can be used to restore from.

After the VMs are selected, click Enable Backup, as shown in Figure 6-66.

**FIGURE 6-66**  Enabling VM backups

When you click the Enable Backup button, behind the scenes the VMSnapshot (for Windows) or VMSnapshotLinux (for Linux) extension is automatically deployed by the Azure fabric controller to the VMs. This allows for snapshot-based backups to occur, meaning that first a snapshot of the VM is taken, and then this snapshot is streamed to the Azure storage associated with the Recovery Services vault. The initial backup is not taken until the day/time configured in the backup policy, however an ad-hock backup can be initiated at any time. To do so, navigate to the Protected Items section of the vault properties, and click Backup items. Then, click Azure Virtual Machine under Backup Management type. The VMs that are enabled for backup are listed here. To begin an ad-hock backup, right-click on a VM and select Backup now, as shown in Figure 6-67.

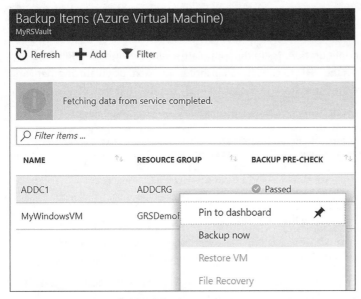

**FIGURE 6-67** Starting an ad-hock backup

# Use of snapshots

Many organizations choose to use Azure Backup to protect their IaaS virtual machines. For those that elect not to use Azure Backup, another strategy is to use blob snapshots to protect virtual machines. Unmanaged VM disks are actually page blobs that are stored within the customer's storage account. A snapshot of these page blobs can be taken, which can then be copied to a storage account in the same or a different Azure Region. If the need arises to recover the virtual machine, it can be recreated from the blob snapshot. To walk through these steps, begin by creating a destination storage account. In this example, the virtual machine to be protected is in West US 2. To ensure the snapshot survives a region-wide outage, it is copied to a destination storage account in a different region. To begin, create a resource group and the destination storage account. The storage account is created and a reference to it is stored in the variable $destStorageAcct. This variable is used later.

```
New-AzureRmResourceGroup -Name MyRecoveryStorageRG -Location eastus2
$destStorageAcct = New-AzureRmStorageAccount -ResourceGroupName MyRecoveryStorageRG
-Name recoverysa0434 -SkuName Standard_LRS -Location eastus2 -Kind Storage
```

Next, create a blob container for the snapshot to exist in. To do this, first set the storage account context.

```
Set-AzureRmCurrentStorageAccount -ResourceGroupName MyRecoveryStorageRG
-Name recoverysa0434
```

Next, create the container.

```
New-AzureStorageContainer -Name recovery -Permission Off
```

Now, create a snapshot configuration. To do this, populate a variable with the URI of the storage account that contains the VHD to collect a snapshot from. Next, populate another variable with the Resource ID of the same storage account. Finally, set the snapshot context.

```
$sourceVHDURI = https://criticalserverrgdisks810.blob.core.windows.net/vhds/
CriticalServer20171005195926.vhd
$storageAccountId = "/subscriptions/<SubscriptionID>/resourceGroups/criticalserverrg/
providers/Microsoft.Storage/storageAccounts/criticalserverrgdisks810"
$snapshotConfig = New-AzureRmSnapshotConfig -AccountType StandardLRS -Location
westus2 -CreateOption Import -StorageAccountId $storageAccountId -SourceUri
 $sourceVHDURI
```

With all these steps in place, create the snapshot.

```
New-AzureRmSnapshot -Snapshot $snapshotConfig -ResourceGroupName CriticalServerRG
-SnapshotName MyCriticalServerDiskSnapshot
```

The snapshot is created in the same resource group as the source storage account (the one containing the VHD from the virtual machine to be protected), as shown in Figure 6-68.

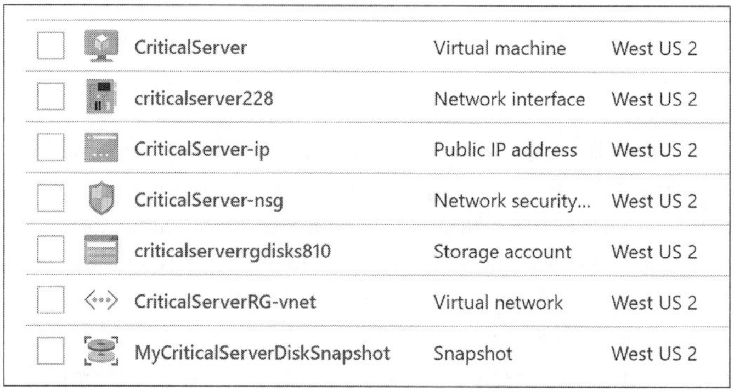

| | | | | |
|---|---|---|---|---|
| ☐ | 🖥 | CriticalServer | Virtual machine | West US 2 |
| ☐ | 📇 | criticalserver228 | Network interface | West US 2 |
| ☐ | ▦ | CriticalServer-ip | Public IP address | West US 2 |
| ☐ | 🛡 | CriticalServer-nsg | Network security... | West US 2 |
| ☐ | ▦ | criticalserverrgdisks810 | Storage account | West US 2 |
| ☐ | ⟨⋅⋅⟩ | CriticalServerRG-vnet | Virtual network | West US 2 |
| ☐ | 💾 | MyCriticalServerDiskSnapshot | Snapshot | West US 2 |

**FIGURE 6-68** New VHD snapshot

Before the snapshot can be copied, the destination storage account key is needed. Obtain this within the Azure portal from the properties of the storage account, as shown in Figure 6-69.

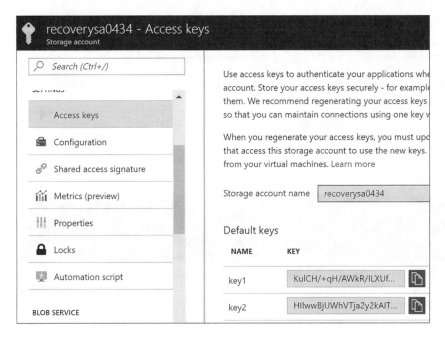

**FIGURE 6-69** Copying the storage key form the destination storage account

Populate the key value into a variable.

```
$storageAccountKey = "<StorageAccountKey>"
```

Several other variables need to be populated to be used in the blob copy command. First populate a variable with the name of the source resource group (where the snapshot exists) and then populate a variable with the name of the snapshot:

```
$resourceGroupName ="CriticalServerRG"
$snapshotName = "MyCriticalServerDiskSnapshot"
```

A shared access signature is created to grant access to the snapshot. Set the duration for the shared access signature (how long it functions).

```
$sasExpiryDuration = "3600"
```

A variable was already populated with the destination storage account earlier in these steps. This serves as the destination storage account name. Now, run the cmdlet to create the shared access signature.

```
$sas = Grant-AzureRmSnapshotAccess -ResourceGroupName $resourceGroupName -SnapshotName
 $SnapshotName -DurationInSecond $sasExpiryDuration -Access Read
```

Now create the destination storage context to use in the snapshot copy.

```
$destinationContext = New-AzureStorageContext -StorageAccountName
$storageAcct.StorageAccountName -StorageAccountKey $storageAccountKey
```

Finally, begin the copy operation. Notice that the snapshot is converted to a VHD in the destination storage account.

```
Start-AzureStorageBlobCopy -AbsoluteUri $sas.AccessSAS -DestContainer "recovery"
 -DestContext $destinationContext -DestBlob "recoveredcriticalserveros.vhd"
```

When complete, the copied VHD is visible in the destination storage account container, as shown in Figure 6-70.

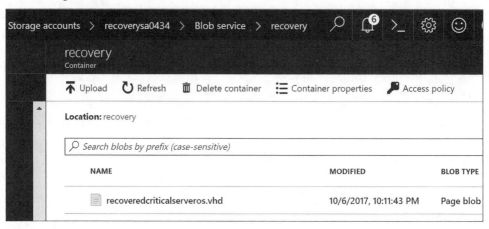

**FIGURE 6-70** Copied VHD blob originating from a blob snapshot

To recover from a VM issue by using the copied VHD in the destination region, create a new resource group for the recovered VM to be created in, convert the VHD to a managed disk, and provision a virtual machine from the managed disk.

```
New-AzureRmResourceGroup -Name RecoveredCriticalServerRG -Location eastus2
$sourceUri =
https://recoverysa0434.blob.core.windows.net/recovery/recoveredcriticalserveros.vhd
$osDiskName = 'myOsDisk'
$osDisk = New-AzureRmDisk -DiskName $osDiskName -Disk (New-AzureRmDiskConfig
-AccountType StandardLRS  -Location eastus2 -CreateOption Import -SourceUri
$sourceUri) -ResourceGroupName RecoveredCriticalServerRG
```

Next, create a virtual network for the VM to exist in.

```
$subnetName = 'mySubNet'
$singleSubnet = New-AzureRmVirtualNetworkSubnetConfig -Name $subnetName
-AddressPrefix 10.0.0.0/24
```

```
$vnetName = "myVnetName"
$vnet = New-AzureRmVirtualNetwork -Name $vnetName -ResourceGroupName
 RecoveredCriticalServerRG -Location eastus2 -AddressPrefix 10.0.0.0/16
 -Subnet $singleSubnet
```

Now, create the network security group that only allows the required network traffic.

```
$nsgName = "myNsg"
$rdpRule = New-AzureRmNetworkSecurityRuleConfig -Name myRdpRule -Description "Allow RDP"
 -Access Allow -Protocol Tcp -Direction Inbound -Priority 110 -SourceAddressPrefix
 internet -SourcePortRange * -DestinationAddressPrefix * -DestinationPortRange 3389
$nsg = New-AzureRmNetworkSecurityGroup -ResourceGroupName RecoveredCriticalServerRG
-Location eastus2 -Name $nsgName -SecurityRules $rdpRule
```

Next, create a public IP address and network interface card for the VM.

```
$ipName = "myIP"
$pip = New-AzureRmPublicIpAddress -Name $ipName -ResourceGroupName
 RecoveredCriticalServerRG -Location eastus2 -AllocationMethod Dynamic
$nicName = "myNicName"
$nic = New-AzureRmNetworkInterface -Name $nicName -ResourceGroupName
 RecoveredCriticalServerRG -Location eastus2 -SubnetId $vnet.Subnets[0].Id
-PublicIpAddressId $pip.Id -NetworkSecurityGroupId $nsg.Id
```

Next, specify the VM name, series, and size, and assign the network interface to the VM configuration.

```
$vmName = "RecoveredCriticalVM"
$vmConfig = New-AzureRmVMConfig -VMName $vmName -VMSize "Standard_D1_V2"
$vm = Add-AzureRmVMNetworkInterface -VM $vmConfig -Id $nic.Id
```

Next, add the OS disk that was created from the snapshot.

```
$vm = Set-AzureRmVMOSDisk -VM $vm -ManagedDiskId $osDisk.Id -StorageAccountType
 StandardLRS -DiskSizeInGB 128 -CreateOption Attach -Windows
```

Finally, create the VM.

```
New-AzureRmVM -ResourceGroupName RecoveredCriticalServerRG -Location eastus2 -VM $vm
```

This final step results in a virtual machine that is created from the copied snapshot. As such, it is an exact replica (from a disk contents perspective) of the source virtual machine that the original snapshot was taken from. If the source VM was shut down prior to the collection of the VM snapshot, the recovered VM would be in an application-consistent state, meaning a state similar to that of a cleanly shut down machine. If the snapshot was collected from a running VM, the recovered VM would be in a crash-consistent state. This means the VM is in a state similar to if the machine was powered off without a clean shut down. In this case the VM will show an unplanned shutdown on the first boot after recovery, as shown in Figure 6-71.

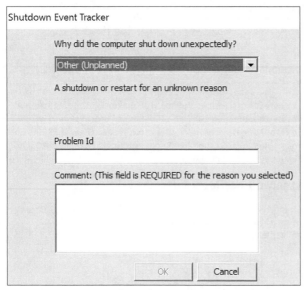

**FIGURE 6-71** Indication of a crash-consistent recovered VM

## Geo-replication for recovery

Azure Storage has several platform-level replication capabilities to help ensure the availability of customer data. One of these replication options is Geo-Redundant storage (GRS). With this option, the Azure platform replicates the customer's data to a paired region hundreds of miles away from the primary copy. This enables recovery of access to data, should the primary region become unavailable. Customers have no access to this second copy of their data until Microsoft declares a persistent outage and accomplishes a geo-failover. This redundancy option is shown in Figure 6-72.

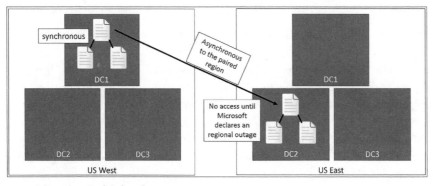

**FIGURE 6-72** Geo-Redundant Storage

Another option for platform-replicated storage is called Read Access-Geo Redundant Storage (RA-GRS). With this option, customers have read-only access to their replicated data. As it pertains to IaaS, unmanaged standard VM disks can be provisioned from storage accounts with GRS or RA-GRS enabled. Keep in mind, that with either GRS and RA-GRS, replication is asynchronous to the paired region. This means the copies in the paired region are behind by a certain number of write operations. Just how far behind is difficult to estimate given that it depends on the data change rate on the replicated disk and the latency/bandwidth between Azure regions.

If an outage of the Azure Storage service occurs that affects a customer's primary data, and if the only strategy for data protection being used is GRS or RA-GRS, there are two potential responses. First, the customer can wait for recovery. Microsoft diligently works to recover access to storage, and customers can monitor the status via the Azure Service Health Dashboard. The second option is valid only if the customer has RA-GRS configured on their storage account. With read access, the customer can create read/write copies of the storage blobs that represent their VM disks. With a read/write copy, they can manually recreate their VMs by using the replicated blobs. This recovery process would be similar to the process described in the Use of snapshots section, earlier in this chapter.

There are two important caveats about VMs recovered in this way. First, the VMs are in a crash-consistent state. Second, because of the asynchronous nature of replication, some recently-changed data on the primary side might be lost.

Because of the caveats mentioned, relying on Geo-Redundant storage is not an effective way to prepare for regional outages. A better strategy is to leverage Azure Backup (backed by a Geo-Redundant storage account) to back up IaaS VMs. Also, for business-critical VMs, use Azure Site Recovery to enable fast failover from the primary to secondary Azure region.

## Implement DR as service, Deploy ASR agent, ASR Configuration & best practices

Azure Site Recovery (ASR) is a disaster recovery service that can protect server workloads from one on-premises datacenter to another on-premises datacenter (D2D), from an on-premises datacenter into Azure (D2A), or from one Azure region to another (A2A). Considering workloads on-premises, ASR can protect physical machines, VMware-based virtual machines, or Hyper-V-based virtual machines. Within Azure, ASR can protect IaaS virtual machines. Because this book is focused on Azure Infrastructure as a Service, this section focuses on the on-premises to Azure (D2A) and Azure to Azure (A2A) scenarios.

As a first step in implementing Azure Site Recovery in any scenario, first create a Recovery Services vault. This vault is the management and configuration resource used with Azure Backup or Azure Site Recovery. Its creation was previously covered in the Create a Recovery Services vault section earlier in this chapter.

## Implementing ASR VMWARE and PHYSICAL Machine Protection

There are several types of information needed to help ensure a successful implementation of Site Recovery. These include the number of servers to protect. It's helpful to break these out by application, so the server count is being based on the needs and dependencies of each application. Also, the number of disks attached to each protected server and an estimate of storage consumed is required information. Another aspect to consider is the daily change rate. This is often called data churn and it represents how much data per disk changes daily. The last consideration is what recovery point objectives are required. This determines how much data is eventually stored in Azure.

The reason for gathering the data points discussed is to arrive at conclusions about how much network bandwidth is required from on-premises to Azure, how much Azure storage will be consumed, what the Azure disk performance requirements are (inputs/outputs per second, or IOPS), how much infrastructure is needed on premises to support replication, and whether the servers to protect are compatible with ASR.

There are tools that can be used to help collect this information. The first is called the Site Recovery Deployment Planner (SRDP). As of this writing, the SRDP only works with VMware-based workloads and is in a public preview status. This planning tool runs within the source datacenter, collecting data about the workloads to protect, including the required bandwidth, Azure storage, and Azure processor cores. Ideally the toolset should run for several weeks to a month so that an accurate representation of performance is collected. A dialog of an SRDP instance collecting data is shown in Figure 6-73.

```
**********
Performing prerequisite checks...
VMware vSphere PowerCLI version installed: 6.0.0.7254
Validated VMware vSphere PowerCLI version successfully.
Checking connectivity to vCenter/ESXi host...
Connectivity to vCenter/ESXi host succeeded.
Validating VMs for profiling...
Prerequisite checks completed.

Total number of profiling virtual machines: 3.
Getting virtual machine details...
VM details stored in file C:\ProfilingData\VMdetailList.xml.

Profiling start time = 7/24/2017 1:05:00 PM and profiling end time = 7/25/2017 1:05:00 PM.
```

**FIGURE 6-73** Site Recovery Deployment Planner collecting data

After the data has been collected, visualizations are created that provide information critical to the planning phase, as shown in Figure 6-74 .

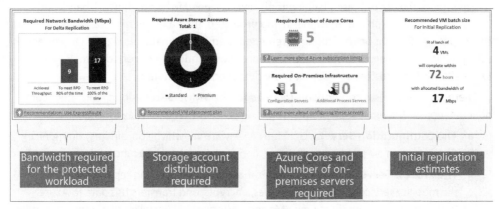

**FIGURE 6-74** Output from the Site Recovery Deployment Planner

Another toolset that is valuable during Site Recovery planning is the ASR Capacity Planner. This is a spreadsheet that allows customers to enter information about their workloads and key planning information is calculated. Figure 6-75 shows a screenshot of the capacity planner spreadsheet.

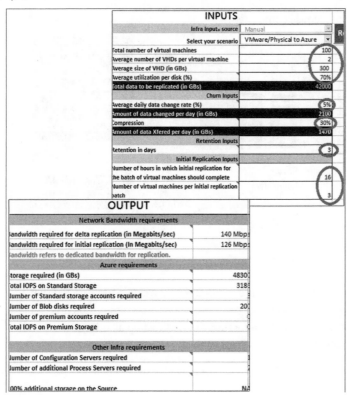

**FIGURE 6-75** ASR Capacity Planner

Commonly, the use of these planning tools reveals a need for more network bandwidth. Depending on the number of machines being protected, their amount of storage, and the data change rate, ASR might be replicating a tremendous amount of data into Azure. Organizations can either increase their outbound internet connection bandwidth or consider implementing ExpressRoute. Refer to Chapter four for more details on ExpressRoute.

There are on-premises components required for the VMware scenario of ASR. These components support the replication of data from on-premises to Azure. They include:

- **The Configuration Server**   Generally a VMware vm which coordinates communications between on-premises and Azure, and manages data replication.

- **The Process Server**   Serves as a replication gateway, receiving replicated data from the mobility service, caches, compresses, encrypts, and transfers this data to Azure. Performs auto-discovery of new VMs and performs push installation of mobility service. Can scale out as needed.

- **Master Target Server**   Handles replication data during failback from Azure. Can scale out as needed.

- **Mobility Service**   Installed on all protected VMs. Intercepts and replicates disk writes to Process Server.

Figure 6-76 shows these on-premise components.

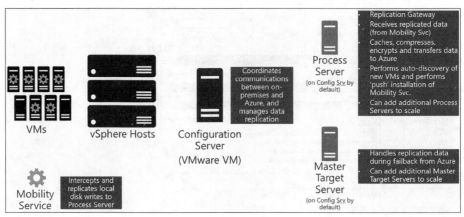

**FIGURE 6-76** ASR VMware scenario on-premises components

By default, all the on-premises server roles are provisioned on a single VMware VM, but the Process Server and Master Target Server can be scaled out as requirements dictate. Table 6-2 gives the server specifications for the Configuration Server (hosting all roles) based on the number of servers that are protected from on-premises.

**TABLE 6-2** Performance requirements for on-premises Configuration Server

| CPU | Memory | Cache disk size | Data change rate | Protected machines |
|---|---|---|---|---|
| 8 vCPUs (2 sockets * 4 cores @ 2.5GHz) | 16 GB | 300 GB | 500 GB or less | Replicate < 100 machines |
| 12 vCPUs (2 sockets * 6 cores @ 2.5GHz) | 18 GB | 500 GB | 500 GB to 1 TB | Replicate between 100-150 machines |
| 16 VCPUS (2 SOCKETS * 8 CORES @ 2.5GHZ) | 32 GB | 1 TB | 1 TB to 2 TB | Replicate between 150-250 machines |
| Deploy another process server (scale out) | | | > 2 TB | Deploy additional process servers if you're replicating more than 200 machines, or if the daily data change rate exceeds 2 TB |

The Configuration server also has network requirements. Remember that ASR is a PaaS service and so it is accessible over the public internet. As such, the configuration server must have direct or proxy-based access to the following URLs:Ports

- *.hypervrecoverymanager.windowsazure.com:443
- *.accesscontrol.windows.net:443
- *.backup.windowsazure.com:443
- *.blob.core.windows.net:443
- *.store.core.windows.net:443
- https://dev.mysql.com/get/archives/mysql-5.5/mysql-5.5.37-win32.msi (for MySQL download)
- time.windows.com:123
- time.nist.gov:123

ASR is ready to be implemented after the planning tools have produced output, any bandwidth increases have been procured, the on-premises infrastructure (Configuration server) is appropriately sized and ready, and the required URLs and ports are allowed from the Configuration server.

To implement the VMware scenario of ASR, start by preparing the VMware environment. This involves preparing for automatic discovery of new VMs for protection and failover of those protected VMs. Both capabilities require a read-only user defined on each vSphere host or on the vCenter server that manages the hosts, as shown in Figure 6-77.

| localhost.corp.microsoft.com VMware ESXi, 5.5.0, 1331820 | Evaluation (51 days remaining) |||
| Getting Started | Summary | Virtual Machines | Resource Allocation | Performance | Configuration | Local Users & Groups | Events | **Permissions** |
| User/Group | Role | Defined in |
|---|---|---|
| readonly | Read-only | This object |
| vpxuser | Administrator | This object |
| dcui | Administrator | This object |
| root | Administrator | This object |

**FIGURE 6-77** vSphere user with Read-Only access

If both failover and failback are features you want, the vSphere or vCenter user requires additional permissions, as shown in Table 6-3. Ideally, a role should be created with the following permissions, and this role should be assigned to a user or group.

**TABLE 6-3** VMware permissions required for Azure Site Recovery integration

| Task | Role/Permission | Details |
| --- | --- | --- |
| VM Discovery | Data Center object –> Propagate to Child Object, role=Read-only | At least a read-only user. User assigned at datacenter level, and has access to all the objects in the datacenter. To restrict access, assign the No access role with the Propagate to child object, to the child objects (vSphere hosts, datastores, VMs and networks). |
| Full replication, failover, failback | Data Center object –> Propagate to Child Object, role=Azure_Site_Recovery Datastore > Allocate space, browse datastore, low-level file operations, remove file, update virtual machine files Network > Network assign Resource > Assign VM to resource pool, migrate powered off VM, migrate powered on VM Tasks > Create task, update task Virtual machine > Configuration Virtual machine > Interact > answer question, device connection, configure CD media, configure floppy media, power off, power on, VMware tools install Virtual machine > Inventory > Create, register, unregister Virtual machine > Provisioning > Allow virtual machine download, allow virtual machine files upload Virtual machine > Snapshots > Remove snapshots | User assigned at datacenter level, and has access to all the objects in the datacenter. To restrict access, assign the No access role with the Propagate to child object, to the child objects (vSphere hosts, datastores, VMs and networks). |

If you want Push installation of the mobility service, an account needs to be provisioned with administrator rights on Windows and/or root access on Linux. The Process server performs the installation of the Mobility service under the context of one of these users.

The next step in implementing ASR is to create the Recovery Services vault in Azure. It is a best practice to create this vault a significant distance from the workload being protected. This helps to ensure that a regional catastrophe does not impact the primary and replicated workload.

After this step, download and install the Unified Setup and vault credentials. These are both available from the properties of the Recovery Services vault, as shown in Figure 6-78.

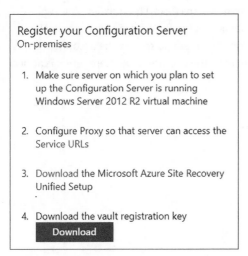

**Register your Configuration Server**
On-premises

1. Make sure server on which you plan to set up the Configuration Server is running Windows Server 2012 R2 virtual machine

2. Configure Proxy so that server can access the Service URLs

3. Download the Microsoft Azure Site Recovery Unified Setup

4. Download the vault registration key
   **Download**

**FIGURE 6-78** Download the ASR Unified Setup and the vault credentials

After the installation completes, the Microsoft Azure Site Recovery Configuration Server program that is used to register the configuration server with the Site Recovery service automatically starts. In this interface specify an account that has admin rights on the Windows systems where the mobility service is installed. Also add a vSphere or vCenter account with appropriate rights in the Vmware infrastructure as discussed previously in this section. This dialog is shown in Figure 6-79.

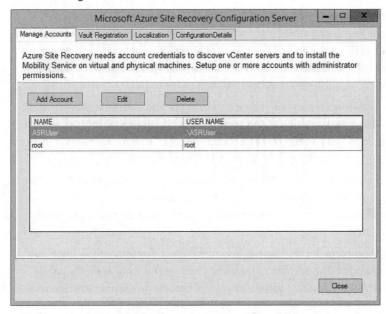

**FIGURE 6-79** Registering the Configuration server and accounts

Add the required accounts and within 10 to 15 minutes, the Configuration Server is registered within the Prepare source blade in the ASR section of the Recovery Services vault. Next, within the same blade click to add the vCenter/vSphere server and specify the account provided earlier with VMware access. Within a few minutes, the vCenter or vSphere server is added as well, as shown in Figure 6-80.

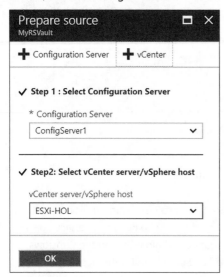

**FIGURE 6-80** Configuration and vSphere server registered

The next configuration step is to set up the target environment in Azure. This includes provisioning or choosing an existing storage account and virtual network. The storage account holds replicated data from the on-premises environment to be used for building virtual machines during a failover. The virtual network provides failed-over VMs with a network context so they can continue to provide the services they did when on-premises.

Following the target environment set up, the next item to configure is the replication policy. This policy defines how long recovery points and application-consistent snapshots should be retained. The replication policy is created and associated with the Configuration server in this step.

The next step is to enable replication. In this interface, the source and target infrastructures are selected. The VMs to protect and which disks per VM to protect are also chosen in this step. Also in this step, the replication policy that was created in the previous step (or a pre-existing replication policy) is selected.

After these steps are complete, replication begins immediately. The initial replication can take many hours, depending on the amount of data, the churn of the data, available bandwidth, and other factors. A fairly accurate estimation of this timeframe should have been an output of the planning phase. Failover is not possible until the replicated VMs show as Protected. In Figure 6-81, the status of the initial replication is seen for two protected VMs.

| NAME | HEALTH | STATUS | ACTIVE LOCATION |
|------|--------|--------|-----------------|
| Web1 | ⊘ OK | 0% synchronized | ConfigServer1 |
| SQL1 | ⊘ OK | 0% synchronized | ConfigServer1 |

**FIGURE 6-81** Protected VMs replicating to Azure

The final item to create when implementing ASR is the Recovery Plan. This is an important construct in Site Recovery because it defines the orchestration of how workloads fail over and are powered on. Some applications need changes to be made via script, such as a connection string change and some applications require certain machines to power on before the others. All of these orchestrations are set up in the recovery plan. A screen shot of a recovery plan is shown in Figure 6-82.

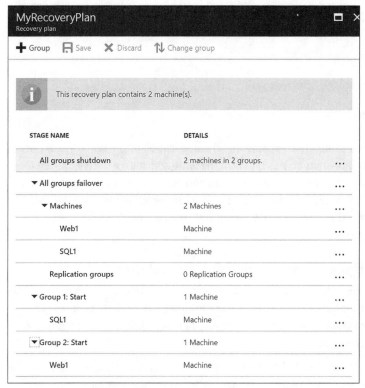

**FIGURE 6-82** ASR Recovery Plan

After the Recovery Plan is completed, ASR is configured and is ready to protect workloads. However, no disaster recovery solution is truly ready until a failover test is accomplished. To perform a test failover, navigate to the Recovery Plan, right-click it and choose Test Failover, as shown in Figure 6-83. Choose the recovery point and the virtual network, and then click OK. Monitor the progress in the Site Recovery Jobs view.

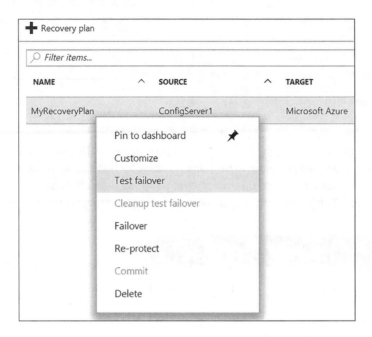

**FIGURE 6-83** Testing the failover

After the test failover has completed, validate that the application is functional. If it is not functional, this is a good opportunity to troubleshoot the issue and learn what is required for a functional failover of the protected application. You can add adjustments to the Recovery Plan to ensure future failovers produce a working instance of the protected application. As a final step, right-click the recovery plan and choose Cleanup test failover. This deletes the resources created during the test failover.

## Implementing ASR Hyper-V virtual machine protection

Protecting Hyper-V-based workloads with ASR requires careful planning, with some of the key considerations being the number of VMs to protect, the number, size, and utilization of disks per protected VM, the data change rate, and the recovery point objectives. The outputs from this planning effort should produce:

- The required network bandwidth for replication
- The required number of storage accounts, Azure CPU cores, and memory
- The on-premises requirements for this ASR scenario
- Whether the VMs to be protected are compatible for ASR protection

The tools that can be used to assist in the planning effort include the Capacity Planner for Hyper-V Workloads and the ASR Capacity Planner. The ASR Capacity Planner was covered in the last section of this chapter, and its use for planning Hyper-V protection is not substantively different from the VMware scenario. As such, only the Capacity Planner for Hyper-V Replica is covered in this section.

The Capacity Planner for Hyper-V Replica can help when planning for either the datacenter to datacenter or the datacenter to Azure ASR scenario. The main data points that help plan the on-premises to Azure scenario include the impact of replication on the primary host's compute, memory, storage disk space, and IOPS. The tool also provides the total bandwidth required for delta replication, which is generated based on the change rate of your data. The recommended approach is to leverage the outputs of this tool to use as inputs in the ASR Capacity Planner. A running instance of the ASR Capacity Planner is shown in Figure 6-84.

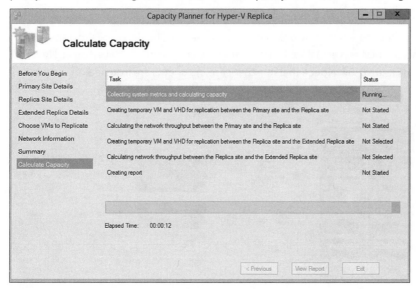

FIGURE 6-84 The Capacity Planner for Hyper-V Replica

As with the VMware scenario, protecting Hyper-V workloads can require a tremendous amount of bandwidth. An increase of outbound internet bandwidth or ExpressRoute can be considered to address this need.

The on-premises components required for the Hyper-V scenario include two agents: The Site Recovery Provider and the Recovery Services Agent. These are installed differently depending on the Hyper-V infrastructure. If there are only individual or clustered Hyper-V hosts, both agents are installed on all hosts, as shown in Figure 6-85.

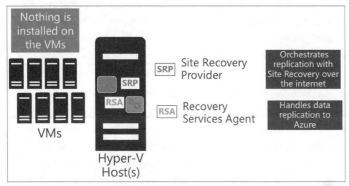

**FIGURE 6-85** ASR agent architecture with only Hyper-V hosts

If System Center Virtual Machine Manager (SCVMM) is being used to manage the Hyper-V hosts, the agent architecture is slightly different. In this case, the Site Recovery Provider agent is installed on the SCVMM server(s) and the Recovery Services Agent is installed on all Hyper-V hosts, as shown in Figure 6-86. Notice that in either case, no agents are installed on the protected VMs.

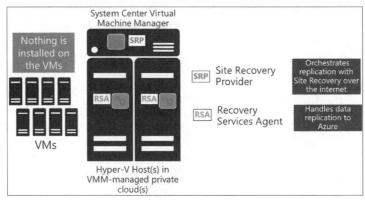

**FIGURE 6-86** ASR agent architecture with SCVMM host management

There are networking requirements for the Hyper-V scenario to consider. Both the Hyper-V hosts and SCVMM (if used) must have direct or proxy-based access to the following URLs:Ports in the internet.

- *.hypervrecoverymanager.windowsazure.com:443
- *.accesscontrol.windows.net:443
- *.backup.windowsazure.com:443
- *.blob.core.windows.net:443
- *.store.core.windows.net:443
- time.windows.com:123
- time.nist.gov:123

After the planning effort is complete, bandwidth upgrades (if required) have been procured, and the networking requirements for internet access from SCVMM and the hosts are met, the implementation steps can begin.

First, create a Recovery Services vault as described in an earlier section of this chapter. Be certain to choose a region that is a significant distance from the primary site. Within the vault, create what is called a Hyper-V site by clicking Site Recovery Infrastructure and then Hyper-V Sites. A Hyper-V site is a management construct that surfaces the Azure Site Recovery Provider and the vault registration downloads, as shown in Figure 6-87. When these are installed on a Hyper-V host, it is associated with the Hyper-V site. Later, the replication policy is also associated with this Hyper-V site.

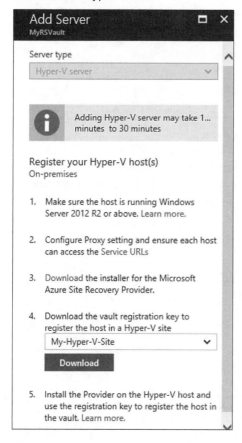

**FIGURE 6-87** Adding a Hyper-V server to a Hyper-V Site

If the Site Recovery Provider is being installed on Hyper-V, it also downloads and installs the Recovery Services Agent, as shown in the progress indication dialog in Figure 6-88.

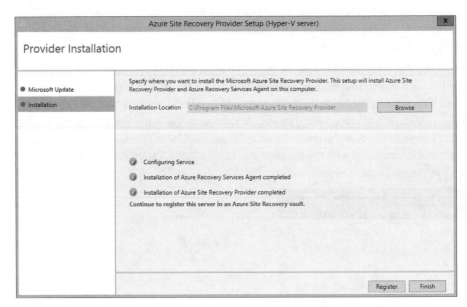

**FIGURE 6-88** Installing the Azure Site Recovery Provider on Hyper-V hosts

After these installations, a dialog box open, allowing the Hyper-V host to be registered with the ASR Hyper-V Site. In the Hyper-V only scenario (no SCVMM) *all* hosts must be registered.

If the Site Recovery Provider is being installed on SCVMM, it alone is installed and then the SCVMM server alone is registered with the Hyper-V Site, as shown in Figure 6-89.

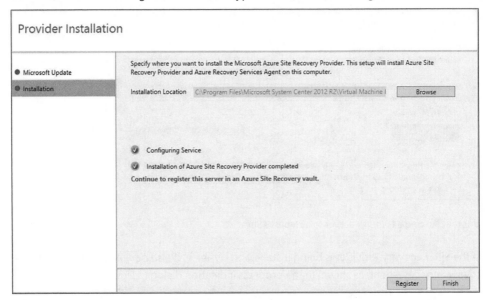

**FIGURE 6-89** Installation of the Site Recovery Provider on SCVMM

A subsequent install of *only* the Recovery Services Agent occurs on the Hyper-V hosts. Note that when SCVMM is managing Hyper-V hosts you *do not register the Hyper-V hosts* with the Hyper-V site. Notice in Figure 6-90 the dialog shows Proceed to registration, but the setup should be closed at this point.

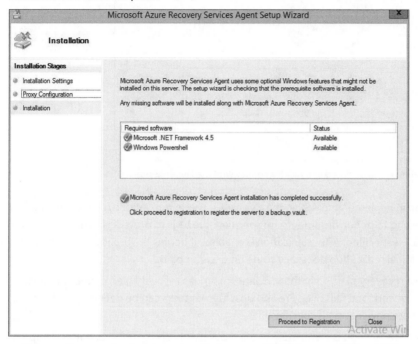

**FIGURE 6-90** Recovery Services Agent installation on an SCVMM-managed Hyper-V host

After the SCVMM server or the Hyper-V hosts are installed and registered, the target environment must be configured. In this step, the Azure storage account and virtual network are selected. The storage account holds the replicated data from on-premises and the virtual network is used to host the networking capabilities of VMs that are failed over.

With the target environment prepared, next configure the replication policy. The replication policy defines how long recovery points and application-consistent snapshots should be retained, and this policy is associated with the Hyper-V site. The screen shot in Figure 6-91 shows the association of the Hyper-V site with a custom replication policy.

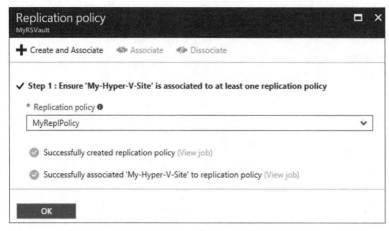

**FIGURE 6-91** Creating and associated a replication policy with the Hyper-V site

The next step in implementing ASR in the Hyper-V scenario is to enable replication. In this step, the source and target environments are specified, the VMs to protect are chosen, and the replication policy is specified. After replication is enabled, it begins the replication process immediately. The initial replication does take some time to complete.

Next, create a recovery plan. As in the VMware scenario, a recovery plan defines the steps that govern how a workload fails over. Pre and post failover tasks can be defined and the order in which servers are powered on is specified.

After the initial replication is complete and the recovery plan is configured, ASR is set up and ready to be tested. To ensure all is working well, perform a test failover by right-clicking the recovery plan and choosing Test Failover. When the failover is complete, validate the functionality of the application and make any necessary tweaks to the recovery plan. Finally, perform a test failover cleanup to delete the failed over resources.

## Implementing ASR Azure to Azure VIrtual Machine protection

The Azure cloud is not without failure, and sometimes a failure can impact an entire region. Thankfully, Azure Site Recovery supports region-to-region VM replication and failover. Earlier, this chapter covered the concept of using disk snapshots as an approach for VM recovery to another region. Now that Site Recovery supports this scenario, a much better level of protection can be achieved with an increased number of recovery points and a dramatically reduced recover time objective. A high-level diagram representing this capability is shown in Figure 6-92.

South Central US        North Central US

**FIGURE 6-92** ASR Region-to-Region Protection

The process to implement Azure-to-Azure Site Recovery is less complex than the on-site to Azure options because it is a completely platform-managed service with no separately installed roles or software to manage. However, there is still planning to accomplish for this scenario.

First, ensure that protected VMs can communicate with the Office 365 authentication and identity endpoints, because the service must authenticate to function. Also, protected VMs must communicate with the source region IP addresses that represent the caching storage account (a concept that is discussed later in this chapter). Finally, protected VMs must communicate with the ASR service endpoint IP addresses to replicate data and orchestration information. We start with this requirement because no Azure to Azure functionality is possible without it.

When Azure-to-Azure VM replication is enabled, a cache storage account is created in the source region (the same region as the replicated VMs). The cache storage account is used by the Mobility extension (installed on the protected VMs) to initially write intercepted disk changes. Also, another storage account is created in the target region. This is where replicated data is eventually replicated and stored awaiting a failover action. A virtual network is created in the target region as well, which hosts the networking requirements of failed over VMs. Lastly, if the source VMs are in an availability set, a target availability set is created

As replication begins, the Mobility service extension is installed on the protected VMs (Figure 6-93, step 1). This service intercepts disk writes and handles the replication of data and then VMs are registered with the Site Recovery service (step 2). Next, the data writes are transferred to the cache storage account in the source region. This transfer is accomplished using the blob endpoint of the cache storage account (step 3). Finally, replicated data is sent by way of the Site Recovery service into the target storage account (step 4).

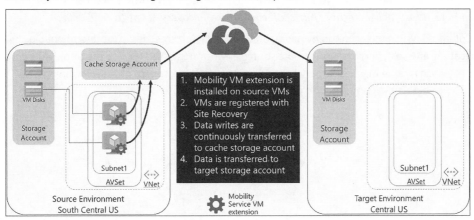

**FIGURE 6-93** ASR Region-to-Region workflow

When a failover is initiated, replication stops and VMs are created within the target region and are configured to participate in the virtual network, subnet, and availability zone.

Some caveats to be aware of with Azure-to-Azure Site Recovery (as of this writing) include:

- The management plan is Azure portal only
- VM Scale Sets are not supported
- Maximum OS disk size is 1023 GB
- Maximum data change rate supported is 6 MBps
- Managed disks are not supported
- Azure disk encryption is not supported
- Cannot replicate/failover between geographic clusters (basically must stay within the same continent)

Though the planning is easier with Azure-to-Azure Site Recovery, there are still things to consider. For example, the target region is a critical concern. Choose this region considering the same criteria as you would in a normal disaster recovery configuration. The replicated data should be a significant distance away from the primary data, and in areas less prone to natural disasters. Also keep in mind the outbound networking requirements mentioned earlier.

To implement Azure-to-Azure Site Recovery, begin by creating a Recovery Services vault in a target region that meets requirements. As in other scenarios, primarily ensure there is sufficient distance from the source region. Create the vault in one of the ways shown earlier in this chapter. This can be done via the Azure portal or PowerShell.

Next, configure the required outbound connectivity so that protected VMs can access the Site Recovery service endpoints, either by URL (if using a URL proxy) or IP address (if using firewall or NSG rules). The protected VMs must also be able to access the IP ranges of the Office 365 authentication and identity IP V4 endpoints and the blob service endpoint of the cache storage account. To make this configuration easier, Microsoft has released a PowerShell script that configures a Network Security Group with all of the required outbound rules. Access this script here: *https://gallery.technet.microsoft.com/Azure-Recovery-script-to-0c950702*.

Configure ASR in this scenario by navigating to the vault properties, choosing to enable replication, and selecting the appropriate source environment. Also choose the deployment model (which is generally Resource Manager), and select the resource group containing the VMs to protect. These configuration options are shown in Figure 6-94.

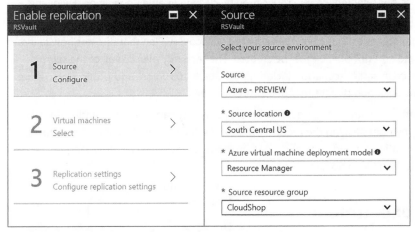

FIGURE 6-94 Selecting the source environment to protect

Next, choose the virtual machines to protect, and then customize the target resources (if required). Site Recovery pre-populates target resource information and a default replication policy, but any of these items can be customized as required. These configuration options are shown in Figure 6-95.

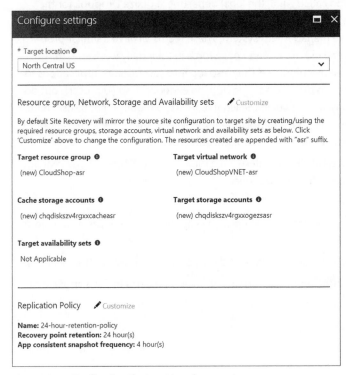

FIGURE 6-95 Configuring the target environment

With these options selected, enable replication by clicking Enable Replication. Failover is impossible until the initial replication is complete.

As in the other scenarios that have been covered, a Recovery Plan that dictates how failed over resources are brought online must be created. The recovery plan has all of the same capabilities discussed in earlier scenarios, including the ability to run pre and post scripts, Azure Automation runbooks, and direct the order VMs power on.

As with the other scenarios, no disaster recovery capability can be trusted until it is tested. Test the failover by right-clicking the recovery plan and selecting Test failover. After failover, validate the application functionality and clean up the test failover, by right-clicking the recovery plan and selecting Clean up test failover.

# Thought experiment

In this thought experiment, demonstrate your skills and knowledge of the topics covered in this chapter. You can find answers to this thought experiment in the next section.

You are the administrator at Fabrikam, and your director has asked you to help solve a problem the users in your organization are experiencing. It seems most users access software as a service (SaaS) applications in their daily work stream. In particular, your project managers are leveraging an application called Aha!, the legal department utilize Dropbox for the storage of their least-sensitive tier of client documents, and HR is piloting the use of Workday to replace an antiquated people management system. These teams all have a similar problem. They must remember several usernames and passwords in their daily work stream. They log into their workstations in the morning, and they also log into several SaaS applications to accomplish their work. You need to provide a single sign-on experience to your users, but do so in a cost-effective, secure way. In particular, the legal team has a requirement to use multi-factor authentication when they access client documents. However, the lawyers are notoriously opposed to having to carry around dedicated authentication tokens.

On a potentially-related note, Fabrikam underwent a migration to Office 365 one year ago, and all is going well with the use of this cloud service.

How do you:

1.  Provide a single sign-on experience for various SaaS applications, and preferably do so by group, instead of by user?

2.  Ensure the single sign-on solution is secure and supports multi-factor authentication?

3.  How will you deal with turnover in your organization as it pertains to SaaS application access?

# Thought experiment answer

This section contains the solution to the thought experiment.

Fortunately, in this scenario, Fabrikam is using Office 365 meaning they are already using Azure Active Directory. Azure AD is the Identity and access management solution for all of Microsoft's cloud properties, including Azure.

1. Azure Active Directory has the capability to provide single sign-on to thousands of SaaS applications. Access can be granted by user with the free and basic SKU, or by group with the premium SKU.

2. Azure Active Directory supports the use of multi-factor authentication with the premium SKU. Multi-factor authentication in Azure AD can use a person's phone as the second factor, either with an authenticator application install or through texts/phone calls.

3. With Azure AD licensed with the Premium SKU, administrators can manage SaaS application access by group. This means an administrator can remove a user from a group representing the application access in the on-premises AD. After synchronization, the user is removed from the Azure AD group and their access to the SaaS application is deprovisioned.

# Chapter summary

This chapter covered a wide variety of security-related topics, including securing and managing company secrets, keys, and certificates, provisioning access to SaaS applications, and ensuring that access to data and services is maintained. Some of the key things to remember include:

- Azure Key Vault is a great way to protect secrets, keys, and certificates. This service can be created and managed via the Azure portal, PowerShell, or the Azure CLI, and includes support for protecting these items with FIPS 140-2 Level 2 validated hardware security modules (HSMs).

- Azure Security Center is enabled by default within your Azure subscription and helps to prevent and detect security issues. Security Center helps secure more than just your Azure deployments. The Microsoft Monitoring Agent can be installed on workloads in other clouds or on-premises to extend the value of this service.

- Azure Active Directory can be used to configure single sign-on access to thousands of SaaS applications and can do so with either federated access or through securely storing and presenting the SaaS application password on behalf of the user.

- Authentication via social providers, such as Facebook, Google, and LinkedIn can be enabled by using Azure Active Directory Business to Consumer (B2C) feature set. This is generally used by developers who want to simplify the addition of robust authentication in their web and mobile apps.

- Azure Backup can be used to protect files and folders, applications, and IaaS virtual machines. This cloud-based data protection service helps organizations by providing offsite backups in the cloud and protection of VM workloads they have already moved to the cloud.

- Azure IaaS VMs can be protected through the use of disk snapshots. These can be copied to storage accounts in other regions and, when required, VMs can be provisioned from these disk snapshots. This can be thought of as a way to provide for disaster recovery of IaaS VMs before Azure Backup and Site Recovery were available. Today, Azure Backup and Site Recovery represent a superior way to protect data and quickly restore service in the case of a sustained outage.

- Azure Site Recovery has several scenarios for enabling the replication and failover of workloads. ASR can protect physical, VMware, and Hyper-V-based workloads from on-premises into Azure. It can also replicate and failover VMs from one Azure region to another.

# CHAPTER 7

# Manage Azure Operations

B uilding workloads in the public cloud brings many benefits to organizations, but some of the same challenges apply in both on-premises environments and the Azure platform. A specific example is the task of managing workloads in the cloud. Of course, this aspect of moving to the cloud is a critical aspect to consider, and one that sometimes requires a differ-ent approach than what was historically used in traditional datacenters. This is the topic that is considered in this chapter.

## Skills covered in this chapter:

- Skill 7.1: Enhance cloud management with automation
- Skill 7.2: Collect and analyze data generated by resources in cloud and on-premises environments

## Skill 7.1: Enhance cloud management with automation

Although the cloud brings a tremendous amount of agility to organizations, the greatest degree of benefit is reserved for organizations that leverage automation. Automation allows machines to do what they are good at (well-defined, repetitive tasks), and frees up humans to do what they do best (creative and abstract work, such as envisioning new solutions to busi-ness problems). In this section, two types of automation are considered, process automation, and configuration automation.

> **This skill covers how to:**
> - Implement PowerShell runbooks
> - Integrate Azure Automation with Web Apps
> - Create and manage PowerShell Desired State Configurations (DSC)
> - Import DSC resources
> - Generate DSC node configurations
> - Monitor and automatically update machine configurations with Azure Automation DSC

# Implement PowerShell runbooks

Azure Automation is the service that exposes features for both process and configuration automation. Within Azure Automation, process automation is handled by runbooks. Runbooks are based on PowerShell or PowerShell Workflow, and so a runbook can do anything that can be accomplished with PowerShell. At the time of this writing, the preview feature of authoring runbooks in Python and Bash are also available. An example of using a runbook for process automation in Azure might be to scale up the size of an IaaS VM based on a schedule during busy times of the year. Another example for using a runbook on-premises might be to automate the creation of a VMware VM. Before creating a runbook, the first step is to create an Azure Automation account.

## Creating an Automation Account (Portal)

Within the Azure portal, click New, and under Monitoring And Management, click Automation. Enter a unique name for the Automation Account, and choose an existing or create a new resource group for the Automation Account to exist in. Choose the Azure region for the account to exist in. Note the region list is truncated because Automation Accounts are not supported in all regions. Under Create Azure Run As Account, select Yes. Finally, click Create as shown in Figure 7-1.

**FIGURE 7-1** Creating an Automation Account in the portal

When the automation account is created, two Run As accounts are automatically created. The first is a service principal in Azure Active Directory along with a certificate. This service principal is granted appropriate rights (Contributor role on the subscription), to invoke automation runbooks. The second is a Classic Run As account. This account uploads a management certificate, which is used to manage classic resources by using runbooks.

## Creating an Automation Account (PowerShell)

The following PowerShell command is used to create an Azure Automation account and place it in an existing resource group.

```
New-AzureRmAutomationAccount -ResourceGroup "MyAutomationRG" -Name "FabrikamAutomation"
 -Location southcentralus
```

This command creates the Automation account, but does not create the Run As accounts. The Run As accounts can be created via PowerShell, but to do so requires the use of a lengthy script. This process is described in the following documentation link: *https://docs.microsoft. com/en-us/azure/automation/automation-update-account-powershell*.

It is also possible to create the Run As accounts within the portal after the Automation Account is created. To do so, navigate to the properties of the Automation Account and click Run As Accounts. Then click Create for the Run As account type that is desired, shown on Figure 7-2.

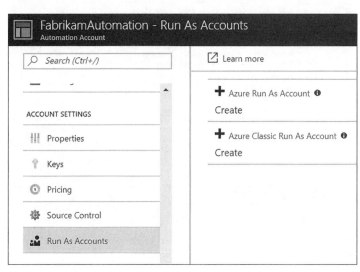

**FIGURE 7-2** Creating Run As accounts in the portal

## Azure Automation runbooks

Once an Automation Account is created, runbooks can be used to automate processes. There are six types of runbooks:

- **Graphical**  PowerShell-based runbooks created and edited within the graphical editor in the Azure portal.
- **Graphical PowerShell Workflow**  These runbooks use PowerShell Workflow and are created and edited within the graphical editor in the Azure portal.
- **PowerShell**  Runbooks that are text-based using PowerShell script.
- **PowerShell Workflow**  Runbooks that are text-based using PowerShell Workflow.
- **Python**  Runbooks that are text-based using Python script (In Preview).
- **Bash**  Runbooks that are text-based using Bash script (In Preview).

The different types of runbooks allow administrators to choose the type that best meets their needs and that uses the scripting language they are most familiar with. The graphical options allow those who are not adept at scripting to still be able to create functional process automation.

To get started with runbooks, a good place to start is the runbook gallery. Within the properties of the Automation Account, under Process Automation, click Runbook Gallery. Choose the type of runbook and publisher (Microsoft or Community), and click OK as shown in Figure 7-3.

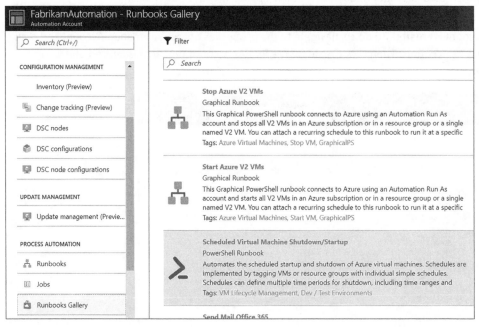

**FIGURE 7-3** Azure Automation Runbook Gallery

| | NAME | AUTHORING STATUS |
|---|---|---|
| | AzureAutomationTutorial | ✔ Published |
| | AzureAutomationTutorialPython2 | ✔ Published |
| | AzureAutomationTutorialScript | ✔ Published |
| | AzureClassicAutomationTutorial | ✔ Published |
| | AzureClassicAutomationTutorialScript | ✔ Published |

**FIGURE 7-4**  Default tutorial runbooks

In the below PowerShell runbook example shown in Figure 7-5, two parameters are collected at run time (a VM name and the resource group where the VM exists); the runbook authenticates using the Run As credentials, and then starts a VM.

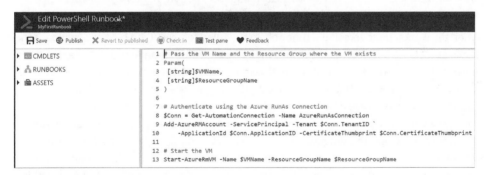

**FIGURE 7-5**  A simple PowerShell runbook

Runbooks can be hybrid in nature, meaning they can be executed in any environment. Of course, runbooks can run natively within Azure, but runbooks can also be run in other public/private clouds or in traditional environments on-premises, using a Hybrid Runbook Worker. A Hybrid Runbook Worker is a designated computer running in an environment where runbooks should be executed, such as in an on-premises datacenter. The Hybrid Runbook Worker polls the Azure Automation account often to see if a runbook has been scheduled for execution on the worker. This means that the Hybrid Runbook Worker requires direct or proxy-based access to the internet over TCP port 443 to either the regional, or the global Azure Automation URLs, as shown in Table 7-1.

**TABLE 7-1** Azure Automation regional and global URLs

| Region | DNS Record |
|--------|-----------|
| Global URL | *.azure-automation.net |
| South Central US | scus-jobruntimedata-prod-su1.azure-automation.net |
| EAST US 2 | eus2-jobruntimedata-prod-su1.azure-automation.net |
| West Central US | wcus-jobruntimedata-prod-su1.azure-automation.net |
| West Europe | we-jobruntimedata-prod-su1.azure-automation.net |
| North Europe | ne-jobruntimedata-prod-su1.azure-automation.net |
| Canada Central | cc-jobruntimedata-prod-su1.azure-automation.net |
| South East Asia | sea-jobruntimedata-prod-su1.azure-automation.net |
| Central India | cid-jobruntimedata-prod-su1.azure-automation.net |
| Japan East | jpe-jobruntimedata-prod-su1.azure-automation.net |
| Australia South East | ase-jobruntimedata-prod-su1.azure-automation.net |
| UK South | uks-jobruntimedata-prod-su1.azure-automation.net |
| US Gov Virginia | usge-jobruntimedata-prod-su1.azure-automation.us |

To provision a hybrid runbook worker in an environment outside of Azure, there is an automated approach and a manual approach, both of which are documented at the following URL: *https://docs.microsoft.com/en-us/azure/automation/automation-hybrid-runbook-worker#installing-the-windows-hybrid-runbook-worker*.

When the worker discovers that a runbook is scheduled for execution by it, it downloads the runbook, executes it, and returns the results to the Azure Automation Account. Note that this is a firewall-friendly operation because it is initiated from the worker within the internal network boundary. In Figure 7-6, the Hybrid Runbook Worker discovers a runbook scheduled for its execution (step 1). In this case it is a runbook that is creating a VMware-based VM. The runbook is copied down to the hybrid runbook worker (step 2) and then executed by the worker (step 3). The VMware host creates the VM based on the automation runbook (step 4). After execution, the worker reports the status back to the Azure Automation service (step 5). This allows the authoring, testing, executing, and monitoring of the status to be accomplished all from within the Azure Automation Account in the Azure portal.

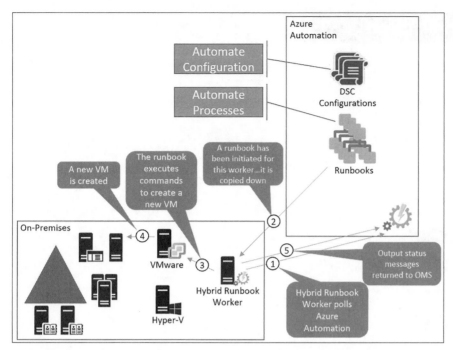

**FIGURE 7-6** The workflow of a Hybrid Runbook Worker executing a runbook

There are several resources that are needed to make runbooks functional. For example, runbooks may need to be scheduled to run at certain intervals, they may need specific PowerShell modules to enable management of non-Microsoft systems (as in the VMware example in Figure 7-6), and they may need variables that can be called at runbook execution. Shared resources enable these capabilities. The next few paragraphs go over these resources.

### SCHEDULES

Schedules are created within Azure Automation to allow runbooks to be executed at a specific start time. Schedules can be configured to run once or on a recurring basis. They can be quite flexible, allowing for execution start time to be defined hourly, daily, monthly, or for specific days of the week or month. To create a schedule in the Azure portal, within the properties of the Automation Account and under Shared Resources, click Schedules, and then click Add A Schedule. Figure 7-7 shows an example of a simple schedule that executes hourly.

**FIGURE 7-7** A simple schedule that executes hourly

Schedules can also be created within PowerShell. The following example shows the creation of a schedule that starts on October 1st, and executes on the first and fifteenth day of each month.

**MODULES**

Modules represent PowerShell modules that can be added to the Azure Automation Account to extend automation capabilities. Many third-party solutions have PowerShell modules that are written by the solution provider. The example of VMware was used earlier in this chapter. These modules can be integrated into the Azure Automation Account to enable runbooks to integrate with many types of solutions. To add a new module from within the Azure Portal, click Modules under Shared Resources. From there, click Add A Module, or to explore options, click Browse Gallery, shown in Figure 7-8.

| | | |
|---|---|---|
| ✚ Add a module | ↻ Update Azure Modules | 🛍 Browse gallery ↻ Refresh |

| NAME | LAST MODIFIED | STATUS |
|---|---|---|
| Azure | 10/9/2017, 9:49 PM | Available |
| Azure.Storage | 10/9/2017, 9:55 PM | Available |
| AzureRM.Automation | 10/9/2017, 9:53 PM | Available |

**FIGURE 7-8** The Azure Automation Modules dialog

Modules can also be imported from the PowerShell Gallery (*www.powershellgallery.com*). This is often necessary because some automation actions require modules that are not imported by default. Manipulating Azure Web Apps is an example because these operations require the AzureRM.Websites module. Locate the module you need at the PowerShell Gallery, and click Deploy To Azure, shown in Figure 7-9.

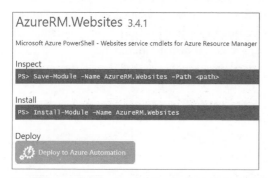

**FIGURE 7-9** Deploying a new PowerShell Module from the PowerShell Gallery

**EXAM TIP**

Modules are updated regularly by the organizations or individuals that wrote them. The default versions in an Automation Account are quite dated and it is likely that scripts that work on a test machine will fail when executed as an Automation runbook simply due to the module being many versions behind that installed on your test machine. The moral is, update the Azure modules when you first begin using Azure Automation and periodically after that. Figure 7-10 shows where to update the modules within the Azure portal.

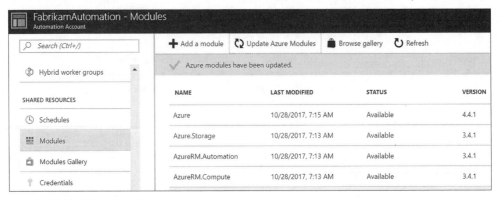

**FIGURE 7-10** Updating Azure Modules

## CREDENTIALS

Azure Automation credentials represent PSCredential objects that contain authentication credentials such as a user name and password. These credentials are stored securely within Azure Automation and they can be invoked during runbook execution, or when using DSC configurations (discussed later in this chapter). To create a credential within the portal, click Credentials under Shared Resources, and then click Add A Credential, shown in Figure 7-11.

**FIGURE 7-11** Adding an Azure Automation credential

To create a new Azure Automation credential with PowerShell, use the following commands to store the Automation Account name and credential information in variables, create a credential object, and then create the automation credential.

```
$automationAccountName = "FabrikamAutomation"
$user = "stever"
$pw = ConvertTo-SecureString "PassWord!" -AsPlainText -Force
$cred = New-Object -TypeName System.Management.Automation.PSCredential `
 -ArgumentList $user, $pw
New-AzureRmAutomationCredential -AutomationAccountName $automationAccountName `
 -Name "MyCredential" -Value $cred -ResourceGroupName "MyAutomationRG"
Connections
```

## CONNECTIONS

The next Azure Automation resource type to consider is connections. A connection is an object that contains the information needed to connect to an external service or application. Connections often include the URL and port required to connect to a service, along with credentials needed to authenticate to that service. Connections can be used with automation runbooks or with DSC configurations. Earlier in this chapter, Run As accounts were discussed. Run As accounts are referenced by automatically created connection objects in Azure Automation Accounts, as shown in Figure 7-12.

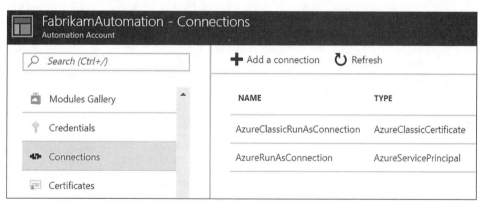

**FIGURE 7-12** Default Connections in Azure Automation

Earlier in this chapter when runbooks were first discussed, an example runbook was shown in Figure 7-5. The runbook example uses a connection object to authenticate to Azure Active Directory so that actions can be taken on Azure resources. Here is the snippet of the connection being referenced by the runbook.

```
$Conn = Get-AutomationConnection -Name AzureRunAsConnection
Add-AzureRMAccount -ServicePrincipal -Tenant $Conn.TenantID `
    -ApplicationId $Conn.ApplicationID `
    -CertificateThumbprint $Conn.CertificateThumbprint
```

To create a new connection within the Azure Portal, click Connections under Shared Resources, and then click Add A Connection. Enter the name, description (optional), and the type. Connection types are defined by Modules (discussed earlier in this chapter). As an example, the SSH PowerShell Module adds an SSH connection type, allowing parameters to be defined for SSH connections to Linux systems. Setting up a connection of this type is shown in Figure 7-13.

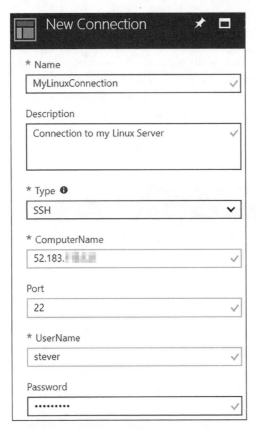

**FIGURE 7-13** Creating a new Azure Automation Connection

### CERTIFICATES

Another Azure Automation resource type is Certificates. Certificates resources are x.509 certificates that are uploaded into Azure Automation and securely stored for authentication by runbooks, or DSC configurations. Creating a new certificate in the Azure Portal involves clicking Add A Certificate within the Certificates section of Shared Resources. Give the certificate a name, optionally a description, and the path to the exported certificate file (.cer or .pfx). This can also be accomplished in PowerShell using the `New-AzureRmAutomationCertificate` cmdlet.

```
$certName = 'MyAutomationCertificate'
$certPath = '.\MyCert.pfx'
$certPwd = ConvertTo-SecureString -String 'Password!' -AsPlainText -Force
$ResourceGroup = "MyAutomationRG"

New-AzureRmAutomationCertificate -AutomationAccountName "FabrikamAutomation"
-Name $certName -Path $certPath -Password $certPwd -Exportable -ResourceGroupName
$ResourceGroup
```

### VARIABLES

Azure Automation Variables are resources that are useful for storing values that can be used by runbooks and DSC configurations. At creation time the variable must be assigned one of several types: String, Integer, DateTime, Boolean, or Null. A common use for a variable is to store the Azure subscription ID so that a runbook can use this during authentication. In Figure 7-14 a parameter is being set in a runbook that utilizes the variable, AzureSubscriptionId.

```
param (
    [Parameter(Mandatory=$false)]
    [String]  $AzureCredentialAssetName = 'AzureCredential',

    [Parameter(Mandatory=$false)]
    [String] $AzureSubscriptionIdAssetName = 'AzureSubscriptionId',

    [Parameter(Mandatory=$false)]
    [String] $ResourceGroupName
)
```

**FIGURE 7-14** A runbook parameter referencing an Azure Automation Variable

To define a variable in the Azure portal, click Variables under Shared Resources within the properties of the Azure Automation Account. Then click Add A Variable. Give the variable a name, optionally a description, specify the variable type, and then enter the value. Also specify whether the variable should be encrypted, and then click Create. Figure 7-15 shows this creation dialog.

**FIGURE 7-15** New Variable dialog

To create a variable using PowerShell, use the New-AzureRmAutomationVariable cmdlet.

```
New-AzureRmAutomationVariable -ResourceGroupName "MyAutomationRG" `
    -AutomationAccountName "FabrikamAutomation" -Name 'MyAutomationVariable' `
    -Encrypted $false -Value 'MyValue'
```

## Integrate Azure Automation with Web Apps

While there are an almost unlimited number of uses cases where Azure Automation can add value, a common example is to integrate Azure Automation with Web Apps. An example scenario is the use of an automation runbook to scale out a basic tier Web App based on site utilization. Basic tier Web Apps can scale out to up to three instances, but this tier only supports manually scaling out the instance count. It is manual, that is, unless Azure Automation is used to automatically scale the instance count. This scenario is unpacked in this section.

### Automatically scaling a basic tier Web App

In this example scenario, an organization is using a basic tier App Service Plan, with one instance. This configuration works well Monday through Thursday, but on Fridays the web app hosted on this App Service gets very busy. So, the business needs to scale the instance count up to two on Fridays, and then scale back down to one on Saturdays. To accomplish this, set up the necessary automation schedules first. PowerShell is used to accomplish this below.

```
$resourceGroup = "MyAutomationRG"
$automationAccountName = "FabrikamAutomation"
$TimeZone = Get-TimeZone
$scaleUpScheduleName = "ScaleAppServiceUpSchedule"
$scaleDownScheduleName = "ScaleAppServiceDownSchedule"

New-AzureRMAutomationSchedule -AutomationAccountName $automationAccountName -Name `
    $scaleUpScheduleName -StartTime "10/29/2017 00:00:00" -WeekInterval 1 `
    -DaysOfWeek Friday -ResourceGroupName $resourceGroup -TimeZone $TimeZone.Id

New-AzureRMAutomationSchedule -AutomationAccountName $automationAccountName -Name `
    $scaleDownScheduleName -StartTime "10/29/2017 00:00:00" -WeekInterval 1 `
    -DaysOfWeek Saturday -ResourceGroupName $resourceGroup -TimeZone $TimeZone.Id
```

Verify that the schedules are created in the Azure Portal, shown in Figure 7-16.

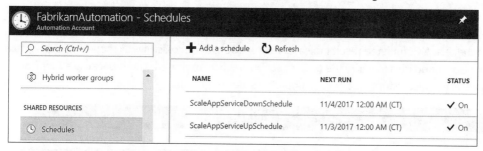

**FIGURE 7-16** Automation Schedules for scaling Azure Web App

Next, add a new PowerShell runbook to perform the scale up operation. The PowerShell code to scale the App Service Plan is as follows and shown in Figure 7-17:

```
Param(
 [string]$myAppServiceName="FabrikamBasicASP",
 [string]$rgName="MyWebAppRG"
)

$Conn = Get-AutomationConnection -Name AzureRunAsConnection
Add-AzureRMAccount -ServicePrincipal -Tenant $Conn.TenantID `
    -ApplicationId $Conn.ApplicationID -CertificateThumbprint $Conn.
CertificateThumbprint

$myAppServicePlan = Get-AzureRmAppServicePlan -ResourceGroupName $rgName `
 -Name $myAppServiceName
Set-AzureRmAppServicePlan -NumberofWorkers 2 -Name $myAppServicePlan.Name `
 -ResourceGroupName $myAppServicePlan.ResourceGroup
```

Once the PowerShell code is entered, click Save.

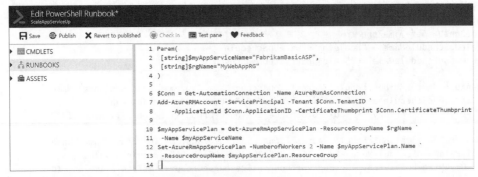

**FIGURE 7-17** Edit PowerShell Runbook dialog

It's always a good idea to test the runbook before publishing it. To test the runbook, click Test Pane. In the example code, the default parameter values are provided, so click Start to begin the test. A Completed result indicates the runbook ran successfully, as shown in Figure 7-18. It is also a good idea to verify the desired action was accomplished. This is because a runbook can execute successfully, but not accomplish the desired result.

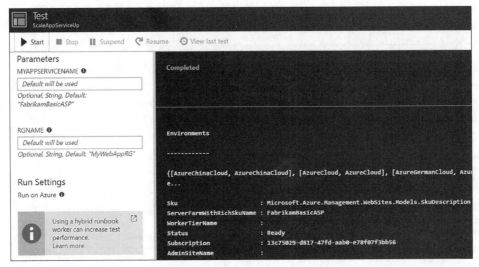

**FIGURE 7-18** A successful runbook execution

In Figure 7-19 the App Service shows as successfully scaled to two instances.

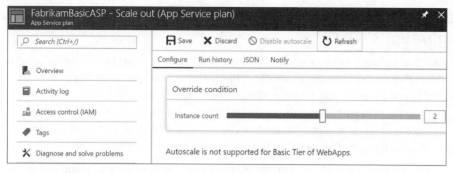

**FIGURE 7-19** The Basic App Service Plan scaled to 2 instances

Now that the runbook has been tested, publish it by clicking on the Publish button. Finally, schedule the runbook to scale up the App Service Plan by associating the runbook with the previously created schedule. To do this, click on Schedule within the runbook properties then click Link A Schedule To Your Runbook. Choose the ScaleAppServiceUpSchedule schedule, then click OK, shown in Figure 7-20.

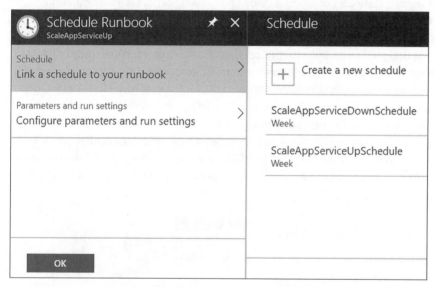

**FIGURE 7-20** Associating a schedule with a runbook

To complete the scenario, create another runbook called ScaleAppServiceDown using the same PowerShell code, but changing the "-"-NumberofWorkers" parameter to 1:

```
Set-AzureRmAppServicePlan -NumberofWorkers 1 -Name $myAppServicePlan.Name `
 -ResourceGroupName $myAppServicePlan.ResourceGroup
```

Then associate this runbook to the previously created schedule called ScaleAppService-DownSchedule.

# Create and manage PowerShell Desired State Configurations (DSC)

So far in this chapter Azure Automation's process automation capabilities have been discussed, however Azure Automation can also automate configurations. Configurations can be defined and assigned to computers within Azure in other cloud environments and on-premises. Once applied, configurations can be monitored so that if configuration drift (undesired changes in the configuration) occurs, then administrators can be notified. If desired, automatic remediation (automatically changing the configuration back to its desired state) can occur.

This section starts off covering a foundational technology that Azure Automation DSC is based on: PowerShell Desired State Configuration. Beginning with PowerShell DSC will aid in understanding DSC configurations, which are used with PowerShell DSC and with Azure Automation DSC. Specifically, creating and managing PowerShell DSC configurations will be discussed.

## Creating PowerShell DSC configurations

A PowerShell Desired State configuration is made up of several parts. Each configuration begins with the configuration statement, which is a special kind of function that was added to PowerShell 4.0. The configuration statement begins a configuration block, or a block of statements and code designed to produce specific configuration outcomes. Within this configuration statement there is the option to add new custom DSC resources. This is accomplished with the dynamic keyword Import-DscResource. Although this looks like a PowerShell cmdlet, it's not. Next in the configuration is the Node section. This defines the machine or machines that the configuration will be applied on. Next comes one or more Resources. A resource is a building block of a configuration that accomplishes or verifies the existence of a configuration item. In Figure 7-21 these components of a PowerShell DSC configuration are shown. This configuration ensures that IIS is installed on the node. If it is not installed, PowerShell DSC will install it.

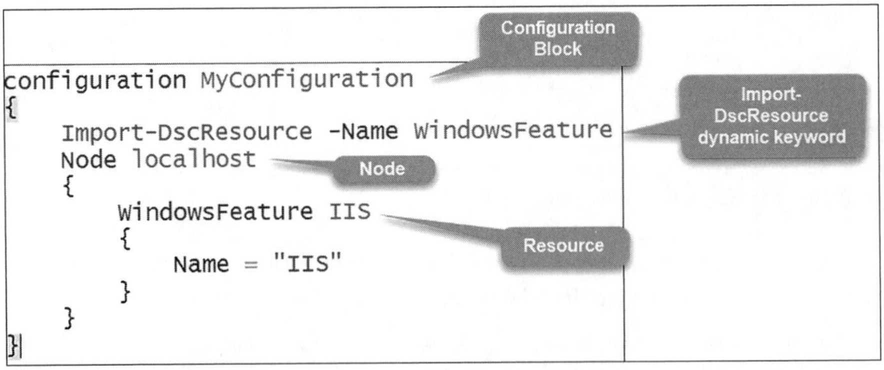

**FIGURE 7-21** An example PowerShell DSC configuration

## Managing PowerShell DSC configurations

DSC configurations are text-based assets that resemble source code. In the world of DevOps, DSC configurations should be managed exactly as source code and infrastructure-as-code (IaC) assets. This means having a repository of configurations maintained in a source-code control system such as GitHub or Visual Studio Team Services. While it is beyond the scope of this book to teach DevOps principles and source code control philosophies, an example work-flow will illustrate managing DSC configurations using a continuous integration/continuous delivery (CI/CD) approach.

Figure 7-22 illustrates an example CI/CD workflow. An administrator creates a new DSC configuration for IIS-based web servers in the organization. This DSC configuration is checked into a source code management system (step 1). The check in action prompts an automatic build, which provisions a VM in Azure and applies the DSC configuration to it (step 2). Next, automated testing occurs to ensure the configuration accomplishes the desired outcome (step 3). A popular testing tool to use with DSC configurations is Pester (https://github.com/pester/Pester). Once testing has validated the outcome, the DSC configuration is added to Azure Automation as a DSC configuration (discussed later in this chapter) (step 4).

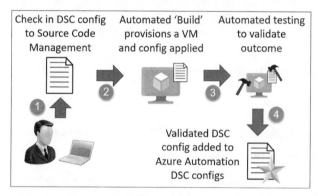

FIGURE 7-22 An example CI/CD workflow approach with DSC configurations

# Import DSC resources

DSC Resources are the building blocks of DSC configurations. They are declarative statements (usually) that are carried out or applied by the Local Configuration Manager. A resource has properties that can be configured and also contains the PowerShell code that the LCM invokes to change or manage the state. Groups of similar DSC resources are combined together into DSC Modules, which were discussed earlier in this chapter.

> **NOTE   THE LOCAL CONFIGURATION MANAGER**
>
> The LCM is the change agent running on every node that applies a DSC configuration. It is responsible for parsing and applying configurations sent to the node.

There are built-In DSC resources and custom resources. Some of the built-in resources include the Archival Resource used to unpack an archive (such as a *.zip file), the File Resource allowing for management of files and folders on target nodes, and the Registry Resource. Custom resources extend the management capabilities of DSC and are authored by Microsoft, partners of Microsoft, and the technical community. An example of a custom resource is included in the xPSDesiredStateConfiguration module. This module contains enhancements to the built-in DSC resources (such as xArchive), and also adds new resources (such as xDSCWebService).

To import resources or modules from within a DSC configuration, use the Import-DscResource dynamic keyword. To import a specific resource, use the following syntax:

```
Import-DscResource <NameOfResource>
```

For example, to import the built-in resource, Service, use this command just before the Node statement:

```
Import-DscResource Service
```

> **NOTE** **BUILT-IN DSC RESOURCES**
>
> You do not have to use the Import-DscResource command to use built-in resources. These can be called natively.
>
> To import an entire module (a collection of resources), use this syntax:

```
Import-DscResource -ModuleName <Module>
```

For example, to import the xPSDesiredStateConfiguration module, use this command:

```
Import-DscResource -ModuleName xPSDesiredStateConfiguration
```

Modules can also be imported into Azure Automation DSC. This was discussed earlier in this chapter in the Modules section under Azure Automation Runbooks.

## Generate DSC node configurations

As mentioned earlier, Azure Automation DSC is built from PowerShell DSC. In a sense, it is simply PowerShell DSC with a "cloud-based" pull server (configurations are pulled rather than pushed). It just so happens that with Azure Automation DSC, the pull server is a platform (PaaS) service rather than a virtual machine that an organization must manage. Earlier in the Creating PowerShell DSC configurations section, the concept of creating DSC configurations was discussed. Once a configuration is created and (ideally) tested, it can be uploaded into Azure Automation DSC as a DSC node configuration. When this is accomplished, the configuration is available to be applied by Azure Automation DSC nodes (computers registered with the Azure Automation DSC service). Creating DSC node configurations will be covered in the next section, while registering machines as DSC nodes will be discussed later in this chapter.

Creating a DSC node configuration begins with creating or downloading a sample DSC configuration. In Figure 7-23 an example DSC configuration checks to ensure the Windows feature Web-Server is present. This is a declarative method of configuration. If the Web-Server feature is absent, then it is installed.

```
configuration TestConfig
{
    Node WebServer
    {
        WindowsFeature IIS
        {
            Ensure              = 'Present'
            Name                = 'Web-Server'
            IncludeAllSubFeature = $true

        }
    }
}
```

**FIGURE 7-23** A simple DSC configuration as shown in the PowerShell ISE

This DSC configuration is added to Azure Automation DSC by clicking on DSC Configurations under Configuration Management, then clicking on +Add A Configuration as shown in Figure 7-24.

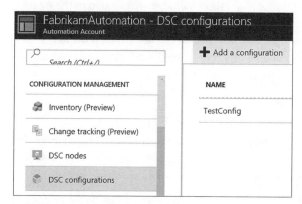

**FIGURE 7-24** Adding a DSC configuration

At the Import Configuration dialog, specify the path to the *.PS1 file containing the DSC configuration code, optionally give a description, then click OK.

Once a DSC configuration has been added it must be compiled. To compile a configuration, click on its name, then click on the Compile button as shown in Figure 7-25.

**FIGURE 7-25** Compiling a DSC configuration

Compiling a DSC configuration places that configuration in a state that DSC nodes can apply it as the desired state of the node. Compiled configurations show up under the DSC node configurations option under Configuration Management.

## Monitor and automatically update machine configurations with Azure Automation DSC

Once a DSC configuration is added to Azure Automation DSC and it has been compiled, it is available to be applied to DSC nodes. When a configuration is applied to a DSC node, the Local Configuration Manager (LCM) ensures that the computer is in compliance with the configuration and it reports status back to the Azure Automation DSC service. A DSC node is a computer that has been configured to reference the Azure Automation DSC service as its DSC pull server. Azure Automation DSC is a hybrid solution, meaning that computers can be configured to be DSC nodes no matter where they exist, including other cloud providers and on-premises. Configuring computers to be DSC nodes will be covered over the next few sections.

### Adding a DSC Node (Azure VM)

Configuring an Azure VM to be a DSC node is by far the simplest of the scenarios. To begin this configuration, click on DSC nodes under the Configuration Management section of the Azure Automation menu options. Next, click on Add Azure VM, then click the VM you wish to add from the list of all Azure VMs in the subscription. Then, click on Connect, and on the Registration screen choose the Node configuration name (the compiled configuration to apply), and the other options as desired. A brief description of the options follows.

#### DSC NODE REGISTRATION OPTIONS

Refresh Frequency refers to how often the LCM on this DSC node will reach out to Azure Automation DSC to see if a new configuration has been assigned to it. Configuration Mode Frequency is how often the DSC node will attempt to apply the current configuration. Configuration Mode refers the way the LCM on the DSC node will configure the client. There are three options.

- **ApplyAndMonitor** is the default option. This mode will apply the assigned configuration and then report any configuration drift as the LCM discovers it during its regular configuration check (Configuration Mode Frequency).

- **ApplyOnly** means that DSC applies the configuration and does nothing further unless a new configuration is assigned to the node.

- **The ApplyAndAutoCorrect** option means that the assigned configuration is applied and at each configuration check if drift has occurred it will be reported, and the LCM will attempt to re-apply the configuration.

Allow Module Override, when selected, will allow existing (on the DSC node) modules to be overwritten when a new configuration is applied that uses updated modules. Reboot Node if Needed allows configuration changes that require a reboot (such as the installation of certain roles or features) to be followed by a reboot. Action after Reboot specifies whether any further steps that are a part of a configuration will be carried out after the restart, or whether the configuration should be stopped. Figure 7-26 shows the Registration dialog with these options.

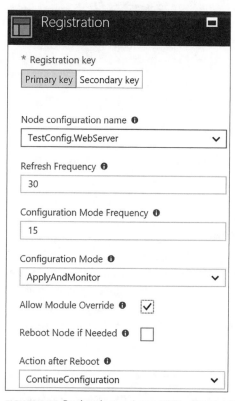

**FIGURE 7-26** Registering an Azure VM to Azure Automation DSC

To register an Azure VM with Azure Automation DSC via PowerShell, use the Register-AzureRmAutomationDscNode cmdlet. The same configuration that is shown in Figure 7-24 is accomplished with the following PowerShell cmdlet and syntax:

```
Register-AzureRmAutomationDscNode -AzureVMName "WebServer" `
    -NodeConfigurationName "TestConfig.WebServer" `
    -RefreshFrequencyMins "30" -ConfigurationModeFrequencyMins "15" `
    -ConfigurationMode ApplyAndMonitor -AllowModuleOverwrite $true `
    -RebootNodeIfNeeded $false -ActionAfterReboot ContinueConfiguration `
    -AutomationAccountName "FabrikamAutomation" `
    -ResourceGroupName "MyAutomationRG"
```

Once a node has been connected to Azure Automation DSC, its compliance with the configuration can be discovered by clicking on DSC Nodes under Configuration Management. A high-level view of the status is available and additional details can be obtained by clicking on the node itself (Figure 7-27).

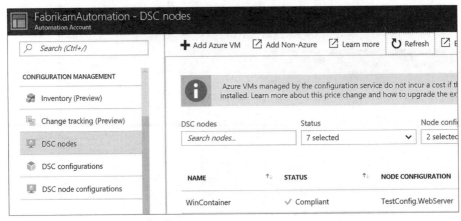

**FIGURE 7-27** Viewing the status of a DSC Node

## Adding a DSC Node (on-premises or other cloud)

It is possible and desirable to add machines as DSC nodes that are not in Azure. This means the Azure Automation DSC service can be a single user interface through which configurations are created, assigned, and managed for all of your computers no matter where they exist. To add a Windows computer that is on-premises or in another cloud environment, first ensure that the latest version of the Windows Management Framework version 5 (WMF 5) is installed. Next, generate a DSC metaconfiguration.

> **NOTE DSC METACONFIGURATIONS**
>
> A DSC metaconfiguration contains the information needed to onboard a computer to the Azure Automation DSC service, including certain secrets. Treat the DSC metaconfiguration like you would a security credential. As a best practice, delete them after use.

### CREATING A DSC METACONFIGURATION

To create a DSC metaconfiguration, from a computer with WMF 5, open PowerShell ISE as an administrator. Next, copy the following code to the script pane of PowerShell ISE:

```
# The DSC configuration that will generate metaconfigurations
[DscLocalConfigurationManager()]
Configuration DscMetaConfigs
{
    param
    (
        [Parameter(Mandatory=$True)]
        [String]$RegistrationUrl,

        [Parameter(Mandatory=$True)]
        [String]$RegistrationKey,
```

```
    [Parameter(Mandatory=$True)]
    [String[]]$ComputerName,

    [Int]$RefreshFrequencyMins = 30,
    [Int]$ConfigurationModeFrequencyMins = 15,
    [String]$ConfigurationMode = "ApplyAndMonitor",
    [String]$NodeConfigurationName,
    [Boolean]$RebootNodeIfNeeded= $False,
    [String]$ActionAfterReboot = "ContinueConfiguration",
    [Boolean]$AllowModuleOverwrite = $False,

    [Boolean]$ReportOnly
)
if(!$NodeConfigurationName -or $NodeConfigurationName -eq "")
{
    $ConfigurationNames = $null
}
else
{
    $ConfigurationNames = @($NodeConfigurationName)
}
if($ReportOnly)
{
$RefreshMode = "PUSH"
}
else
{
$RefreshMode = "PULL"
}
Node $ComputerName
{
    Settings
    {
        RefreshFrequencyMins = $RefreshFrequencyMins
        RefreshMode = $RefreshMode
        ConfigurationMode = $ConfigurationMode
        AllowModuleOverwrite = $AllowModuleOverwrite
        RebootNodeIfNeeded = $RebootNodeIfNeeded
        ActionAfterReboot = $ActionAfterReboot
        ConfigurationModeFrequencyMins = $ConfigurationModeFrequencyMins
    }
    if(!$ReportOnly)
    {
    ConfigurationRepositoryWeb AzureAutomationDSC
        {
            ServerUrl = $RegistrationUrl
            RegistrationKey = $RegistrationKey
            ConfigurationNames = $ConfigurationNames
        }
        ResourceRepositoryWeb AzureAutomationDSC
        {
        ServerUrl = $RegistrationUrl
        RegistrationKey = $RegistrationKey
        }
    }
```

```
        ReportServerWeb AzureAutomationDSC
        {
            ServerUrl = $RegistrationUrl
            RegistrationKey = $RegistrationKey
        }
    }
}


# Create the metaconfigurations
# TODO: edit the below as needed for your use case
$Params = @{
    RegistrationUrl = '<fill me in>';
    RegistrationKey = '<fill me in>';
    ComputerName = @('<some VM to onboard>', '<some other VM to onboard>');
    NodeConfigurationName = 'SimpleConfig.webserver';
    RefreshFrequencyMins = 30;
    ConfigurationModeFrequencyMins = 15;
    RebootNodeIfNeeded = $False;
    AllowModuleOverwrite = $False;
    ConfigurationMode = 'ApplyAndMonitor';
    ActionAfterReboot = 'ContinueConfiguration';
    ReportOnly = $False;  # Set to $True to have machines only report to AA DSC but not
pull from it
}
# Use PowerShell splatting to pass parameters to the DSC configuration being invoked
# For more info about splatting, run: Get-Help -Name about_Splatting
DscMetaConfigs @Params
```

Next, fill in the RegistrationUrl, RegistrationKey and ComputerName(s) sections in the metaconfiguration script. The RegistrationUrl and the RegistrationKey values can be found in the properties of the Automation Account, by clicking on Keys under Account Settings, shown in Figure 7-28. The ComputerName section should reflect the computer or computers that are to be onboarded as DSC nodes.

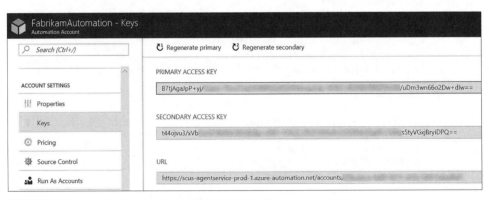

**FIGURE 7-28** Automation Account Keys and service URL

Next, run the script. This will create a folder called DscMetaConfigs in the directory where the script was run. Copy this folder to the computer to be onboarded, then run the following command:

```
Set-DscLocalConfigurationManager -Path ./DscMetaConfigs
```

Within a few minutes, the computer will show up under DSC nodes within the Automation Account. From this point, a DSC node configuration can be assigned to the new DSC node.

# Skill 7.2: Collect and analyze data generated by resources in cloud and on-premises environments

As IT administrators, one of the major challenges to deal with is making efficient use of machine data in the environments under management. Machine data is a wealth of valuable information, but gaining value from it is hindered by at least three challenges. First, machine data is distributed all around the organization. Every server, storage device, network appliance, etc. is generating machine data. In such a distributed from it is very hard to get value from this data. Also, the sheer amount of machine data is enormous. Millions and millions of lines of semi-structured data to parse through makes discovering insights challenging. Finally, machine data is complex. It takes specialized skills to comprehend valuable, actionable information from esoteric machine data files. Thankfully, Microsoft has provided an approach to dealing with these challenges so as to make machine data produce valuable insights with little effort. The service that solves these challenges is Azure Log Analytics.

> **This skill covers how to:**
> - Collect and search across data sources from multiple systems
> - Build custom visualizations
> - Visualize Azure resources across multiple subscriptions
> - Transform Azure activity data and managed resource data into an insight with flexible search queries
> - Monitor system updates and malware status
> - Track server configuration changes by using Azure Log Analytics

## Collect and search across data sources from multiple systems

Azure Log Analytics allows administrators to search across their data sources from various systems and environments. It accomplishes this by ingesting these data sources into a central repository in Azure. Once the data is stored, it is indexed and categorized so that searching through millions of records takes seconds. In some cases, data is collected by agents installed on systems. In other cases, such as that of Azure platform services, data is collected by the platform itself. In still other cases, products can be data sources. For example, System Center Configuration Manager (SCOM) can forward monitoring and performance data it collects to the Log Analytics service. In Figure 7-29, an on-premises environment is sending machine data to Log Analytics by way of an OMS Gateway. In the AWS, and Azure environment machine data is flowing into Log Analytics also by way of an OMS Gateway. Finally, in the Azure environment data sources are forwarding machine data to the Log Analytics service directly. Insights from this collected data are surfaced from the Azure portal.

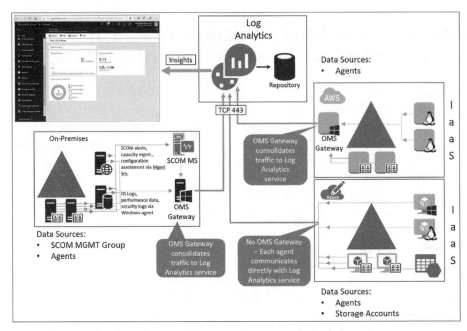

**FIGURE 7-29** Data flow from diverse environments into Azure Log Analytics

The process to collect machine data begins with choosing whether to use the default Log Analytics workspace or to create a new one. In every Azure subscription with IaaS VMs provisioned, a default Log Analytics workspace will be created automatically (Figure 7-30.

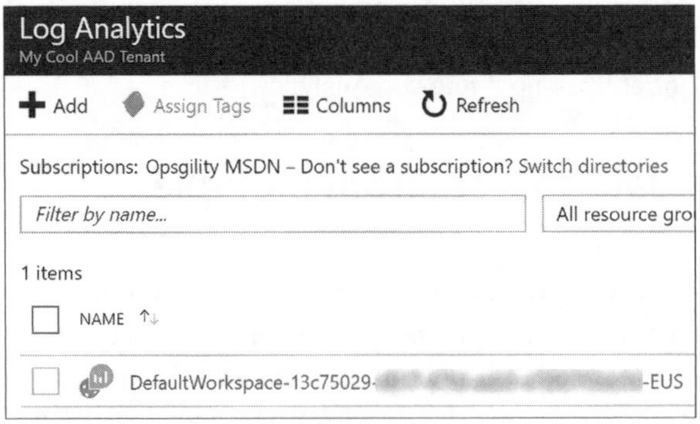

**FIGURE 7-30** Default Log Analytics workspace

Initially, this workspace is only used for storing security-related data, but it can be extended to accomplish all of the features available with Log Analytics. In the next few sections, the assumption is made that a new Log Analytics workspace will be created. Once created, systems must be connected to it connecting systems to the Log Analytics service. The process to connect systems varies based on the system type and where it is hosted. Several potential scenarios are considered in the next few sections. First, creating a Log Analytics workspace will be covered, and then the process to connect data sources to the workspace will be discussed.

## Creating a Log Analytics workspace (Azure portal)

To create a Log Analytics workspace from the Azure portal, click on the New button and under Monitoring and Management, click Log Analytics. Give the workspace a name, specify the subscription, create or specify an existing resource group, choose the location (Azure region), and the pricing tier. Then click OK to begin creation. Normally, the workspace creation occurs in under a minute.

When choosing the location, notice there are fewer options than for most resources that can be created in Azure. Choose a region that is close to or as centralized as possible relative to the resources it will monitor. The choice of pricing tier depends upon whether an organization has licensed Operations Management Suite or will pay for this feature per node. Choosing the Free tier allows all features, but the organization pays the stand-alone pricing for each service deployed. These options are shown in Figure 7-31.

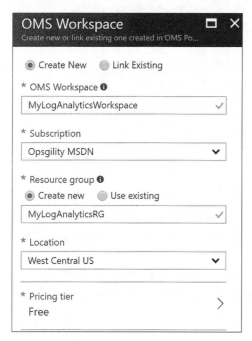

FIGURE 7-31 Creating a new Log Analytics workspace

## Creating a Log Analytics workspace (PowerShell)

Creating a Log Analytics workspace with PowerShell requires using the New-AzureRmOperationalInsightsWorkspace cmdlet. Log Analytics was formerly named Operational Insights, but the PowerShell cmdlets have not been renamed. To create a workspace with the same parameters and options as are shown in Figure 7-31, use the following PowerShell code.

```
$ResourceGroup = "MyLogAnalyticsRG"
$WorkspaceName = "MyLogAnalyticsWorkspace"
$Location = "westcentralus"
New-AzureRmResourceGroup -Name $ResourceGroup -Location "westcentralus"
New-AzureRmOperationalInsightsWorkspace -Location $Location `
 -Name $WorkspaceName -Sku Free -ResourceGroupName $ResourceGroup
```

## Connecting Log Analytics Data Sources (Azure VMs)

Connecting an Azure VM to a Log Analytics workspace is quite easy. Navigate to the properties of the workspace and under Workspace Data Sources, click Virtual Machines. You will notice a listing of all the virtual machines in the subscription and whether they are connected to this workspace, another workspace, or not connected at all (Figure 7-32).

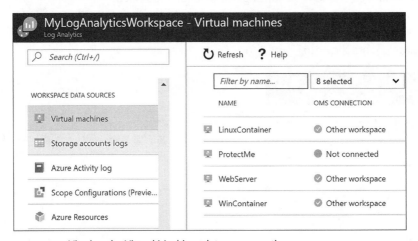

**FIGURE 7-32** Viewing the Virtual Machines data source option

Notice that most of the VMs are connected to another workspace. Remember that a default Log Analytics workspace is created when virtual machines are added to the subscription. VMs will be connected to this workspace by default.

To connect a virtual machine to the newly created workspace, click on it and click Disconnect. This will disconnect it from the default workspace, enabling it to be connected to the new workspace.

***NOTE*** **COMPUTERS AND LOG ANALYTICS WORKSPACES**

A computer can only be connected to a single Log Analytics workspace at a time.

Disconnecting a computer takes several minutes because the configuration is changing within the Microsoft Monitoring Agent in the VM. Once this operation is complete, click Connect. Because the focus is the newly created workspace, the VM will be connected to it, as shown in Figure 7-33.

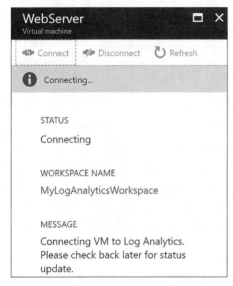

**FIGURE 7-33** Connecting an Azure VM to a Log Analytics workspace

This connection operation installs the Microsoft Monitoring Agent (if necessary) and automatically configures it to connect to the targeted workspace. Once connected, the VM will begin to forward machine data from the VM to the workspace. This will be visible within Log Analytics within a few minutes. To validate data flowing in from the VM, click on Log Search under General within the workspace properties. Run the query search * and within a few minutes you should see data from the connected VM (Figure 7-34).

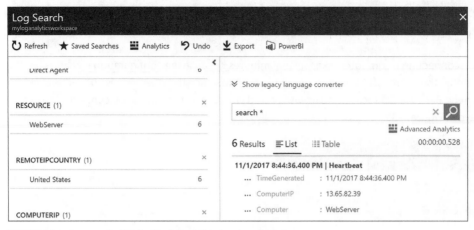

**FIGURE 7-34** A connected VM with data visible in a Log Search

## Connecting Log Analytics data sources (non-Azure computer)

To connect a computer to a workspace that is outside of Azure, the Microsoft Monitoring Agent (MMA) must be installed and configured to connect to the desired Log Analytics workspace. This can be done manually or it can be automated. The MMA supports an unattended installation and configuration to support automation. A common way of addressing this installation and configuration is to leverage Azure Automation (discussed earlier in this chapter). In this chapter, the manual method will be covered and an EC2 virtual machine instance within Amazon Web Services will be connected to the workspace.

To begin, collect the Log Analytics workspace ID and primary key, as you will need this information when installing the MMA.

> **NOTE**  **LOG ANALYTICS WORKSPACE ID AND KEYS**
>
> The Log Analytics workspace ID and keys are credentials that allow connecting to and writing data into the workspace, so protect them as such.
>
> Obtain the workspace ID and key from the Advanced settings menu option under the Settings section of the workspace properties. Record the ID and primary key in a safe place. Next, log into the computer that will be connected to the workspace and download and run the MMA. It can be downloaded here: *https://go.microsoft.com/fwlink/?LinkId=828603*. Click Next until the Agent Setup Options dialog is reached. Here, select Connect the agent to Azure Log Analytics (OMS), as shown in Figure 7-35, then click Next.

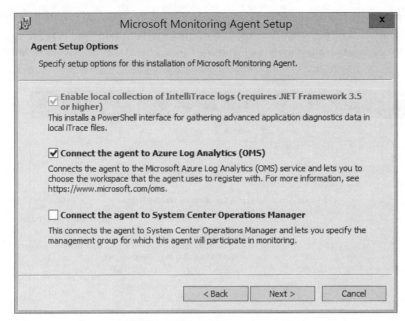

**FIGURE 7-35** MMA setup dialog, choosing the agent connection type

On the Azure Log Analytics dialog, enter the workspace ID and primary key. Choose Azure Commercial for the Azure Cloud selection. The agent will need to communicate to the Log Analytics service over TCP port 443. If a proxy is required for this connection click Advanced to configure this. These options are shown in Figure 7-36.

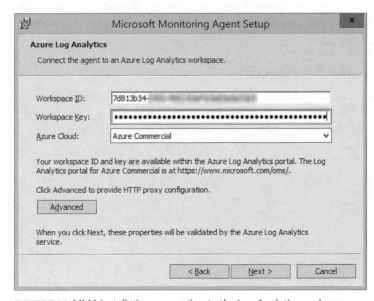

**FIGURE 7-36** MMA installation connecting to the Log Analytics workspace

Click Next and choose whether to allow Windows Update to keep the agent up to date (this is recommended). Finally click Install. Once the install completes, machine data should be forwarded into the workspace within a few minutes. Figure 7-37 shows data from the AWSWinVM computer.

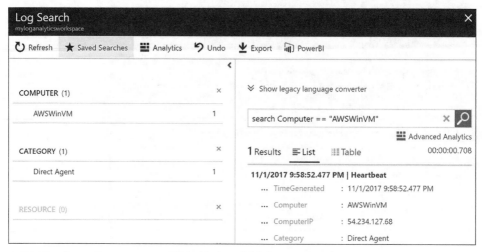

**FIGURE 7-37** A non-Azure connected VM with data visible in a Log Search

## Other Data Sources

Other data sources besides computers can be configured to connect and send data to Log Analytics. Some examples include Azure Storage Accounts, Azure Activity Logs, Network Security Groups, and others. Having as many data sources connected as possible helps to maximize the potential value of Log Analytics.

## Log Analytics Management Solutions

One of the promises of Log Analytics is that it helps administrators to gain insights from complex machine data. The components of Log Analytics that accomplishes this are management solutions. Management solutions are pre-built visualizations and queries that help to surface valuable insights from collected machine data. There are many of these solutions, each focusing in on a specific technology or business need. A few solution examples are:

- Change tracking
- Antimalware assessment
- Update management
- AD assessment
- SQL assessment

To see all of the management solutions that can be deployed in a Log Analytics workspace browse to the Azure Marketplace (*https://azuremarketplace.microsoft.com/en-us*), under Product Category select Monitoring and Management, then select Management Solutions, shown in Figure 7-38.

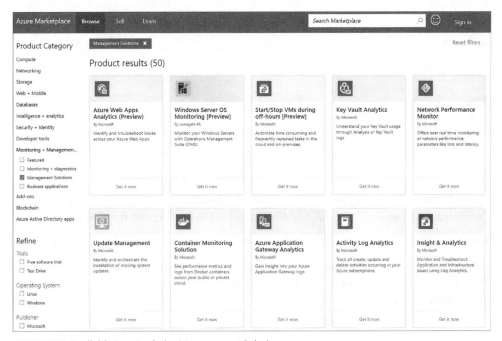

**FIGURE 7-38** Available Log Analytics Management Solutions

## Searching across Log Analytics data sources

As mentioned, all of the machine data is collected into a repository and is indexed and categorized. This makes searching through the data for the specific information needed much easier and less time intensive. To accomplish ad hock queries, use the Log Search feature. Open the Log Search feature from the Log Analytics properties within the General section. Start with a simple example to see the records collected by Log Analytics. In the search dialog, enter the following:

```
search *
```

As shown in Figure 7-39, this query returns all collected records across all data sources.

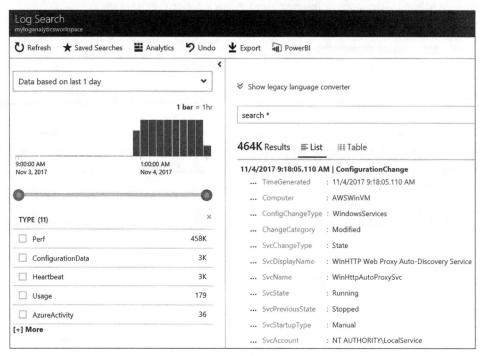

**FIGURE 7-39** The Log Search dialog show all records returned

To get more specific, imagine the need to see all computers that require operating system updates. To search across all records and all data sources to find this out, use this query:

```
search * | where Type == "Update"  | where ( UpdateState == "Needed" )
```

This query searches all records (search *) and within that dataset looking only for records of the type "Update" (where Type == "Update") and within that data set looking only for records where UpdateState is equal to "Needed" (where ( UpdateState == "Needed" ). The result of this query is seen in Figure 7-40.

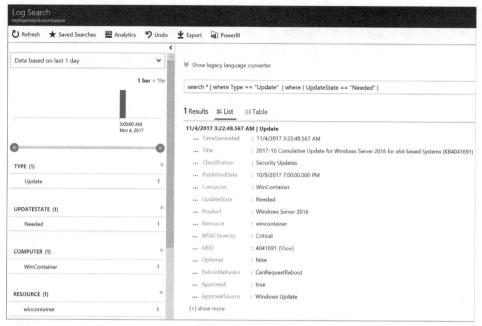

**FIGURE 7-40** Log Search showing required operating system updates

Keep in mind that management solutions contain pre-built queries to help those new to Log Analytics quickly find the needed data. An example query included in the Change Tracking management solution looks for changes to Linux Deamons.

```
ConfigurationChange | where ConfigChangeType == "Daemons"
```

Once an administrator becomes proficient in writing custom queries, often there is a requirement to save these queries for future reference. For example, if an administrator needed to know if services that have a startup type of Automatic but are in a stopped state, they may write a query like this one.

```
search * | where Type == "ConfigurationData"  | where ( SvcStartupType == "Auto" )   |
where ( SvcState == "Stopped" )
```

To save such a query, from within the Log Search dialog, click Saved Searches, click Add, and then enter a meaningful name, a category, the query syntax, and optionally a Function Alias (a short name given to a saved search). Then click OK. This dialog is shown in Figure 7-41.

**FIGURE 7-41** Saving a useful custom query

# Build custom visualizations

Custom visualizations can be created within Log Analytics and added to the Overview section. This feature allows organizations to populate the Overview section with an at-a-glance data that is relevant to their business. To begin creating a custom visualization, click View Designer under the General section within the Log Analytics properties. An example custom visualization is created here using the same query that was saved in the last section.

```
search * | where Type == "ConfigurationData"  | where ( SvcStartupType == "Auto" )  |
where ( SvcState == "Stopped" )
```

Within the View Designer, an overview tile and a Dashboard tile is created. The overview tile ideally is a view of the desired data at the highest level. In the case of this example, a number view works best. The dashboard tile will be a deeper dive into the data, showing a breakout of information by computer and allowing the user to click on a result to get more detail.

## Creating the Overview tile

Within the View Designer there is a gallery of overview templates to choose from. The example use case is best suited to a number view. From the Gallery, and click the Number option. Enter a descriptive name because this helps other users to understand what the value being displayed represents. Ideally, enter a description, and change the Legend text to Number Of Computers In State. Finally, enter the following query syntax in the Query section.

```
search * | where Type == "ConfigurationData"  | where ( SvcStartupType == "Auto" )  |
where ( SvcState == "Stopped" ) | summarize AggregatedValue = count() by Computer |
 count
```

Notice the highlighted portion of the query is different from the saved query. This section summarizes the query output by count of computers, giving the value to display in the Overview tile. The Overview tile setup is displayed in Figure 7-42.

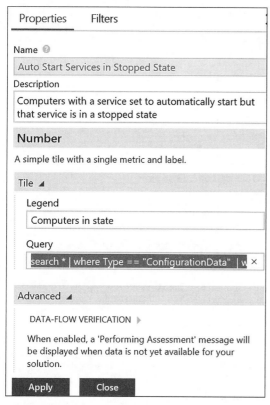

**FIGURE 7-42** Adding the Overview tile in a custom visualization

Click Apply, and then click the View Dashboard tab to begin configuring the Dashboard tile.

## Creating the Dashboard tile

In the View dashboard section, there are several gallery views to choose from. For the purposes of this example, the Number And List view was chosen. The configuration blade for this view is broken out by sections. In the Group Title section, enter a group title that describes the dashboard. These options are shown in Figure 7-43.

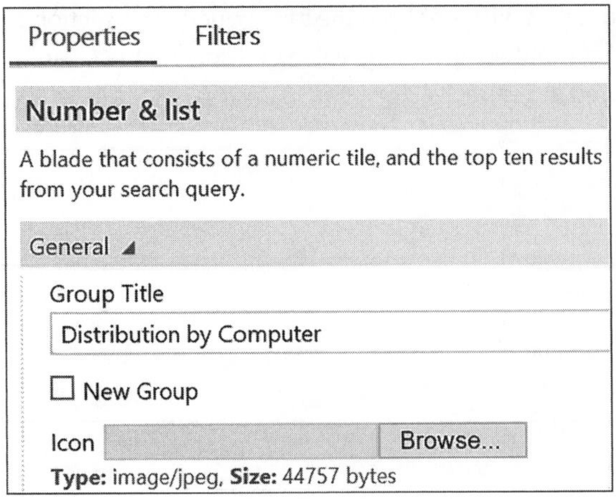

**Properties**     Filters

**Number & list**

A blade that consists of a numeric tile, and the top ten results
from your search query.

**General** ◢

Group Title

Distribution by Computer

☐ New Group

Icon                **Browse...**
**Type:** image/jpeg, **Size:** 44757 bytes

**FIGURE 7-43** The General section of the Number and List dashboard visualization

In the Title section enter a legend value that describes the data and a query that summarizes the data. In the case of this example, the same query is used that was specified in the
Overview tile. In the List section enter a query that displays the computers that have services in
this state, as shown in Figure 7-44. The query syntax is like before.

```
search * | where Type == "ConfigurationData"  | where ( SvcStartupType == "Auto" )   |
where ( SvcState == "Stopped" ) | summarize AggregatedValue = count() by Computer
```

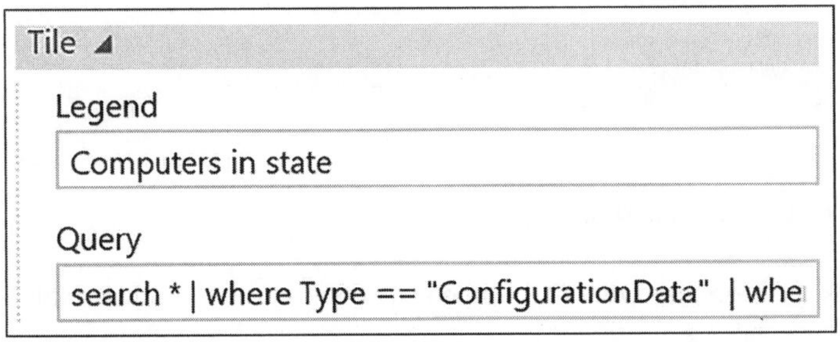

**Tile** ◢

Legend

Computers in state

Query

search * | where Type == "ConfigurationData"  | whe

**FIGURE 7-44** The Tile section of the Number and List dashboard visualization

The only difference is that the final count statement is removed so that the list of computers is shown. For the column titles, the defaults of Name = Computer and Value = Count are
appropriate as shown in Figure 7-45.

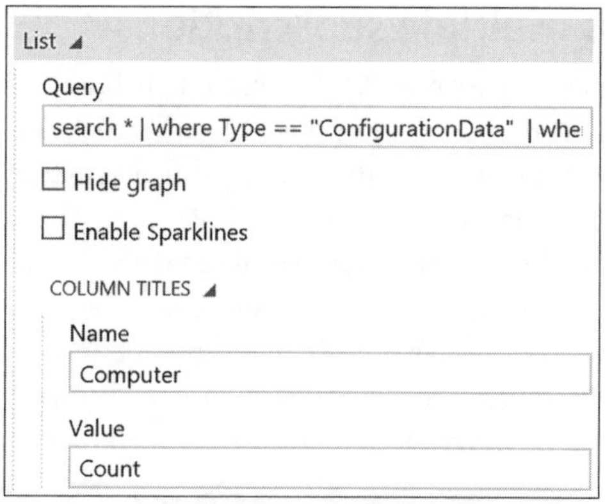

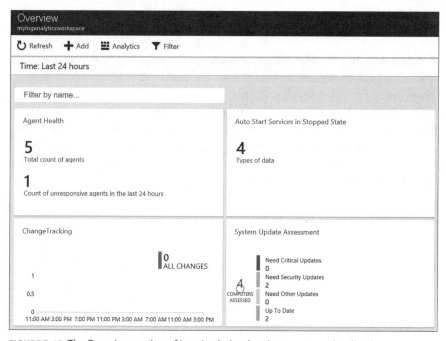

FIGURE 7-45 The List section of the Number and List dashboard visualization

Finally, the Navigation query is entered so that Log Analytics knows what data to return when the visualization is clicked.

```
search {selected item}  | where ( SvcStartupType == "Auto" )   | where ( SvcState ==
  "Stopped" )
```

The highlighted section uses as a value whichever line item was clicked in the visualization to perform a log search against that specific computer. Finally, click Apply, and then click Save at the top of the View Designer. Now, as shown in Figure 7-46, the Overview section shows the custom visualization that was just created. Clicking it reveals a greater depth of information.

FIGURE 7-46 The Overview section of Log Analytics showing a custom visualization

# Visualize Azure resources across multiple subscriptions

Smaller organizations are able to comfortably exist within a single Azure subscription, but often, larger organizations use many subscriptions. Larger enterprises often license their Azure consumption through an Enterprise Agreement, and it is common that these companies assign one or more Azure subscriptions to their different business units or geographical offices. This practice helps to manage cost distribution across an organization. However, it can create management and monitoring difficulties. Fortunately Log Analytics helps in these scenarios as well. Although a Log Analytics workspace is a resource that exists in a single Azure subscription, it can monitor and manage resources in multiple subscriptions. In Figure 7-47 two activity logs from different subscriptions are connected to the same workspace.

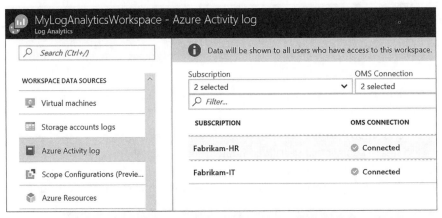

**FIGURE 7-47** Connected Azure Activity Logs from different subscriptions

With resources from multiple subscriptions connected to the same Log Analytics workspace, it is possible to perform searches, create queries, and build visualizations that surface insights comprehensively across the organization. The previous query used for example purposes displayed computers with automatically starting services that are in a stopped state. Extending that example, there is now a Fabrikam-IT subscription and a Fabrikam-HR subscription. A virtual machine was added to the Fabrikam-HR subscription HRWebSrv), however the Log Analytics workspace is in the Fabrikam-IT subscription. With the same query syntax servers are returned from both subscriptions, as shown in Figure 7-48.

**FIGURE 7-48** Log Search showing results with resources from multiple subscriptions

# Transform Azure activity data and managed resource data into an insight with flexible search queries

The Azure Activity Log is the audit facility with an Azure subscription to track creation, renaming, updating, and deletion of CRUD operations. The Activity Log can be viewed from within the Monitor node of Azure and under the Shared Services section. All Azure Resource Manager resources write their CRUD activity to the Activity Log, making it a reliable record of the actions taken. The Activity Log maintains 90 days of information.

As mentioned, the Activity Log can be configured to write activity into Log Analytics, which brings several benefits. Some of these include using pre-defined visualizations, analyzing log data from several subscriptions, and keeping log data for longer than 90 days (assuming the Log Analytics workspace is configured to retain data for longer than 90 days). To begin realizing these benefits, first connect the Activity Log to Log Analytics.

## Connect the Azure Activity Log to a Log Analytics workspace

To connect the Azure Activity Log to a Log Analytics workspace, navigate to the Workspace Data Sources section within the properties of the workspace, and click the Azure Activity Log. The Activity Logs for all subscriptions the authenticated user has access to are displayed. To connect an Activity Log, click it, and then click Connect, shown in Figure 7-49. Note that there is no agent involved in sending this data (as with virtual machines), but rather the date is sent directly from the platform.

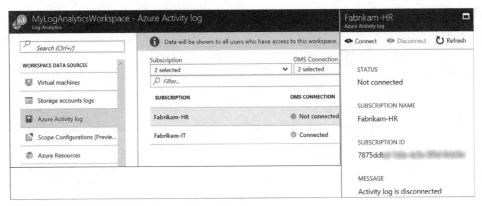

FIGURE 7-49  Connecting the Activity Log to a Log Analytics workspace

## Gaining insights with Log Analytics Queries

Starting from the Log Analytics Overview, click the Azure Activity Logs tile. Click the bar chart on the Azure Activity Log Entries tile (Figure 7-50). This opens the Log Search dialog and displays the results for the query:

```
search "AzureActivity"
```

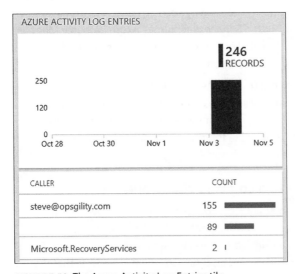

FIGURE 7-50  The Azure Activity Log Entries tile

To the left under the custom time range section of Log Search, click the Azure Activity type. Notice that this dynamically changes the Log Analytics search, which now shows:

```
search "AzureActivity" | where Type == "AzureActivity"
```

Now click the Succeeded type under ActivityStatus, and notice that this is also added to the query automatically.

```
search "AzureActivity" | where Type == "AzureActivity"  | where ActivityStatus ==
"Succeeded"
```

Next click a user under the Caller section, again automatically creating a more precise query.

```
search "AzureActivity" | where Type == "AzureActivity"  | where ActivityStatus ==
"Succeeded"  | where Caller == "steve@opsgility.com"
```

The resulting query shows all Azure Activity Log entries where the status is succeeded and the caller is a specific user. Figure 7-51 shows the results of this query. Notice that the log search shows that this user successfully deleted a virtual machine. This virtual machine was in a different subscription from the Log Analytics workspace.

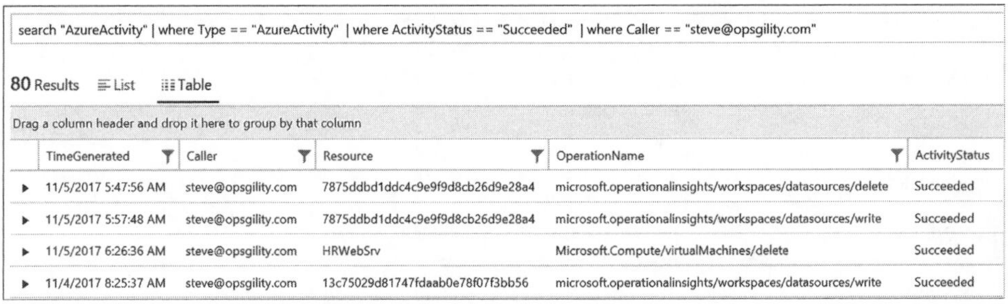

| TimeGenerated | Caller | Resource | OperationName | ActivityStatus |
|---|---|---|---|---|
| 11/5/2017 5:47:56 AM | steve@opsgility.com | 7875ddbd1ddc4c9e9f9d8cb26d9e28a4 | microsoft.operationalinsights/workspaces/datasources/delete | Succeeded |
| 11/5/2017 5:57:48 AM | steve@opsgility.com | 7875ddbd1ddc4c9e9f9d8cb26d9e28a4 | microsoft.operationalinsights/workspaces/datasources/write | Succeeded |
| 11/5/2017 6:26:36 AM | steve@opsgility.com | HRWebSrv | Microsoft.Compute/virtualMachines/delete | Succeeded |
| 11/4/2017 8:25:37 AM | steve@opsgility.com | 13c75029d81747fdaab0e78f07f3bb56 | microsoft.operationalinsights/workspaces/datasources/write | Succeeded |

search "AzureActivity" | where Type == "AzureActivity" | where ActivityStatus == "Succeeded" | where Caller == "steve@opsgility.com"

80 Results    List    Table

Drag a column header and drop it here to group by that column

**FIGURE 7-51** Searching the Azure Activity Log via Log Analytics

# Monitor system updates and malware status

Azure Log Analytics can be used to monitor the computers in an environment and report when system updates are needed. This functionality is enabled through the System Update Assessment management solution. An administrator can also keep tabs on whether malware is present on monitored systems, via the Antimalware Assessment management solution. Each of these capabilities are considered in the following sections.

## Monitoring System Updates with Log Analytics

The System Update management solution for Azure Log Analytics detects missing updates for both Windows and Linux systems, and provides for remediation through automated installation of missing updates. The solution works by configuring computers that are connected to the workspace to perform a compliance scan, and report the results back to the workspace. The solution reports how up-to-date the computer is based on the service it is configured to synchronize with (Windows Update or Windows Server Update Services if Windows or a Linux update repository). The results of this scan are displayed on the built-in tiles within the System Update management solution (Figure 7-52).

**FIGURE 7-52** System Updates Assessed Computers visualization

Clicking into a visualization provides more insights, and ultimately reveals the log search behind the visualization data. For example, the following log search produces a view of missing security updates for all systems being monitored by Log Analytics.

```
Update | where OSType!="Linux" and Optional==false and Classification=~"Security
Updates" | summarize hint.strategy=partitioned arg_max(TimeGenerated, *) by
Computer,SourceComputerId,UpdateID| where UpdateState=~"Needed" and Approved!=false |
render table
```

This query results in the following table view (Figure 7-53).

**FIGURE 7-53** Missing security updates query in log search

It is also possible to set up alerts based on the results of log search queries. This feature is not currently available in the Azure portal so it must be accomplished from the OMS portal. To access the OMS portal easily from the Azure portal, navigate to the OMS Workspace option under the Log Analytics properties, and then click OMS Portal. This opens the OMS portal and automatically authenticates the user with the credentials used to log into Azure. In this example, an alert is set up that sends an email if the number of security alerts missing in the environment are above two. Within the OMS portal home screen, click the System Update Assessment tile. Under the Missing Updates tiles, click the Security Updates classification. In the Log Search screen showing the results, click Alerts in the upper left part of the dialog. Under General, give the alert a name, description, and select the severity. The query is already populated and the time window is set to 15 minutes. Under Schedule set the frequency the alert is checked for and choose Number Of Results for the Generate Alert Based On option. For Number Of Results, leave the option set to Greater Than and enter 2. Select Suppress Alerts and under Suppress Alerts For, set the number to 24 hours. This means we will get one alert for this condition each day while it is active. Finally, under the Actions section set Email Notification to Yes and ensure a valid email is configured. Note, there are other actions that can be taken, such as executing a runbook or calling a webhook. These options are displayed in Figure 7-54.

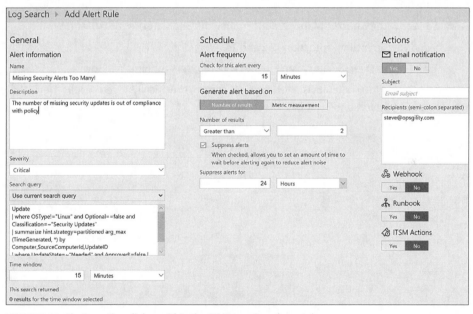

**FIGURE 7-54** Alert creation dialog within the OMS Log Search portal

## Monitoring malware status with Log Analytics

Using the Antimalware Assessment management solution Log Analytics also allows for monitoring the status of malware protection and infestations in the environment. Of course, the first step in realizing these benefits is to all the Antimalware Assessment. As with other management solutions, from the Azure portal click New, and in the Search The Marketplace dialog enter Antimalware Assessment, and then click the Returned option. Once the solution is installed, the MMS agent on each connected virtual machine begins assessing whether an antimalware solution is installed and whether it is enabled, is running regular scans, and is using signatures not older than seven days. This solution also reports on malware activity if a supported antimalware product is installed. These include:

- Windows Defender on Windows 8, Windows 8.1, Windows 10, and Windows Server 2016 TP4 or later
- Windows Security Center (WSC) on Windows 8, Windows 8.1, Windows 10, Windows Server 2016 TP4 or later
- Servers running System Center Endpoint Protection (v4.5.216 or later), Azure virtual machines with the antimalware extension, and Windows Malicious Software Removal Tool (MSRT)
- Servers with Windows Management Framework 3 (or later) WMF 3.0, and WMF 4.0.
- Symantec Endpoint Protection 12.x and 14.x versions
- Trend Micro Deep Security version 9.6 on computers running Window

In Figure 7-55, the four default visualizations are shown, specifically Threat Status, Detected Threats, Protection Status, and Type of Protection.

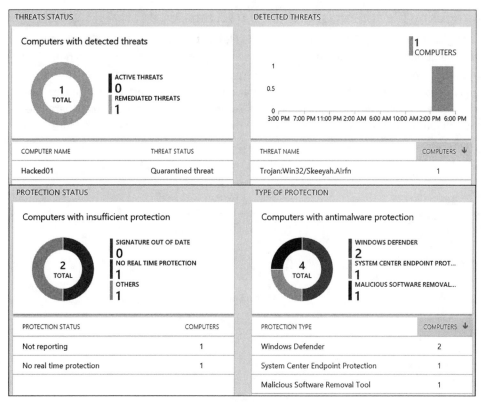

**FIGURE 7-55** The Antimalware Assessment default visualizations

Log Analytics alerts can be set up in a similar way to what was described earlier under Monitoring System Updates with Log Analytics.

## Track server configuration changes by using Azure Log Analytics

One of the most common quandaries that IT administrators face when troubleshooting problems is determining what changed in the environment. Thankfully Azure Log Analytics helps to address this issue as well. By installing the Change Tracking management solution, changes to both Windows and Linux systems can be tracked. The solution specifically can track changes to software, Windows files and registry keys, Windows services, and Linux files and daemons. It is the MMS agent on connected computers that tracks these changes once the management solution is installed into the workspace.

## Configuring file and registry change tracking

Tracking changes to the Windows registry and to files on both Windows and Linux requires additional configuration. As of this writing, this configuration must be carried out in the OMS portal. This capability will be added to the Azure portal eventually. Open the OMS portal as describe previously in this chapter (there are several links to the OMS portal within the properties of the Azure Log Analytics workspace), and click Settings (the gear symbol). From there, click either Windows File Tracking, Windows Registry Tracking or Linux File Tracking (Figure 7-56).

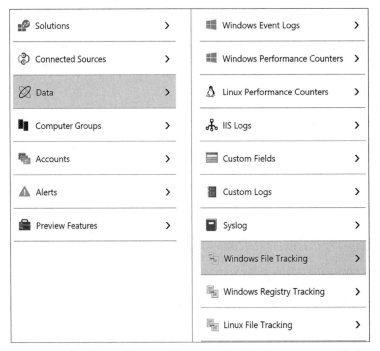

**FIGURE 7-56** Configuring Windows File and Registry Tracking, and Linux File Tracking

In either case, the process to enable change tracking for these objects is to click the configuration area and enter in the path to the files or registry keys that must be monitored for changes. In addition to the path, additional properties are available for Linux file change tracking, including Type (File or Directory), Links (how Linux simlinks are handled), Recurse (tracking all files under the specified path), and Sudo (enables tracking of files that require sudo privilege).

## Viewing configuration changes

To view the changes that have occurred on connected computers, navigate to the Change Tracking solution from the Overview section of the Log Analytics workspace properties. Several tiles contain the default visualizations for this solution, including Configuration Changes Summary, Changes by Configuration Type, and Software Changes. Figure 7-57 shows the Configuration Changes Summary.

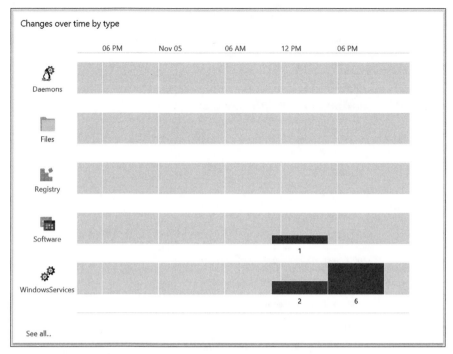

**FIGURE 7-57** The Configuration Changes Summary visualization

Clicking See All runs a log search query that returns all recorded changes. The query syntax looks like this.

```
search in (ConfigurationChange) ConfigChangeType == "Daemons" and (SvcChangeType ==
"StartupType" or SvcChangeType == "Path" or SvcChangeType == "Runlevels") or
ConfigChangeType == "Files" or ConfigChangeType == "Registry" or ConfigChangeType ==
"Software" and SoftwareName !contains_cs "KB2461484" and SoftwareName !contains_cs
"KB2267602" or ConfigChangeType == "WindowsServices" and SvcChangeType != "State" and
not (SvcName == "BITS" and SvcChangeType == "StartupType")
```

An example of a software installation entry is shown in Figure 7-58. Note the software name, previous and current values, showing the software as a new install.

| | |
|---|---|
| $table | ConfigurationChange |
| Computer | Hacked01 |
| ConfigChangeType | Software |
| ChangeCategory | Added |
| SourceComputerId | 09d292b0-e76a-4a79-84e0-4a343d6986ad |
| SoftwareType | Application |
| SoftwareName | System Center Endpoint Protection |
| Previous | Not installed |
| Current | 4.10.209.0 |
| Publisher | Microsoft Corporation |
| SourceSystem | OpsManager |
| MG | 00000000-0000-0000-0000-000000000001 |
| ManagementGroupName | AOI-7d813b34-2400-4982-83ef-b3e83a5e51b5 |
| TenantId | 7d813b34-2400-4982-83ef-b3e83a5e51b5 |
| TimeGenerated | 2017-11-05T22:06:09.06Z |
| VMUUID | 035549ee-dc0b-4383-a512-e0d8bf35f670 |
| Type | ConfigurationChange |

**FIGURE 7-58** A software installation change

# Thought experiment

In this thought experiment, demonstrate your skills and knowledge of the topics covered in this chapter. You can find answer to this thought experiment in the next section.

You are the administrator at Fabrikam and your HR contact has asked you to help solve several problems they have been experiencing with their Time Reporting application. The application runs on a single IaaS VM in Fabrikam's Azure subscription and because it is a legacy application it cannot be clustered nor host multiple instances. The problem they have been experiencing is load-related slowness during end of the month timeframes, when employees are most likely to use the application. The HR department could choose a different IaaS VM series/size with more CPU cores and RAM, but they want to avoid running with too much capacity during slow times (most of the month). "Over-provisioning the server during slow periods would be a waste of money," says Helen Wilson, the HR Director.

An additional problem is that the application has been brought down three times over the past 12 months. In each case, a change was made to the server that impacted the application, but this conclusion only was discovered after hours of troubleshooting. The HR department needs your help.

How will you:

1. Help the HR department address their performance issue without over-provisioning the virtual machine during the slower times over most of the month?

2. Protect the configuration of the application server to maximize its availability?

3. Help administrators quickly discover the root cause whenever the next 'mystery' outage occurs?

# Thought experiment answers

This section contains the solution to the thought experiment.

Fortunately, Azure brings features that help address the HR department's single-instance application server challenges.

1. Azure Automation runbooks are a great way to scale up the IaaS VM's size during heavy usage periods. A runbook can be written to accomplish this scale up operation, and it can be scheduled to perform the scale up a day before the high-load periods. Another runbook can be authored and scheduled that scales the VM back down to the original size during the slower periods.

2. Azure Automation DSC is a way to address the configuration drift on the application server. The server can be added as a DSC Node, and then a DSC configuration can be authored, tested, and applied to the server. DSC can be set up automatically remediate any configuration drift or simply report it to administrators.

3. To quickly discover the root cause of change-related application issues, Log Analytics Change Tracking can be used. Any changes of software, services, key files, or registry areas, etc. will be recorded in the Log Analytics service. An alert can be set up to email administrators should a change be detected.

# Chapter summary

This chapter covered a wide variety of topics related to automating processes and configurations, and collecting and analyzing machine logs and data from cloud-based on-premises deployments in order to gain insights from this data. Some of the key things to remember include:

■ Azure Automation runbooks can automate processes within on-premises or cloud-based deployments. Any process that can be accomplished with PowerShell, Python or Bash, can be automated with Azure Automation runbooks.

■ Azure Automation DSC automates the configuration of computers in on-premises or cloud environments. This solution can automatically correct or alert on configuration drift and can work with Windows or Linux computers.

- Azure Log Analytics can consolidate machine data from on-premises and cloud-based workloads and this data is indexed and categorized for quick searching.

- Azure Log Analytics has many management solutions that help administrators gain value out of complex machine data. These solutions contain pre-built visualizations and queries that help surface insights quickly.

- One of the key management solutions included with Log Analytics is the Antimalware Assessment solution. This helps organizations find out about systems missing malware protection, or discover malware infestations.

- Another important Log Analytics management solution is the Change Tracking solution. This solution enables organizations discover "what changed" quickly, helping in the troubleshooting of outages.

# CHAPTER 8

# Manage Azure Identities

Microsoft has long been a leader in the identity space. This leadership goes back to the introduction of Active Directory (AD) with Windows 2000 before the cloud even existed. Microsoft moved into cloud identity with the introduction of Azure Active Directory (Azure AD), which is now used by over five million companies around the world. The adoption of Office 365 led this extended use of Azure AD. These two technologies however have very different purposes, with AD primarily used on-premises and Azure AD primarily used for the cloud.

Microsoft has poured resources into making AD and Azure AD work together. The concept is to extend the identity that lives on-premises to the cloud by synchronizing the identities. This ability is provided by a technology named Azure AD Connect. Microsoft has also invested in extending those identities to enable scenarios such as single sign-on by using Active Directory Federation Services (ADFS), which is deployed in many large enterprises.

Microsoft has continued pushing forward by developing options for developers to leverage Azure AD for their applications. Microsoft provides the ability for developers to extend a company's Azure AD to users outside of the organization. The first option is known as Azure AD B2C (Business to Consumer). This allows consumers to sign into applications using their social media accounts, such as a Facebook ID. A complementary technology, known as Azure AD B2B (Business to Business), extends Azure AD to business partners.

As the cloud becomes more popular and Azure AD adoption continues to pick up, there are some legacy applications that require you to use the traditional AD, even in the cloud. For this, Microsoft has developed a service called Azure AD Domain Services. This allows for traditional Kerberos and LDAP functionality in the cloud without deploying Domain Controllers into a VNet.

This area of the 70-533 exam is focused on the management of identities by using Azure, as well as monitoring their health and functionality by using Azure AD Connect Health.

- Skill 8.1: Monitor On-Premises Identity Infrastructure and Synchronization Services with Azure AD Connect Health
- Skill 8.2: Manage Domains with Azure Active Directory Domain Services
- Skill 8.3: Integrate with Azure Active Directory (Azure AD)
- Skill 8.4: Implement Azure AD B2C and Azure AD B2B

# Skill 8.1: Monitor On-Premises Identity Infrastructure and Synchronization Services with Azure AD Connect Health

Azure AD Connect Health is a monitoring tool integrated into the Azure portal. Azure AD Connect Health can be used to monitor your on-premises identity infrastructure and synchronization services to the cloud.

Maintaining your users' identities is critical to ensure their ability to leverage Azure, Office 365, and any other Microsoft Online services. Azure AD Connect Health Services can be used to monitor Active Directory Federation Services (ADFS) servers, Azure AD Connect servers (also known as Sync Engine), Active Directory Domain Services, and traditional AD Domain Controllers. Azure AD Connect Health can also provide usage data which helps you better understand how your users are leveraging the cloud.

**This skill covers how to:**

- Monitor Sync Engine & Replication
- Monitor Domain Controllers
- Setup Email Notifications for Critical Alerts
- Monitor ADFS Proxy and Web Application Proxy Servers
- Generate Utilization Reports

## Monitor Sync Engine & Replication

Replication is a critical service that must be monitored and maintained to ensure reliable access to your cloud. Without healthy replication, directory objects are not available or updated on a regular basis, which makes deploying services to the Microsoft cloud unreliable.

When you synchronize AD with Azure AD, users are more productive because they leverage a common identity across both cloud and on-premises resources. Azure AD Connect Health monitors and provides visibility into your on-premises identity infrastructure used to access Office 365 and Azure AD applications. It is as simple as installing an agent on each of your on-premises identity servers. Figure 8-1 shows the Azure AD Connect Health blade in the Azure portal.

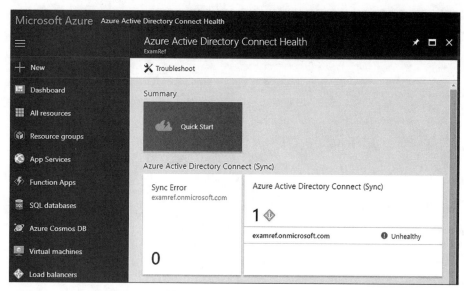

FIGURE 8-1  Azure AD Connect Health

**EXAM TIP**

Azure AD Connect Health requires Azure AD Premium, either P1 or P2 SKU. The first Azure AD Connect Health agent requires at least one Azure AD Premium license. Each additional registered agent requires 25 additional Azure AD Premium licenses.

In Figure 8-1, there is an unhealthy message for the examref.onmicrosoft.com Domain. To examine the Domain, click its name which brings you to the monitoring page. Here, you can review the status of this Domain, as shown in Figure 8-2.

**FIGURE 8-2** Azure AD Connect Health Domain Monitoring

To determine the cause of the unhealthy state, you can review the alerts and click through to Alerts Details. Figure 8-3 shows the details of the following alert, stating the Health service data is not up to date.

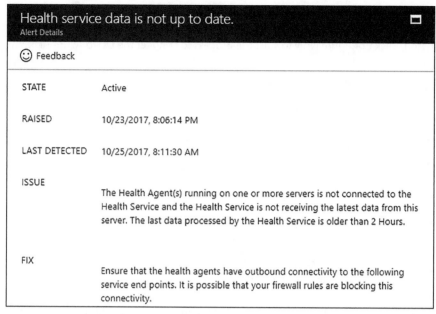

**FIGURE 8-3** Azure AD Connect Health Alert

## Monitor Domain Controllers

The Azure AD Connect tool is installed on one Domain controller (DC), to synchronize the identities of an on-premises AD Domain to Azure AD. In most AD installations there are many DCs. The first DC installed with AD Connect will automatically have the Azure AD Connect Health Agent installed and reports status updates on the Azure portal.

The Azure AD Connect Health tool can also monitor other AD DCs on-premises or running in a VNet in Azure. To configure these DCs you need to install the Azure AD Connect Heath agent for AD DS. Figure 8-4 shows, the links available in the Quick Start area of the Azure AD Connect Health blade in the Azure portal.

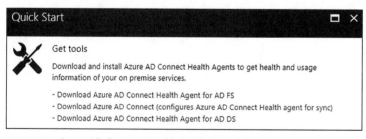

**FIGURE 8-4** Azure AD Connect Health Quick Start Links

The health agent installer should be downloaded to the DC you want to add to the Azure AD Connect Health monitoring portal. Figure 8-5 shows the tool after the initial install has been completed. Click Configure Now to start the process to connect the DC to Azure AD Connect Health.

**FIGURE 8-5** Azure AD Connect Health agent for AD DS

After clicking Configure Now, you are prompted to log in to your Azure AD tenant by using a global admin account, as shown in Figure 8-6.

**FIGURE 8-6** Azure AD Connect Health agent for AD DS Authentication

After a successful authentication, a PowerShell window appears running the configuration. Figure 8-7 features a resemblance of what you will see during the installation.

```
Administrator: Windows PowerShell

Executing Elevated PowerShell Command: Register-AzureADConnectHealthADDSAgent
2017-10-25 14:24:03.355 ProductName: Microsoft Azure AD Connect Health agent for AD DS,
TC Time: 2017-10-25 14:24:03Z

2017-10-25 14:24:03.371 AHealthServiceUri (ARM): https://management.azure.com/providers

2017-10-25 14:24:03.371 AdHybridHealthServiceUri: https://adds.aadconnecthealth.azure.c

2017-10-25 14:24:03.371 AHealthServiceUri (ARM): https://management.azure.com/providers

2017-10-25 14:24:03.371 AdHybridHealthServiceUri: https://adds.aadconnecthealth.azure.c

2017-10-25 14:24:04.16 AHealthServiceApiVersion: 2014-01-01

2017-10-25 14:25:01.98 Detecting AdDomainService roles...

2017-10-25 14:25:02.058 Detected the following role(s) for examref.com:

2017-10-25 14:25:02.058          Active Directory Domain Services

2017-10-25 14:25:13.232 Aquiring Monitoring Service certificate using tenant.cert

2017-10-25 14:25:15.594 Successfully aquired and stored Monitoring Service certificate:
76-f84b-4d74-af5b-797175ebdb50. OU=Microsoft ADFS Agent, Issuer=CN=Microsoft PolicyKeyS
mbprint=]

2017-10-25 14:25:15.625 Fetched and stored agent credentials successfully...

2017-10-25 14:25:16.444 Started agent services successfully...

Test-AzureADConnectHealthConnectivity completed successfully...

2017-10-25 14:25:22.181 Agent registration completed successfully.
```

**FIGURE 8-7** Azure AD Connect Health agent for AD DS Registration using PowerShell

After this is completed, the on-premises domain appears in the Azure AD Connect Health Portal, as shown in Figure 8-8.

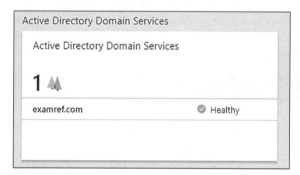

**FIGURE 8-8** Azure AD Connect Health showing the monitoring domain

When you click through to the next blade in the portal, important information about the Domain and its DCs appears, as shown in Figure 8-9. This blade includes information about the Domain, DC errors, and monitoring of authentications along with other performance monitors.

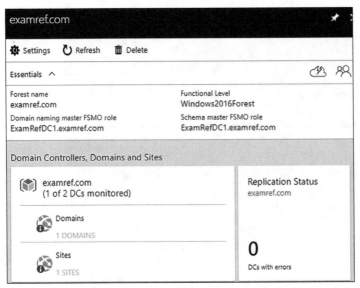

**FIGURE 8-9** Azure AD Connect Health monitoring on-premises forest, domain, and DCs

## Setup Email Notifications for Critical Alerts

One of the important functions of the Azure AD Connect Health tool is the ability to make notifications when errors are detected. In the portal's Sync Error section, different types of errors can be located, investigated, and the notification settings can be configured. Figure 8-10 shows the Sync Error blade where both of these activities can take place.

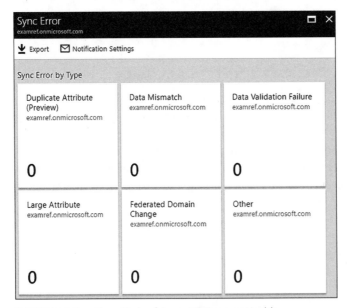

**FIGURE 8-10** Sync Error Blade of Azure AD Connect Health

You can configure email alerts by clicking Notification Settings on the blade. By default, the notifications are enabled and setup to send email to global administrators. Figure 8-11, shows that another email address has been configured to send email to a distribution group named vmadmins@examref.com.

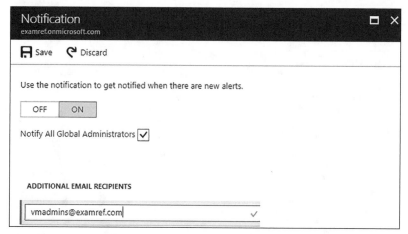

**FIGURE 8-11** Email Notifications configured in Azure AD Connect Health

## Monitor ADFS proxy and Web Application proxy Servers

Azure AD Connect Health for ADFS supports ADFS 2.0 & 3.0 on Windows Server 2008 R2, Windows Server 2012, Windows Server 2012 R2, and Windows Server 2016 respectively. It also supports monitoring the ADFS proxy or web application proxy servers that provide authentication support for extranet access. These services are provided after the Azure AD Connect Health for ADFS agent is installed on those servers.

**EXAM TIP**

The following are some important capabilities that Azure AD Connect Health for ADFS and App Proxy provide:

- Monitoring with alerts to know when ADFS and ADFS proxy servers are not healthy
- Email notifications for critical alerts
- Trends in performance data, which are useful for ADFS capacity planning
- Usage analytics for ADFS sign-ins with pivots (apps, users, and network location), which are useful to understand how ADFS is used
- Reports for ADFS, such as top 50 users who have bad username/password attempts and their last IP address

The Azure AD Connect Health Alerts for ADFS shows a list of active alerts. You can open an alert and additional information is provided to information can include steps that you can take to resolve the alert and links to documentation. You can also view historical data on alerts resolved in the past. Figure 8-12, shows alerts for an ADFS installation in the Azure AD Connect Health portal.

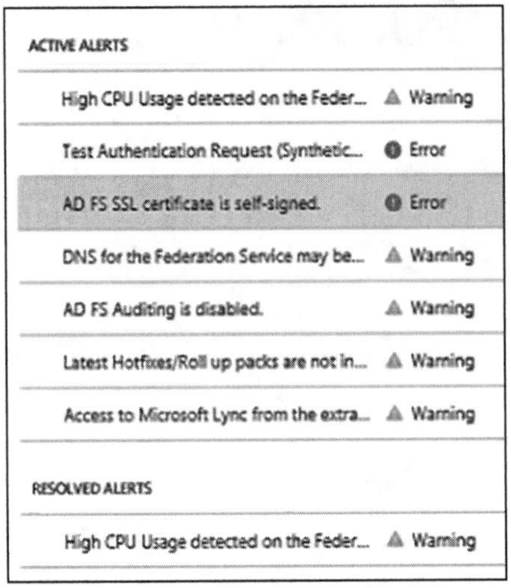

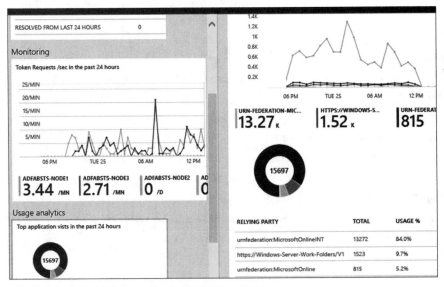

**FIGURE 8-12** Azure AD Connect Health monitoring ADFS Alerts

Azure AD Connect Health Usage for ADFS provides detailed information on authentication traffic of your federation servers. You can drill into the data by opening the usage analytics blade as shown in Figure 8-13, showing several metrics and groupings.

**FIGURE 8-13** Azure AD Connect Health ADFS Usage metrics

# Generate Utilization Reports

Azure AD reporting can be used to better understand how your environment is functioning. You can gain visibility into how your apps and services are being utilized by the users. Risks impacting the environment's health can also be detected. This empowers administrators to troubleshoot issues preventing users from accessing applications and systems.

There are two types of reports available:

- Security reports
- Activity reports

## Security Reports

By using the security reports in Azure AD, you can protect your organization's identities. Azure AD detects suspicious activities that are related to your user accounts. For each detected action, a record called *risk event* is created and shown in the reports.

There are two types of security reports in Azure Active Directory:

- **Users flagged for risk**   Report showing an overview of user accounts that might have been compromised.
- **Risky sign-ins**   Report showing indicators for sign-in attempts that might have been performed by someone who is not the legitimate owner of a user account.

## Activity Reports

The **audit logs report** provides you with records of system activities that are generally used for compliance purposes.

There are two types of activity reports in Azure Active Directory:

- **Audit logs**   The audit logs activity report provides you with access to the history of every task performed in your tenant.
- **Sign-ins**   With the sign-ins activity report, you can determine who has performed the tasks reported by the audit logs report.

# Skill 8.2: Manage Domains with Active Directory Domain Services

Azure AD Domain Services is a cloud based service that provides managed Domain activities, such as Domain Join, Group Policy management, LDAP, and Kerberos/NTLM authentication, which are fully compatible with Windows Server Active Directory. Azure AD Domain Services functionality works if your directory is a cloud-only Azure AD tenant or synchronized to your on-premises AD.

You can leverage these services without the need to deploy, manage, and patch Domain Controllers in the cloud. Azure AD Domain Services integrates with your existing Azure AD tenant making it possible for users to log in by using their corporate credentials.

Existing groups and user accounts can then be used to secure access to resources. This means that moving on-premises resources to Azure Infrastructure Services is quicker and less complex.

> **This skill covers how to:**
> - Implement Azure AD Domain Services
> - Join Azure virtual machines to a Domain
> - Securely Administer Domain-joined virtual machines by using Group Policy
> - Migrate On-premises Apps to Azure
> - Handle Traditional Directory-aware Apps along with SaaS Apps

## Implement Azure AD Domain Services

Azure AD Domain Services is provisioned and managed using the Azure portal. You need to select your region and VNet where it should be deployed before starting the provisioning process. Part of this process requires you to create a new subnet in the VNet where you are deploying domain services. After the deployment, you are not able to make any changes to this subnet. In this example, a new subnet was created named DomainServices in a VNet named ExamRefVNET.

On the Azure portal, click New and then search for Azure AD Domain Services. Click Domain Services and then click Create. As shown in Figure 8-14, complete the Basics blade, consisting of the DNS domain name, Resource group, and Location fields.

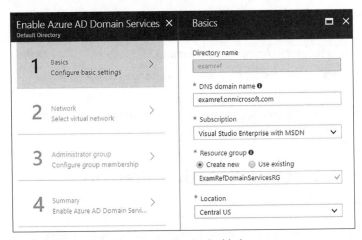

**FIGURE 8-14** Azure AD Domain Services Basics blade

> **IMPORTANT  AZURE AD DOMAIN SERVICES**
> When selecting the DNS domain name for Azure AD Domain Services, you should only use the default name or a custom domain already added to your Azure AD tenant.

On the Network blade, choose the VNet where domain services should be deployed. Then, select the subnet, as shown in Figure 8-15.

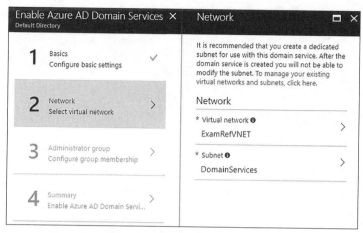

**FIGURE 8-15** Azure AD Domain Services Network blade

On the Administrator group blade, you need to add a user or group to the new AAD DC Administrators group to be provisioned. You should select at least one global admin for this group. Figure 8-16 shows that the user CloudAdmin, a global admin for this Azure subscription, is selected.

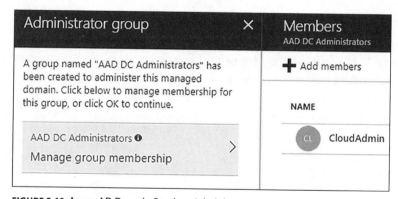

**FIGURE 8-16** Azure AD Domain Services Administrator group blade

The final step is to click OK after you review the Summary blade. Following the completion of the provisioning, you can review the Domain Services object.

After the Domain Services blade is opened, next you need to configure your DNS servers for the VNet to point to the domain services as the DNS servers. As shown in Figure 8-17, click Configure DNS Servers to update them with the IP addresses that are shown. Notice these addresses are in the dedicated DomainServices subnet.

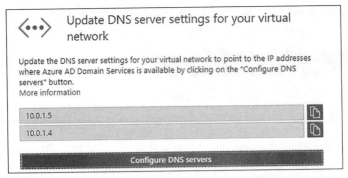

**FIGURE 8-17** Azure AD Domain Services Configure DNS Servers

The final step is to enable password synchronization to Domain Services. The process is different for user accounts synchronized from an on-premises directory and for those that are cloud user accounts created in Azure AD.

> **MORE INFORMATION   PASSWORD SYNCHRONIZATION SETTINGS**
>
> To understand the details of setting up the password synchronization, review this article: *https://docs.microsoft.com/en-us/azure/active-directory-domain-services/active-directory-ds-getting-started-password-sync-synced-tenant.*

## Join Azure virtual machines to a Domain

After the Azure AD Domain Services are deployed and active, you can add VMs that are running in your VNet to the Domain. These machines must not be deployed to the DomainServices subnet. When you are ready to add these machines, follow the same steps as you normally would when adding a machine to an AD.

Figure 8-18, shows the Server Manager program on a VM named ExamRefServer1. To add the machine to the domain servers, select WORKGROUP.

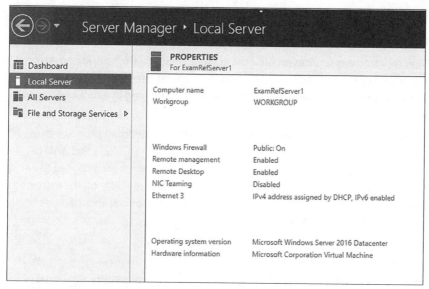

FIGURE 8-18  Windows Server 2016 Server Manager

Next, select Change on the System properties window followed by Member of Domain, and type in the DNS Domain name of the Azure AD Domain Services Domain. Figure 8-19 shows examref.onmicrosoft.com entered in this dialog box.

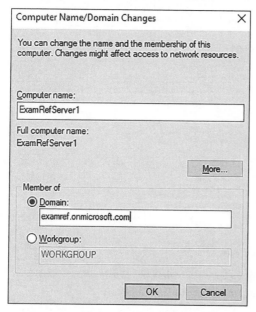

FIGURE 8-19  Adding ExamRefServer1 to the Azure AD Domain Service Domain

# Securely Administer Domain-joined virtual machines by using Group Policy

Azure Active Directory Domain Services provide the ability to manage Domain-joined Azure VMs by using Group Policy Objects (GPOs). You cannot manage on-premises machines of any type by using these GPOs because they are only for VMs that are running in Azure and joined to the Domain services.

When the Domain Services is configured by Azure it will create two Organization Units (OUs) for the management of users and groups. These are named: AD DC Users and AAD DC Computers. There are two built-in GPOs used to manage these OUs which are assigned to each respectively. You can customize these built-in GPOs to configure Group Policy on the managed Domain. You can also create your own custom OUs in the managed Domain and then create custom GPOs to manage these new OUs.

> **IMPORTANT** AAD DC GROUP POLICY
>
> Users belonging to the AAD DC Administrators group are granted Group Policy administration privileges on the managed Domain.

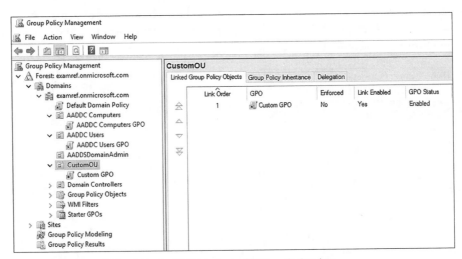

FIGURE 8-20 Group Policy Objects (GPOs) in Azure AD Domain Services

> **MORE INFRORMATION** OUS IN DOMAIN SERVICES
>
> For more information on managing OUs in Domain Services review this article *https://docs. microsoft.com/en-us/azure/active-directory-domain-services/active-directory-ds-admin- guide-administer-group-policy.*

# Migrate On-premises Apps to Azure

Applications running in a traditional AD environment require the AD authentication services such as LDAP, NTLM and Kerberos. Given this requirement, these applications cannot be moved to the cloud into Azure IaaS. By using Azure AD Domain Services, you are able to migrate legacy directory-aware applications running on-premises to Azure without having to worry about those identity requirements.

When using the Azure AD Domain Services, users can submit their corporate credentials to authenticate with the managed Domain. This makes the transition of these applications to the cloud seamless to the users without the complexities of deploying DCs into Azure. Their credentials are kept in sync with the Azure AD tenant. For synced tenants, Azure AD Connect ensures that changes to credentials made on-premises are synchronized to Azure AD.

# Handle Traditional Directory-aware Apps along with SaaS Apps

Another issue that some deployments face is providing SaaS applications with the ability to do LDAP reads of your AD. Azure AD Domain Services provides this feature, so your traditional directory-aware applications can run alongside your modern cloud apps.

# Skill 8.3: Integrate with Azure Active Directory (Azure AD)

Integrating an on-premises AD with Azure AD is the lifeblood for hybrid cloud deployments. This section focuses on how to accomplish this by using Azure AD Connect and then leveraging that setup to provide more complex scenarios, such as multi-factor authentication in the cloud.

---

**This skill covers how to:**

- Add Custom Domains
- Implement Azure AD Connect and Single Sign-on with On-premises Windows Server
- Multi-Factor Authentication (MFA)
- Config Windows 10 with Azure AD Domain Join
- Implement Azure AD Integration in Web and Desktop applications
- Leverage Microsoft Graph API

---

# Add Custom Domains

When creating an Azure AD, it always has an initial Domain name in the form of domainname.onmicrosoft.com. This name cannot be changed or deleted, but it is possible to add a registered internet domain names to your Azure AD. Companies typically have domain names they use to do business and users who sign in by using their AD Domain name. Adding custom domain names to Azure AD allows you to assign user names familiar to users. This means they could log in by using their email address billg@contoso.com, instead of billg@contoso.onmicrosoft.com.

The process to add a customer domain is simple:

- Add the custom domain name to your directory.
- Add a DNS entry for the domain name at the domain name registrar.
- Verify the custom domain name in Azure AD.

To add a customer domain by using the Azure portal, open the Azure AD that you wish to add a custom domain. Next, select Domain names followed by +Add domain name, then enter a domain, such as examref.com. Upon completion, you can see a screen resembling the screen shown in Figure 8-21 with instructions on adding a DNS record to your authoritative NS server which Azure will use to verify you are the owner of the domain.

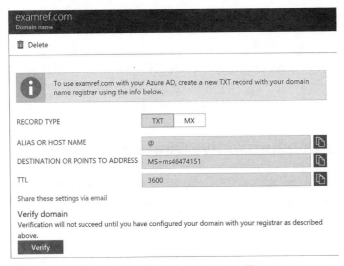

**FIGURE 8-21** Adding a Custom Domain to an Azure AD

After the records are added, click Verify, and the domain is added to the list of domains that can be used with this Azure AD.

---

*IMPORTANT* **ON-PREMISES CREDENTIALS**

You should add your custom domain and verify it prior to synchronizing the directory to an on-premises Active Directory. This allows your users to log in to Azure AD by using their on-premises credentials.

# Implement Azure AD Connect and Single Sign-on with On-premises Windows Server

Integrating your on-premises AD with Azure AD provides a common identity for accessing both cloud and on-premises resources. Users and organizations can take advantage of using a single identity to access on-premises applications and cloud services, such as Office 365.

To make this integration possible, Microsoft provides the Azure AD Connect tool, and when it's installed and configured on a DC, it synchronizes the local identities found in the on-premises AD to the Azure AD.

In this example, the Active Directory Forest and Domain and Azure AD have already been created, and they are ready for Azure AD Connect to be installed and configured on a DC named ExamRefDC1. Using an enterprise admin account from the forest, sign into to the Domain controller. Next open internet Explorer, and sign into your Azure subscription using the global admin account to the Azure AD you want to synchronize. Next, open the Azure AD in the Azure portal and, click Azure AD Connect which loads the Azure AD Connect configuration screen, as shown in Figure 8-22.

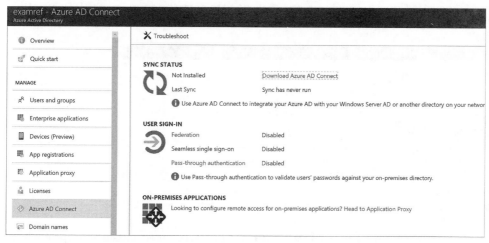

**FIGURE 8-22** Azure AD Connect in the Azure Portal prior to being configured

Click Download Azure AD Connect. This downloads the software to your local DC. After the software downloads, start the program, and click continue. In this example, there is only one forest, so you can select the Use Express Setting option.

### EXAM TIP

If your network has more than one Active Directory Forest, you must use the customized settings option in Azure AD Connect.

As shown in Figure 8-23, you are challenged for the global admin credentials for the Azure AD you want to synchronize.

**FIGURE 8-23** Enter the Global Admin Credentials for the Azure AD

As shown in Figure 8-24, you are now challenged to enter the on-premises AD Domain Enterprise Admin credentials.

**FIGURE 8-24** Enter the Enterprise Admin Credentials for the Active Directory Domain

You can now complete the confirmations, and Azure AD Connect installs and synchronizes the identities. After this is complete, the users and groups from the on-premises AD appear in the Azure AD portal.

## Multi-Factor Authentication (MFA)

Azure Multi-Factor Authentication (MFA), is Microsoft's multi-step account credentials verification solution. Azure MFA helps safeguard access to data and applications while providing a simple sign-in process. MFA delivers a strong authentication via a range of verification methods, including phone call, text message, or mobile app. MFA does require that Azure AD Premium licenses be applied to the users you want to use the service. All the Azure AD Premium SKUs include the MFA feature.

One requirement that must be met prior to assigning an Azure AD Premium license and enabling MFA for the user is the usage location must be set in the user's profile. Figure 8-25 shows that the Usage location field for the user CloudAdmin has been set to the United States.

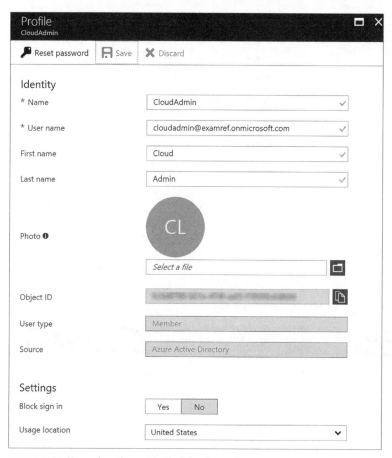

**FIGURE 8-25** Usage location set to their local country

Using the Azure portal on the Azure AD that is being configured, click the Licenses link then, select Product. When Azure AD Premium is listed, select it and then, click +Assign. Select the user. In this case the CloudAdmin user is selected, as shown in Figure 8-26.

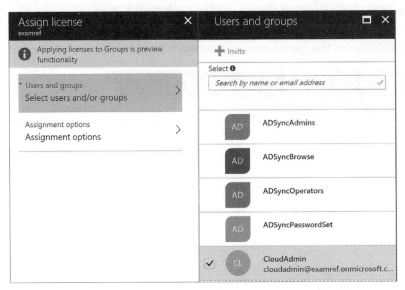

**FIGURE 8-26** The CloudAdmin user is selected for an Azure AD Premium License

After you select the user(s), next click Assignment options. The portal loads, as shown in Figure 8-27. Click On for each of the three options, and then click Assign. By assigning this license it is now possible to enable MFA feature for CloudAdmin user.

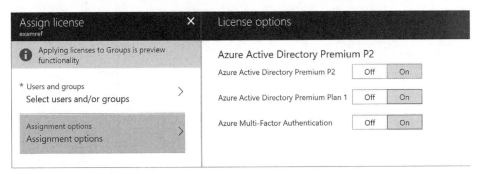

**FIGURE 8-27** The Azure AD Premium License options are selected including MFA

To force the user to use MFA, you need to create a Conditional Access Policy. To create this policy by using the Azure portal, click Conditional Access under the Security section of your Azure AD. Next, click +New Policy and provide a name and select the users, the groups, or all users for this policy to apply to in the Assignments section. Then click All Cloud Apps to have this policy impact the applications in this Azure AD. Next, under Access Controls, click Grant access and then select the Require multi-factor authentication option, as shown in Figure 8-28.

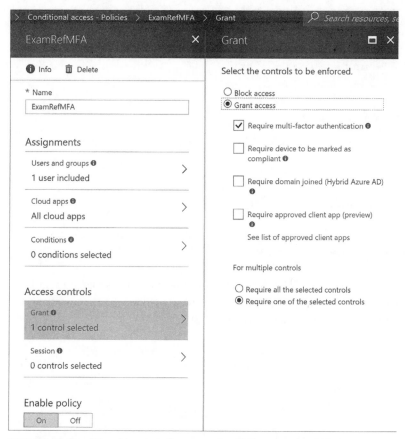

**FIGURE 8-28** Conditional Access Policy to require All Users to using MFA

After this is complete, upon their next login to any Azure or Office 365 service the users are required to enroll with the MFA service. Figure 8-29 shows the MFA enrollment screen that the users see when they first enroll.

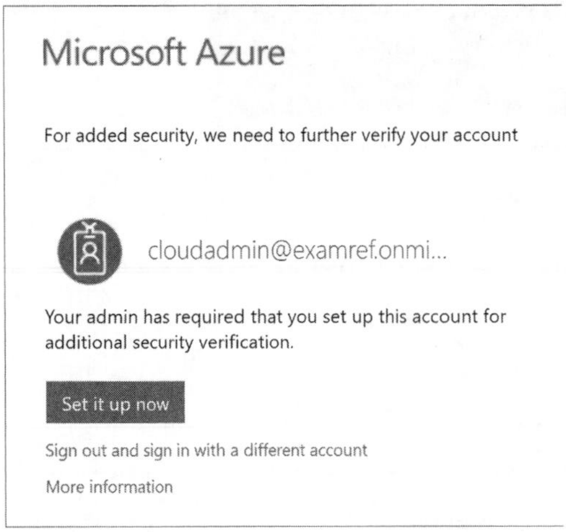

**Microsoft Azure**

For added security, we need to further verify your account

cloudadmin@examref.onmi...

Your admin has required that you set up this account for additional security verification.

Set it up now

Sign out and sign in with a different account

More information

**FIGURE 8-29** Azure requiring a user to enroll in MFA

After it is set up, every time users authenticate to one of the applications that are a part of your Azure AD, they need to complete a two-step login. The user enters their username and password and are then challenged, as shown in Figure 8-30.

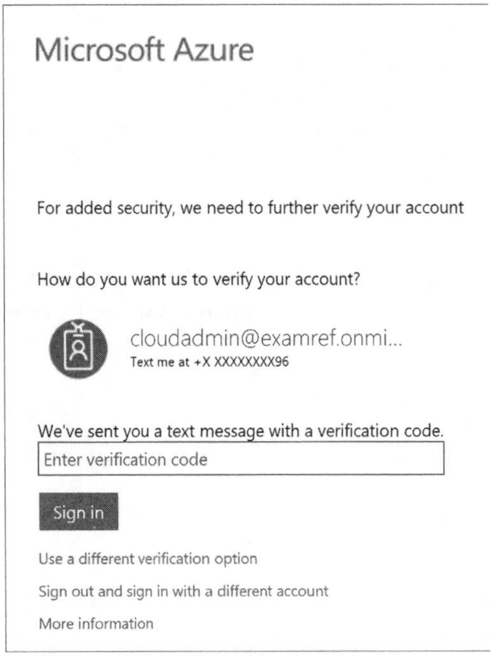

**Microsoft Azure**

For added security, we need to further verify your account

How do you want us to verify your account?

cloudadmin@examref.onmi...
Text me at +X XXXXXXXX96

We've sent you a text message with a verification code.

Enter verification code

Sign in

Use a different verification option

Sign out and sign in with a different account

More information

**FIGURE 8-30** Azure MFA challenging a user for a code sent to a mobile phone

To verify their identity, a code is sent to the user's mobile phone via SMS message. After the user receives the code on their mobile phone, as shown in Figure 8-31, the code must be entered into the webpage to complete the sign in process to access the Azure AD application.

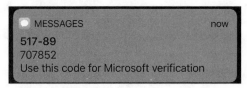

**FIGURE 8-31** Azure MFA verification code sent to a user on a mobile phone

## Config Windows 10 with Azure AD Domain Join

Azure AD allows you to add and manage devices in the directory. This management then allows you as the administrator to ensure that your users are accessing resources from devices that meet your standards for security and compliance.

If you want all your users to leverage a Bring Your Own Device (BYOD) policy, you can accomplish this by configuring Azure AD registered devices. In Azure AD, you can configure Azure AD registered devices for Windows 10, iOS, Android, and macOS. For the exam, you need to understand the process as it relates to Windows 10 devices.

To allow the registration of a Windows 10 device, the device registration service must be configured. In addition, to having permission to register devices in your Azure AD tenant, you must have fewer devices registered than the configured maximum.

To allow users to join devices to Azure AD, open the directory in the Azure portal and click Devices. Next, click Device settings and set the Users may join devices to Azure AD option to All. Figure 8-32 shows this configuration.

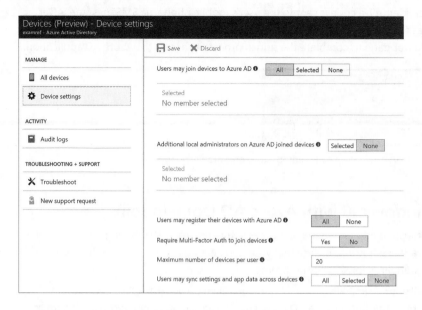

FIGURE 8-32  Device Settings set to allow Users to join devices to Azure AD

Now, that the Azure AD is configured to allow devices to the directory, adding a Windows 10 device is done from the device. On Windows 10, open the All settings menu and then open Accounts, as shown in Figure 8-33.

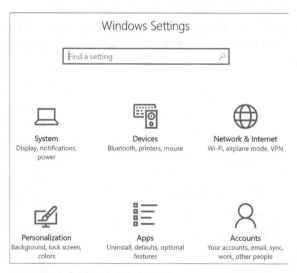

FIGURE 8-33  Settings in Windows 10

Click Access work and school and then click connect, as shown in Figure 8-34.

Access work or school
Connect to work or school
Get access to resources like email, apps, and the network. Connecting means your work or school might control some things on this device, such as which settings you can change. For specific info about this, ask them.
Connect

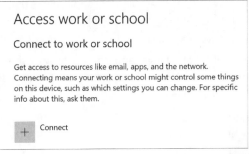

**FIGURE 8-34** Click Connect to add the Windows 10 device to Azure AD

Next, sign in by using your account. If the users are set up for MFA, they are challenged, which is to be expected for this type of sign in, as shown in Figure 8-35.

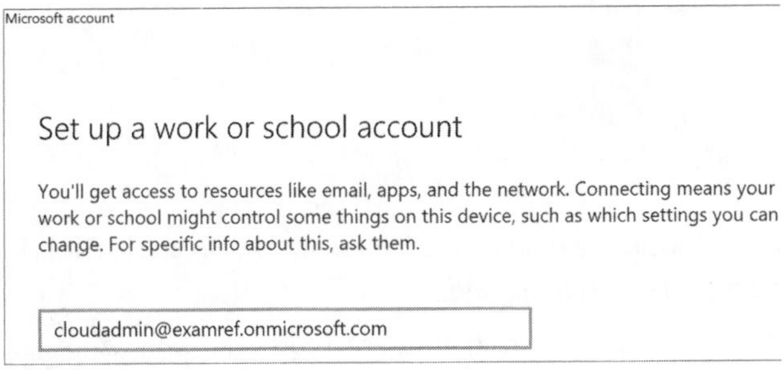

Microsoft account
Set up a work or school account
You'll get access to resources like email, apps, and the network. Connecting means your work or school might control some things on this device, such as which settings you can change. For specific info about this, ask them.
cloudadmin@examref.onmicrosoft.com

**FIGURE 8-35** Azure AD Account used to add the device to Azure AD

The device is now added to Azure AD and appears in the Azure AD portal as a managed device.

## Implement Azure AD Integration in Web and Desktop Applications

Independent Software Vendors (ISV), enterprise developers, and software as a service (SaaS) providers can develop cloud applications services that can be integrated with Azure Active Directory (Azure AD) to provide secure sign-in and authorization for their services. To integrate an application or service with Azure AD, a developer must first register the application with Azure AD.

Any application that wants to use the capabilities of Azure AD must first be registered in an Azure AD tenant. This registration involves providing Azure AD details about the application, such as the URL where it's located, the URL to send replies to after a user is authenticated, and the URI that identifies it.

To register a new application by using the Azure portal in the Azure AD blade, click App registrations, and click +New application registration. Next, enter your application's registration information, including Name, Application type: "Native" for client applications that are installed locally or "Web app / API" for client applications and resource/API applications that are installed on a secure server.

As shown in Figure 8-35, you need to complete the Sign-on URL field. If the application is a "Web app / API" you should provide the base URL. For "Native" applications, provide the Redirect URI used by Azure AD to return token responses. Notice the app shown in Figure 8-36 is registered by using a sign-on URL of http://localhost:30533.

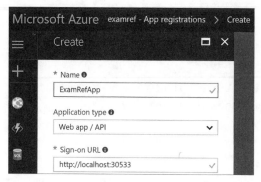

**FIGURE 8-36** Azure AD Application Registration

When finished, click Create. Azure AD assigns a unique application ID to your application, and you're taken to the application's main registration page.

Keep in mind there are different types of applications that can be registered with Azure AD. Depending on whether your application is a web or native application (client installed), different options are required to add additional capabilities to your application.

## Leverage Microsoft Graph API

You can use the Microsoft Graph API to interact with the user data in the Microsoft cloud. Microsoft Graph can be leveraged to build apps for organizations that connect to many types of resources, relationships, and intelligence. There is a single endpoint for using the Graph API, which is *https://graph.microsoft.com*.

Microsoft Graph can access Azure AD resources to enable scenarios like managing roles or inviting external users to your directory. The Graph API also provides methods that applications can use to find information about users, groups, or role memberships.

To use the Graph APIs on Azure AD resources, your application needs the appropriate permissions. Many of the APIs exposed on Azure AD resources require one of more directory permissions be assigned to function properly.

# Skill 8.4: Implement Azure AD B2C and Azure AD B2B

Azure AD Business to Consumer (B2C) and Business to Business (B2B) are unique Azure directories that enable authentication scenarios in support of consumer based applications or enterprises that want to partner with other companies. This section focuses on these directories as well as some other more advanced features, including Multi-Factor Authentication (MFA) and self-service password reset features provided to users by Azure.

**This skill covers how to:**

- Create an Azure AD B2C Directory
- Register an Application
- Implement Social Identity Provider Authentication
- Enable Multi-Factor Authentication (MFA)
- Set up Self-service Password Reset
- Implement B2B Collaboration and Configure Partner Users
- Integrate with Applications

## Create an Azure AD B2C Directory

Azure AD B2C is a cloud identity management solution for your web and mobile applications. It is a highly available global service that scales to hundreds of millions of identities.

With minimal configuration, Azure AD B2C enables your application to authenticate:

- Social Accounts (such as Facebook, Google, LinkedIn, and more)
- Enterprise Accounts (using open standard protocols, OpenID Connect, or SAML)
- Local Accounts (email address and password, or username and password)

### Create an Azure AD B2C tenant in the Azure Portal

To create a new Azure AD B2C tenant by using the Azure portal, first click New and then search the marketplace for Azure Active Directory B2C and click Create. Next, click Create a new Azure AD B2C Tenant, as shown in Figure 8-37.

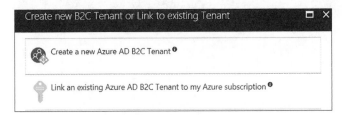

**FIGURE 8-37** Create a new B2C Tenant

Next, you need to enter the Organization name, enter the Initial domain name, and select your country or region. In Figure 8-38, the name ExamRefB2C is used for the Organization name and the Initial domain name (must be globally unique to the Microsoft cloud). Next, click Create.

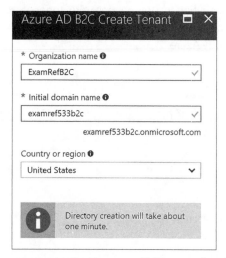

**FIGURE 8-38** Creating a new B2C Tenant using the Azure portal

After the directory is created, a link appears that says Click here, to manage your new directory. Click the link, as shown in Figure 8-39, to open the Azure AD B2C tenant that was just created.

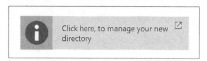

**FIGURE 8-39** Link to the new B2C Tenant

The next step is to register this B2C tenant with your subscription. When the window loads after clicking the link shown in Figure 8-39, you land on the management page. Note that no subscription has been linked to the B2C tenant, as shown in Figure 8-40.

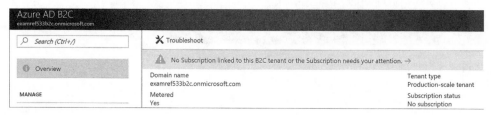

**FIGURE 8-40** The Azure B2C Tenant showing No Subscription linked

To link the new Azure AD B2C tenant to an Azure subscription by using the Azure portal, first click New in the Azure portal and then search the marketplace for Azure Active Directory B2C and click Create. Next, click Link an existing Azure AD B2C Tenant to my Azure subscription, as shown in Figure 8-41.

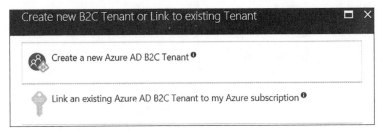

FIGURE 8-41 Link an existing Azure AD B2C Tenant to my Azure subscription

After clicking the link, you need to select your Azure AD B2C tenant, create a resource group, New Resource Group and select a region, as shown in Figure 8-42. When this is complete, click Create.

FIGURE 8-42 Completed details Linking Azure AD B2C Tenant to a subscription

After this has completed, you are directed to the B2C page. As shown in Figure 8-43, you can then click the Settings link.

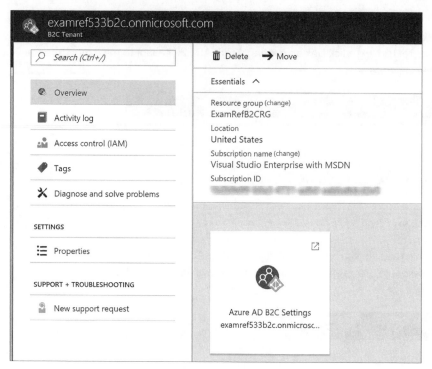

**FIGURE 8-43** B2C Tenant to a subscription after linked to the Azure Subscription

The settings for the Azure AD B2C tenant are then used for registering applications, implementing social identity providers, enabling multi-factor authentication, and other configurations. These settings can be selected from the Azure portal, as shown in Figure 8-44.

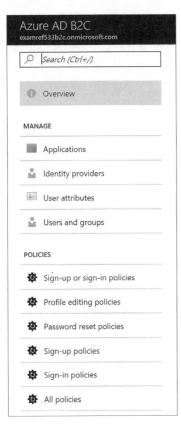

**FIGURE 8-44** B2C Tenant settings in the Azure portal

You can also switch to this Azure AD tenant by using the Azure portal and selecting the B2C directory in the top-right corner of the portal. Figure 8-45 shows the ExamRefB2C directory being selected as the Directory being viewed in the Azure portal.

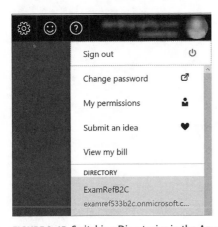

**FIGURE 8-45** Switching Directories in the Azure portal

# Register an Application

To build an application that accepts consumer sign-up and sign-in, first you need to register the application with an Azure Active Directory B2C tenant.

Applications created from the Azure AD B2C blade in the Azure portal must be managed from the same location.

You can register the following types of applications:

- Web Applications
- API Applications
- Mobile or Native Applications (Client Desktop)

From the B2C Settings in the Azure portal, click Applications and then click +Add. To Register a Web App, use the following settings, as shown in Figure 8-46.

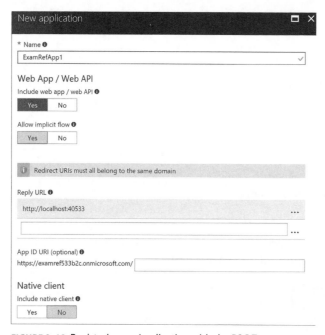

**FIGURE 8-46** Registering an Application with the B2C Tenant

**EXAM TIP**

Reply URLs are endpoints where Azure AD B2C returns any tokens that your application requests. Make sure to enter a properly formatted Reply URL. In this example, the app is running locally and listening on port 40533 as represented by the *http://localhost:40533 URL*.

After the application is created you can view its properties by clicking the name in the portal. Changes can be made to the configuration of the application registration. Also, the Application ID is shown and this is required for the code of the application to call this application from your B2C. The application created in this example is shown in Figure 8-47.

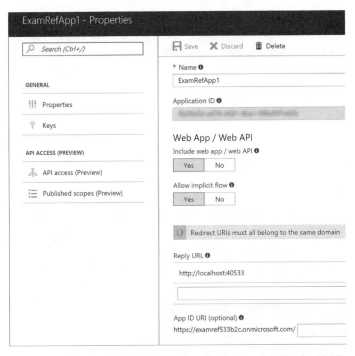

**FIGURE 8-47** The Application Registration after being added to the B2C Tenant

# Implement Social Identity Provider Authentication

Azure AD B2C is an identity management solution for web and mobile applications focused toward consumers. The feature allows your application's users to leverage an existing account that they already have in place on a social media site instead of creating a new user ID on your site.

The process to enable a social identity provider is a multi-step process that involves setting up the provider that you want to integrate with for this application. For example, to allow users to leverage their Facebook ID with your application, you need to sign up as a Facebook developer and create an application on their site, as shown in Figure 8-48.

**FIGURE 8-48** Facebook Application

After you complete this process, you are provided an App ID and an App Secret, as shown in Figure 8-49. These are used to add the social provider to your B2C tenant by using the Azure portal.

**FIGURE 8-49** Facebook Application App ID and App Secret

To enable Facebook, the last step is to add it as an identity provider. This is done by clicking the identity provider's link in the settings of the B2C tenant and then clicking +Add. From here you need to enter the name you want to give the provider, select the provider from the list of supported providers, and then enter the App ID and App Secret as the Client ID and Client Secret respectively. When this is complete, click Create to add Facebook as an identity provider for your application, as shown in Figure 8-50.

**FIGURE 8-50** Adding Facebook as a Social Identity Provider

After the identity provider is created, you need to create a Sign-up or Sign-in Policy. This is done by using the Azure portal and clicking Sign-up or Sign-in Policy and clicking +Add. From here, provide a name for the policy and select the providers, along with the attributes and claims that you need for your application. After it is configured, the portal page will resemble Figure 8-51.

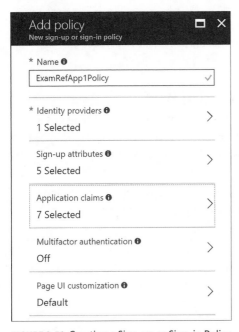

**FIGURE 8-51** Creating a Sign-up or Sign-in Policy

After you save this policy, you can open it and click Run Policy. Running the policy then opens a new web browser to show the user experience when users connect their Facebook accounts to your application, as shown in Figure 8-52.

**FIGURE 8-52** The Facebook Login Page as an Identity Provider to the B2C Tenant Application

## Enable Multi-Factor Authentication (MFA)

Azure AD B2C integrates directly with Azure MFA, so that you can add a second layer of security to sign-up and sign-in consumer-focused applications. This can be achieved without needing to write any additional code in the application. Microsoft currently supports phone call and text message verification for these applications.

To change the multi-factor authentication settings, open Sign-up or Sign-In Policy and click Edit in the Azure portal on the B2C directory. A simple change to the settings turns on multi-factor authentication, as shown in Figure 8-53.

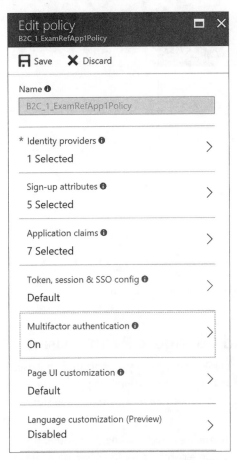

**FIGURE 8-53** Enabling Multi-Factor Authentication

## Set up Self-Service Password Reset

You can set up Self-Service Password Reset by adding a Password Reset policy. By using the Azure portal with the B2C directory open, click Password Reset Policies and then click +Add. When the blade for the password reset policy loads, supply the appropriate information as shown in Figure 8-54.

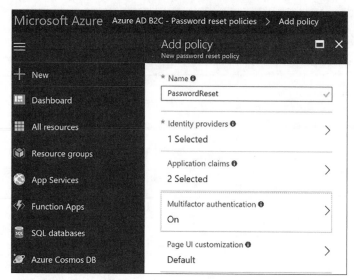

**FIGURE 8-54** Enabling Self-Service Password Reset using Multi-Factor Authentication

## Implement B2B Collaboration and Configure Partner Users

Azure AD Business to Business (B2B) collaboration capabilities enable any organization that uses Azure AD to work safely and securely with users from any other organization. The partner companies that are invited to use Azure AD B2B can be set up with or without their own Azure AD for this to work properly.

Companies that use Azure AD can provide access to applications, documents, or other resources to their partners, but they always maintain complete control over their own data. Also, it's easy for users to navigate, which minimizes helpdesk calls.

> **EXAM TIP**
>
> **Azure AD B2B works with any type of partner directory. Partners use their own credentials. There is no requirement for partners to use Azure AD and no external directories or complex setup is required. The invitation to join is the critical action that makes this scenario work.**

Global admins and limited admins can use the Azure portal to invite B2B collaboration users to the directory, to any group, or to any application.

To add a B2B user, open Azure AD in the Azure portal and click through to All-Users. From this point, click +New Guest User, as shown in Figure 8-55.

**FIGURE 8-55** Adding a New Guest User

The next step is to add the user's email address and then include a welcome message, as shown in Figure 8-56.

**FIGURE 8-56** Adding a Guest User's Email and Welcome Message

The user receives an invite in their inbox to the Azure AD as a B2B user, as shown in Figure 8-57. They can click through and then complete a process to add their user name to the directory.

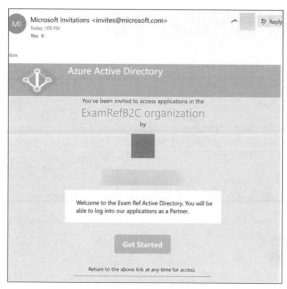

**FIGURE 8-57** Email Invitation received by a B2B user added to Azure AD

## Integrate with Applications

Adding users to applications in Azure AD is required for them to have access. After the users are added, the applications show up on their MyApps portal. To add a B2B external user, or any user for that matter, open the Azure AD in the Azure portal and click Enterprise Applications. Next, open the application that you want to give the user access to. In the example shown in Figure 8-58, you see the application DocuSign has been added to the Azure AD.

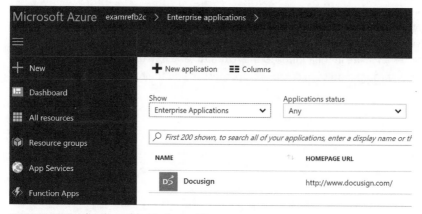

**FIGURE 8-58** Application added to Azure AD

Click the application to open it and then click Users and Groups. Next, click +Add User as shown in Figure 8-59.

**FIGURE 8-59** Click +Add User to add the B2B user

From the list of users, add the B2B user, as shown in Figure 8-60. Click Assign and the user is added to the application.

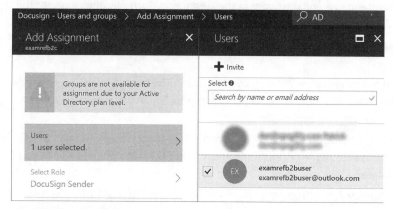

**FIGURE 8-60** Adding a B2B user to an Azure AD Application

The user can now point their web browser to *http://myapps.microsoft.com* where the application shows up as an option after they sign in. Figure 8-61 shows that the user can now access the application.

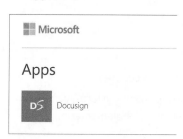

**FIGURE 8-61** MyApps portal showing an Azure AD application assigned to a user

# Thought experiment

In this thought experiment, apply what you have learned in this chapter. You can find answers to these questions in the "Answers" section at the end of this chapter.

You are the new IT Administrator at TailSpin Toys, which is a global leader in selling and distributing toys around the globe. Recently TailSpin purchased one of the leading online websites for gaming. As a part of this transition, your CIO has determined that you will use Azure and Office 365 moving forward.

As a result, you have been put in charge of setting up the identity with Azure AD for the following systems:

- Any TailSpin user needs to be able to authenticate to Azure solutions and Office 365 by using the same user name and password as they use today. Currently, they log in to the on-premises AD domain, which is running Windows Server 2012R2 Native mode.

- The online gaming system should use Azure AD and allow users to use their social media accounts.

- TailSpin's main ordering system will be moved to Azure. The security team has advised you that partners can no longer have accounts in the TailSpin AD, so you need a way to provide them access to this application.

1. What Azure tools should you use to securely synchronize the AD accounts from the AD Domain on-premises to Azure? How should you monitor this replication as well as your domain controllers?

2. What type of directory should you deploy for the online gaming site? How will you allow for the users to sign-up and sign-in to the application by using their social media identities?

3. What type of directory should you use for the ordering system? What user login IDs should the partners use since security is taking away the IDs that had been provided to partners in the past?

# Thought experiment answers

This section contains the solution to the thought experiment for this chapter.

1. Use Azure AD Connect to synchronize the users and groups from the local AD to Azure AD. Use Azure AD Connect Health to monitor all the directory implementation at TailSpin Toys.

2. An Azure B2C tenant should be deployed to support the online gaming system. Social media providers should be added to the Azure AD application to allow users to leverage their social media IDs. Since their IDs are held by the social media provider, there should not be any helpdesk calls for password resets.

3. Use Azure AD B2B for the ordering system. New invitations are emailed to users. By using their own IDs, users are now able to gain access to the TailSpin ordering system. This allows for the removal of their partner accounts that are a part of the on-premises AD and thus meets the security team's requirements.

# Chapter summary

Below are some of the key takeaways from this chapter:

- All versions of Active Directory can be managed by using Azure AD Connect Health
- On-premises domain controllers can be managed by using Azure AD Connect Health
- Email notifications can be set up to send emails to alert of issues found while monitoring your different AD directories
- Azure AD Domain Services allows for joining Azure VMs to a directory without the need to deploy DCs into Azure IaaS
- Azure AD Domain Services supports the use of GPOs
- Traditional AD aware applications can be deployed to the cloud and use LDAP and Kerberos authentications with the support of Azure AD Domain Services
- Custom domains can be added to Azure AD, such as contoso.com, but there is always a default contoso.onmicrosoft.com domain
- Multi-Factor Authentication (MFA), requires users to supply another form of verification other than just user name and password. This is in the form of phone call, text message, or verification app on a mobile phone.
- MFA requires a Premium license for each user and their location must be set prior to enabling the service
- Windows 10 can be added to Azure AD as a device to be managed, enabling BYOD or corporate cloud only deployments
- Azure AD B2C allows developers to leverage the social identity of users such as Facebook and Microsoft ID amongst others
- Azure AD B2B allows administrators to invite partner companies to gain access to their cloud resources

# Index

## A

access control  178–184, 310–321. *See also* security
  access policies  338
  ARM authentication  311–315
  lock resources  319–321
  management policies  315–318
  role-based  192–195, 322–330
  SaaS applications  370–371
  Shared Access Signatures  180–182
  stored access policy  182–183
  Virtual Network Service Endpoints  183–184
access control lists (ACLs)  193
access panel extension  368
ACE. *See* access control entries
ACLs. *See* access control lists
ACR. *See* Azure Container Registry
ACS. *See* Azure Container Services
Active Directory (AD)  311, 469
  registering application in  311–313
  service principals in  313–314
Active Directory Federation Services (ADFS)  469
  proxy monitoring  477–478
activity data  457–459
activity log alerts  119, 122–123
activity logs  456–459
activity reports  479
AD. *See* Active Directory
Adaptive application controls  357–358
Add-AzureRmAccount cmdlet  66
Add-AzureRmVirtualNetworkPeering cmdlet  221
Add-AzureRmVirtualNetworksubnetConfig cmdlet  237
Add-AzureRmVmssExtension cmdlet  134
ADFS. *See* Active Directory Federation Services
Alert Rules  189–190

alerts  39
  activity log  119, 122–123
  Azure Storage  189–190
  based on log search queries  461
  configuration  119–123
  critical, email notifications for  476–477
  metric  119–121
  security  359–361
Allow Gateway Transit option  258–259
Antimalware Assessment management solution  462–463
append blobs  158
application delivery controller (ADC)  232
Application Gateway (App Gateway)
  cookie-based session affinity  233
  creating  234–239
  deployment into virtual networks  234
  design and implementation  285–286
  end to end SSL  233
  implementing  232–239
  internal load balancers and  262
  load balancing  233
  secure sockets layer (SSL) offload  233
  sizes  234
  URL-based content routing  234
  web application firewall  233
application gateways  266
Application Insights  6, 35–39, 111, 116–117
application logs  115
applications. *See also* Web Apps
  Adaptive application controls  357–358
  adding users and groups to  369–370
  availability tests  37–39
  deploying to web apps  14
  desktop  495–496
  diagnostic logs  28–29

# D

# O

# P

# Y

# Z

# About the authors

**RICK RAINEY** is Principal Program Manager in Microsoft's Azure Customer Advisory Team (CAT).

**MICHAEL WASHAM**, Microsoft Azure MVP, Insider and Advisor, is CEO of the cloud readiness company Opsgility. Michael has extensive history in the IT Industry where he has worked as an IT Professional, developer, Evangelist, and Program Manager before turning to his passion of enabling companies of all sizes make the digital transformation to the cloud. Michael is an avid blogger, author speaker, and trainer on cloud computing, debugging, and DevOps

**DAN PATRICK** is the Chief Cloud Strategist for Opsgility http://www.opsgility.com. He has an extensive background in the IT industry with a focus on Virtualization, Networking and Identity management. Dan is a 15 year veteran of Microsoft, where was a Principal Consultant and Practice Manager. Today he still works with Microsoft as an Azure MVP and advisor. He regularly speaks about the cloud all over the world, and you can follow him on twitter @deltadan.

**STEVE ROSS** is Partner Technology Strategist with Microsoft's One Commercial Partner Technology Team and is heavily involved in helping partners build services using cloud technologies. Steve has also been a Principal Cloud Solution Architect with Opsgility, building Microsoft Azure training content and teaching enterprise customers and Microsoft partners and employees all around the world.